THE NEW
URBAN
SOCIOLOGY
THIRD EDITION

THE NEW
URBAN
SOCIOLOGY

THIRD EDITION

MARK GOTTDIENER
University at Buffalo

RAY HUTCHISON
University of Wisconsin–Green Bay

Westview Press
A Member of the Perseus Books Group

Designed by Brent Wilcox

Library of Congress Cataloging-in-Publication Data
Gottdiener, Mark.
The new urban sociology / Mark Gottdiener, Ray Hutchison.— 3rd ed.
p. cm.
Includes bibliographical references and index.
ISBN–13: 978–0–8133–4318–1 (pbk.)
ISBN–10: 0–8133–4318–6 (pbk.)
1. Metropolitan areas—United States. 2. Suburbs—United States. 3. Urbanization—
United States—History. 4. Sociology, Urban—United States. 5. Sociology, Urban. 6. Ur-
banization. I. Hutchison, Ray. II. Title.
  HT334.U5G657 2006
  307.76'0973—dc22

2005023650

06 07 08 / 10 9 8 7 6 5 4 3 2 1

Mark Gottdiener dedicates this third edition to the memory of his lifelong friend, Eric Monkkonen. Kind, compassionate, intelligent, understanding to a fault, but possessing a shared intolerance for nonsense, Eric was a rarity among scholars. Mark cherished their conversations and will miss him very much.

CONTENTS

PREFACE TO THE THIRD EDITION

The New Urban Sociology was the first textbook to present the sociospatial model and to apply this model to the study of urban sociology. The theoretical discussion and applied study of "urban space" have emerged as the dominant paradigm not only in urban sociology but also in the various disciplines within urban studies, such as geography, architecture, and planning. New books by established scholars in the field, as well as special issues of scholarly journals and edited collections, offer insights into the social production and meaning of urban space. These developments reflect not simply a long-standing critique of earlier models of urban structure and process but a growing recognition that the emergence of global capitalism and the accompanying changes in the international division of labor have altered the social, political, economic, and cultural landscapes of metropolitan areas in the United States as well as in developing and industrialized nations around the world.

At the beginning of a new century, more than 3 billion persons live in urban areas around the world. By 2030 this number is expected to increase to more than 5 billion persons—some 60 percent of the total world population. Most of this growth will occur in cities in the developing world, much of it in cities where many if not most persons live in shantytowns, with incomes below the poverty level. This will be the first urban century in human history, and the well-being not just of families and households but of human society more generally will depend on our creating a safe and just urban environment—something that human populations have not been particularly adept at doing. A beginning point in this very significant challenge is the study of urban sociology.

The third edition of *The New Urban Sociology* has evolved from our commitment to the study of urban sociology, a commitment forged over many years of experience in graduate school education and teaching in the classroom. We both were introduced to urban sociology in graduate school by several well-known scholars and became passionately committed to the discipline.

Mark studied with David Street and Gerald Suttles at SUNY–Stony Brook, and Ray studied with Morris Janowitz, Gerald Suttles, and William Julius Wilson at the University of Chicago. Urban sociology seemed to offer everything that was attractive about sociology: It required an interdisciplinary understanding of economics, politics, and culture. It was concerned with the reality of everyday life. It possessed great themes of immigrant adjustment, the making and unmaking of fortunes, active and exciting politics, the rise and decline of community ties, and even the dark side of human existence in the form of crime and vice. As graduate students, we were eager to learn about it all. From our experience, we came to an understanding that remains at the core of our work: Urban sociologists must be interested in actual reality. We must be inspired by the routines of everyday life, and we must seek to explain life in its full complexity. We agree with Robert Park that to understand urban life, one must move beyond the ivory tower of the university and "get the seat of your pants dirty" by doing research and becoming involved in urban communities.

In graduate school, we learned about the theory of urban ecology. That was the only explanatory paradigm taught at universities in the United States. Our doctoral dissertations were case studies of suburban development on Long Island (a suburban area adjacent to New York City) and of black suburbanization in Harvey, Illinois (an older suburb just south of Chicago). It became increasingly clear to both of us—even though we had not yet met each other—that the urban ecological paradigm could not adequately explain the changes occurring in the post–World War II period in metropolitan areas across the United States. Our dissatisfaction with mainstream urban sociology and our passionate interest in explaining the social, political, and economic changes that we observed in our field studies led us to reconceptualize the field. Over the past decade and a half, we have devoted our work to introducing new ideas about the role of economics, politics, and culture in urban analysis. This effort culminated in a new kind of urban theory and a new paradigm for the discipline, as well as the first edited series devoted to urban sociology. Our work joined the efforts of others, such as Lefebvre, Castells, Harvey, and Pickvance, in what has come to be called the new urban sociology.

Over this same period, we have also devoted ourselves to the teaching of urban sociology. The limitations of the textbooks that presented urban ecology as a global paradigm made it difficult to instruct our students in understanding the complexities of urban life. Slowly we began to frame specific concepts and arguments that we felt improved the approach of urban sociology. The first edition of this book represented the culmination of Mark's efforts over several decades to develop a new theoretical model that was better suited to contemporary urban society and the systematic application of this theory to the topics studied by urban sociologists. The third edition represents our joint effort to expand the earlier material by including new topics and examples that demonstrate the applications of sociospatial theory to the reality of urban life not just in the United States but around the world.

The central organizing concepts of this text were devised in response to the limitations of other textbooks in the field. Without exception, urban sociologists focus principally on the large central city as an object of analysis. Suburban considerations may be treated, but they are usually consigned to a separate chapter. This urban bias distorts reality. In the United States, the majority of people now live, work, and shop in the suburbs rather than in large central cities. Our text focuses on the entire metropolitan region, including cities, suburbs, industrial parks, shopping malls, recreational sites, and small towns. We believe this approach presents a more balanced account of contemporary urban life.

Too often, textbooks are written as a series of disconnected chapters reporting facts about one topic after another without providing a compelling vision. This book is an exception. The sociospatial perspective is an integrated paradigm of thinking about metropolitan life. Its basic premise is that spatial or environmental and locational considerations are always part and parcel of everyday social relationships. We cannot talk about one without also talking about the other. The sociospatial perspective is not urban ecology. It does not propose that explanation should follow biological principles, nor does it suggest that metropolitan development can be reduced to the effects of technological change alone. The sociospatial perspective presents a synthesis of class, race, gender, lifestyle, economics, culture, politics, and environmental considerations to explore the development of metropolitan regions. Each chapter borrows from this thematic perspective to discuss specific topics ranging from crime to Third World development and, when possible, makes comparative distinctions.

The goal of this text is not just to be innovative but to be up to date. Its chapter topics are comparable to those found in other urban texts. The fruits of our discontent with the outdated mainstream perspective are realized in the execution of the material. When discussing the development of ancient cities, for example, cultural and political factors are considered to be as important as economic ones. The urban history of the United States is presented as high drama involving fortunes made through real estate speculation as much as through industry. Social problems are depicted as metropolitan and regional concerns rather than as the exclusive products of city living. The diversity of daily life is presented in terms of the full spectrum of race, class, and gender considerations. And finally, when we turn to metropolitan policy and the environment, we want to know why programs fail, what ideologies govern metropolitan growth, and how we can improve metropolitan life.

Some chapters, however, depart somewhat from the typical fare of other presentations. We consider the metropolitan changes occurring in the United States since 1960 to be so unique that we have devoted a separate chapter to their discussion. Furthermore, in the chapters on urban history and contemporary development, it is necessary to take a global perspective and provide comparative material. While a discussion of the development of Third World cities is now standard in urban texts, we have added a new discussion of metropolitan development in Europe and Japan to more fully incorporate a global perspective and provide comparative material. Finally, unlike most urban sociology texts, this book has a separate chapter on metropolitan politics and another chapter on metropolitan policy and the environment. Both are important for understanding how people manage and how they might improve the space of everyday life.

In the third edition, we have updated the material in the first two editions and include important new research. The reader will find not only a more complete discussion of earlier theoretical work but also an extension of the sociospatial model to incorporate both older and emerging areas of research.

Specific changes and additions to the third edition include the following:

- general reorganization of the textbook to bring chapters on the development of urban theory and of the new urban sociology to the front of the text;
- consolidation of three chapters on the development of American cities into two chapters;
- addition of a new chapter on ethnic groups in cities and suburbs;
- extensive additions to chapters on world urbanization and metropolitan regions in the industrialized nations and in the developing world;
- a new concluding chapter on the prospects for urban sociology in the new urban century.

The development of *The New Urban Sociology* through three editions has been an extended project stretching over many years. It could not have been accomplished without the crucial help provided by a number of people. We wish to thank friends in academia for their support: Andrew Austin, Bob Antonio, Marcelo Cruz, David Diaz, Joe Feagin, Kevin Gotham, Harvey Kaye, Chigon Kim, Nestor Rodriguez, Eric Monkkonen, Peter Muller, Leonard Wallock, Georjeanna Wilson-Doenges, and Talmadge Wright in the United

States; Phil Gunn, Lena Lavinas, Sandra Lincioni, Czaba Deek, and Sueli Schiffer in Brazil; Alexandros Lagopoulos, Thomas Maloutas, Cheistos Kousidonis, and Nikos Komninos in Greece; Leslie Budd in England; Dorel Abraham in Romania; Jens Tonboe in Denmark; Gustavo Mesch and Noam Skoval in Israel; Jésus Leal in Spain; and José Luis Berand Lozano in Mexico. Randy Roethle and Tanya Krall (University of Wisconsin–Green Bay) provided editorial support for the second edition.

We are pleased to see the third edition of this text coming out under the Perseus Books imprint. We thank the editing/design/production team of Laura Stine, Michelle Mallin, and especially Steve Catalano.

We would like to thank our colleagues who served as reviewers for earlier editions: Brian Aldrich, Winona State University; Brian Barry, Rochester Institute of Technology; Craig Calhoun, then at the University of North Carolina, Chapel Hill, and now at New York University; Robert L. Carroll, University of Cincinnati; Scott Ford, Florida State University; Anthony Filipovitch, Minnesota State University at Mankato; Karl Flaming, University of Colorado–Denver; Judith Friedman, Rutgers University; Kevin Fox Gotham, Tulane University; Geoffrey Grant, South Dakota State University; George Kephart, Pennsylvania State University; Jerry Lembcke, College of Holy Cross; Anthony Mendonca, Community College of Allegheny County; Charles Price Reavis, CUNY–John Jay College of Criminal Justice; Nestor Rodriguez, University of Houston; Thomas Shannon, Radford University; Steven L. Vassar, Mankato State University; and J. Talmadge Wright, Loyola University.

THE NEW URBAN SOCIOLOGY

People speak about the city or the suburban town they live in, but rarely about the region. Yet the best way to understand urban growth is that it is regional in scale. Today we work, shop, attend schools, go to churches, synagogues, or mosques, and pursue recreation in an increasing variety of locations, all within an expanding metropolitan area. Urban texts in the past have addressed this issue, but they do not take it to heart as the central organizing principle of the discussion as this text does. In Eric Bogosian's brilliant film *Suburbia,* actress Parker Posey portrays an L.A. record promoter on tour who grew up in the affluent southern California suburbs. When asked by a group of small-town teenagers where she is from, she replies, "I come from an area." Bogosian insightfully understands that the words *city* and *suburb* fail to connect with the more contemporary reality of daily life.

The metropolitan regions of the United States contain an incredible array of people. Circumstances vary according to social class, race, gender, ethnicity, age, family status, and religion, among other factors. These important social variables, which are often treated as the traditional subject matter of sociology, in reality interact with locational, or spatial, factors such as the clustering of homes according to family income, the journey to work or school, the diverse ways people pursue a particular lifestyle, the particular patterning of our social networks, the regional search for cultural experiences, and the daily pattern of commuting. Consequently, this text captures the reality of contemporary life by studying daily phenomena as embedded within the urban and suburban settlement spaces that make up the multicentered metropolitan region. These settlement spaces are given special cultural meanings and value by the people living within them. Discovering how these settlement

1

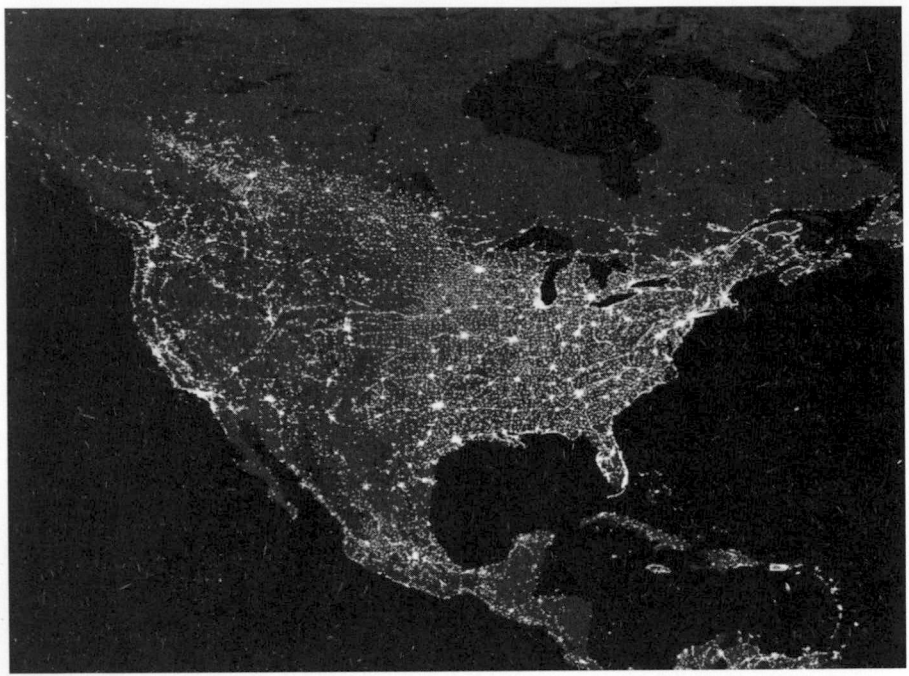

FIGURE 1.1 Satellite image of the United States at night showing metropolitan areas. *Source:* NASA.

spaces have come to be, the role that economic, political, and social institutions play in creating and destroying these spaces, and the processes by which these spaces are given meaning by local inhabitants is all part of the *sociospatial perspective* of the new urban sociology.

If we flew over our metropolitan regions, we would be struck most strongly by the immensity of scale. Urbanized development characteristically extends for one hundred miles around our largest cities. The built-up region contains a mix of cities, suburbs, vacant space, industrial parks, intensely farmed agricultural land, shopping malls, and recreational areas—all of which are interconnected and bridged by communication and commuter networks including highways, rail, telecommunications, and satellite- or cellular-based links. The satellite image of the United States at night shown in Figure 1.1 shows the extensive regional development of urban areas across the United States. Along the eastern seacoast of the United States, the Boston-New York-Washington megaopolis described by Jean Gottman is clearly visible. Similar urban agglomerations can be seen in the Buffalo-Toronto area around Lake Ontario, the Detroit-Toledo-Cleveland area around Lake Erie, the Milwaukee-Chicago-Gary area on Lake Michigan, and the San Francisco-San Jose-Oak-

TABLE 1.1   Most Populated Cities in the United States, 1980–2000

	1980	1990	2000	1990–2000	% change
New York City	7,077,000	7,323,000	8,008,000	686,000	9.4
Los Angeles	2,967,000	3,485,000	3,695,000	209,000	6.0
Chicago	3,005,000	2,784,000	2,896,000	112,000	4.0
Houston	1,595,000	1,631,000	1,954,000	256,000	15.1
Philadelphia	1,688,000	1,586,000	1,518,000	- 68,000	- 4.3
Phoenix	790,000	989,000	1,321,000	332,000	33.6
San Diego	876,000	1,111,000	1,223,000	112,000	10.1
Dallas	904,000	1,007,000	1,189,000	182,000	18.1
San Antonio	786,000	997,000	1,145,000	147,000	14.8
Detroit	1,203,000	1,028,000	951,000	- 77,000	- 7.5
San Jose	629,000	783,000	895,000	112,000	14.2
Indianapolis	701,000	732,000	782,000	50,000	6.9
San Francisco	679,000	724,000	777,000	53,000	7.3
Jacksonville	541,000	635,000	736,000	101,000	15.8
Columbus	565,000	636,000	712,000	75,000	11.8

SOURCE: Population figures from U.S. Bureau of the Census, *Statistical Abstract of the United States*, for years shown.

land area in California. The population of these areas ranks in the millions. Interestingly, most of the people residing in metropolitan regions live outside the large central cities and in the suburbs. The dominant position of the suburbs relative to the central cities has existed since at least the 1970s, when census figures brought this change to our attention. At present, some 90 percent of all Americans live in metropolitan regions. But this pattern of urban growth, and the dominance of the suburban region, was not characteristic of cities in the past.

Cities used to be highly compact spatial forms with a distinct center that dominated, in both an emotional and economic sense, the urbanized area surrounding it. Once inhabitants went outside the city, they would be traveling in the countryside. As the famous urban historian Lewis Mumford (1961) once observed, cities served as both huge magnets and containers that concentrated people and economic activities or wealth within well-defined, bounded spaces. Table 1.1 lists the 15 most populated cities in the United States. Some of the figures are impressive, such as a total of more than 8 million persons for New York City and more than 3.7 million for Los Angeles, and they demonstrate the great variability in urban growth, with cities like Houston and Phoenix growing by more than 250,000 persons over the past decade, while Philadelphia and Detroit both lost some 70,000 people. But these numbers do not illustrate the massive regional growth of metropolitan areas and their population concentration in the United States. Compare this table with Table 1.2, which shows the metropolitan regions associated with

TABLE 1.2   Most Populated Metropolitan Regions in the United States, 1970–2000

	1970	1980	1990	2000	1980–1990 % change	1990–2000 % change
New York-NJ–Long Island NECMA	18,071,522	17,412,203	17,830,586	21,200,000	3.4	8.4
Los Angeles–Anaheim–Riverside CMSA	9,980,850	11,497,549	14,531,529	16,374,000	26.4	12.7
Chicago–Gary–Hammond CMSA	7,778,948	7,973,290	8,239,820	9,158,000	1.5	11.1
San Francisco–Oakland–San Jose CMSA	4,754,366	5,367,900	6,249,881	7,039,000	16.4	12.6
Philadelphia–Trenton CMSA	5,749,093	5,680,509	5,893,019	6,188,000	4.3	5.0
Detroit–Ann Arbor MSA	4,788,369	4,762,764	5,187,171	5,456,000	- 2.0	5.2
Washington PMSA	3,040,307	3,250,921	4,222,830	4,923,000	21.4	16.6
Dallas–Ft. Worth CMSA	2,351,568	2,930,568	4,037,282	5,222,000	32.5	29.3
Boston–Lawrence–Salem NECMA	3,709,642	3,662,888	5,685,763	5,819,000	6.5	6.7
Houston–Galveston–Barzoria NECMA	2,169,128	3,099,942	3,731,029	4,670,000	19.6	25.2
Miami–Ft. Lauderdale MSA	1,887,892	2,643,766	3,192,725	3,443,501	20.8	21.4
Atlanta MSA	1,684,200	2,138,136	2,959,500	3,431,983	32.5	38.9
Cleveland–Akron–Lorain CMSA	2,999,811	2,834,062	2,859,644	2,903,808	- 2.7	3.0
Seattle–Tacoma CMSA	1,836,949	2,093,285	2,970,300	3,265,139	23.3	19.7
San Diego MSA	1,357,854	1,861,846	2,498,016	2,644,132	34.2	12.6
Minneapolis–St. Paul CMSA	1,981,951	2,137,133	2,538,776	2,723,137	15.4	16.9
St. Louis MSA	2,429,376	2,376,968	2,492,348	2,547,686	3.2	4.5
Baltimore MSA	2,089,438	2,199,497	2,382,172	2,553,000	8.3	7.2
Pittsburgh–Beaver Valley CMSA	2,556,029	2,423,311	2,394,811	2,394,702	- 6.9	- 1.5
Phoenix MSA	971,228	1,509,175	2,238,498	2,563,582	39.9	45.3

SOURCE: U.S. Bureau of the Census, *Statistical Abstract of the United States*, for years shown.

NOTE: MSAs are metropolitan statistical areas; CMSAs are consolidated metropolitan statistical areas; NECMAs are New England county metropolitan areas, which are based on townships and require a separate way of aggregating areas in the metropolitan region.

these large cities. The New York metro region, for example, contains 18 million people, while the area around Los Angeles is home to 16.4 million residents.

Today the city has exploded. There is no one focus or "downtown," as there was in the past. People live and work in widely separated realms. Most of the U.S. population is urban, so most live in or near some city. But progressively fewer people each year live within the large central cities that were the population foci of the past. Instead, we now call home the expanding regions of urbanization that are associated with a mix of cities, towns, suburbs, and exurban areas. This new form of settlement space is called the *multicentered metropolitan region (MCMR)*, and it is the first really new way people have organized their living and working arrangements in 10,000 years. In contrast to the characteristics of the bounded city, the new form of space can be typified by two features: It extends over a large region, and it contains many separate centers, each with its own abilities to draw workers, shoppers, and residents.

Some geographers have also begun to speak of multicentered urban regions. According to Peter Muller (1981), the urban region can be understood best as composed of different *realms*. Realms are differentiated according to four factors: physical terrain, physical size, the level and kinds of physical activity within the realm (most particularly the kinds of minicenters), and the character of the regional transportation network. Commuting flows are particularly critical both for the creation of multinucleated regions and for the connection and interaction of people within the regions. In addition to the physical features of the region, it is important that people living within each realm often have a shared sense that they occupy an urban space that is different from other areas within the metropolitan region.

For example, Los Angeles contains six distinct realms within a region of approximately 50 square miles and a metro population in 2003 of more than 16 million persons. Urban development is sandwiched between several mountain ranges, especially the long escarpment created by the San Gabriel and San Bernardino mountains to the north that runs east more than one hundred miles into the desert. On the West Coast is the Pacific Ocean, another barrier. The six realms are central Los Angeles (the old city center), the San Fernando Valley (the "valley"), the Pacific foothills (Santa Monica to Pasadena), the Pacific lowlands (beach cities—Hermosa, Redondo Beach), eastern Orange County (a separate metropolitan region that is exclusively suburban), and the San Gabriel and Pomona valleys (extending eastward and including Pomona, Ontario, and San Bernardino). See Figure 1.2.

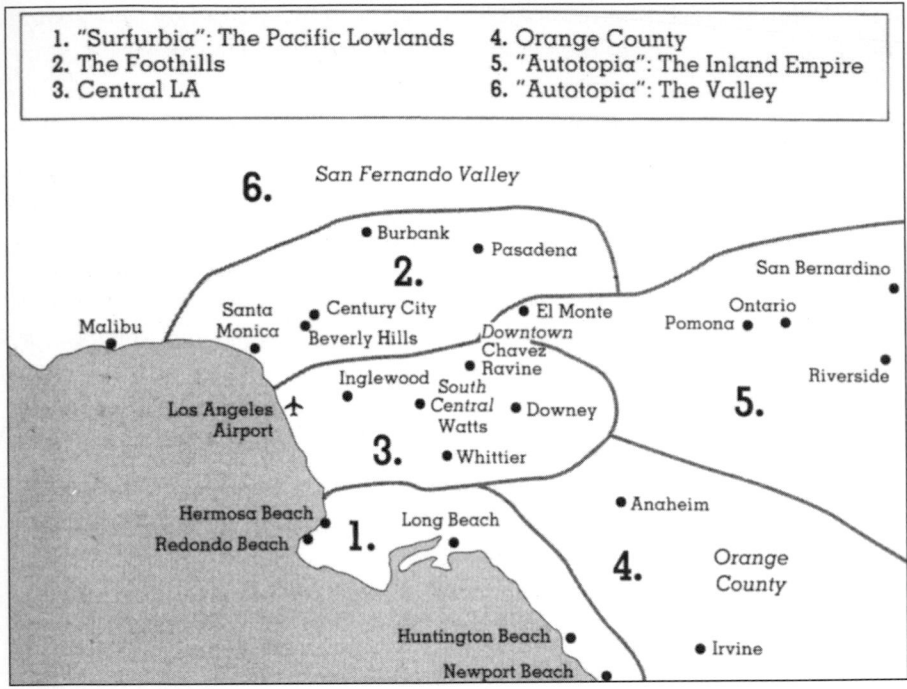

FIGURE 1.2   The Urban Realms of Los Angeles

DEFINING THE METROPOLITAN REGION

For much of U.S. history, it was sufficient to report information about the population of the central city. Most economic and commercial activity was focused in and around the central business district. By the early 1900s suburban and regional growth, including planned suburban communities, satellite cities, and other developments began to challenge the dominant role of the city. As early as the 1940s the U.S. Bureau of the Census sought to capture regional and multicentered growth within metropolitan areas by use of the term *standard metropolitan area (SMA)*. The SMA included a city with a population of at least 50,000 persons and the surrounding suburbs and towns. In 1959 this definition was expanded to better reflect the regional growth patterns that included population in centers in two or more counties. The *standard metropolitan statistical area (SMSA)* was defined as a county or counties with a central city of 50,000 or more (or twin cities with a combined population of 50,000 or more) as well as adjacent counties that are linked economically and socially with the central city.

This is determined by measuring the extent to which people in outlying counties travel to work to the designated SMSA. If enough people commute to work from outside city boundaries, the county they reside in becomes part of the SMSA. In 1983 the SMSA was relabeled *metropolitan statistical area (MSA)*. While the number of MSAs in the United States continues to grow (the number increased from 254 to 258 between the 1990 and 2000 censuses), two states, Wyoming and Vermont, still do not contain any. The 73 largest MSAs have been designated *primary metropolitan statistical areas (PMSAs)*. Because county boundaries vary widely across the United States (except in New England where there are no counties), the usefulness of the MSA classification is somewhat questionable. In the 2000 census, for example, New Jersey is the most urbanized state, with 100 percent of its population living in MSAs. But it is followed by Arizona (88 percent) and Nevada (86 percent), states where there are one or two large population centers and most of the state is rural.

The regional growth and the sociospatial integration of cities is even more extensive than the social, economic, and political links suggested by the MSA concept. The U.S. Office of Management and Budget created yet another term, the *standard metropolitan consolidated area (SMCA)* to better capture the expansion of the multinucleated urban regions. The SMCA was used for the first time in the 1980 census. It is defined as having a population of at least 1 million persons in two or more PMSAs *and* represents a higher order of integration for metropolitan areas that contain several adjacent metropolitan areas, such as the Los Angeles/Orange County/Riverside/San Bernardino complex in southern California or the New York/New Jersey/Connecticut complex on the East Coast. Both of these regions contain more people than the entire country of Canada. In the 2000 census there were eighteen consolidated metropolitan statistical areas in the United States. They are prime illustrations of the concept of the multinucleated metropolitan region that is so important for the new urban sociology.

Table 1.2 reveals important aspects of metropolitan growth in the United States. First, the urban system includes a significant number of metropolitan areas that have large populations rather than only one or two as is often found in developing nations (see Chapter 12 on primate cities). Second, the population in the suburban region is often much greater than that of the older central city. Philadelphia had a population just over 1.5 million persons in 2000, but its metropolitan region contained some 6.1 million persons, nearly four times as large. Phoenix had a population of 1.3 million in 2000, but the total metropolitan area included a population of more than 2.6 million, and San Diego had a population of 1.2 million, but its total metropolitan area included

BOX 1.1 Census Designations for Metropolitan Areas

Consolidated metropolitan statistical area (CMSA) A geographic entity defined by the Federal Office of Management and Budget (OMB) for use by Federal statistical agencies. An area becomes a CMSA if it meets the requirements to qualify as a metropolitan statistical area (MSA), has a population of 1,000,000 or more, if component parts are recognized as primary metropolitan statistical areas (PMSAs), and local opinion favors the designation. Whole counties are components of CMSAs outside of New England, where they are composed of cities and towns instead.

Metropolitan area (MA) A collective term, established by the Federal OMB and used for the first time in 1990, to refer to metropolitan statistical areas (MSAs), consolidated metropolitan statistical areas (CMSAs), and primary metropolitan statistical areas (PMSAs). In addition, there is an alternative set of areas termed NECMAs.

Metropolitan statistical area (MSA) A geographic entity, defined by the Federal OMB for use by Federal statistical agencies, based on the concept of a core area with a large population nucleus, plus adjacent communities having a high degree of economic and social integration with that core. Qualification of an MSA requires the presence of a city with 50,000 or more inhabitants, or the presence of an MA and a total population of at least 100,000 (75,000 in New England). The county or counties containing the largest city and surrounding densely settled territory are central counties of the MSA. Additional outlying counties qualify to be included in the MSA by meeting certain other criteria of metropolitan character, such as a specified minimum population density or percentage of the population that is urban. MSAs in New England are defined in terms of cities and towns, following rules concerning commuting and population density.

New England county metropolitan area (NECMA) County-based areas defined by the Federal OMB to provide an alternative to the city- and town-based MSAs and CMSAs in New England. A NECMA includes the county containing the first-named place in an MSA/CMSA title (this county may include the first-named places of other MSAs or CMSAs), and each additional county having at least half its population in the MSA(s)/CMSA(s) whose first-named place is in the county identified in the previous step. NECMAs were first defined in 1975.

Primary metropolitan statistical area (PMSA) A geographic entity defined by the Federal OMB for use by Federal statistical agencies. If an area meets the requirements to qualify as a metropolitan statistical area (MSA) and has a population of one million or more, two or more PMSAs may be defined within it if statistical criteria are met and local opinion is in favor. A PMSA consists of a large urbanized county, or a cluster of such counties (cities and towns in New England) that have substantial commuting interchange. When one or more PMSAs have been recognized, the bal-

(continues)

ance of the original, larger area becomes an additional PMSA; the larger area of which they are components then is designated a consolidated metropolitan statistical area (CMSA). PMSAs were first defined and effective on June 30, 1983.

Standard consolidated area (SCA) The SCA was a forerunner of the CMSA. Two SCAs (for the New York and Chicago areas) existed between 1959 and 1975. These SCAs were combinations of SMSAs, although the New York SCA also included two counties that were not within any SMSA. The SCA was replaced by the SCSA.

Standard consolidated statistical area (SCSA) The SCSA was a forerunner of the CMSA. An SCSA was a combination of two or more SMSAs that had substantial commuting between them and where at least one of the SMSAs had a population of 1,000,000 or greater. SCSAs were first defined in 1975 and used until June 1983.

Standard metropolitan area (SMA) SMA was the first term used for official metropolitan areas as defined by the then Bureau of the Budget. SMAs were first defined in 1949 for the 1950 decennial census, and the term was used until replaced in 1959 with the term SMSA.

Standard metropolitan statistical area (SMSA) In 1959, the term SMSA replaced SMA for the official metropolitan areas defined by the then Bureau of the Budget. The term SMSA was used until MSAs, CMSAs, and PMSAs were introduced in 1983. See also consolidated metropolitan statistical area, metropolitan area, metropolitan statistical area, primary metropolitan statistical area, standard consolidated area, standard consolidated statistical area, standard metropolitan area.

SOURCE: U.S. BUREAU OF THE CENSUS

2.6 million persons. Third, while metropolitan areas across the Northeast and Midwest have grown slowly or even lost population since the 1970s, the multinucleated metropolitan regions of the South and Southwest have grown rapidly. This illustrates the Sunbelt shift, discussed in Chapter 6. For example, the Los Angeles, San Francisco, Dallas, Houston, San Diego, and Phoenix metropolitan regions have all seen double-digit population increases in each decade since 1970.

MEGACITIES AROUND THE WORLD

The world's urban population was 1 billion in 1960, 2 billion in 1985, and 3 billion in 2003. It is expected to increase to 5 billion persons by 2030—a 60 percent increase in just 25 years. In 2003 about 48 percent of the world's population lived in urban areas. This number is expected to increase to 61 percent by 2030. For the first time in human history, a majority of the world's population will live in urban areas. At the current rate of growth, the urban population will double every 38 years. Almost all of this growth will occur in cities and metropolitan regions in the developing world. Migration from rural areas and the transformation of rural settlements into urban places will account for much of the increase (United Nations, 2003).

Not every country of the world is experiencing the new form of multicentered metropolitan growth found in the United States, but all countries are subject to a process of urban development that produces gigantic cities and regional urbanization. According to Dogan and Kasarda (1988), only 78 cities across the globe had populations of 1 million or more in 1950. In 1975 there were 65 metropolitan areas with 10 million or more persons, and by 2000 this number had increased to 251. The growth of large metropolitan regions is also expected to accelerate. In 2015 it is anticipated that there will be 358 urban agglomerations with populations of at least 10 million persons and that more than a third of the world's urban population will live in slums. Table 1.3 indicates the 15 largest *megacities* in the world with their projected populations to the year 2015.

Urban growth is very unequally distributed across the globe. According to census estimates from the United Nations, the largest urban agglomerations in the United States and other developed nations will lose population or grow slowly, whereas those in other areas of the world will experience explosive growth. Thus, the population estimates for the year 2015 for Tokyo, Osaka, New York, and Los Angeles suggest that these urban agglomerations will experience relatively slow growth. In contrast, Mumbai (Bombay), Calcutta, Dhaka, and Delhi (all in India), and Karachi (in Pakistan) are expected to grow by some 4–8 million persons each, and São Paolo, Mexico City, and Manila are expected to grow by some 2–3 million persons.

Although the potential benefits from urbanization cannot be overlooked, the speed and scale of this second urban revolution presents many challenges. The rapid growth and overwhelming sprawl of cities in the developing nations, particularly in Asia, has been given a new term—*hyperurbanization* (see Chapter 12). New groups of policymakers and organizations are emerging to take up responsibilities of urban governance in developing nations around the globe. As national governments in many such countries have sought to decentralize their functions, or even to cut back their participation, programs in poverty, health, education, and public services are increasingly being deposited in the hands of untested municipal and regional governments. While the acceleration of urban growth in developing countries suggests staggering social costs for many persons around the world, the continuing expansion of multinucleated metropolitan regions in the United

TABLE 1.3 World's Largest Urban Agglomerations, 1975–2015

Agglomeration	Country	Population (millions)			Rank			Average annual rate of change (percent)		Population residing in agglomeration, 2003, as percentage of	
		1975	2003	2015	1975	2003	2015	2000–2005	2010–2015	Total population	Urban population
Tokyo	Japan	26.6	35.0	36.2	1	1	1	0.5	0.2	27.4	41.9
Mexico City	Mexico	10.7	18.7	20.6	4	2	4	1.0	0.8	18.0	23.9
New York	United States of America	15.9	18.3	19.7	2	3	6	0.7	0.6	6.2	7.7
São Paulo	Brazil	9.6	17.9	20.0	6	4	5	1.4	0.7	10.0	12.0
Mumbai (Bombay)	India	7.3	17.4	22.6	15	5	2	2.6	2.0	1.6	5.8
Delhi	India	4.4	14.1	20.9	25	6	3	4.2	2.8	1.3	4.7
Calcutta	India	7.9	13.8	16.8	11	7	10	1.8	1.7	1.3	4.6
Buenos Aires	Argentina	9.1	13.0	14.6	7	8	12	1.2	0.8	34.0	37.7
Shanghai	China	11.4	12.8	12.7	3	9	15	−0.3	0.3	1.0	2.5
Jakarta	Indonesia	4.8	12.3	17.5	23	10	8	3.6	2.5	5.6	12.3
Los Angeles	United States of America	8.9	12.0	12.9	8	11	14	0.6	0.6	4.1	5.1
Dhaka	Bangladesh	2.2	11.6	17.9	73	12	7	4.2	3.3	7.9	32.5
Osaka–Kobe	Japan	9.8	11.2	11.4	5	13	18	0.2	0.0	8.8	13.5
Rio de Janeiro	Brazil	7.6	11.2	12.4	13	14	17	1.2	0.7	6.3	7.6
Karachi	Pakistan	4.0	11.1	16.2	28	15	11	3.3	3.1	7.2	21.2
Beijing	China	8.5	10.8	11.1	10	16	20	0.0	0.4	0.8	2.2
Cairo	Egypt	6.4	10.8	13.1	19	17	13	1.4	1.7	15.1	35.8
Moscow	Russian Federation	7.6	10.5	10.9	12	18	21	1.1	0.1	7.3	10.0
Metro Manila	Philippines	5.0	10.4	12.6	22	19	16	1.4	1.7	12.9	21.2
Lagos	Nigeria	1.9	10.1	17.0	90	20	9	5.0	3.9	8.1	17.4

SOURCE: Adapted from United Nations Department of Economic and Social Affairs, Urban Agglomerations 2003.

States and other developed nations also presents serious challenges for policy-makers, governments, and those of us who live in the urban world.

A NEW APPROACH TO URBAN SOCIOLOGY

How did these changes come about? What is daily life like in the multinucle-ated metropolitan region? How does life there differ from that in the past? How has the city construction process, or *urbanization*, given way to the re-gional process of concentrated central city development, dispersed minicen-tered districts, and sprawling suburbanization? What is metropolitan culture like in the new regional spaces, and how does it differ from city life of the past? The answers to these and other questions are the subject of this book. Our discussion is about urban sociology, but it is not about the city alone. On the pages that follow we take an integrated perspective according to the re-gional focus of multicentered regional space. We consider both life in the city (urban settlement space) and life in the suburbs (suburban settlement space). But there is much more.

The new urban sociology has three additional dimensions: the shift to a global perspective, attention to the political economy of pull factors in urban and suburban development, and appreciation for the role of culture in metro-politan life and in the construction of the built environment.

GLOBAL CAPITALISM AND THE METROPOLIS

The contemporary metropolis is the consequence of the complicated and continuing interaction of economic, political, and cultural forces. In recent years, urbanists have come to appreciate just how important the link is be-tween cities or suburbs and changes in the economy. Prior to the 1970s, dis-cussions about urban political economy assumed that the most critical influence on urban growth and development was the behavior of local busi-ness people. A resident of a town might open up a store or factory. The owner would be known by others in the area. Jobs would be created, and local resi-dents would apply for and fill them. Products of factories might be sold na-tionally, but locals would take pride in homegrown commodities and support the businesses of neighbors with their patronage, often because there was no place else to go.

This state of affairs no longer exists. Economic activity in metropolitan communities has become increasingly controlled by decisions made at the global level. Businesses are owned and managed by people from distant lo-cations. The local TV repair shop, for example, may represent a manufacturer, such as Sony, whose headquarters are in another country, say Japan. The TV sets themselves may be assembled in Korea or Malaysia. Finally, the selling and repairing of the company's product may be supervised by foreign representatives of the manufacturer living in this country. Reversing this example, many U.S. companies, such as Ford and General Motors, engage in such manufacturing, marketing, and administrative activities overseas. In short, economies today are linked across the globe, and the small, local factory with ties to the adjacent community has given way to the multinational corporation and to the global flow of investment as the dominant economic forces.

The global perspective has important implications for the study of metropolitan regions. Prior to the 1970s, urban sociologists saw changes in the city as emerging from the interaction of many local interests in a shared and common space. According to the sociologist Gerald Suttles (1972:8), this *ecological* approach, as it is called, meant that the organization of the city was not caused by "the planned or artificial contrivance of anyone." Rather, it emerged out of the "many independent personal decisions based on moral, political, ecological, and economic considerations." Today we possess a different understanding of urban organization as being caused by the actions of powerful interests, many of which have their home bases in places far removed from local areas. Their decisions, for example, to open a plant somewhere, close one down someplace else, buy up farms to build houses, or tear down existing housing to create minimalls or apartment buildings are all so important that they affect the well-being of the entire community.

The perspective adopted in this text, however, does not suggest that all important influences on metropolitan development derive from the global level. Important economic and political forces also arise from within community territory that can account for change. In the following chapters, therefore, we will consider the contribution to metropolitan development of all sociospatial levels: the global, the national, and the local. It is the interplay of the forces from the different levels within the local space that is the most interesting.

Since the 1970s, urban scholars have paid increasing attention to the relationship between capitalism and the metropolis (see Chapter 4). Competition among businesses that may not have a direct effect on space has been overshadowed by the competition among different places for their share of global investment (see Chapters 5, 12, and 13). Local populations and community well-being are also affected by changes in job needs, the level of economic activity, and growing lifestyle disparities between low-skilled or semiskilled workers and professionals living in the metropolis (see Chapter 10). All of these aspects constitute a new dimension to the study of urban sociology.

THE PRODUCTION OF THE MULTICENTERED
METRO ENVIRONMENT: PULL FACTORS

Prior to the 1970s, urban scholars looked at city and suburban growth as an expression of individual desires. For example, people moved from the city to the suburbs, it was believed, because they preferred the latter's lifestyle. In another case, investors picked a particular plot of land to develop because they liked its size and location. Individual actions based on individually held beliefs or needs might be termed the *demand-side* or push factor view of market activity, because they express the ways in which people and business act on their own desires. Urban sociology prior to the 1970s viewed growth almost exclusively in this manner.

At present, we are aware of several factors that operate to promote development in specific ways and thereby mold individual desires through incentives. These factors represent the *supply-side* or pull factor view of individual choice. Powerful social forces can create opportunities that persuade people to follow courses of action that they otherwise might not. Two supply-side sources of incentives in the development of metropolitan regions are government and the real estate industry.

The Role of Government in Urban Development

The abstract model of capitalism represents this economic system as involving limited government intervention. This is not the case for modern economies. The United States, like other industrialized nations, has an economy that is influenced greatly not only by government regulations but also by the direct spending of government tax dollars on particular public projects. The combined action of laws or regulations and direct investment provides incentives for both businesses and individual consumers to behave in certain ways.

When city dwellers who are renters announce that they want to move to the suburbs, they are expressing their own personal preference. This decision may be occasioned by push (demand-side) factors such as problems with the public schools and high rents. Movers may also cite that the suburb they have chosen contains single-family homes that are affordable. Furthermore, due to government tax incentives on mortgage payments, it pays to own your home rather than rent. Government programs provide an enticement that pulls people in the direction of homeownership in the suburbs.

So the decision to move to the suburbs is a complex one that is prompted by both demand- and supply-side factors. For years urbanists neglected the latter dimension. Today we have a greater appreciation, in particular, for the way government at the local, state, and federal levels has operated to create opportunities and incentives that channel behavior in specific ways. In subsequent chapters we will see how this "political economy," the linked actions of business and government in the development of metropolitan regions, promotes growth.

Another major and recent change in the population distribution of the United States has been the rise of the Sunbelt. By the 2000 population census, the majority of Americans lived in the Sunbelt and western states. This transformation represents a phenomenal shift of residential location. Historically, the Midwest and the East Coast contained the bulk of the U.S. population, and this remained true until the past few decades.

According to the old urban sociology, the shift to the Sunbelt would have been produced by technological factors, such as inexpensive airline travel and demand-side preferences for a mild climate. To be sure, these factors are part of the equation. However, the pull factors created by the political economy of the United States and its government spending cannot be ignored. They are, in fact, the major reasons for Sunbelt growth because this federal outlay created millions of jobs. The employment, in turn, provided the base for Sunbelt growth and expansion. One aspect alone tells a good part of the story. Beginning with World War II, the United States spent billions of dollars on military installations in locations in the West and in the Sunbelt. California, Florida, Georgia, and New Mexico, among others, were recipients of vast sums of spending. Even Las Vegas, which had been growing as the gambling mecca of the country after the war, benefited from large-scale government spending that created jobs, first, with the construction of Boulder Dam and then with the placement of the gigantic Nellis Air Force base in the region. Later, the Korean and Vietnam wars reinforced this pattern. The states of Texas and Florida benefited greatly from the NASA space program, as we know from the familiar names of "Houston Control" and "Cape Kennedy."

The old urban sociology simply ignored the effects of government spending and tax incentives, that is, the *political economy* of the United States. Our sociospatial perspective considers this factor of central importance.

The Role of the Real Estate Industry in Development

With some notable exceptions (Hoyt, 1933; Hughes, 1928; Form, 1954), early urban sociologists have neglected the critical role the real estate industry plays in metropolitan development. Recall from the discussion above that at one time, urban organization was viewed not as the product of any particular interest but as the interplay of many separate ones (the ecological approach). Presently, we understand that the opposite is often the case. Special interests such as global corporations can make or break a town depending on where they decide to invest new capital. But the single most important source of special interests in the development of the metropolis is the real estate industry.

The real estate sector includes all those corporations and banks, as well as land developers and construction companies, that invest in the development of land use and housing, including the land and the built environment themselves. The construction of new spaces proceeds through the actions of all those individuals, financial conduits, and corporations that make money from the change (turnover) in land use. Because a great deal of money often can be made through this type of activity, real estate interests are powerful special actors in the development of the metropolis, and their influence is greatly felt.

At any given time and on any piece of land, real estate forces can converge to turn over the existing use and engage in development that changes the utilization of local space. All of this is done in the pursuit of profit that comes as a consequence of development. Thus, in addition to understanding the political economy of production, it is important to understand the political economy of real estate.

THE IMPORTANCE OF CULTURE IN METROPOLITAN LIFE

Many of the discussions of urban issues involve economic and political concerns. As we have seen, some of the more important aspects of the new urban sociology emphasize a greater attention to political economy. But this is not all there is to the new approach. People live in a symbolic world that is meaningful to them. They possess sentiments and ideas and attempt to communicate with others using common concepts.

Much of this interaction is organized through the direct use of spoken or written language. A significant part, however, employs expressive symbols that are used to convey meanings. One of the principal sources of symbolic life involves aspects of the built environment. For example, cities and suburbs are the sites of many subcultures—ethnic, religious, racial, gender specific, and age related. Neighborhoods within the metropolis can readily be identified by objects that are signs of subcultural status. For example, ethnic areas of the city advertise themselves by the signs in front of restaurants, bakeries, specialty shops, and religious institutions (see Chapter 8). Urban subcultures may produce graffiti to show the boundaries of their neighborhood or to make claims over social space within the metropolis (see Figure 1.3). People use such signs to orient themselves in the act of engaging in metropolitan life.

FIGURE 1.3   Urban Semiotics

The study of culture and the role of objects as signs constitutes a significant part of the new urban sociology. Sociologists have studied metropolitan life as culturally meaningful for some time. What is new and different is the way such meanings are associated with objects in addition to words. For example, cities often try to develop an image that boosts attention in order to attract investment and tourists. A variety of images have been used, such as signs of industry ("motor city"), signs of regional growth ("the twin cities"), signs of vision ("the city of tomorrow"), and signs of life's good quality ("the city of leisure"). Slogans such as these are often linked to images or objects, such as a skyline or graphic logo of some kind. In this way, a particular symbolic identity is created for a place that gives the impression that it is special. The study of culture that links symbols to objects is called *semiotics,* and the special subfield that studies the built environment in this manner is called *spatial semiotics.*

In the past, approaches to urban sociology have neglected the symbolic aspect of space, although some interesting early exceptions exist (see Wohl and Strauss, 1958). The perspective we will follow in this book integrates the symbolic nature of environments with more traditional factors that make up social behavior, such as class, race, gender, age, and social status. Space, then, is another compositional factor in human behavior. We call this new perspective on metropolitan life the *sociospatial* approach.

SUMMARY: THE SOCIOSPATIAL APPROACH

In the past, urbanists have regarded space as only a container of social activities. But this view is limited. Space not only contains actions but also acts as a meaningful object to which we orient our actions. The factor of space constitutes a part of social relations and is intimately involved in our daily lives. It affects the way we feel about what we do. In turn, people alter space and construct new environments to better fit their needs. Hence, a dual relationship exists between people and space. On the one hand, human beings act according to social factors such as gender, class, race, age, and status within and in reaction to a given space. When a city converts a vacant lot into a basketball court, the type of activity and interaction of groups of persons within that space will change. On the other hand, people also create and alter spaces to express their own needs and desires.

The sociospatial perspective connects the dual relationship between people and space with the social factors that are the bases of individual behavior. The most basic concept of this approach is *settlement space,* which refers to the built environment in which people live. Settlement space is both constructed and organized. It is built by people who have followed some meaningful plan for the purpose of containing economic, political, and cultural activities. Within it, people organize their daily actions according to the meaningful aspects of the constructed space. In subsequent chapters we will discuss how sociospatial factors determine the construction and use of settlement space. Over time we will also see how change has occurred and how constructed environments are in turn molded by sociospatial factors.

In summation, the sociospatial perspective consists of attention to the following dimensions of daily life:

1. The urban and suburban settlement spaces that make up the built environment have developed within a larger metropolitan region. We adopt a regional perspective to study the older central cities, suburban communities, and new growth poles that make up the metropolitan region of the twenty-first century. We call this new form of social space the multicentered metropolitan region. We ask how and why multicentered metropolitan regions in the United States and across the globe came to be structured the way they are.

2. Settlement spaces are considered not only within their local and national contexts but as linked to the global system of capitalism. We pay special attention to the powerful forces of economics and politics, whose decisions influence the well-being of local areas. These economic and

political decisions may derive from the metropolitan, the national, or even the international level.

3. Settlement spaces are affected by government policies and by the actions of developers, financiers, and other organizations and individuals that make up the real estate industry. These supply-side forces provide incentives and opportunities that pull and mold the behaviors, preferences, and choices of individual consumers and channel metropolitan development in certain specific ways. The real estate market does not simply respond to consumer demand; government policy (or the absence of such policy) at the local, state, and national levels has important consequences for metropolitan development.

4. The urban and suburban settlement spaces that make up the built environment are the products of human thought and action and are always meaningful places. Everyday life is organized according to cultural symbols and material objects that are part of the built environment; these symbols and objects are likely to have different meanings to different individuals or groups. We call the study of these symbols and objects urban semiotics.

5. Sociologists recognize that social class groups are an essential element of industrial and postindustrial societies. Social class groups differ from one another with respect to lifestyle, attitudes, beliefs, and access to political power and influence. As a consequence, these groups have more or less influence on decisions about how social space is allocated and structured within and across the metropolitan region.

6. The sociospatial perspective emphasizes the interaction between society and space. To class, gender, race, and other social characteristics that define difference among groups in contemporary society we add the element of space itself. The spatial arrangements found in urban and suburban settlement space have both manifest and latent consequences: They influence human behavior and interaction in predictable ways, but also in ways the original planner or developer may not have anticipated. But individuals, through their behaviors and interactions with others, constantly alter existing spatial arrangements and construct new spaces to express their needs and desires.

KEY CONCEPTS

multinucleated metropolitan region
geographic realms
standard metropolitan statistical area

standard metropolitan consolidated area
megacity
global capitalism
demand-side (push) factors
supply-side (pull) factors of development
political economy of real estate
built environment
urban signs and urban semiotics
sociospatial perspective
settlement space

DISCUSSION QUESTIONS

1. What is meant by the concept of the "multinucleated metropolitan region"? How is the multinucleated metropolitan region different from urban development of the past? Why is the metropolitan regional perspective important for understanding urban growth around the globe?

2. The authors suggest that most of the time we do not consciously think about or identify the metropolitan region from which we come. What are some of the characteristics of the metropolitan region in which you grew up?

3. The authors believe that other approaches to urban sociology, which focus upon urban neighborhoods and urban ethnic groups, are no longer useful for understanding metropolitan life in the United States. Why do they hold this point of view?

4. The sociospatial approach to urban sociology emphasizes the links with the global system of capitalism, the actions of the real estate industry, government policies, pull factors of development, the social organization of urban and suburban settlement space, and the importance of culture. Pick two of these factors and explain how they have influenced the development of the multinucleated metropolitan region that you live in.

5. The concept of "space" is important in our understanding of metropolitan life. List two important characteristics of this concept and discuss their significance for our understanding of daily life in urban and suburban settlement spaces of the multinucleated metropolitan region.

THE ORIGINS OF
URBAN LIFE

Five thousand years of urban history and perhaps as many of proto-urban history are spread over a few score of only partly exposed sites. The great urban landmarks Ur, Nippur, Uruk, Thebes, Helopolis, Assur, Ninevah, Babylon, cover a span of three thousand years whose vast emptiness we cannot hope to fill with a handful of monuments and a few hundred pages of written records.

LEWIS MUMFORD, *THE CITY IN HISTORY*

The origins of urban life—the period when humankind was transformed from hunters and gatherers to city dwellers—is shrouded in the distant past. Yet we know that cities and urban civilizations appeared in many different areas of the world independent of one another in the relatively recent past. Urbanization, or the building of and living in compact densely populated places, appeared as early as 10,000 years ago. Continuously used, densely populated settlements can be found in the Middle East that date back over 6,000 years and in the Indus Valley in India that date back over 4,000 years. Other centers of ancient urban life include the Minoan civilization of Crete (1800 BC) and the cities of China (circa 2000 BC). The origins of the earliest cities are shown in Table 2.1.

The population of ancient cities tended to be small by present-day standards. Mohenjo-Daro in the Indus Valley had a population at its height of approximately 20,000 inhabitants. At its peak in the fifth century BC, classical Athens, the birthplace of Western art, architecture, and philosophy, had no more than 150,000 inhabitants. Until the late Middle Ages, no city could compare with ancient Rome, which housed over 1 million people in the first century AD.

TABLE 2.1   World's Earliest Cities

Region	Location	Approximate Date
Mesopotamia	Tigris and Euphrates Rivers	3900 BC
Egypt	Nile River valley	3200 BC
India	Indus River valley	2400 BC
Eastern Mediterranean	Crete	1600 BC
China	Yellow River valley	1600 BC
Mexico	Yucatan Peninsula	200 BC

SOURCE: Adapted from Ivan Light, *Cities in World Perspective* (New York: Macmillan, 1983), p. 13.

Lewis Mumford, the great scholar of urban history and culture, has suggested that the first human settlements were cities of the dead—the Thanatopolis. The dead were the first to have a permanent dwelling (the caverns and mounds where Paleolithic hunters buried their dead). Men and women would return to these ritual spaces to worship ancestors, and it is here that humankind first drew pictographs and paintings of not only animals for the hunt but also formalized figures of men and women. Mumford writes (1961:10), "The first germ of the city, then, is in the ceremonial meeting place that serves as the goal for pilgrimage: a site to which family or clan groups are drawn back, at seasonable intervals, because it concentrates, in addition to any natural advantages that it may have, certain 'spiritual' or supernatural powers, powers of higher potency and duration, of wider cosmic significance, than the ordinary processes of life."

Several ancient cities possessed remarkable structural features that made urban living not only possible but also quite comfortable. Mohenjo-Daro in ancient India had a grid street system that made maximum use of space and an open sewer system for the elimination of waste and rainwater. Baked clay sewer pipes and roofing tiles have been unearthed at the site of this early city that are identical to the materials used in modern construction. Two-story houses were constructed around a central courtyard with balconies on the second floor. The courtyard provided private space for families but also allowed for the circulation of air through the building—important for the hot climate of the region. Jericho, in ancient Israel, possessed a system of canals that aided the irrigation of fields outside the city. The palace at Knossos, on Crete, which is over 3,000 years old, was several stories high and was designed to allow light to enter from the roof as well as the sides. However, it is easy to overemphasize these special cases. Most ancient cities, such as Athens, were plagued by unsanitary housing conditions and streets.

The citizens of the early towns lived an urban life that was fragile. Precariousness was, perhaps, an inevitable consequence of the growth of cities. Ac-

---

BOX 2.1 Lamentations (the Bible)

How doth the city sit solitary, that was full of people! How is she become as a widow! She that was great among the nations, and princess among the provinces, how is she become tributary!

She weepeth sore in the night, and her tears are on her cheeks; she hath none to comfort her among all her lovers; all her friends have dealt treacherously with her, they are become her enemies.

Her adversaries are become the head, her enemies are at ease; for the Lord hath afflicted her for the multitude of her transgressions; her young children are gone into captivity before the adversary.

And gone is from the daughter of Zion all her splendour; her princes are become like harts that find no pasture, and they are gone without strength before the pursuer.

Jerusalem remembereth in the days of her affliction and of her anguish all her treasures that she had from the days of old; now that her people fall by the hand of the adversary, and none doth help her, the adversaries have seen her, they have mocked at her desolations.

For these things I weep; mine eye, mine eye runneth down with water; because the comforter is far from me, even he that should refresh my soul; my children are desolate, because the enemy hath prevailed.

SOURCE: LAMENTATIONS 1 (THE BIBLE)

---

cording to Gideon Sjoberg (1960), cities were the sites of power. In order to be secure, it was necessary for early cities to exercise their strength and dominate the hinterland, the relatively less developed area outside the boundaries of the large city. Then, in order to prosper, it was necessary to expand the hinterland sphere of domination. As sites of wealth, ancient cities were protected by fortifications, and warfare between cities was quite common. Average town citizens lived under the constant threat of attack by roving bands of warriors or the armies of other towns. Often victors simply killed off or enslaved defeated city populations, and then the city itself was burned to the ground. In Judges we read, "And he took the city, and slew the people therein, and he beat down the city and served it with salt."

We have many accounts of the destruction of early cities in the great writings that have come down to us from the earliest urban civilizations. The section of the Old Testament called Lamentations was written by the prophet Jeremiah, who was a court official in Jerusalem when the city was conquered by the Babylonian ruler Nebuchadnezzar in 587 BC. In Lamentations the ancient Hebrews lament the loss of their city from their exile in Babylonia (see

Box 2.1). In *The Trojan Women*, the Greek author Euripides writes about the destruction of the ancient city of Troy. After its defeat by the Greeks, the Trojan men were killed or taken into slavery, and the women were parceled out to the victors. These two stories illustrate the unhappy fate of the inhabitants of the early cities in the face of war among competing city-states (see Box 2.2).

The domination of urban settlements by successful rulers led, in turn, not only to increased trade and commerce but also to more war and the exercise of power over the countryside. Early urban existence constituted a drama involving such interwoven spheres of everyday life as agricultural production, regional and foreign trade, military conquest and rule, and the pursuit of arts and sciences based on the relative success of economic and political activities.

Most discussions of early cities focus on the apparent division of labor and economic activities around which the concentrated population was organized. In this way, city life is discussed as a progression from limited to complex specialization of work and functional organization. Not only were cities the locus of social functions; they created *social spaces* that had religious meaning and significance. Cities did not simply appear because certain fundamental social activities had matured. Cities had to be produced, or constructed, by humans through the conscious intent of individuals and groups. In ancient societies, urban settlements were built using a shared set of symbols and a model of space that was inherently meaningful to each group (Lagopoulos, 1986). Early cities, such as Ur in ancient Babylon, were produced using cosmological codes that mandated geometrical relations between the city and the heavens, such as an east-west axis, and within the city through geometrical arrangements of the buildings. In this way, the built environment of even the earliest urban settlements had important social, political, and religious connections that created a sense of shared history and identity among the urban inhabitants.

Religious codes distinguished between sacred and profane spaces and endowed particular structures and spaces with the protection of the gods. Around 500 BC, the Etruscans, ancestors of the Romans, built cities by first plowing a "sacred furrow" as a large enclosure in a religious ceremony. The city could be built only within this space, signifying the sacred domain, separated from the profane space of the rest of the world. Only later, in fourteenth- and fifteenth-century Europe, did cities first appear without religious or cosmological codes guiding the construction of space. At this time, and continuing to the present day in Europe (and the United States), the meaning of a building (such as a bank) corresponded to the function it performed in the society with no necessary connection to any particular social or religious meaning. In contrast, in the earliest human settlements, and through at least the time of the medieval city, there was a strong connection between

BOX 2.2 The Fate of the Trojan Women

Scene: The action takes place shortly after the capture of Troy. Priam, the king of the Trojans, has been killed. All of the men have been put to the sword; all of the women and children have been made captive. The following dialogue takes place in an open space in front of the city, which smolders in the background. The speaker is Hecuba, the former Queen of Troy:

Lift thy head, unhappy lady, from the ground; thy neck upraise; this is Troy no more, no longer am I queen in Ilium. Though fortune change, endure thy lot; sail with the stream, and follow fortune's tack, steer not thy barque of life against the tide, since chance must guide thy course. Ah me! ah me! What else but tears is now my hapless lot, whose country, children, husband, all are lost? Ah! the high-blown pride of ancestors! How cabined now, how brought to nothing after all. What woe must I suppress, or what declare? What plaintive dirge shall I awake? Ah, woe is me! The anguish I suffer lying here stretched upon this pallet hard! O my head, my temples, my side! Ah! could I but turn over, and he now on this, now on that, to rest my back and spine, while ceaselessly my tearful wail ascends. For 'en this is music to the wretched, to chant their cheerless dirge of sorrow.

Ah! hapless wives of those mail-clad sons of Troy! Ah! poor maidens, luckless brides, come weep, for Ilium is now but a ruin; and I, like some mother-bird that o'er her fledglings screams, will begin the strain; how different from that song I sang to the gods in days long past, as I leaned on Priam's staff, and beat with my foot in Phrygian time to lead the dance!

Oh! do not bid the wild Cassandra leave her chamber, the frantic prophetess, for Argives to insult, nor to my griefs add yet another. Woe to thee, ill-fated Troy, thy sun is set; and woe to thy unhappy children, quick and dead alike, who are leaving thee behind!

SOURCE: FROM EURIPIDES, *THE TROJAN WOMEN*

buildings and the way individuals living within the city conceived of the meanings of those buildings.

As the sociospatial perspective suggests, the ancient city was the combined product of political power, economic functions, and overarching symbolic meanings that expressed deeply held beliefs of the inhabitants.

ANCIENT URBANIZATION

Social scientists are interested in the origin of cities because the process of early urbanization holds insights into the origins of social structure. In particular, the origin of the first urban communities provides clues for an understanding of how complex social relations arose and how strong bonds were maintained among residents who were often unrelated. The best-known theory of the rise of cities was proposed by V. Gordon Childe (1950, 1954). According to Childe, the first cities developed a form of social organization that differed from rural society in many respects and provided the social basis for modern life.

Childe viewed the development of society in terms of distinct stages and considered the emergence of urban life as a critical evolutionary phase in the rise of modern civilization. City building was part of an "urban revolution" that also brought a set of special social relations that are characteristic of modern life. The first step toward an urban society occurred when hunting and gathering societies shifted to food production in relatively stable and sedentary groups. Once the urban revolution began, civilization progressed and evolved to more complex forms of social life sustained by an urban economy based on trade and craft production. It is principally from Childe that we have derived the idea that urbanization develops through specialization of work and the separation of different functions through increasing interdependence of societal tasks. These social relations were considered different from those found in rural society, and they provided the basis for modern civilization.

The urban revolution possessed a number of distinct characteristics, including (1) a large population of several thousand inhabitants; (2) craftspeople, merchants, priests, and state functionaries who worked full time in these specialized occupations; (3) control of food production in the hinterland and the storage of the surplus; (4) a ruling class that possessed absolute control over the society; (5) numerical and alphabetical notational systems for information processing; (6) cultural forms of expression that were progressively refined, such as art and music; and (7) the existence of trade with other centers, some of which were at a considerable distance. In short, the large ancient city was the "cradle of civilization."

Childe's theory of early urbanization was quite influential and may be accurate as a descriptive interpretation of ancient city life based on evidence from cities in Mesopotamia. Like other models of its day, it asserted an evolutionary view of development according to which civilization passes first through the stage of hunting and gathering, then to agriculture, and finally to urban-based economies, with an ever more complex and interdependent form of social organization leading up to a contemporary, "modern" stage. However, other evidence suggests a discontinuous process of development.

Archeologists have known for some time that signs of civilization, such as the production of pottery in quantity or the use of writing, coexisted with the development of agriculture rather than appearing at the later stages of agriculturally based societies as evolutionary theories maintain. Jane Jacobs (1970) notes that some of the earliest human settlements, such as Catal Hyuk in present-day northern Turkey, developed as commercial trade centers, not because of an agricultural surplus. For example, one of the oldest cities, Jericho, already possessed a complex urban culture based on trade and crafts more than 4,000 years ago, *prior to* the domestication of grain in the surrounding region (Eisenstadt and Shachar, 1987:27). Because of the need to create a livelihood on marginal agricultural lands, early residents of towns innovated alternative economic activities including trade, full-time craft work, and even religion, whose products could then be exchanged for essential goods, thereby providing the basis for a city-based economy that could survive on trade.

While the social division of labor and its growing complexity certainly contributed to urban development, economic factors alone did not produce the first cities. The market by itself can never provide adequate control or guidance—that is, *regulation*—for social organization. In fact, the classical sociologists Emile Durkheim, Karl Marx, and Max Weber all argued that everyday actions in a market society generate problems and conflict that call for regulation by political and cultural means. "The most important of such problems were the construction of trust or solidarity (stressed by Durkheim), the regulation of power (Marx and Weber) and the provision of both meaning and legitimation for social activities so prized by Weber" (Eisenstadt and Shachar, 1987:50).

CLASSICAL CITIES

The earliest cities in Mesopotamia and in China were built according to complex belief systems and symbolic codes, reflected in, for example, city gates devoted to specific deities that were oriented to the cardinal points of the compass (north, east, south, and west) and streets that would prevent spirits from moving directly to the center of the city. In ancient Greece, cities were constructed according to a cosmological code that incorporated sacred spaces and religious symbols linked to the pantheon of Greek gods. The city of Athens was built to honor the goddess Athena, and all buildings followed geometrical design principles in accordance with the "golden mean." In the center of the circle that encompassed the city was the *agora,* which was not simply the marketplace but the public hearth or *hestia koine,* the center of the community. Over a period of 200 years, the agora at the base of the acropolis took form, as public buildings—courts, libraries, temples, gymnasium—

gradually closed in the open area, creating an enclosed space where the public life of the city was focused. The public hearth was considered to be the *omphalos*, the center of the world.

Visitors would pass through the agora along the Pan-Athenaic Way, walk past the *stoa* (public marketplace), and then ascend the *propylaea*, the gateway to the sacred temples at the top of the acropolis, designed and built by the architect Mnesicles in 430–420 BC. Robin Rhodes (1995:53) describes the ascent of the acropolis:

> Its architecture, in concert with the Panathenaic procession, progressed step by step from the west, from the realm of the secular, the human, the realm of stories, of human explanation, to the elemental religious experience of divine epiphany at the east side of the tenemos, at the front of the major temples to Athena.

Active participation in all parts of public life was the central organizing concept for Athenians, and urban space within Athens was overlaid by a political code that supplanted the earlier cosmological/religious one. The radial street network emanating out from the center of the *omphalos* would connect all citizens to the central public space. This development is very different from both the precocious early grid network found in cities in the Indus Valley and the haphazard organic growth of urban settlements in Mesopotamia. Radial development was dictated not by the economic concern of easy access to the market but by the political principle that all homes should be equidistant from the center because all Athenian citizens were equal. Within the center were placed the citizen assembly hall, the city council hall, and the council chamber, all structures linked to the institution of city politics.

Classical Rome was constructed using a different model, one that developed from an imperial code that stressed grandeur, domination, and (eventually) excess. The construction of urban space in Rome was based not on the political equality of its citizens but on the military power of the state. Functional space within the Roman forum serving economic functions was embedded in a larger, meaningful space governed by political and cultural symbols.

Initially, the buildings of the Republican Forum at the center of Rome were built on a human scale and formed the focal point for social interaction, public ceremony, and political activity within the city. As the empire expanded and the republic was replaced first by a dictatorship and then by a monarchy, Rome was refashioned by the imperial code to a gargantuan scale. The city of Rome became a physical representation of the empire itself. Monuments and public buildings were constructed to honor the personal accomplishments of each emperor. At its height in the third century, Imperial Rome contained a population of some 1 million people, many of them slaves (including secretaries, clerks, accountants, and foremen, in addition to laborers). It encompassed a total area of eight square miles, much of which was given over to public space. The majority of the population lived in the 46,000 *insulae* (apartment buildings) within the city; these buildings usually were three stories tall and contained five apartments, housing five to six people each. There were only 4,000 private homes within the city. Eight aqueducts brought the more than 200 million gallons of water needed to service 1,200 public fountains, 926 public baths, and the public latrines. The streets were narrow, twisting, and dark, averaging 6 to 15 feet wide; the largest street was just 20 feet wide. The city fire department consisted of some 7,000 men. The *circus maximus,* where chariot races took place, seated more than 100,000 people and was surrounded by taverns, shops, and eating places. The famous Colosseum rose more than 180 feet above the city and seated more than 80,000 people.

Rome was very different from Athens and other Greek city-states in that it was the capital of the first urban civilization, with roads linking the city to administrative centers across Europe and the Middle East. These cities served as centers of political power, economic control, and cultural diffusion. By AD 200, more than 5 million people lived in Roman cities. As the empire prospered, the 1 million or more residents of Rome lived off the great wealth that poured into the city. Eventually the center became known for its decadence and idleness. At one time, a full 159 days out of the Roman year were declared public holidays! Of these, 93 days, or one-fourth of the entire year, were devoted to games at the emperor's expense. Alongside this parasitic existence emerged immense urban problems that we commonly associate with the modern city: the deterioration of housing, widespread poverty, public corruption, and a dangerous lack of proper sanitation facilities and other services for the residents.

With the expansion of the empire, Rome increasingly became a city of the rich and the poor, a society wedded to spectacle and consumption rather than commerce and trade. By 300 AD the emperor Constantine moved the capital of the empire to Constantinople, and Rome began a long period of decline. The ebb and flow of human civilization, and of the urban centers that serve as the symbolic markers of those civilizations, is both remarkable and sobering. In many cases we have only the briefest of archeological evidence and written information about the earliest urban civilizations. Babylon, perhaps the best known of the Old Testament cities, lay buried for

TABLE 2.2   Population History of Selected Cities

Location	Population	Notes
Rome		
AD 100	650,000	World's largest city
600–800	50,000	Invasion by Germanic tribes
1000	35,000	
1300	15,000	Exile of Popes to Avignon
1500	35,000	
1600	120,000	Pope Sixtus and the Rebirth of Rome
Mexico City		
1500	80,000	Capital of Aztec Empire
1524	30,000	Destruction by Spanish conquistadors
1600	75,000	Colonial center of Spanish Empire
Baghdad		
765	480,000	Following establishment of Caliphate in 750
900	1,100,000	Largest city in the world; first city of 1,000,000
1400	125,000	Sacked by Tamerlane in 1401
1650	30,000	
Peking		
1200	150,000	
1300	400,000	Capital of China
1500	670,000	World's largest city
1800	1,100,000	World's largest city
London		
1700	350,000	
1800	1,000,000	Second largest city in the world
1900	6,480,000	Largest city in the world
New York		
1800	80,000	
1900	4,240,000	Largest city in United States
1950	19,800,000	World's largest city

SOURCE: Adapted from Ivan Light, *Cities in World Perspective* (New York: Macmillan, 1983). Population estimates rounded to nearest 10,000.

centuries beneath the sands of Iraq. Baghdad, the largest and wealthiest city of the early Middle Ages, was destroyed in the 1300s and has never achieved the dominance and influence of the earlier era. The history of urban civilizations represents an ongoing cycle of growth and decline and, in many cases, permanent end due to the ecological damage that urban civilization has brought to many areas of the globe.

URBANIZATION AFTER AD 1000

After the decline of centralized control from the Roman Empire beginning in 500, urban space in Europe was reclaimed by the countryside and a new form of feudal relations. Towns needed to defend themselves in the absence of a central authority. Many became small, fortified settlements—like the walled hill towns of central Italy—while in northern Europe small towns survived only in the shadow of the medieval castle. The level of urbanization was low in Europe during the Middle Ages, and few places exceeded 10,000 in population. In contrast, the cities of Asia, the Near East, and what is now Latin America housed thriving communities during this same period.

Most historians contend that the cities that emerged after AD 1000 were the products of powerful national rulers and the success of regional trade rather than deriving from social relations that were uniquely urban in nature, as Childe's theory suggests. City life remained precarious and dependent on social relations that emanated from state power. It was not until the seventeenth century, with the rise of capitalism in Western Europe, that urban life appeared to be propelled by forces emerging from within cities themselves. In China, for example, towns were organized by the state under the infallible rule of the emperor and for the principal purpose of administration. These were secular kingdoms united under a political hierarchy to harness the economic wealth of the countryside. Under the imperial capital, the provincial capitals were dispersed throughout the kingdom, and under these were clustered the still smaller county capitals of the Chinese empire. In sum, commerce and trade combined with the power of the state to produce the towns of the Orient.

Much the same story characterized the Middle East, which also contained places with populations that eclipsed those in Europe after AD 1000. With the coming of Islamic hegemony, cities appeared that solidified the control of territory under the Muslim rulers, or caliphs (see Chapter 12). Islam also took over older cities built by the Romans, such as Constantinople. To these it added two types of "new" towns across North Africa and the Near East: *Villes crées* were fortress cities constructed by Islamic rulers as administration centers, and *villes spontanées* arose as trading centers constructed without preconceived plans but sanctioned by the caliph. Thus, Islamic society possessed a robust system of cities, but these were all products of state-directed territorial expansion and administration. As in the Chinese case, the rulers needed cities to control the territory and commerce of the hinterland.

The experience of India during this same period (from 1000 to 1700) replicates the combined role of royal administration, on the one hand, and the importance of local trade, on the other, in the sustenance of Oriental cities. As elsewhere in Asia and the Middle East, the size and well-being of Indian cities were a consequence of the power of central state authority rather than of social relations emanating from the urban community itself. Fernand Braudel (1973:413) provides an interesting illustration of the dependency of the city on the power of the state in his examination of India during the seventeenth century:

> The example of India shows how much these official towns were bound up with the prince—to the point of absurdity. Political difficulties, even the prince's whim, uprooted and transplanted the capitals several times. . . . As soon as its prince abandoned it the town was jeopardized, deteriorated and occasionally died.
>
> When a Mogul prince left Delhi on a journey to Kashmir in 1663, the whole town followed him because they could not live without his favors and liberality. An improbable crowd formed, estimated at several hundred thousand people by a French doctor who took part in the expedition. Can we imagine Paris following Louis XV during his journey to Metz in 1744?

Finally, in Latin America, the Aztec and Inca civilizations achieved impressive heights during this same period. As late as the 1600s, Spanish explorers marveled at the awesome scale of New World urbanization. Yet, as the example of Aztec civilization in Mexico shows, these places were closely connected to the agricultural relations of the hinterland and could not be considered modern cities. According to Murray Bookchin (1974:7–8),

> An illustration of the earliest cities can be drawn from descriptions of the Aztec "capital" of Tenochtitlán, encountered by Spanish *conquistadores* only three centuries ago. At first glance, the community is deceptively similar in appearance to a modern city. . . . The city's resemblance . . . rests on its lofty religious structures, its spacious plazas for ceremonies, its palaces and administrative buildings. Looking beyond these structures, the city in many respects was likely a grossly oversized pueblo community.

As Bookchin points out, in the case of Aztec cities, the horticulturally based activities of the family clans organized social relations within the city. These clan-based social orders reached into the very heart of city life. Integration around the agricultural economy was so complete that Aztec cities did not even develop money but retained a barter system. Just as in the Orient, commercial and craft activities carried on within Tenochtitlán could not explain either its immense physical space or the size of its population. The principal role of the city was to serve as the center for the Aztec rulers and their administrative functions.

It was not until the late Middle Ages in Europe that towns acquired political independence from the state. The classical sociologist Max Weber (1966) considered this autonomy to be necessary for the establishment of an urban community. For Weber, the key to city life was the creation of an independent urban government that was elected by the citizens of the city itself. Classical Athens and early Rome were two examples. Weber believed that in the late Middle Ages, Europe also developed cities of this type. For Weber, an urban community consisted of three elements: a fusion of the fortress and the marketplace where trade and commercial relations predominated, a legal court of its own that had the authority to settle local disputes, and partial political autonomy that allowed residents to elect authorities who could administer daily affairs.

If the cities of the later European Middle Ages enjoyed autonomy, it was relatively short-lived. By the eighteenth century, nation-states had acquired control of territory, and the commercial-trading economy was global in scale, thereby making individual places dependent on one another. Weber's remarks about the city were meant to suggest that there may once have been uniquely urban social relations that characterized city life and helped to transform society from a rural, agriculturally based system of social organization to one that is considered "modern." For example, urban life was sustained by a mode of social organization that, when compared to rural areas, consisted of greater emphasis on specialized jobs, the decline of family authority and the rise of contractual and political relations, and a replacement of the strong ties binding people together based on kinship with those based on the interdependence of sharing the same fate as the city. In addition to Weber, other classical sociologists developed ways of studying the contrast between premodern and modern societies. Ferdinand Tönnies, for example, called this the shift from *gemeinschaft* to *gesellschaft,* or the change from a traditional society based on trust and mutual aid to a modern one in which self-interest predominates. Emile Durkheim considered modernization to be a change from a society based on mechanical solidarity, or a low degree of specialization, to one based on organic solidarity, or a high degree of specialization and interdependence.

THE MEDIEVAL ORDER AND THE RENAISSANCE CITY

Just as classical cities developed around the agora and the forum, the medieval city developed around a central symbolic space. Buildings on each side of the central square represented the dominant social, economic, and political interests in medieval society: the cathedral, the town hall, and the merchants' hall and trade guilds. Medieval cities often competed with one another for economic and political dominance, and many were protected by city walls. Because the walls prevented the cities from expanding outward, the cities built upward, and by the late Middle Ages, four- and even five-story buildings overhanging crowded streets were not uncommon. As trade prospered, cities grew more crowded—and so did the problems of poverty, crime, poor sanitation, and ultimately disease. Daniel Defoe, in *A Journal of the Plague Year* (1722), described the ravages of the great plague that devastated London in the seventeenth century, when houses containing persons suffering from the Black Death were boarded up by city authorities with the victims still inside!

By the mid-1500s, Rome had been restored to its position as the capital city of the Catholic world, and it grew in size and significance as trade and commerce in cities across Europe produced a new merchant class with the wealth and leisure time necessary to support pilgrimages to this most holy of sites. But continued growth and an aging infrastructure produced a medieval city of narrow streets, overcrowded housing, and massive traffic problems; in the last decades of the sixteenth century, nearly 450,000 pilgrims traveled to Rome each year. Pope Sixtus V (1585–1590) began an ambitious plan of urban redevelopment. Edmund Bacon (1970:117) described the plan that would create Renaissance Rome:

> Sixtus V, in his effort to recreate the city of Rome into a city worthy of the church, clearly saw the need to establish a basic over-all design structure in the form of a movement system as an idea, and at the same time the need to tie down its critical parts in positive physical forms which could not easily be removed. He hit upon the happy solution of using Egyptian obelisks, of which Rome had a substantial number, and erected these at important points within the structure of his design.
>
> The seven holy pilgrimage sites within the city were linked by broad boulevards, providing for a new sense of movement and spatial ordering within the city. This plan for urban redevelopment was celebrated in engravings by the leading artists of the day. Implementing this plan would take more than 60 years and result in the destruction of neighborhoods of crowded medieval housing, but it produced a new city that would attract pilgrims from across Europe. New squares were built and monuments erected to symbolize the power of the church.

The redevelopment of Rome served as a model for urban planning during the Renaissance. New squares would be constructed with monuments to historical events and public figures; boulevards would connect these urban spaces with one another and direct traffic through the city. Older housing, now a crowded eyesore, would be demolished to make way for urban devel-

TABLE 2.3 World's Largest Cities, 1200 BC–AD 1850

	City	Present Location	Estimated Population
1200	Memphis	Egypt	50,000
600	Ninevah	Iraq	120,000
450	Babylon	Iraq	200,000
200	Patna	India	400,000
100	Rome	Italy	650,000
350	Constantinople	Turkey	300,000
600	Constantinople	Turkey	500,000
800	Changan	China	700,000
900	Baghdad	Iraq	1,100,000
1000	Córdoba	Spain	450,000
1100	Kaifeng	China	440,000
1200	Hangchow	China	250,000
1300	Hangchow	China	430,000
1400	Nanking	China	490,000
1500	Peking	China	670,000
1600	Peking	China	710,000
1800	Peking	China	1,100,000
1850	London	Great Britain	2,320,000

SOURCE: Adapted from Ivan Light, *Cities in World Perspective* (New York: Macmillan, 1983).

opment. The design of the new metropolis would be replicated in Renaissance cities across Europe in the 1700s and would serve as a model for urban planning in many other areas of the world, including Detroit and Washington, D.C. (Girouard, 1985).

The change in urban fortunes is clearly shown in Table 2.3, which shows the largest city in the world in each century from 1200 BC to 1850—a documentary history of the development of urban civilization across the globe. In the first half of the table, the cities and civilizations correspond to what we have learned in high school and college courses on Western history: Babylon was the largest city in Mesopotamia in biblical times, Memphis the largest city in ancient Egypt, and Rome the largest city of the Roman Empire. But urban life during the Middle Ages shifted to the great Moslem empires of the Middle East (Baghdad and Damascus in 900 and 1100) and then North Africa and Spain (Córdoba in the 1200s and 1300s) and then to the great Chinese civilizations of the 1500s through 1700s. The rise of first European and later American cities did not occur until the advent of the Industrial Revolution in the 1800s.

In retrospect, it seems clear that the force that propelled the development of cities in Europe after the late Middle Ages did not involve the same process of urban growth that led to the urban civilizations of earlier centuries. When we examine the historical record put forward in Table 2.2, we realize that the expansion of urban civilization in Europe was a direct consequence of the rise of capitalism and industrialization. It is this change that defines the development from the relatively autonomous urban community in Europe of the seventeenth and eighteenth centuries to the large industrial and postindustrial cities that we know today.

CAPITALISM AND THE RISE OF THE INDUSTRIAL CITY

Throughout the world, especially in North Africa, Asia, and the Near East, cities were the sites of vigorous trade and the economic activities associated with commerce. However, trade by itself did not sustain the rise of cities in Western Europe. Distinguishing the developing towns of the late Middle Ages from other such places was the emergence of capitalism based on a money economy.

The economy of the feudal manor, for example, was characterized by *simple commodity production;* that is, craft products were produced for exchange, and the owners were the producers of the products. Exchange took place among owners/producers and could be facilitated using any object or service that was equivalent according to the cultural judgment of the society. This barter system prevailed for several hundred years in Europe after the fall of Rome and existed elsewhere in the Middle East and Asia.

In the later Middle Ages, beginning in the twelfth century, the general and accepted use of money and a fully developed commodity market within the city that was regulated by local government allowed the people with capital to hire both labor and resources to produce goods. The classical sociologist Karl Marx was the foremost student of the rise of capitalism. He called the type of economy made possible by capital and city regulation of markets *extended commodity production.* That is, unlike simple commodity production, which ended in the exchange of goods or services, extended production began with money, or capital, and, after production and exchange, ended with still more money, which was then invested in a new cycle of accumulation.

In this manner, commercial relations supported the accumulation of capital, and cities with such economies began to prosper beyond anything experienced up to that time. In addition, social and cultural relations changed in the cities to sanction the pursuit of wealth through the accumulation of money. For example, the early Catholic Church prohibited the loaning of money, except within restricted guidelines, and limited the role of banks (see Vance, 1990). In the sixteenth century, the Protestant Reformation swept away these cultural and social restrictions on the free flow of investment, providing a cultural basis for capitalist development (Weber, 1958). Once that point was reached, the accumulation process spilled out into the surrounding area as

TABLE 2.4 Largest Cities in Europe, 1000–1800 (in 1,000s)

1050		1200		1330		1500		1650		1800	
Córdoba	150	Palermo	150	Granada	150	Paris	225	Paris	400	London	948
Palermo	120	Paris	110	Paris	150	Naples	125	London	350	Paris	550
Seville	90	Seville	80	Venice	110	Milan	100	Naples	300	Naples	430
Salerno	50	Venice	70	Genoa	100	Venice	100	Lisbon	150	Vienna	247
Venice	45	Florence	60	Milan	100	Granada	70	Venice	140	Amsterdam	217
Regensburg	40	Granada	60	Florence	95	Prague	70	Milan	120	Dublin	200
Toledo	37	Córdoba	60	Seville	90	Lisbon	65	Amsterdam	120	Lisbon	195
Rome	35	Cologne	50	Córdoba	60	Tours	60	Rome	110	Berlin	172
Barbastro	35	Leon	40	Naples	60	Genoa	50	Madrid	100	Madrid	168
Cartagena	33	Ypres	40	Cologne	54	Ghent	55	Palermo	100	Rome	153
Naples	30	Rome	35	Palermo	51	Florence	55	Seville	80	Palermo	140
Mainz	30	Bologna	35	Siena	50	Palermo	55	Florence	74	Venice	138
Merida	30	Toledo	35	Barcelona	48	Rome	55	Vienna	70	Milan	135
Almeria	17	Verona	33	Valencia	44	Bordeaux	50	Granada	70	Hamburg	130
Grenada	26	Narbonne	31	Toledo	42	Lyon	50	Marseille	70	Lyon	109
Speyer	25	Salerno	40	Bruges	0	Orleans	50	Copenhagen	65	Copenhagen	101
Palma	25	Pavia	30	Malaga	40	London	50	Genoa	64	Marseille	101
Leon	25	Messina	00	Aquila	40	Bologna	50	Bologna	63	Barcelona	100
London	25	Naples	30	Bologna	40	Verona	50	Antwerp	60	Seville	96
Elvira	22	Genoa	30	Cremona	40	Brescia	49	Brussels	60	Bordeaux	96

SOURCE: Adapted from De Long and Shleifer (1992) and based upon the work of Bairoch, Batou, and Chevre (1988) and Russell (1972).

the new, money-based capitalist economy penetrated relations in the countryside. The history of the Occidental city, as Braudel, Weber, and Marx all agreed, became the history of capitalism.

The full impact of the changes described by these authors may be best understood by looking at the location and size of the largest cities in Europe from 1000 to 1800 (roughly the period from the onset of the Middle Ages up to the start of the Industrial Revolution). The population figures presented in Table 2.4 illustrate the shift of economic activity and urban life from southern Europe to the north. In the early Middle Ages, the largest urban areas were found in the Moorish empire in Spain and in the early Italian city-states. By the 1500s the influence of the Moorish empire was declining, and the early textile manufacturing cities of the north were ascending. Soon thereafter, the port cities of the Hanseatic League made their appearance. By 1800, the metropolitan centers of the new European powers and the cities of the industrial north predominated.

As Adam Smith and Karl Marx would note in their complementary works, *The Wealth of Nations* and *Das Kapital,* industrial capitalism would forever change the nature of social relations and set in motion the powerful economic forces that resulted in global capitalism and the emerging world city. Occupations became specialized, and the division of labor grew ever more complex as mercantile capitalism was replaced by industrial capitalism. Aided by emergent nation-states, the political and legal relations of capitalism began to dominate the countryside in Europe. To be successful, the emerging forms of capitalism required the legal sanctification of private property, and this resulted in the "commodification" of many aspects of society. All this buying and selling meant that many new markets were formed and existing ones expanded, providing people with even more ways to make money.

Land, for example, which was once held only by the nobility and the church, became commodified and available for purchase by anyone with money. A real estate market emerged that cut up and parceled out land for sale. A second market, this one for labor, emerged as the serfs, who had been bound by feudal traditions to their masters, were freed only to become commodities in the new system of wage labor. As feudal relations of dependence and reciprocity were broken down by capitalism and the pursuit of monetary accumulation, immense numbers of people were forced out of rural, farming areas and into cities, where they looked for work by selling their labor for a wage on the labor market.

With the coming of the Industrial Revolution, this "urban implosion," or shift of population from rural to urban places, reached truly astounding proportions. According to Lewis Mumford (1961), the cities of the late eighteenth century contained relatively few people, numbering fewer than 600,000 (see Table 2.2). By the middle of the nineteenth century, capitalist industrialization had created cities of a million or more all across Western Europe. The most dramatic changes were experienced in England and Wales, because it was there that the scale of industrialization and capitalist development was most advanced. According to Geruson and McGrath (1977:25), urban counties in Britain grew by 30 percent between 1780 and 1800 and again by approximately 300 percent between 1801 and 1831. Commercial and industrial counties experienced a net population increase of 378,000 between 1781 and 1800 and an additional 720,000 between 1801 and 1831. At the very same time, agricultural counties lost 252,000 people during the first period and lost 379,000 between 1801 and 1831.

Census figures at the time of the nineteenth century were not always accurate. Nevertheless, Braudel (1973:376) suggests that around the turn of the century, several regions in Europe tipped their population balance from rural to urban, especially in England and the Netherlands, a truly momentous occurrence. In short, for the first time in history, several nations changed from populations that were predominantly rural to ones dominated by urban location, and this is why the urbanization process in Western Europe after the 1700s was so significant.

By the middle 1800s, Western Europe possessed many industrialized cities. What was life like in them? The cities that emerged in the nineteenth century, unlike the ancient places, were not conceived according to some overarching symbolic meaning, such as religious or cosmological codes. Development was a haphazard affair. Individual capitalists did what they willed, and real estate interests operated unchecked by either legal code or cultural prescription. Land was traded like other goods. About the only clear pattern that emerged involved the spatial separation of rich and poor. The industrial city of Western Europe became the site of a clash of classes: the workers against the capitalists. Observing the excesses of the time and the utter devastation visited on working-class life by the factory regime of capitalism, Karl Marx (1967) recognized that class struggle would become the driving force of history. It was left for Friedrich Engels (1973), Marx's close friend, to document in graphic terms the pathological nature of uneven development characterizing urban growth under capitalism. In his classic account, *The Condition of the Working Class in England,* Engels describes the separation of residences for the bourgeoisie and the proletariat in Manchester, rivers polluted with the intestines of slaughtered cattle and other manufacturing waste, pollution from the giant factories that settled over residential areas of the city, and the location of the immigrant workforce in an area known as Little Ireland. One of the most telling scenes of his firsthand observational account of life in the new industrial city was of tenements housing dozens of families, with only two outdoor latrines (outhouses)—resulting in children playing in a courtyard several inches deep in urine. In fact, several books were written in the nineteenth century cataloging the hardships caused by industrialization, including Henry Mayhew's *London Labour and the London Poor* and Charles Booth's *Life and Labour of the People in London.* These works, and many more, described what Booth called "the problem of poverty in the midst of wealth."

By the seventeenth century, destitution had been accepted as the normal lot in life for a considerable part of the population. Without the spur of poverty and famine, they could not be expected to work for starvation wages. Misery at the bottom was the foundation for luxury at the time. As much as a quarter of the urban population in the bigger cities, it has been estimated, consisted of casuals and beggars; it was this surplus that made for what was considered, by classic capitalism, to be a healthy labor market, in which the capitalist hired labor on his own terms, or dismissed workers at will, without notice, without concern about what happened to either the worker or the city under such inhuman conditions. In a memorandum dated 1684, the chief of police of Paris referred to the "frightful misery that afflicts the greater part of the population of this great city." Between forty and sixty-five thousand were reduced to outright beggary. There was nothing exceptional about Paris.

In the chapters to follow, we will see that many of the ideas associated with modern life have their origins in observations made about industrial cities. The problem of uneven development—the graphic contrast between the wealthy and the poor, for example, and the contradictions between progress and misery—remains very much at the center of the urban dynamic in cities around the globe. On the one hand, the city represented hope to all those laboring under meager conditions in the countryside. It was the site of industrialization and the great dream of modernization and progress. On the other hand, the powerful forces of urbanism dwarfed the individual and crushed the masses into dense, environmentally strained spaces. In time, the built environment of the industrial city would replace that of the feudal town. The city rhythm, so unlike that of the country, would replace earlier cycles of life dominated by nature. Life was worth only as much as the daily wage for which it could be exchanged. The processes of urbanization and capitalism that created large cities in Europe during the nineteenth century also thrived in the United States at the same time, and in many ways, U.S. cities were governed by the same dynamic.

KEY CONCEPTS

Thanatopolis
agora
Republican Forum / Imperial Forum
Childe Hypothesis
rise of capitalism
simple commodity production
extended commodity production
urban implosion

IMPORTANT NAMES

V. Gordon Childe
Jane Jacobs
Lewis Mumford
Gideon Sjoberg

Max Weber
Karl Marx
Friedrich Engels
Henry Mayhew
Charles Booth

DISCUSSION QUESTIONS

1. V. Gordon Childe's description of the urban revolution is often said to be an evolutionary theory. What does this mean? What factors did Childe believe were necessary for the urban revolution to take place? What evidence have other scholars used to critique his theory?

2. The roles of culture and political power were important for the development of both Athens and Rome, yet these forces produced two very different patterns of urban settlement. What might account for the differences between Athens and Rome, and for the changes that took place in the development of republican and imperial Rome?

3. Early cities were built by groups using a distinctive set of symbols and a model of space meaningful to the group. Explain how the redevelopment of Renaissance Rome by Pope Sixtus followed these same ideas.

4. The well-known saying that "city air makes one free" dates from the development of European cities in the medieval period. What does this saying represent? Why was it important for European cities to develop political autonomy from the surrounding economic and political system?

5. The rise of the industrial city in Europe is linked to the development of capitalism. Discuss two characteristics of early capitalism and show how this influenced the growth of the industrial city.

6. Urban historians have long debated whether capitalism resulted in better living conditions for the average worker. What evidence do we have from the development of the industrial city to answer this question?

THE RISE OF
URBAN SOCIOLOGY

A **special inquiry devoted to** urban phenomena was the premier achievement of early U.S. sociology. The first sociology department in the country was founded by Albion Small at the University of Chicago in 1893. Robert Park joined the department in 1914 and quickly took on a prominent role. Albion Small and Robert Park had something in common. They had both traveled to Germany as graduate students to take courses with Max Weber. In the 1890s only France and Germany had professional sociologists. Emile Durkheim, a sociologist at the Sorbonne in Paris, had developed a growing reputation in France. But Max Weber was acknowledged as the leading social thinker of his day. And another important sociologist, Georg Simmel, had a growing reputation as the most innovative social philosopher on the continent.

The first generation of sociologists was concerned with the impact of urbanization on European society. The political revolutions of the 1800s brought an end to earlier ideas that the social and political order reflected a divine plan—but what exactly would the new social order, created by widespread changes in the economic and social structure, look like? In the wake of the French Revolution, questions about how social order itself could be maintained were not simply a matter of idle speculation. These questions were essential to understanding the very nature of the new industrial society that was transforming European cities.

Ferdinand Tönnies (1855–1936) is one of the early German social philosophers who addressed these questions. In *Gemeinschaft und Gesellschaft* (published in 1887 and often translated as "community and society," although "community and association" more accurately reflects the original meaning), Tönnies sketched out an evolutionary view of the development of human society. The great period of industrialization that transformed European societies beginning in the late 1700s signified a change from community to association. His ideas are often used to highlight differences between village life of the preindustrial period and urban life of the industrial period, and between small-town life and that of the large city more generally. Tönnies saw that the transition from community (where individual families have long histories, individuals interact with one another on a personal basis because they often work together or are related to one another, and all jobs are interdependent on one another) to society (where individuals often interact with others whom they do not personally know and work at jobs that are seemingly unrelated to one another) resulted in a weakening of social ties and the loss of a shared sense of belonging to a meaningful community.

Emile Durkheim (1858–1917), who was the first chair of sociology at the Sorbonne in Paris in 1883, also wrote about the changes brought about by industrialization. In *The Division of Labor in Society*, Durkheim discussed many of the same issues presented in Tönnies's earlier essay, this time under the labels of *mechanical solidarity* and *organic solidarity*. In the preindustrial village, individuals were held together by the mechanical bonds of kinship and social interdependence—mechanical because they were predetermined and could not be changed as long as the individual remained within the local village. In the industrial city, individuals were no longer bound by the mechanical bonds of kinship; instead they could work at new types of jobs and have greater opportunities for interaction with a wider range of people. These were organic bonds that flowed naturally from the increased social differentiation brought about by the division of labor. If these terms seem to be counterintuitive (we often think of work in factories as being mechanical), it is important to realize that Durkheim was convinced that the new industrial economy was an improvement over the limited opportunities of feudal society, and he may have deliberately chosen words with a positive connotation to represent the modern city. Durkheim was certain that the new industrial order would replace the earlier ways of life: "with the coming of the industrial economy, village society has disappeared, never to come again."

The perspective of the German sociologist Friedrich Engels (1820–1895) was very different from that of Durkheim. Engels lived in England in the mid-1800s and wrote *The Condition of the Working Class in England in 1844*. This seminal work in urban sociology devoted a chapter to "The Great Towns." According to Engels, the evils of industrialization and capitalism were intensified by the space of the city. This is a perspective to which we will return in the next chapter.

The most influential European thinker in U.S. urban sociology during this early period was Georg Simmel (1858–1918). Simmel viewed the city in cultural terms and wrote about how urban life transformed individual consciousness: Everyday existence within the city altered the way people thought and acted compared to traditional society. Robert Park and Albion Small were familiar with Simmel's work and brought this "interactive" perspective back to the University of Chicago. In the United States, the work of the early Chicago School was less concerned with historical and comparative studies in the manner of Weber and more focused on social behavior and interaction within the urban milieu in the manner of Simmel.

Any thorough discussion of the development of urban sociology in the United States must begin by explaining the important difference between the two organizing topics in the field: urbanization and urbanism. *Urbanization* refers to city formation or city building process. It studies the way social activities locate themselves in space and according to interdependent processes of societal development and change. Its analyses are often historical and comparative. When we study the process of urbanization, we are interested in charting the rise and fall of great cities and urban civilizations. Our discussion of the emergence of cities, the largest cities in the world, and the changing location of large cities in Europe presented in Chapter 2, was about urbanization. *Urbanism,* in contrast, takes the city formation process as given and seeks instead to understand the ways of life that transpire within this container. Urbanism deals with culture, with meanings, symbols, patterns of daily life, and processes of adjustment to the environment of the city, but also with conflicts, with forms of political organization at the street, neighborhood, and city levels.

While both Weber and Engels emphasized the relation between the historical development of the city and its ways of life, Simmel was more concerned with patterns of activity and ways of thinking that were found in the city. The work of the early Chicago School followed Simmel closely and focused on patterns of activity within cities rather than addressing the topic of U.S. urbanization or city formation. Yet for Simmel, the study of life within the city was not meant as an "urban sociology." Simmel was instead concerned with *modernity,* or the transition from a traditional society characterized by social relations based on intimacy or kinship (known as "primary" relations) and by a feudal economy based on barter to an industrial society situated within cities and dominated by impersonal, specialized social relations based on compartmentalized roles (known as "secondary" relations) and by a money economy based on rational calculation of profit and loss. For Simmel, the subtle aspects of modernity were displayed most clearly within the large city or metropolis and through consciously directed behaviors. Simmel gives us a social psychology of modernity that Robert Park took to be the sociology of urbanism, or "urban sociology."

SIMMEL ON THE CITY

What was it like to confront modernity and why was Simmel so impressed with the city as the vehicle for change? Consider, if you will, a German farmer from Bavaria. His life was tuned to the daily rhythms of agriculture. Nature and his own physical labor provided the boundaries within which the farming endeavor was framed. The regime of labor on the land was early to bed, because darkness meant little work could be done, and early to rise, because it was necessary to use every second of daylight for work—even dawn and twilight. This farmer was immersed in a social world of primary kinship relations. His principal contacts were members of his family, both immediate and extended. Perhaps several generations and families lived together in the same location and worked the land. Beyond this primary network, the farmer would interact with individuals who aided his enterprise. Most typically he visited a local service center, perhaps a small town. There he was surely involved in a network of people who knew him well. In this kind of traditional society, it was entirely possible that no money changed hands while farm produce and needed commodities were exchanged. Barter, credit, and informal agreements among known persons characterized the social relations of this world.

As Simmel might suggest, suppose this individual—call him Hans—lost the farm and his family in some personal tragedy. With a small amount of money, he now traveled to Berlin to begin a new life. He went to this modern city precisely because it offered him an alternative to the traditional rural existence of farming. Karl Marx, writing in the nineteenth century, would have focused on Hans's conversion to an industrial worker. He would have taken us into the factory with Hans and described his encounter with abstract capital (the machine), with the relations of production (the factory building, the assembly line, and the daily schedule of work), and with class relations (interaction with the workers and the boss). Simmel, writing in the early twentieth century, virtually ignored this entire domain of the factory, which could be termed the immediate environment of capitalism, and focused instead on the larger context of daily life, the extended environment—namely, the city.

Hans stands on the corner of a large boulevard in Berlin teeming with daytime auto traffic. He has to dodge the steady stream of pedestrians just to stand still and watch, since everything else is in constant motion. At first shock, Hans would be paralyzed by the "excess of nervous stimulation," according to Simmel. Haven't we all had a similar experience upon visiting a large city? Loud noises from traffic, people in the crowds calling after one another, strangers touching him as they passed without an acknowledgment, and more—noise, noise, and noise. Hans would find himself in a totally new environment that demanded an adjustment and a response.

According to Simmel, small-town life required Hans to develop strong, intimate ties to those with whom he interacted. Here in the city, the excess of stimulation requires a defensive response. These are the characteristics of urbanism noted by Simmel. Hans would (1) develop what Simmel called a "blasé" attitude—a blurring of the senses, a filtering out of all that was loud and impinging but also irrelevant to Hans's own personal needs. Emotional reserve and indifference replace acute attention to the details of the environment.

Hans would require the satisfaction of his needs. Yes, he would encounter capitalism and, no doubt, sell his labor for a wage, as Marx had observed. Simmel agreed with Marx about the necessity of that transaction. It would (2) reduce the quality of Hans's capabilities simply to the quantity of his labor time—the time he spent at work, for a wage. It would make his work equivalent to a sum of money, no more, no less. That sum of money exchanged for Hans's labor time would be all the employing capitalist would provide. Hans would quickly see that absolutely no concern for his health-related, spiritual, communal, sexual, or any other type of human need would be involved in his relationship with his employer. In short, the world of capitalism was (3) an impersonal world of pure monetary exchange.

Simmel, unlike Marx, showed how the impersonal money economy extended outside the factory to characterize all other transactions in the city. Hans would use his paycheck to buy the needs of life, but in these transactions, too, impersonal or secondary social relations prevailed. Unless he went to a small store and frequented it every day, he would simply be viewed as (4) an anonymous customer being provided with mass-produced items for purchase. As a city dweller, he might find himself more frequently going to a department store where (5) a mass spectacle of consumption would be on display.

In all these transactions, Hans would have to be very careful. His weekly paycheck could go only so far. He would have to count how much each item cost and then budget himself accordingly. This (6) rational calculation would be at the heart of his daily life. Everything would be measured by him, just as costs were carefully measured at the factory. Rational calculation of money would require knowledge and technique. If Hans mastered it successfully along with gaining mastery over the consumer world of the city, he could look down at his country-bumpkin cousins. City life, for Simmel, was a life of the intellect, and everywhere the relation between the money economy and the rational calculation needed to survive in the world of capitalism prevailed. Those in the city who could not master the technique of money management would surely be lost.

We are not finished with the example of Hans. In the traditional society of the country, the rhythm of life was provided by nature. The city environment required (7) adjustment to a second nature—the orchestration of daily activities as governed by clock time and as played out within a constructed space. All life in the city followed the schedule of capitalist industrialization or modernity. If Hans didn't own a watch before coming to the city, he now needed one. Time and money constituted the two types of calculation necessary for survival in the second nature of the urban milieu—the built environment of concrete, steel, and glass that is the city.

Finally, Simmel also commented on the qualitative value of an experience like Hans's. He did not see the transformation as something that was necessarily bad. Hans would be cast in a calculating and impersonal world, but he would also be (8) freed from the restrictions of traditional society and its time-bound dictates. Hans would be free to discriminate about the types of friends he chose, about the job he took (within strong constraints, of course), and about where he lived. To Simmel, modernity meant the possibility of immense individual freedom in addition to constraint.

For Simmel, the freedom of the city meant, above all else, that Hans would be free to pursue and even create his own individuality. Provided he had the money, of course—an actuality that Marx would doubt—Hans could cultivate himself. He could dress according to some distinct fashion, develop hobbies he could share with others, perhaps take up the violin and join a neighborhood string quartet; he could enjoy a certain brand of cigar or shoes or attend night classes at the university—even Simmel's own lectures. Could Hans and Simmel have eventually met? The city allowed the possibility of attaining such cultural freedom, and the signs of individual cultivation—the clothes, cigars, friends, lovers, discussion groups, opera, art, novels—were collectively the signs of modernity that we may also call urbanism.

LOUIS WIRTH AND URBANISM AS A WAY OF LIFE

As we have seen, Georg Simmel had an important impact on the development of urban sociology in the United States. Albion Small and Robert Park had attended lectures by Simmel while they were studying in Germany, and Park included some of the first English translations of Simmel's work in the sociology textbook (titled *The Science of Society*) used at the University of Chicago. Louis Wirth was born in Germany but was sent to live with relatives in Chicago, where he attended high school and then the University of Chicago. Wirth's doctoral research reflected his knowledge of the development of Chicago's Jewish community. Published in 1926 with the title *The Ghetto*, Wirth's work describes the Maxwell Street neighborhood where recently arrived Russian immigrants had settled (the ghetto) and the area of second settlement where the older German immigrants had moved (Deutschland). Wirth became a faculty member in the sociology department at the University of Chicago and was one of the important figures in the later development of the Chicago School.

Louis Wirth was inspired by the work of Simmel. The Chicago sociologists came to view spatial patterns in the city as the result of powerful social factors, such as competition and the struggle for survival among individuals and groups within the city. Thus, Robert Park and his associates viewed urban space as a container, a built environment that encloses the action. Wirth's idea was different. He emphasized the way the city, as a spatial environment, influenced individual behavior. Wirth wanted to know what it was about the city itself that produced unique behaviors that might be called an "urban way of life." Given his study emphasis, Wirth naturally returned to Simmel. However, while Simmel (and Weber and Marx) attributed much of the city way of life to the influence of larger systemic forces, especially capitalism and its money economy, Wirth aimed for a general theory that ignored forces having origins outside the city. He studied the characteristics of people in the city and how life there might produce a distinct "urban" culture. Hence, "urbanism," or an urban way of life, became the dependent variable to be explained.

In his important essay "Urbanism as a Way of Life" (1948), Wirth focused on three factors. Urbanism was produced in relatively large and densely populated settlements containing groups of persons of different backgrounds; that is, urbanism was a product of large *population size, density,* and *heterogeneity*. Wirth's approach was an important advance because he provided a set of factors that could be analyzed statistically according to their effects. It was a theory with true predictive power. Given a sample of cities, the higher each one scored on the three factors of size, density, and heterogeneity, the more one could expect it to house a true urban culture.

Wirth's theory was impressive for the time because of its predictive potential. Problems arose when he tried to define what precisely an urban culture would be like. Recall the example of Hans. Simmel gave us a detailed picture

BOX 3.1   Wirth's Urbanism as a Way of Life: The Effects of Size, Density, and Heterogeneity

The effect of size:
1. The larger the population, the greater the chances for diversity and individualization.
2. Competition and formal mechanisms of social control would replace primary relations of kinship as a means of organizing society.
3. The larger the population, the greater the specialization and functional diversity of social roles.
4. Anonymity and fragmentation of social interaction increase with size.

The effect of density:
1. Greater density intensifies the effects of large population size.
2. Greater density creates the blasé attitude and the need to tune out excessive stimulation.
3. Greater density produces greater tolerance for living closely with strangers, but also greater stress.
4. Escape from density produces development of the fringe and greater land value in suburbia.
5. Density increases competition, compounding the effects of size.

The effect of heterogeneity:
1. The greater the heterogeneity, the more tolerance among groups.
2. Heterogeneity allows ethnic and class barriers to be broken down.
3. Individual roles and contacts become compartmentalized according to different circles of contacts. Anonymity and depersonalization in public life increase.

that contained both negative and positive aspects. Essentially, Simmel viewed the city as simply different. In his formulation, Wirth stressed the dark side of Simmel's vision: Urbanism as a culture would be characterized by aspects of social disorganization. Most central to Wirth's view was the shift from primary to secondary social relations. Wirth tended to see urban anonymity as debilitating. More specifically, the effects of the three factors on social life can be expressed as a series of propositions, as indicated in Box 3.1.

Wirth's work has been exhaustively tested, mainly because it was so clearly stated (Fischer, 1975). Unfortunately, the core assertion that size, density, and heterogeneity cause behaviors considered urban has not been borne out. If we look at the propositions presented in Box 3.1, many of the assertions appear to be accurate descriptions of social interaction in the large city, and they help to provide a more detailed picture of what urbanism as a culture is like.

However, while the theory contains some truth, we cannot be certain that these factors produce specific results. Cities merely concentrate the effects of societal forces producing urban culture. Surely we know that small towns are affected by many of the same social forces as the central city, although the types of behaviors that we observe in these environments may differ in type and intensity.

Finally, Louis Wirth held strongly to the view that the true effects of urbanism would occur as a matter of evolution as cities operated on immigrant groups to break down traditional ways of interacting over time. He did not see the larger city acting as an environment to bring about immediately the change he predicted. These things would take time, perhaps a generation. "Urbanism as a Way of Life" would inspire other urban sociologists to analyze the development of new suburban lifestyles ("Suburbanism as a Way of Life"; see Fava, 1980) and to compare urban and suburban lifestyles ("Urbanism and Suburbanism as Ways of Life"; Gans, 1968). We will return to the topic of urbanism and continue discussing the refinement of Wirth's ideas up to the present in Chapter 9. Wirth's work also inspired a subsequent generation to plow through census data and derive the statistical regularities of urban living. Much urban research is similarly conducted today.

THE CHICAGO SCHOOL OF URBAN SOCIOLOGY

Robert Park and Human Ecology

Robert Park (1865–1944) attended the University of Michigan and began his career as a newspaper reporter, first for the *Minneapolis Journal* and later for the *New York Journal*. He was assigned to the "police beat" where he would have to pound the streets of the city to develop leads and check facts for his newspaper articles. He later became city editor for the *Detroit Tribune* and drama critic and reporter for the *Chicago Journal*.

Park returned to graduate school. He studied first at Harvard University and then at Heidelberg University in Germany, where he attended lectures by Georg Simmel. He returned to the United States in 1903 and met Booker T. Washington, the most influential African American leader of the day and the founder of the Tuskegee Institute. For the next decade Park served as Washington's personal secretary, revising papers and speeches. Park used his spare time to investigate lynching in the American South and to write about race relations in the United States. In 1912 Park organized a conference on race relations at Tuskegee. He was approached by W. I. Thomas, who had recently completed his graduate work and now was teaching at the University of Chicago. Thomas wanted to know if Park would come to the university and join other scholars in the newly formed department of sociology (Blumer, 1984; Mathews, 1977).

In 1914, at age forty-nine, Park joined the faculty of the University of Chicago on a part-time basis. Park's approach to the sociological study of the urban environment was clear: He urged his students to "get the seat of their pants dirty" by getting out into the neighborhoods of the city, studying the many different groups of people who had come there. While Park worked on his own study of the development of the immigrant press in the United States, he and Ernest Burgess conducted undergraduate classes and graduate seminars that required students to go into the community, collect data from businesspeople, interview area residents, and report back with their information.

From the very first, the Chicago School sociologists adopted a conceptual position that we know as human ecology—the study of the process of human group adjustment to the environment. Whereas European thinkers such as Weber, Marx, and Simmel viewed the city as an environment where larger social forces of capitalism played themselves out in a human drama, Chicago School sociologists avoided the study of capitalism per se, preferring instead a biologically based way of conceptualizing urban life. For them urban analysis was a branch of human ecology. Their ideas brought them closest to the work of the philosopher Herbert Spencer, who also viewed society as dominated by biological rather than economic laws of development. Economic competition, in this view, was a special case of the struggle for survival. All individuals in the city were caught up in this struggle and adjusted to it in various ways.

According to Park, the social organization of the city resulted from the struggle for survival that then produced a distinct and highly complex division of labor, because people tried to do what they were best at in order to compete. Urban life was organized on two distinct levels: the biotic and the cultural. The *biotic level* refers to the forms of organization produced by species' competition over scarce environmental resources. The *cultural level* refers to the symbolic and psychological adjustment processes and to the organization of urban life according to shared sentiments, much like the qualities Simmel also studied.

In Park's work, the biotic level stressed the importance of biological factors for understanding social organization and the urban effects of economic competition. In contrast, the cultural component of urban life operated in neighborhoods that were held together by cooperative ties involving shared cultural values among people with similar backgrounds. Hence, local community life was organized around what Park called a "moral order" of cooperative, symbolic ties, whereas the larger city composed of separate communities was organized through competition and functional differentiation. In Park's later work, however, the complex notion of urbanism as combining competition and cooperation, or the biotic and the cultural levels, was dropped in favor of an emphasis on the biotic level alone as the basic premise of urban ecology. This led to some of the earliest critiques of the ecological perspective, faulting it for ignoring the role of culture in the city, or what Simmel would call the important influence of modernity, and for neglecting the basis of community (Alihan, 1938), which was social and not biological.

Other members of the early Chicago School translated the social Darwinism implicit in this model into a spatially attuned analysis. For Roderick McKenzie, the fundamental quality of the struggle for existence was position, or location, for the individual, the group, or institutions such as business firms. Spatial position would be determined by economic competition and the struggle for survival. Groups or individuals that were successful took over the better positions in the city, such as the choicest business locations, or the preferred neighborhoods. Those less successful would have to make do with less desirable positions. In this way the urban population, under pressure of economic competition, sorted itself out within the city space. McKenzie explained land-use patterns as the product of competition and an economic division of labor, which deployed objects and activities in space according to the roles they played in society. Thus, if a firm needed a particular location to perform its function, it competed with others for that location. The study of urban patterns resulting from that process would be studied by a new group of sociologists known as ecologists.

Burgess's Model of Urban Growth

Ernest W. Burgess developed a theory of city growth and differentiation based on the social Darwinist or biologically derived principles that were common in the work of Park and McKenzie. According to Burgess, the city constantly grew because of population pressures. This, in turn, triggered a dual process of central agglomeration and commercial decentralization; that is, spatial competition attracted new activities to the center of the city but also repelled other activities to the fringe area. As activities themselves located on the fringe, the fringe itself was pushed farther out from the city, and so on.

The city continually grew outward as activities that lost out in the competition for space in the central city were relocated to peripheral areas. This sorting led, in turn, to further spatial and functional differentiation as activities were deployed according to competitive advantages. In Burgess's theory, the city would eventually take on the form of a highly concentrated central

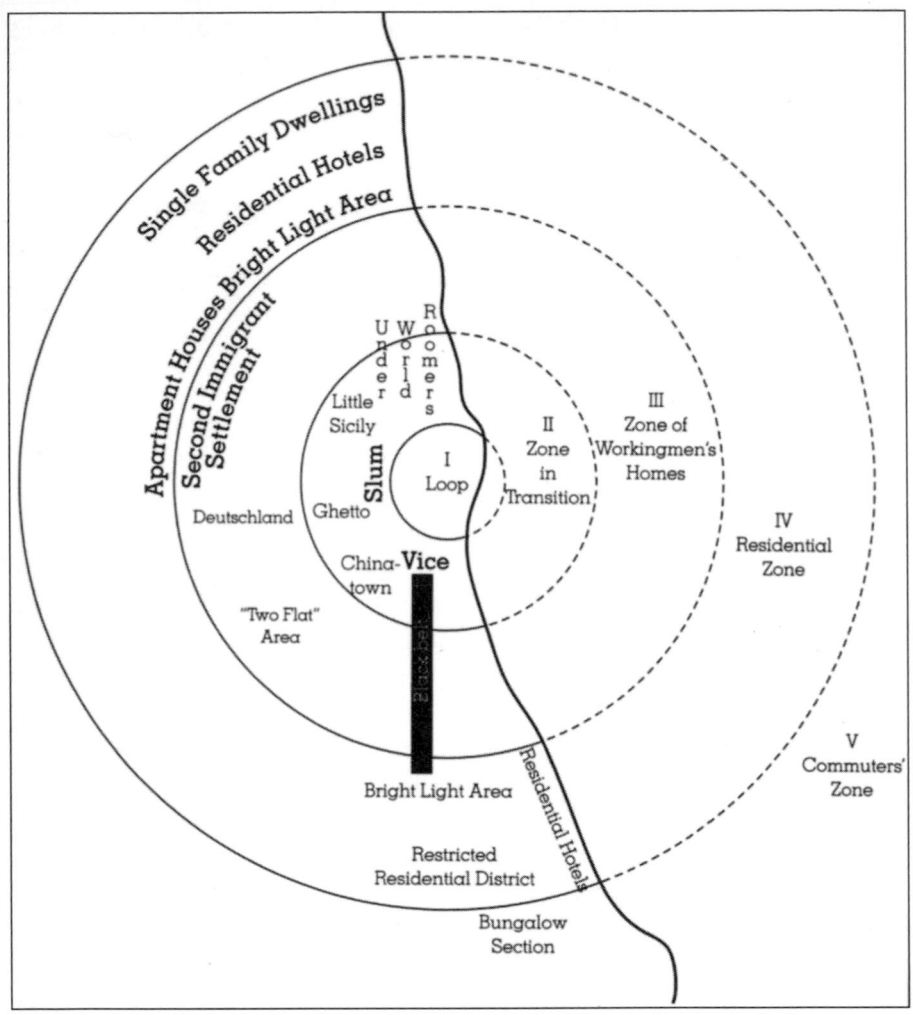

FIGURE 3.1   Ernest Burgess's Model of Concentric Zones

business district that would dominate the region and be the site for the highest competitive land prices, while the surrounding area would comprise four distinct concentric rings (see Figure 3.1).

The importance of Burgess's model cannot be overemphasized. First, he explained the pattern of homes, neighborhoods, and industrial and commercial locations in terms of the ecological theory of competition over "position," or location. In short, competition produced a certain space and a certain social organization in space. Both of these dimensions were pictured in the concentric zone model. Those who could afford it lived near the center; those who could not arranged themselves in concentric zones around the city center.

Second, Burgess's model explained the shifting of population and activities within the space of the city according to two distinct but related processes: centralization and decentralization. His theory explicitly related social processes to spatial patterns—a most important link for all theorizing about the city that was to follow and a view that is quite compatible with the aims of the new urban sociology.

Finally, Burgess revealed that the characteristics of the social organization of the urban population were spatially deployed. A gradient running from the center to the periphery characterized the attributes of the urban population. Individual traits such as mental illness, gang membership, criminal behavior, and racial background were found to be clustered along the center/periphery gradient of the city. Cutting across the urban form from the central business district (known as the CBD) to the outskirts, Chicago School researchers, using census data, found that the incidence of social pathology decreased, while homeownership and the number of nuclear families increased. The inner zones, therefore, were discovered to be the sites of crime, illness, gang warfare, broken homes, and many other indicators of social disorganization or problems.

In practice, however, research on the internal structure of cities contradicted Burgess's view of concentric zones. Other models of the city argued that cities had multiple centers rather than a single urban core. The first critique of Burgess's model was proposed by Homer Hoyt (1933) and was called "sector theory." Hoyt suggested that cities were carved up not by concentric zones but by unevenly shaped sectors within which different economic activities tended to congregate together, that is, agglomerate. Hoyt suggested that all activities, but especially manufacturing and retailing, had the tendency to spin off away from the center and agglomerate in sectors that expanded outward. Thus, the city grew in irregular blobs rather than in Burgess's neat circles.

The idea of multiple nuclei as the shape of the city further developed Hoyt's break with Burgess and is similar to the current multicentered approach used in this book (see Chapter 1). It was introduced in a classic paper by Chauncy Harris and Edward Ullman (1945). They suggested that within any city, separate functions and their particular needs require concentration within specific and specialized districts. Thus, within cities, similar activities often locate in the same area, forming agglomerations, or minicenters. Cities often grow asymmetrically around these multiple nuclei.

A common assumption of all of these models is that the city remains the central place that dominates all other areas. In recent years this way of thinking about urbanized areas has declined, and a focus on the individual city has given way to the regional perspective, which stresses the relative independence of multiple centers within the larger metropolitan region. While ecologists were concerned with location and with thinking of social activities as located in space, their biologically based explanation for perceived activities and spatial patterns has been rejected in recent years in favor of the new urban sociology (see Gottdiener and Feagin, 1988).

The Chicago School Studies

The work of the early Chicago School dominated urban sociology in the prewar years. For about a decade, beginning in 1925, a veritable flood of work poured out of the sociology department. Surveying just the books alone (that is, ignoring master's and Ph.D. theses produced at that time), the following list samples their accomplishments. All of these books were published by the University of Chicago Press: F. Thrasher, *The Gang* (1927); Louis Wirth, *The Ghetto* (1928); Ruth S. Cavan, *Suicide* (1928); Clifford S. Shaw, *The Jackroller* (1930); Harvey W. Zorbaugh, *The Gold Coast and the Slum* (1929); E. Franklin Frazier, *The Negro Family in Chicago* (1932); Paul G. Cressey, *The Taxi-dance Hall* (1932); Walter C. Reckless, *Vice in Chicago* (1933); Norman Hayner, *Hotel Life* (1936); and then later, St. Clair Drake and Horace R. Cayton, *Black Metropolis* (1945). Regarding this list, it can also be said that although gender issues were not well articulated at that time, women were involved in the Chicago School.

This marvelous output was produced with a similar stamp. It took an important social phenomenon, such as suicide, and located the distribution of its incidence in the space of the city. Chicago researchers then analyzed it in terms of the relation between the individual and the larger social forces of integration/disintegration. Most often this meant that phenomena were explained as products of social disorganization, particularly the breaking up of primary social relations through city living, as Wirth's theory suggested. As a result, the Chicago School was eventually criticized for reinforcing a negative view of city life.

Despite their limitations, we can appreciate the positive aspects of these early efforts. First, Chicago School researchers explicitly connected social phenomena with spatial patterns; that is, they thought in sociospatial terms. Second, they took an interactionist perspective. Individuals were studied in interaction with others, and the emergent forms of sociation coming out of that interaction were observed closely. Finally, they tried to show the patterns of adjustment to sociospatial location and developed a rudimentary way of speaking about the role of individual attributes in explaining urban phenomena. It was true that they focused almost exclusively on social disorganization and pathology; the breakup of family integration, for example, was given much more attention than questions of race or class.

BOX 3.2   Case Study: Gangland Chicago, 1927

The population of gangs in the 1920s was composed principally of recent immigrants to this country. Of the total gang census taken by Thrasher amounting to 25,000 members in a city of 2 million, roughly 17 percent were known as Polish gangs, 11 percent were known as Italian, 8.5 percent were Irish, 7 percent were black, another 3 percent were mixed white and black, 2 percent were Jewish, and so on, with the largest percentage of all gangs composed of "mixed nationalities" known exclusively for their territory, not for their ethnicity (1927:130). According to Thrasher, roughly 87 percent of all gang members were of foreign extraction! The gang phenomenon was explained in part by the lack of adjustment opportunities for immigrants, in part by the carryover of Old World antagonisms, and also by the need to defend territory against "outsiders."

Thrasher's study demonstrates sociospatial thinking. As Robert Park (Thrasher, 1927:vii) comments in his introduction: "The title of this book does not describe it. It is a study of the gang, to be sure, but it is at the same time a study of "gangland," that is to say, a study of the gang and its habitat, and in this case the habitat is a city slum."

Note Parks's grounding of the study in a biological metaphor by his use of the word habitat. Today we would adopt the sociospatial perspective and say territory or space. Gangland is the city space where gangs lived. Their influence was felt all over. What Thrasher did was locate gangs in their space. In fact, he found "three great domains" of gangdom—the "northside jungles," the "southside badlands," and the "westside wilderness." Using Ernest W. Burgess's map of Chicago (see Figure 3.1), Thrasher provided details for each of these areas and the gangs they contained. Within gangland, "the street educates with fatal precision" (1927:101). The northside covered an area directly north of the downtown, or the "loop" on the Burgess map, and behind the wealthy neighborhoods that lined the shore of Lake Michigan. It was home to the "Gloriannas," the site of "Death Corner" and "Bughouse Square," and a gang so threatening that Thrasher disguised its real name.

The westside was the most extensive slum area producing gangs, and it encompassed the area west of downtown, spreading out both northward and southward. The westside was home to the "Blackspots," the "Sparkplugs," the "Beaners," and the "hard-boiled 'Buckets-of-Blood'" (1927:9). On the southside of Chicago are located the stockyards and miles of railroad yards. Most of the blacks settled there, but the area remained dominated by Poles and Italians. The latter gangs were known as the "Torpedoes" or the "So-So's." Black gangs of the time were the "Wailing Shebas" or the "Wolves."

(continues)

As a territorially divided area, the city of Chicago and its environs pulsed with the give-and-take confrontations among the various gangs. Only the relative scarcity of killing weapons such as handguns kept the constant confrontations from erupting into the type of carnage characteristic of many cities today. For students of contemporary urban sociology, there can be no better example of spatially sensitive research than Thrasher's original study. It is doubtful, too, that in today's urban environment anyone could carry out the kind of exhaustive census on street gangs that Thrasher did. Certainly his study is now outdated. But like the pyramids, it remains an inspiration across time.

Another way to appreciate their achievements is by returning to the original case studies. A particularly vivid ethnography is Frederick M. Thrasher's 1927 study of *The Gang*. Thrasher spent eight years tracking down the youth gangs of Chicago and in the end was able to identify 1,313 of them. Today media coverage tends to associate street gangs with black or Hispanic teenagers in the inner city and lament their violent ways, as exemplified by such films as *Boyz N The Hood* and *Colors*. Thrasher's work takes us back to the city of some seventy years ago when gangs were as much of a problem, but they were almost all white. Thrasher's study is described in more detail in Box 3.2.

McKenzie and the Metropolitan Community

Roderick McKenzie, a student of Park and Burgess, sought to apply the principles of human ecology to a regional metropolitan approach. He viewed the development of the metropolitan region as a function of changes in transportation and communication that produced new forms of social organization. These stages of development were the pre-railway era (before 1850), the railway era (1850–1900), and the motor transportation area (1900 to present). McKenzie considered technological change to be the key variable in producing spatial patterns in urban society, as he states in his introduction to *The Metropolitan Community:*

> Formerly independent towns and villages and also rural territory have become part of this enlarged city complex. This new type of super community, organized around a dominant focal point and comprising a multitude of differentiated centers of activity, differs from the metropolitanism established by rail transportation in the complexity of its institutional division of labor and the mobility of its population. Its territorial scope is defined in terms of motor transportation and competition with other regions. (1933:6–7)

McKenzie's ideas were recognized as a significant contribution to the field at the time. In some respects, his approach may be viewed as a precursor to the general concept of the multicentered metropolitan region emphasized by the sociospatial approach. But McKenzie did not have a great influence on later sociologists, and he is sometimes overlooked even by contemporary human ecologists. It is interesting to speculate on the reasons for this oversight. In the 1950s a new field of study, regional science, began investigating metropolitan regions from the perspective of economic geography, an approach with less appeal to urban sociologists. McKenzie's focus on the metropolitan region conflicted with the more general tendency of urban sociologists to focus their research and writing, as well as fieldwork, on the central city. A serious consideration of his regional perspective would have led urban sociology out of the city and into the suburban region, something that would not happen for several decades but is a central focus of this text.

FROM HUMAN ECOLOGY TO URBAN ECOLOGY

In 1945, Walter Firey published a study of land use in Boston titled "Sentiment and Symbolism as Ecological Variables." He noted that large areas of land in downtown Boston were reserved for noneconomic uses. Parks and cemeteries, as well as a 48-acre area in the center of the city that had formed the original "commons" of the community, had never been developed. In addition, an upper-class residential neighborhood known as Beacon Hill retained its privileged position as a home to wealthy and established Boston families despite its location near the downtown area. Each of these observations ran counter to the concentric zone model. Firey suggested that "sentiment" and "symbolism" were important ecological factors that influenced spatial patterns of development in urban space (Firey, 1945). Although other sociologists offered little systematic elaboration of the ideas Firey presented in this important piece of research, his work is often referred to as the "sociocultural school" of human ecology.

After World War II, the ecological approach enjoyed something of a renaissance because ecologists paid careful attention to the census of population and how demographic locational patterns had changed. By 1950, it was found that the U.S. population had matured and spread out across metropolitan regions. In addition to altering population dispersal, the war years had changed the locational patterns of U.S. industry. Many industrial plants dispersed to the countryside during the 1940s. As a result of the war effort against Japan, heavy industry was also decentralized and relocated to the

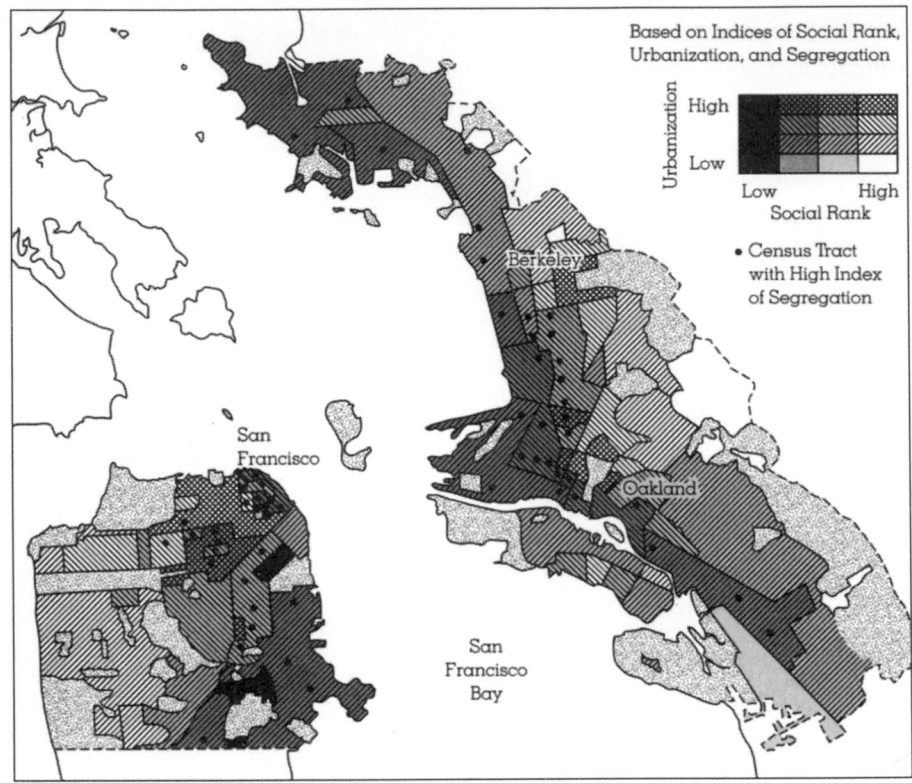

FIGURE 3.2   Shevky and Bell's social area analysis of the San Francisco Bay region

West. Los Angeles in particular became both a focal point for the burgeoning aerospace industry and an important port for trade with the Pacific Rim markets. All of this restructuring and change called for new research that would chart the emergent patterns.

Social Area Analysis

Social area analysis is associated with the work of Eshrev Shevky and Wendell Bell (1955). This method of urban analysis ranked areas within a city or metropolitan area on the basis of the social characteristics of the population, including social status (education, occupation, and income) and family status (number of children, whether the mother worked, and type of dwelling unit). Areas that scored high on social status and family status (typically suburban communities) could be compared with areas that scored low on the same measures. Social area analysis produced detailed maps showing the location of class and ethnic groups in the San Francisco Bay area, as shown in Figure 3.2; especially noticeable in this mapping are the minority neighborhoods in Richmond, Oakland, and San Francisco, as well as the upper-class suburban neighborhoods in the foothills of the East Bay. But as a more general contribution to human ecology and urban sociology, social area analysis was found to be lacking. It was a descriptive methodology, this time with a visual application, but it did not provide an analytical model that could explain why particular groupings of sociological variables (ethnicity, social class, and family status) might be mapped in one area of the metropolitan region and not in another.

Factorial Ecology

The development of new computer technologies brought sweeping changes to the field of human ecology. Urban sociologists no longer had to limit their research to field studies of urban communities; now they could assemble data for entire cities and look for associations among, for example, the educational levels, incomes, and employment status of urban and suburban residents. Factorial ecology made use of these techniques and, through the 1950s and 1960s, produced a large number of studies that greatly increased our knowledge of the structure of cities, not just in the United States but across the world.

In the usual model, data concerning the social, economic, and family status of urban residents are examined for commonalities among households living in different areas of the city. Each census tract or community area has specific information as to the educational levels, incomes, and employment status of area residents (economic status); the age, marital status, and presence of children (family status); and racial and ethnic characteristics (urbanism). A computer-generated analysis of this information then reveals the structure of urban areas. The factorial analysis of data for American cities and their suburbs indicated that economic status is the most important determinant of residential location, followed by family status and then social status. Because of their increasing focus on these variables and an associated decrease in the field research and community studies, which employed a very different sort of research methodology, urban sociologists working in this tradition became known as urban ecologists rather than human ecologists.

Having examined the ecological structure of urban areas in the United States, it was only a matter of time before urban ecologists turned their attention to the structure of cities in other areas of the world (see Schwirian, 1974). In a sense, they were out to prove a very important point: Urban ecology was in fact a research paradigm that could be applied to human settlement spaces across time and across space. They believed this model could explain not only the structure of cities in Europe (which had evolved out of a feudal mode of production and with a physical structure very different from that of American cities) but also that of cities in developing nations. According to this theory, residential dissimilarity and segregation among groups (based on religion, ethnicity, caste, or occupation) is universal, and modernization or industrialization will have no effect on this pattern (Mehta, 1969).

Although the evidence from studies of cities in India, Finland, and Egypt was sometimes inconsistent, urban ecologists still believed they had discovered a universal model of urban structure. In "The Factorial Ecology of Calcutta," Brian Berry and Albert Rees (1969) presented an "integrated model of land use" that combined the concentric zone, sector, and multinuclei models of the past and stated their belief that once the additional effects of local geography or history had been taken into account, their model could be applied to any city to explain where any group or business activity is located.

CONCLUSION

All theoretical paradigms are beset with potential problems and contradictions. Theoretical models borrow concepts and models from other fields of study; they are creatures of the concerns and beliefs of sociological scholars at a particular historical moment. Robert Park borrowed from models of plant ecology to formulate a model of human ecology. He incorporated the idea of conflict among competing land uses and competition among population groups, although it is unlikely that he envisioned the particular forms of conflict among class, ethnic, and racial groups that beset American society at the present time. Later ecologists incorporated new methods of analysis and answered new and even more challenging questions concerning urban life than the early Chicago sociologists could have imagined. But human ecology and its offspring, social ecology and urban ecology, confront numerous obstacles when studying the complexities of the multicentered metropolitan regions that now characterize urban society in the United States and across the globe.

The human ecology paradigm gives undue prominence to one factor—technological innovation—in explanations of urban growth and change. As noted earlier, Roderick McKenzie viewed changes in the metropolitan region as the product of shifts in transportation technology. This approach created problems for other human ecologists who followed McKenzie. Amos Hawley, for example, was interested in explaining two aspects of change in the postwar period: the massive growth of suburbanization and the restructuring of central city areas away from manufacturing and toward administration. In explaining these changes, he dropped the early ecologists' concern for space itself. He viewed social organization as fundamentally produced by the technologies of communication and transportation. As the technology of these means of interaction changed, so did the patterns of social organization.

The ecological perspective remains active in urban sociology. The core biological metaphor has been retained, as well as the central view that social organization should be understood as a process of adaptation to the environment. As we have seen, ecologists avoid any mention of social groupings such as classes or ethnic, racial, and gender differences. Urban ecologists see life as a process of adaptation rather than competition over scarce resources that often brings conflict. They have a limited conception of the economy, which still is viewed as simply the social organization of functions and division of labor—a conception that neglects the dynamics of capitalism and the global system. Although they emphasize ecological location, they ignore aspects of the real estate industry and its role in developing space. Finally, urban ecologists often ignore the important political institutions that administer and regulate society and affect everyday life through the institutional channeling of resources. Their emphasis is on the push factors or the demand-side view, which neglects the powerful supply-side causes of growth and change in the metropolis. We will examine the factors responsible for the development of the multicentered metropolitan region in the next chapter as we explore the new urban sociology.

KEY CONCEPTS

gemeinschaft / gesellschaft
mechanical solidarity / organic solidarity
modernity
urbanism
rational calculation
blasé attitude
human ecology
concentric zones
sector theory
multiple nuclei
size / density / heterogeneity
Chicago School of urban sociology
social area analysis
factorial ecology
urban ecology

DISCUSSION QUESTIONS

1. Early sociologists shared a common vision of the consequences of industrialization and urbanization for social organization. What did Georg Simmel, Ferdinand Tönnies, Emile Durkheim, and others see as the consequences of the shift from village life to the modern city?

2. Georg Simmel ultimately felt that urban life would result in greater individual freedom. Why is this likely to be the case?

3. In the text you have examined several competing models of urban structure: concentric zones, sector theory, and multiple nuclei. Explain how each of these models could be used to explain the development of the city that you live in. Which of these models gives the best explanation for the development of your city?

4. Roderick McKenzie wrote about the development and importance of metropolitan regions. Why was this important work overlooked by other human ecologists? How is McKenzie's work similar to the discussion of the multinucleated metropolitan region emphasized in this textbook?

5. In the 1960s and 1970s human ecologists sought to apply new computer technologies to the study of urbanization. What are some of the results of this research? What did human ecologists see as the limitations of their theoretical model and of its application for studying urbanization in other parts of the world?

CONTEMPORARY URBAN
SOCIOLOGY

A t the beginning of this text, we discussed several conceptual changes that are the hallmark of the new urban sociology. These include a shift to a global perspective on capitalism and the metropolis; the inclusion of factors such as class exploitation, racism, gender, and space in the analysis of metropolitan development; an attempt, when possible, to integrate economic, political, and cultural factors of analysis; special attention to the pull factors of real estate investment and government intervention; and the shift to a multicentered, regional approach to cities and suburbs. These concepts constitute the *sociospatial* approach.

Since the 1970s, a great deal of creative work has been accomplished by numerous writers who have challenged orthodox ideas of city development. One of the most interesting observations about this effort is that much of it has been carried out by people in other fields and even in other countries. Only recently has U.S. urban sociology been influenced by new theories. Second, regardless of the international scope and intellectual diversity, most of the new theories have their origin in the ideas of Max Weber, Karl Marx, and Friedrich Engels and their analyses of capitalism. This chapter examines this "political economic" approach. Although this perspective represents a considerable advance over those discussed in the previous chapter, mainly because the latter simply ignore the important role of economic and political factors, it also has its limitations. Sociologists have tried to tailor the approach of political economy to the needs of their discipline. In the concluding sections of this chapter, we discuss those attempts and our perspective, the sociospatial approach of this text.

POLITICAL ECONOMY AND THE CITY

Marx, Weber, and Engels

The classical sociologists Karl Marx and Max Weber turned to historical analysis in exploring their ideas regarding the general laws of social development. Both understood that societies were organized around integrated systems of economics, politics, and culture. Marx emphasized the dominance of economic considerations in analysis, whereas Weber explored the way cultural and political factors affected individual behavior and social history along with economic activity. The two approaches served to complement each other.

Marx also recognized that the interests of capital and labor are not the same. Because profit results from the difference between the costs of production (raw material, machinery, and labor) and the price for which a commodity can be sold in the market, capitalist producers look for any way possible to reduce the costs of production (Marx, 1967). Marx's analysis is as relevant for the monopoly capitalism of the present day as it was for the industrial capitalism of his time. In the past several decades, we have seen the displacement of workers by automation, a dramatic increase in immigration, and the movement of manufacturing to Third World countries—all of which are consequences of corporations seeking to lower their labor costs, and all of which dramatically impact the people and the built environment of urban and suburban settlement space across the world.

Marx wrote very little about the city in his classic *Capital* (1967; originally published in 1867), whereas Weber included some passages about the nature of the city in a much larger text, *Economy and Society* (1968; originally published as separate pieces beginning in the 1880s). For Marx, the early history of capitalism was a struggle between social relations located within urban areas and those situated in the countryside within feudal manors. For Weber, the city developed because of its political power—in particular, the independence of city residents and their local government from feudal authority. In both cases, Marx and Weber showed how modes of social organization, such as feudalism or capitalism, work through a form of space—the city—and the social relations situated within that spatial form. It is this perspective that informs the approach of political economy to settlement space.

For example, Weber argued that during the feudal period in the European Middle Ages, traders and craftspeople set up towns and bargained for protection from the king against the activities of local feudal lords. In these towns, capitalism began to thrive through trade in goods and eventually overtook the feudal economy. Thus, as capitalism became a dominating force in Europe, it also created the modern city. The political economy perspective studies social processes within urban space and links them to processes occurring at the general level of society.

Whereas Marx and Weber had comparatively little to say about the industrial city of capitalism, Friedrich Engels devoted extensive attention to the topic. We already mentioned his study of the conditions of the working class in nineteenth-century England and his field observations of the "great towns," Manchester in particular. For Engels, the industrial city was the best place to study the general aspects of capitalism as a social system, just as the factory was the best place to study the specific details of the relationship between capital and labor. Engels picked the city of Manchester because it was built up as capitalism developed in England, as opposed to other cities, such as London, which had a long-established history.

Engels observed several aspects of capitalism at work within the urban space. First, he noted that capitalism had a "double tendency" of concentration: It concentrated capital investment, or money, as well as workers. This centralizing process made industrial production easier because of the large scale and close proximity of money and people. Second, Engels observed that as Manchester developed, investment moved away from the old center and extended farther out to the periphery. Unlike Burgess, but very much like Harris and Ullman and the sociospatial approach, Engels pictured growth as a multiplication of centers. For him this followed no particular pattern, and he observed that capitalism unregulated by government planning produced a spatial chaos of multiplying minicenters.

Third, among other important observations, Engels focused on the social problems created by the breakdown of traditional society and the operation of capitalism. In Manchester, he noticed examples of extreme poverty and deprivation: homelessness, orphan beggars, prostitution, alcoholism, and violence. For him this misery was the result of exploitation at the place of work, which went largely unseen in the factory itself, along with the failure of capitalism to provide adequate housing for everyone. Engels connected conditions in the workplace with those in the living space, or what Marxists call the *extended conditions* of capital accumulation, which involve the reproduction of social relations that ensure the continued use of the working class across the generations. For example, if problems such as poverty and homelessness become too severe, they can threaten the ability of working-class families to produce new generations of workers. This would then threaten the future of the capitalist system. Hence, neighborhood or living-space relations and the quality of daily life are just as important to the survival of capitalism as are relations at the place of work.

In addition to the problems of poverty, Engels observed that the city of Manchester was a segregated space. Rich and poor lived in separate neighborhoods. Engels concluded that capitalism produces this spatial isolation of the classes. The sum total of all these social problems is described by the term uneven development, which conveys both the disparity between rich and poor and their segregation in space. We use this concept frequently in subsequent chapters.

Uneven Development

Urban and suburban settlement spaces grow and develop because of capital investment. The ebb and flow of money determines community well-being. It is not simply the fact that jobs are created; the resulting economic activity generates tax revenue that is used partly by local government to fund public projects that improve the quality of community life. But spending, both public and private, is not uniformly distributed across metropolitan space. Some places receive much more investment than others. Even within cities there are great differences between those sections that are beehives of economic activity and those that seem scarcely touched by commerce and industry.

Within any given business, there are also great disparities between workers who are well paid and those who get the minimum salary. Wages are carried home to neighborhoods, and a significant portion is spent in the local area. Hence, the well-being of a place depends not only on the amount of investment it can attract but also on the wealth of its residents.

In the metropolitan region, the variation in the affluence of particular places is called *uneven development*. It is a characteristic of our type of society with its economic system of capitalism, but, as we will see in Chapters 12 and 13, it is also characteristic of other societies, some of which have communist rather than capitalist economies. People with money seek to invest in places and enterprises that will bring them the highest rate of return. Profit drives the capitalist system. But this profit making is usually expected to occur in a short time period and with the largest return possible. Consequently, investors look carefully at opportunities and always try to invest their money where it will achieve its greatest return. This process causes uneven development. Impacts on quality of life increase as capital becomes increasingly mobile. At present, capital is more mobile than ever before in history. The ability to move capital investments from one country or region to another in search of the lowest costs and highest profit margins has immense consequences for individual places.

The changes that have occurred since the late 1960s in Silicon Valley, the high-tech showcase of California, illustrate this pattern. In the 1960s, when the printed-circuit industry was first expanding, all operations, including manufacturing, research and development, and marketing, were located within Silicon Valley. By the late 1960s, one of the leading manufacturers, Fairchild, transferred its manufacturing operations to plants in Mexico, leaving thousands of U.S. workers jobless. Soon, other electronic assembly plants followed the Fairchild lead, and by the 1970s most of the manufacturing operations of Silicon Valley had been transferred to other countries with cheaper labor. By that time, too, Western owners of corporations had discovered that operating in Mexico was not as cheap as production in Asia. Hence, many plants were shut down and work was transferred to Hong Kong, South Korea, and Singapore, then to Malaysia and Indonesia, and more recently to Sri Lanka. Silicon Valley residents lament the speed with which the boom and bust cycle played itself out in that region. Recently, the region has rebounded with a new boom that has been reflected in high housing prices.

As a result of the disincentive to invest in places that offer little in the way of economic returns, uneven development usually becomes more acute over time. This pattern increases the polarization between those places that are poor and those that are thriving. These spatial disparities result in different life chances for metropolitan residents. As Engels observed in Manchester, inequities create a problem of social justice as the less affluent members of the working class find it difficult to raise families that will acquire a reasonable, productive status in society.

Because of uneven development, society tends to degenerate into a two-tiered structure in which a small group of affluent people is surrounded by a sea of poverty. In the United States, however, government has intervened and provided a safety net of programs that attempts to prop up the bottom stratum. Unemployment insurance, aid to families, subsidized housing, and job training are a few of the ways government agencies use tax revenues to fight the inherent tendency of capitalist activities to produce uneven development. Over the years, however, despite periods of prosperity, the problems of the poor have been little ameliorated by government programs (Jencks, 1992). Thus, new techniques of public policy are sorely needed.

Metropolitan areas today are besieged by the uneven nature of capitalist development. Job security and planning for the future are jeopardized for people in communities across the nation. Extremes of poverty and wealth characterize metropolitan life. This clash between rich and poor in the city was also observed more than one hundred years ago by writers in the industrial towns of England. What is new and different today is the global extent of un-even development and the way the cyclical nature of growth affects people and places across the world.

THE REVIVAL OF URBAN POLITICAL ECONOMY: HENRI LEFEBVRE

In the late 1960s and early 1970s, the Marxian tradition was revived in social science. Urban analysis was initially affected minimally in this country but was greatly affected in France by the philosopher Henri Lefebvre. Lefebvre is without question the seminal source of new thinking on the city from a critical and Marxian perspective (Lefebvre, 1991). His accomplishments can be viewed as encompassing major four ideas:

1. He went back to the work of Marx and Engels on the city and extracted from their writing an urban political economy. That is, Lefebvre showed how it was possible to use economic categories such as capital investment, profit, rent, wages, class exploitation, and uneven development in the analysis of cities. In effect, he argued that the city development process was as much a product of the capitalist system as anything else—the production of shoes, for example. The same operation of the economy applies in both cases.

2. Lefebvre showed how Karl Marx's work on the city was limited. He introduced the idea of the circuits of capital, particularly the notion that real estate is a separate circuit of capital. For example, we often think of economic activity as involving the use of money by an investor of capital, the hiring of workers, their production of products in a factory, and the selling of the goods in a market for a profit, which can then be used for more investment. Automobile production would be a good example of this circuit. Lefebvre called all such industrial activity the "primary circuit of capital."

Much of the wealth created in a capitalist society is of this type. But for Lefebvre there was a "second circuit of capital," real estate investment. For example, the investor in land chooses a piece of property and buys it; the land either is simply held onto or is developed into some other use; it is then sold in a special market for land, the real estate market, or developed as housing for a profit. The circuit is completed when the investor takes that profit and reinvests it in more land-based projects. Lefebvre argued that the second circuit of capital is almost always attractive as investment because there usually is money to be made in real estate. As we have seen in the development of the United States, investment in land was an important means for the acquisition of wealth. But in addition, investment in real estate pushed the growth of cities in specific ways.

3. Lefebvre introduced the idea that real estate is a special case of the dynamics of settlement space. For Lefebvre, social activities are not only about interaction among individuals but about space as well. Social activities take place in space. They also produce a space by creating objects. The city-building process, for example, creates a certain space. When we visit a city, we experience particular attributes of the space that was created in that area. Other city spaces may be different, although places produced by similar social systems tend to resemble each other, such as the close resemblance of suburbias in California and Virginia or the similarities between the United States and Australia.

Lefebvre therefore introduced the idea of space as a component of social organization, as we discussed in Chapter 1. When people discuss social interaction, they are implicitly talking about behavior in space as well. Space is involved in a dual sense: as an influence on behavior and, in turn, as the end result of construction behavior, as people alter space to suit their own needs.

4. Finally, Lefebvre discussed the role of government in space. The state uses space for social control. Government places fire stations and police departments in various locations across the metropolis in order to respond quickly to distress. The state controls a large amount of land and utilizes it in its administration of government. It dispenses resources and collects taxes according to spatial units such as cities, counties, individual states, and regions. Government also makes decisions and relays them to individuals across the network of administrative units, that is, from the national level back down to the separate regions, individual states, counties, cities, and ultimately neighborhoods.

Lefebvre argued that the way capital investors, or businesspeople, and the state think about space is according to its abstract qualities of dimension—size, width, area, location—and profit. This he called "abstract space." In addition, however, individuals use the space of their environment as a place to live. Lefebvre called this interactively used space of everyday life "social space." For him the uses proposed by government and business for abstract space, such as in the planning of a large city or suburban development of new houses, may conflict with the existing social space, the way residents currently use space. Lefebvre said that the conflict between abstract and social space is a basic one in society and that it ranks with the separate conflict among classes, though it is often different. With this view, he departed from the Marxian perspective, which holds that class conflict is the basic force in the history of capitalism.

Lefebvre is responsible for many of the ideas that inform the sociospatial perspective. He also influenced the thinking of other urbanists and encouraged them to develop ideas of their own. In the following sections, we survey some contemporary urban approaches and describe how the ideas of Lefebvre, in some cases, and those of the classical thinkers Marx, Engels, and Weber, in other cases, have influenced new theories of urban development.

CLASS CONFLICT THEORIES:
GORDON, STORPER AND WALKER, AND CASTELLS

A class conflict approach to urban development was introduced by the economist David Gordon (1977, 1984). He suggested that the locations chosen by capitalists for factories were affected not only by economic needs but also by the desire to remove their workers from areas of union organizing. According to Gordon, owners of businesses prefer to locate in places where workers are not as militant as they are in cities with a long labor tradition.

To prove his point, he studied a period in U.S. history when workers were especially militant: the late 1800s through the early 1900s. He calculated the number of workers engaged in strikes during those years and matched it with the number of times owners of factories decided to relocate to the suburbs or to more isolated satellite cities. The matchup was significant for the years between 1880 and 1910. Hence, the need to control labor conflict by relocating to the outlying areas of large cities was a very early reason that urban development assumed a regional, multicentered form, because it led to the suburbanization of factories (see Chapter 6).

Two geographers, Michael Storper and David Walker, have expanded Gordon's approach (Storper, 1984; Storper and Walker, 1983). They view labor-force considerations as the principal locational variable. By doing so they argue against the received wisdom of traditional location theory, which asserts that businesses choose to locate in a specific place because of marketing and production costs (including transportation), a view that is similar to that of urban ecologists (see Chapter 3).

For example, studies of the shift in manufacturing to Asia note that it is caused predominantly by labor-force considerations (Peet, 1987). These include not only the presence of cheap labor but also the particular qualities of the workers. In the case of the electronics and garment industries in Asia, the workforce is overwhelmingly female, young, and unmarried. These laborers are advertised by development officials as providing a docile, easily controlled workforce (Fuentes and Ehrenreich, 1987).

According to the class conflict approach, then, any given nation has regions that vary with regard to the quality of labor. In part, the quality of schools and training facilities is responsible for this. However, the presence of a union tradition in the local area is also considered. Finally, particular cultural conditions, such as extreme patriarchy that subjugates women workers, are also important for creating a docile labor force.

An interesting variation on the conflict perspective was devised by the European sociologist Manuel Castells (1977, 1983). He was familiar with the early work of Lefebvre since they both lived in Paris, but Castells broke with him and followed the ideas of more orthodox Marxists. Castells suggested, however, that traditional Marxian analysis was limited when dealing with social movements in cities. In particular, advanced countries had highly developed welfare states; that is, the national government supported a variety of social programs for all workers, such as unemployment insurance and subsidized housing, that sustained people's quality of life. Most often welfare programs were administered by local, that is, city governments. Struggles for resources by residents of the city therefore often took the form of conflicts aimed at local government rather than the capitalist class.

For Castells, the unique aspects of urban sociology as a special field of inquiry were defined by the issues arising from city government's administration of worker subsidies, such as housing, mass transportation, education, health, and welfare. This created the conditions for a special kind of conflict that did not fall into the traditional Marxian category of disputes between labor and capital. Yet state-supported resources were necessary for the reproduction of the working class; that is, state intervention provided for the "extended conditions" of capitalism, as we discussed in the case of Engels. Thus, urban struggles were a new form of conflict (Castells, 1983) produced by the modern form of capitalist social organization—namely, welfare capitalism. Such social movements are highly significant for the study of urban sociology.

CAPITAL ACCUMULATION THEORY: DAVID HARVEY

When sociologists discuss economics, they usually think in general terms and focus on individuals such as wealthy businesspeople who own companies. Class conflict theory goes beyond individuals to discuss group behavior—particularly, the structural clash between the capitalist class of owners or investors and the class of workers who sell their labor for a wage.

David Harvey applied this structural Marxian economic analysis to the condition of the cities. He was especially influenced by the earlier writings of Lefebvre on the urban analysis of Karl Marx and Friedrich Engels.

In his case study of urban development in Baltimore, Harvey asks how returns to the ownership of land or property can be understood when "the distinction between capitalist and landlord has blurred concomitantly with the blurring of the distinctions between land and capital and rent and profit" (1985:65). Harvey defines a specific category called "class-monopoly rent" as the return on property owned in cities. He suggests that the ability to earn this money is contingent on a combination of factors involving both a variety of financial institutions and government subsidies. Hence, the process of earning money from real estate is quite complex and varies from location to location. Thus, the structural or institutional aspects of the real estate market and the quest for a profit explain differences in population location.

To demonstrate this point, Harvey divided Baltimore City into eight real estate submarkets. Each of these submarkets had its own dynamic of investing and selling. Harvey used data for 1970 and obtained the following results.

First, urban development is not some monolithic process of growth (as the growth machine perspective suggests; see next section). The second circuit of capital is composed of a variety of arrangements, each with its own set of social factors, conflicts, and possibilities in determining the level and quality of investment in real estate.

Second, the second circuit of capital consists of a combination of private financial institutions, community banks, and assorted government programs that support housing in different ways. Real estate is not a pure case of private enterprise but involves the government in direct ways. Speculators, developers, homeowners, and renters react differently in these separate environments, and while some people are simply interested in owning a home, others are out to make money any way they can.

Third, the housing market in the United States discriminates against African Americans and the poor. Inner-city African Americans have it the worst. They must finance most of their transactions by cash payment. Banks will not lend to them. Poor white ethnics also have trouble obtaining bank support, but they have managed to establish community savings and loans to help them out. Only the middle and upper classes have free access to loans, with fully 75 percent of such households obtaining bank financing.

Finally, the discrimination against poor and/or African Americans people is also revealed in the data on government-sponsored insurance. Inner-city and ethnic areas cannot obtain such support. However, more affluent sections have no trouble getting FHA or VA insurance. In short, the real estate market not only works through a complex assortment of combined public and private resources but also reinforces the inequities and uneven development of the society.

Harvey took a detailed look at the capitalist class and how it made money within the space of the city. He borrowed the concept of circuits of capital from Lefebvre and elaborated on his ideas. In particular, Harvey argued that capitalists involved in the first industrial circuit (that is, manufacturing and commerce) are principally interested in location within the urban environment and in reducing their costs of manufacturing. Capitalists in the second circuit hold a different set of priorities relating to the flow of investment and the realization of interest on money loaned or rent on property owned. These differences are reflected in the different ways capital investment circulates within the two circuits.

Whereas investment in factories is often located in places with cheap housing, capitalists in the second circuit often refuse to invest in poorer areas and seek out only the higher-rent districts of the city. As a consequence, areas of the city can become run-down and abandoned not because of the actions of industrial capital, the faction that we usually think of as determining city fortunes, but because of actions taken by investors in real estate, as the sociospatial perspective suggests. In the Baltimore study, both suburbanization of the population and central city decay were linked to the priorities of the second circuit of capital as assisted by government programs. Harvey's work bears out the importance of Lefebvre's ideas concerning the real estate industry and of Engels's central insight into the production of uneven development under capitalism.

In sum, both the class conflict and capital accumulation approaches of the new urban sociology provide impressive improvements over more traditional perspectives. The world today is a volatile one where the predictable accommodations of work, shopping, and residential living characteristic of the industrial city have been shattered. Economic factors such as the ebb and flow of real estate investment and the changing structure of manufacturing in a global system affect the sociospatial features of daily life. So do the activities of workers involved in the struggle lying at the heart of the capital/labor relationship, and the residents of communities who are concerned about maintaining their quality of life. Each of these aspects helps determine the pattern of sociospatial organization.

THE GROWTH MACHINE

The approach that views cities as "growth machines" is most closely associated with the work of Harvey Molotch and his collaboration with John Logan (Logan and Molotch, 1987). Molotch was dissatisfied with the traditional ecological approach to urban development and was highly influenced by new work carried out among French urbanists inspired by Lefebvre and Castells (Pickvance, 1976). Molotch was especially taken with the studies by Lamarche (1976) on the role of property development in the city. The focus of urban change involves the activities of a select group of real estate developers who represent a separate class that Marx once called the "rentiers." This concept is at direct odds with Harvey's view of the capitalist class, because under capitalism anyone can invest in real estate simply by purchasing land or buying a house.

For Molotch, the interests of the rentier class mesh well with the needs of local government, because government is in constant need of new tax revenue sources. As increasing numbers of people enter an urban area, their demand for services strains fiscal budgets. Without new sources of revenue, city governments cannot maintain the quality of life, and the region is threatened with a decrease in prosperity. Property development is a major source of new tax revenue. New people also bring new demands for city goods and services, which aids the business community and, in turn, increases revenues to local government. In short, according to Molotch, cities are "growth machines" because they have to be. Pushed from behind by demands for community quality and pulled from the front by the aggressive activities of the rentiers, city governments respond by making growth and development their principal concerns.

Molotch's approach might be considered the exact opposite of the one advocated by David Harvey. For Harvey, spatial development is explained by the structural drive for capital accumulation in real estate. For Molotch, structural factors have little to do with urban change. Both perspectives focus on only one aspect of the more complex development process.

THE SOCIOSPATIAL PERSPECTIVE

How can we make sense of the various ideas offered by new urban theories? This text adopts the sociospatial perspective (SSP), which takes what is best from the new ideas while avoiding the endemic reductionism characteristic of both traditional ecology and recent Marxian political economy. It does not seek explanation by emphasizing a principal cause such as transportation technology (Hawley), capital circulation (Harvey), or production processes (Scott). Rather, it takes an integrated view of growth as the linked outcome of economic, political, and cultural factors. At one time, it might have been suggested that such an integrated view derives from the tradition of Weber. However, since the 1950s, even Marxists have looked for ways to advance an integrated perspective (see Althusser, 1971), and this is especially important for the understanding of space (see Lefebvre, 1991).

Real Estate and Government Intervention

The sociospatial perspective (SSP) is inspired by the work of Lefebvre as applied to the needs of urban sociology by Feagin (1983, 1988) and Gottdiener (1977, 1985) and their collaboration (1988). The SSP can be distinguished from other approaches by the following characteristics. First, it considers real estate development as the leading edge of changes in the metropolitan region. Whereas other approaches tend to focus only on economic changes in industry, commerce, and services, the SSP adds to these important dimensions an interest in the way real estate molds metropolitan growth. Second, the sociospatial perspective considers government intervention and the interests of politicians in growth as a principal factor in metropolitan change. Traditional urban ecology and the newer approaches of urban political economy either ignore completely the role of government in channeling growth or treat the state as simply derivative of economic interests. The SSP considers the state to be relatively autonomous—that is, with officials having interests of their own—and, more specifically, considers politics to be highly linked to the concerns of property development (Gottdiener, 1986).

Third, the sociospatial perspective considers the role of cultural orientations as critical for an understanding of metropolitan life. Because of the importance of this subject, the role of urban cultures is considered in more detail in Chapters 8 and 9.

Finally, the SSP takes a global view of metropolitan development. Most local areas today are tied to the activities of multinational corporations and banks. Changes in the way they invest affect every resident. By emphasizing global economic changes, however, the sociospatial perspective also seeks to understand how local and national factors interrelate with international links. All spatial levels of organization are important in understanding metropolitan development. In the following section, let us review some of these features while keeping in mind the differences between the SSP and other sociological perspectives discussed in this and previous chapters. In particular, we will see how the sociospatial perspective is much more sophisticated and useful than either the growth machine approach or the traditional ecology paradigm.

Real Estate Investment as the Leading Edge of Growth

From the earlier chapters on urbanization in the United States, we have seen that interest in real estate profits played a central part in urban development.

George Washington not only was the first president of the country but also participated in the innovative scheme to develop the swampland that became the site of the nation's capital. During the 1800s, great profits were made by businesses as the country industrialized, but they were also made through investment in land. Cyrus McCormick earned millions from the manufacture of his famous reaper, but millions more from his activities in real estate. Railroad tycoons competed with one another by building the infrastructure that opened up the great landmass of the United States to development, but they also established towns and developed real estate as they went along. Finally, over the past several decades, we have seen that the shifts to suburbia and the Sunbelt were fueled in part by the phenomenal expansion of the single-family home industry and the development of lands outside the large central cities of the Northeast and Midwest.

The sociospatial perspective argues that other perspectives have neglected the important role played by investment in real estate in the process of regional development. Traditional urban sociology or ecology, for example, overemphasizes the push factor of technology as an agent of change. Marxian political economy pays special attention to the activities of capitalists and the way changes in industrial investment patterns affect local spaces. The SSP acknowledges push factors, such as changes in economic production and transportation innovations, but also highlights the role of pull factors, such as government intervention and the action of real estate—the second circuit of capital—as crucial explanations of metropolitan growth. Both demand-side and supply-side dynamics are studied in detail.

The sociospatial perspective stresses the human dimension along with structural arrangements. The model identifies who the actors are and how they behave, not just the facts or figures about aggregate levels of growth and change. Activities involve people acting as part of socioeconomic class factions, or of gender, racial, and ethnic interests. How people come together in the struggles that sometimes emerge over the impact of urban development is an important question for anyone interested in the study of urban sociology (see our discussion of community movements in the United States and in developing nations in Chapters 11 and 15) But the sociospatial perspective does not view these movements simply as the result of a single political movement or machine.

Feagin (1983), for example, discusses specifically the variety of ways real estate developers and speculators create development projects and channel money to real estate investment. Agents of growth include financial conduits such as commercial banks and trust or pension funds, savings and loan associations, insurance companies, mortgage companies, and real estate investment trusts; real estate brokers and chamber of commerce members; and public utilities and other relatively immobile public service agencies that must work to maintain the attractiveness of specific places. Real estate, therefore, is composed of both individual actors and a structure of financial conduits that channel investment into land.

Gottdiener (1977) has also shown how both structure and agency are important for an understanding of real estate activities. His case study of suburban Long Island, New York, identifies the following types of social roles assumed by investors in the built environment:

1. Land speculators who purchase land or buildings simply to be sold at a later date for a profit.
2. Land developers who purchase land with or without housing and then develop it by constructing housing or other built structures such as factories or malls. To this type can be added developers who restructure the uses of land and buildings, such as those who convert rental units into condominiums, single-family housing into multifamily dwellings, and residential housing into office space.
3. Homeowners and individuals who invest in property as part of an overall scheme for the protection of income and not just to acquire shelter.
4. Local politicians who are dependent on campaign funds from the real estate industry, and lawyers or other professionals who make money from government-mandated requirements that necessitate legal services.
5. Individual companies or corporations that do not specialize in real estate but develop choice locations for their respective businesses, such as office towers or industrial plants, and a host of financial institutions, such as savings and loans, that channel investment into land.

The preceding list of institutional and private interests involved in the development of the metropolitan region reveals that growth is not simply determined by economic "push" factors of production, as both the class conflict and capital accumulation perspectives maintain, or by a special class of people called rentiers, as the growth machine approach emphasizes. Development is caused by the pull factor of people's activities involved in the second circuit of capital, real estate. This sector is not simply a select group of investors, as adherents to the growth machine model assert, but is composed of both *actors* interested in acquiring wealth from real estate and a *structure* that channels money into the built environment. The latter consists of a host of financial intermediaries such as banks, mortgage companies, and real estate investment trusts, which allow a large variety of people to put their money in land.

Because the second circuit of capital enables anyone, even individual homeowners, to invest money in real estate for profit, it is erroneous to divide society into the select few who seek to make money in real estate (exploiting its exchange value) and the great majority who seek only to enjoy the built environment as a staging ground for everyday life (the exploitation of space's use value). Instead, space can be enjoyed for its uses and for its investment potential by both business and local residents. In fact, that's what makes the relationship of society to space so complicated. Space is *simultaneously* a medium of use and a source of wealth under capitalist commodity arrangements.

Because developing the built environment involves so many different interests, growth or change is always a contentious affair. These inherently conflicting interests have vital theoretical and empirical implications for the study of urban sociology, especially the role of the state, which we discuss next.

Government Intervention and Political Agency

The sociospatial perspective suggests that metropolitan growth is the outcome of negotiations and contending interests, rather than the product of some well-oiled machine without conflict. Developers, for example, must negotiate with government planners and politicians, citizen groups voice their concerns in public forums, and special interests such as utility companies or religious organizations also interject their stakes and culturally defined symbolic visions in metropolitan growth. The end result of these negotiations is a built environment that is *socially constructed*, involving many diverse interests.

The absence of a separate class of growth mongers means that the conceptualization of local politics by the growth machine perspective is limited. Feagin (1988) shows how powerful economic interests use the state to subsidize growth; hence development often reflects the direct interests of industrial and financial capital rather than some select, separate class of rentiers. Gottdiener (1977, 1985) indicates how local politicians are intimately involved with development interests. The purpose of this alliance is not growth and increased public revenues per se, as it is viewed by the growth machine, but *profit*. In this sense, those with an interest in growth comprise two groups: factions of capital involved in the accumulation process, and community interests concerned about growth's impact on quality of life. It is this melding of profit taking and environmental concerns that is most characteristic of settlement space development, and it involves a second source of complexity in the society/space relationship.

The interests aligned around issues of change in the built environment should be seen as *growth networks* rather than as the monolithic entities suggested by the concept of a "machine" (Gottdiener, 1985). The idea of networks captures the way alliances can form around a host of issues associated with development, often splitting classes into factions. The concept of network captures the diversity of people who may join, often only temporarily, to pursue particular growth paths. What counts is not necessarily the push for growth but the way different community factions perceive the form growth will take and how they evaluate their own environmental needs. There is a rich complexity of people and interests involved in metropolitan growth and change that is captured neither by the ecological or political economy perspectives—because they ignore particular agents—nor by the growth machine approach, which reduces conflict to a simple dichotomy of pro- and anti-growth factions.

The Global Economy

Finally, the sociospatial approach agrees with all other perspectives in acknowledging the important role of the global economy, the new mobile or "flexible" arrangements in production, and their effects on the restructuring of settlement space. Often perspectives identified with the "new" urban sociology stress the effect of the global system as the key determinant of metropolitan change (see Smith and Feagin, 1987; Palen, 1991). But the push factors of capital mobility and the considerations regarding the international division of labor, discussed earlier, are not the only determinants of growth. The pull factors of state policies and the second circuit of capital are also important, particularly as manifested at the local, regional, and national levels.

The sociospatial approach gives us a more integrated view of push and pull factors associated with growth. The influence of the global system does have a profound effect on the fortunes of place, but unlike other approaches (see Logan and Molotch, 1987; Sassen, 1991; Smith and Feagin, 1987), the sociospatial perspective does not assert that it has a sole determining effect. This can be seen in the development of the Sunbelt. Although the U.S. economy had become integrated into the world system in the postwar period, development patterns of deconcentration to suburbs and Sunbelt regions had been going on for many years, even prior to the 1960s when the restructuring of the global system began to be felt. The shifts to the suburbs and the Sunbelt are the two most important sociospatial changes in recent U.S. history, but neither can be said to have been produced by the power of the global economy. These shifts have their roots in growth trends that have been going on for years and that involve important aspects of both government intervention and the phenomenal draw of real estate investment.

Changes in the global economy have had a profound effect on the built environment. The decline of manufacturing in the United States and the transfer of many production activities abroad have wiped out the traditional relation between central city working-class communities and their capitalist employers. The economy of our largest cities has restructured away from manufacturing and toward specialization in advanced services and information processing, particularly those business services required by the finance capital faction that coordinates investment activity for the global economy (Sassen, 1991). The record high of the stock market and record low in unemployment through the 1990s did not alter this longer-term trend of restructuring of the urban economy and increasing economic polarization of urban space. All these changes have affected the nature of the local labor force and altered living and working arrangements. We discuss some of these effects on the people of the metropolis in Chapters 8 and 9. Other effects of the restructuring initiated within the context of a global economy are considered in Chapters 10 and 11 when we look at metropolitan problems and policies, respectively. Finally, in Chapters 12 and 13, we discuss the effects of global restructuring on Third World cities and settlement spaces in European countries and Japan.

SUMMARY: THE SOCIOSPATIAL PERSPECTIVE

The sociospatial perspective involves ideas that distinguish it from previous sociological approaches.

First, it incorporates a number of different factors, instead of emphasizing one or two, that can account for development and change. It particularly seeks to provide a balanced account of both *push* and *pull* factors in metropolitan and regional growth.

Second, it considers the role of real estate in development as the combined activities of both agency and structure. Investment in land is a sector of capital accumulation with its own factions and cycles of boom and bust. The categories of political economy, such as profit, rent, interest, and value, are just as applicable to metropolitan development as to any other part of the economy.

Third, the sociospatial perspective strives for a detailed view of politics that emphasizes the activities of individuals and groups in the development process. The SSP focuses on the activities of certain *growth networks* that form coalitions interested in choices that must be made concerning the direction and impacts of change.

The sociospatial perspective considers cultural factors, such as race, gender, and the symbolic context of space, to be just as important as economic and political concerns. It also deals specifically with the special qualities of spatial forms and their role in the organization of society. At present, metropolitan life is played out within the context of an ever-expanding multicentered region. We have discussed the historical significance of this form of settlement space in previous chapters and discuss its significance for contemporary daily life in chapters to come.

Finally, the sociospatial perspective, along with other approaches, adopts a global view of development but does not claim that the world economy alone is responsible for the restructuring of settlement space. Global changes are particularly relevant for an understanding of how cities, suburbs, and regions have been affected by the economy in recent years. New spaces of industry, commerce, and services have helped redefine settlement patterns as multicentered regional development. Historically, however, the pull factors of government intervention and investment in real estate have also played an essential part in the restructuring of space.

KEY CONCEPTS

political economy
international division of labor
capital accumulation
flexible production
uneven development
second circuit of capital
abstract space
social space
labor theory of location
growth machine
use value / exchange value
financial conduits
urban growth networks
sociospatial perspective

DISCUSSION QUESTIONS

1. The new urban sociology has developed in part from earlier theoretical work in what is known as political economy. Who are some of the earlier sociologists identified

with this theoretical perspective? What did they write about? How were their ideas incorporated into urban sociology and into sociological thinking more generally?

2. What is meant by *uneven development*? What causes uneven development to occur within a metropolitan region? What are the effects of uneven development on metropolitan growth? What are some examples of uneven development that you can see within the metropolitan region where you live?

3. Henri Lefebvre stands as the major theoretical figure in the development of urban political economy. What was his contribution to recent work in the new urban sociology? Identify three ideas that Henri Lefebvre wrote about and explain how they are used in urban sociology.

4. There are important differences between the class conflict and capital accumulation approaches of the new urban sociology. Discuss the work of one theorist from each of these approaches and explain the differences in their approaches to studying metropolitan regions.

5. John Logan and Harvey Molotch have suggested that urban development is driven forward by a *growth machine* that emphasizes the "exchange value" of urban property against the "use value" that local residents assign to their property. What are some of the limitations of this approach? How is the idea of the growth machine different from the sociospatial approach more generally?

6. What is meant by the *sociospatial approach* to urban sociology? Pick three features of this perspective and discuss how these are used to study metropolitan regions.

URBANIZATION IN
THE UNITED STATES

Then the Lord rained down burning sulfur on Sodom and Gomorrah—from the Lord out of the heavens. Thus he overthrew those cities and the entire plain, including all those living in the cities—and also the vegetation in the land.

GENESIS 19

Americans have a long-standing distrust of cities and of city life. Thomas Jefferson (1977) suggested that cities were the source of evil and corruption that would threaten the young democracy's political system. Despite such sentiments, the growth of urban centers in the United States has been prolific and, as we already have seen in Chapter 1, has increased in recent decades. For much of our history, the everyday life of Americans has been defined in urban terms.

In many respects, development in the United States mirrors the same trends and effects of social forces unleashed in Western Europe. We experienced, for example, the same Industrial Revolution that swept through European countries in the late 1700s and 1800s and even contributed significantly to its technological breakthroughs. Everyone has probably heard of McCormick's reaper or Thomas A. Edison's light bulb. Such inventions helped the United States compete with industrial giants like England in the nineteenth century.

Yet, for all its close links to the Old World, the city-building process in the United States has exhibited several features that are different from urbanization found elsewhere. These include (1) the lack of walls or fortifications around cities; (2) real estate development as a major component in the economy of capitalism; (3) the ideology of privatism, which limits the role of the state and emphasizes individual accomplishments as the basis of community; (4) large-scale foreign immigration and massive population turnover within cities; and (5) the regional dispersal of the metropolis. This chapter discusses urbanization and the development of the industrial city within the larger context of U.S. urban history.

THE STAGES OF URBAN GROWTH

Many factors have contributed to urban expansion in the United States. These include economic forces; transportation, construction, and communication technology; political changes; immigration policy; and expansion into a global superpower. *The best explanation for urban patterns is found when connection is made between the production of settlement space and the society's political economy.* According to the sociospatial perspective, this does not mean stages of metropolitan growth are directly correlated to particular stages of economic development; rather, it means only that important features of each period of economic development are directly associated with important factors in the social and political change of metropolitan space.

Four distinct stages of urban growth in the United States have resulted in the formation of the multicentered metropolitan region. These are (1) the colonial period, 1630 to 1812; (2) the industrial period, 1812 to 1920; (3) the metropolitan period, 1920 to 1960; and (4) the deconcentration and restructuring of settlement space within the multicentered metropolitan region that has taken place since 1960.

Urban and suburban settlement space within the United States has developed within a free-market economy based on private property and capital accumulation. We know this type of economic system by the name of *capitalism.* As both Adam Smith and Karl Marx emphasized, capitalism is a dynamic system that brings about changes in the social relations and political

---

BOX 5.1   Stages of Capitalism and Urbanization in the United States, 1630 to the present

Stages of Capitalism	*Stages of Urbanization*
Mercantile-colonial period	Colonial period: 1630 to 1812
Industrialization period	Industrial period: 1812 to 1920
Monopoly capitalism period	Metropolitan period: 1920 to 1960
Global capitalism period	Multicentered expansion: 1960 to today

systems with which it comes in contact. The stages of urban development correspond to growth periods in the development of American capitalism. These stages of development are often referred to as (1) mercantile capitalism, (2) industrial capitalism, (3) monopoly capitalism, and (4) global capitalism. But these periods do not represent an evolutionary theory of development such as that suggested by V. Gordon Childe in Chapter 2. Although cities in the United States experienced progress through these periods, there is no reason that another society has to pass through exactly the same sequence, as indeed other countries' economic transformations differ from ours. The stages of urban growth and change in political economy are only loosely coupled. Nonetheless, the discussion of distinct phases of city building is an effective way to organize our analysis of the connection between developments in the American political economy and the forms of settlement space over time.

THE COLONIAL PERIOD: 1630 TO 1812

The United States was colonized by European societies engaged in the political economy of *mercantilism,* an early stage of global capitalism. In this system, the countries of Europe organized the expansion of their local economies at a time when manufacturing was not industrialized and with the aid of the political apparatus of the nation-state. The wealth of nations, it was believed, depended on the well-being of commerce or trade, while domestic manufacturing was protected from foreign competition by government tariffs. Mercantilist theory called for the colonization of resource-rich but undeveloped areas of the globe accomplished through the state's own military and naval power. Wealth would increase if raw materials could be plundered from the undeveloped colonies, while manufactured articles would be produced exclusively in the home countries. Through these arrangements, the maximum amount of work could be provided to the nation's own laborers, and excess population could be drained off to the colonies.

In the 1700s the cities of the United States were little more than colonial outposts of England, France, and Spain located on the shores of a country with an unknown and unsettled interior. The attention and the energies of the colonists were directed eastward across the Atlantic Ocean toward the colonial powers and events in Europe. The existence of these cities was guaranteed by the might of the colonial powers' navies and military organization.

Colonial cities were port cities. The docks and warehouses and the shipping, insurance, and trading companies constituted the focus of urban development. Farther back from the port facilities, merchant and counting houses

TABLE 5.1   The Most Populated Urban Areas in the United States, 1790–1850

1790		1820		1850	
New York, NY	33,100	New York, NY	123.700	New York, NY	515,500
Philadelphia, PA	28,500	Philadelphia, PA	63,800	Baltimore, MD	169,000
Boston, MA	18,300	Baltimore, MD	62,700	Boston, MA	136,900
Charleston, SC	16,400	Boston, MA	43,300	Philadelphia, PA	121,400
Baltimore, MD	13,500	New Orleans, LA	27,200	New Orleans, LA	116,400
North Liberties, PA	9,900	Charleston, SC	24,800	Cincinnati, OH	115,400
Salem, MA	7,900	North Liberties, PA	19,700	Brooklyn, NY	96,800
Newport, RI	6,700	Southwark, PA	14,700	St. Louis, MI	77,900
Provincetown, RI	6,400	Washington, DC	13,200	Spring Garden, PA	58,900
Marblehead, MA	5,700	Salem, MA	12,700	Albany, NY	50,800
Southwark, PA	5,700	Albany, NY	12,600	North Liberties, PA	47,200
Gloucester, MA	5,300	Richmond, VA	12,100	Kensington, PA	46,800
Newburyport, MA	4,800	Providence, RI	11,800	Pittsburgh, PA	46,600
Portsmouth, NH	4,700	Cincinnati, OH	9,600	Louisville, KY	43,200
Nantucket, MA	4,600	Portland, ME	8,600	Charleston, SC	43,000

SOURCE: Adapted from Campbel Gibson, *Population of the 100 Largest Cities and Other Urban Places in the United States, 1790–1990*. Washington, D.C.: U.S. Bureau of the Census, Population Division, Working Paper. No. 27, June 1998.

were located, while behind the port district, the beginnings of residential quarters, principally for the colonial businessmen and their families, were located. Artisans of all kinds who engaged in handicraft manufacture of the simple implements required for daily life were also located in the town. Their shops and residences were situated throughout the port district.

The colonial cities of the United States prospered because of the success of British mercantilism. Each of the largest towns filled a niche in the European mercantile trade economy. Boston was the center for colonial provisions; Newport specialized in shipbuilding and slave trading; New York focused on the trade of flour and furs; Philadelphia focused on meat, wheat, and lumber; and Charleston was known for the export of rice and indigo. Initially, Baltimore had few natural advantages, and it lagged behind the growth of these five cities, but by the late 1700s its businesses specialized in the flour-exporting trade, and it prospered. However, towns such as Williamsburg, Virginia, which were laid out solely as political centers, never grew.

Table 5.1 shows the development of cities in the period 1790–1850, from the colonial period through the decade just before the Civil War. The table gives us some important information about the growth of early cities under the mercantilist system and the later replacement of these cities by industrial towns in the years following the Civil War. In the early colonial period, we see New York City, Boston, and Philadelphia but also a number of smaller port cities in the northeast. None of these cities was very large by European standards (compare the figures here with those for European cities shown in Table 2.3). Some cities, such as Philadelphia and Boston, remain important population centers today. Most of the others, however, like Newburyport or Southwark, would never develop into metropolitan centers.

By the time of the Revolutionary War, American cities played a crucial role due to their demographic and economic power. The first confrontations, such as the Boston Tea Party, took place in cities. The wealth concentrated in New York, Boston, Philadelphia, and Newport also financed the revolt. Colonial cities became centers of propaganda that disseminated antiloyalist views throughout the colonies. At the time of the revolution, for example, thirty-six newspapers actively operated in the colonies (not all of which opposed the Crown). Finally, cities played a major role because they nurtured new political organizations. These organizations became part of the colonial militia when war finally broke out.

One legacy of colonial dependency was the absence of autonomous government and the concomitant lack of political responsibility among the citizens of the cities. As colonies they were administered by agents of the English king. Precisely this lack of political influence may have contributed to the revolutionary fervor, because the growing wealth and population of the colonies had no democratic recourse in the administration of port cities. In any event, the absence of autonomy, according to the historian Sam Bass Warner Jr. (1962), fostered a "laissez-faire" economic and social milieu that developed into the culture of *privatism* that so closely characterizes U.S. cities even today (see Chapters 14 and 15).

Privatism, a legacy of our colonial history, refers to the civic culture that eschews social interests in favor of the private pursuit of individual goals. From the very beginning of our urban experience, residents already believed their principal responsibility lay in the pursuit of self-interest. Unlike the citizens of ancient Athens, for example, who were obligated to pledge their indebtedness to the city that gave them birth, residents of the American colonies were not responsible to the city but only to the colonial power. Over the years, this has greatly restrained the development of a civic culture that fosters community values and social responsibility. Instead, the limited vision of privatism remains in place. According to Warner:

> To describe the American tradition of privatism is not to summarize the entire American cultural tradition. . . . The tradition of privatism is, however, the most important element of our culture for understanding the development of cities. The tradition of privatism has always meant that the cities of

the United States depended for their wages, employment, and general prosperity upon the aggregate successes and failures of thousands of individual enterprises, not upon community action. It has also meant that the physical forms of American cities, their lots, houses, families, and streets, have been the outcome of a real estate market of profit-seeking builders, land speculators, and large investors. (Warner, 1968:4)

A second legacy of colonial dependency was the absence of independent city economic rights. European cities of the late Middle Ages were powerful economic enterprises because they possessed independent charters of governance as well as the legal right to mint their own currency and conduct trade in their name. Colonial America granted no such privileges to its cities, and the cities did not possess chartered rights. There were no city trade monopolies, no special currency, and no city property rights beyond city borders, unlike Western Europe. Trade was organized by the large European conglomerates such as the Hudson's Bay Company. Any individual or group of entrepreneurs could break away from an American city and settle in the hinterland, forming a separate town. The varied reasons for such fragmentation could be religious, political, or economic. What mattered was only the relative ability to split off and settle elsewhere under the protective umbrella of the colonial powers. Laissez-faire, privatism, and the ease of settlement characterized city life during the colonial period. Hence, the legacy of the colonial period remains very much with us today in the form of weak city government and limited city political power.

A third legacy of colonialism was the physical absence of city walls. Max Weber's ideal city of the Middle Ages possessed defensible fortifications or walls. Elsewhere, forts usually defined the old city center. Thus, the words *Kremlin* in Russian and *Casbah* in Moroccan both mean "fortress." Few American cities built by colonial powers exhibited this trait (although some did have temporary stockades) because the home country provided for the general defense of the region by sustaining a standing army (Monkkonen, 1988). Consequently, unlike the walled cities of Europe in the late Middle Ages, American towns provided immense locational freedom. Land could always be developed at the fringe. To the clean-cut speculators' grid of the colonial port city was added a surrounding fringe that could always grow by accretion and land speculation. This particular pattern remains very much with us today as growth occurs constantly at the fringe of development in a pattern of sprawl.

A final legacy of the colonial city was the role played by land development as a singular source of wealth in the economy. For the residents of the American colonies, land was plentiful and cheap—a sharp contrast to the situation in Europe. Very early in the history of this country, it became clear to enterprising Europeans with money to invest that land development was a principal way to acquire greater wealth. But the very nature of exploiting this resource requires concomitant locational activities of a group of people and the ultimate attraction of residential and commercial users. It does little good to stake a land claim, no matter how large, in a wilderness with no friendly residents, without an attendant scheme for the eventual development of the land, including state protection for the influx of population. Hence, early in American history, land developers adopted the practice of working closely with politicians and colonial authorities to promote the development of select places. This pattern of *boosterism,* involving speculators, developers, politicians, and state authorities, or a *growth network* (Gottdiener, 1985) composed of varied individuals who are like-minded developers of land, was repeated many times in our history and remains characteristic of development today (see Chapter 7).

THE ERA OF INDUSTRIAL EXPANSION: 1812 TO 1920

The settlement of the vast U.S. territory following the Revolutionary War constituted a magnificent drama involving individuals representing the very legends of our country itself. As Gary Nash (1974) has observed, this drama was colored in red, white, and black, because it involved a three-way clash among white former colonists, Native Americans, and black slaves. Frontiersmen such as Davy Crockett shouldered hunting muskets and fought the Indian Wars. Native Americans such as the Apache chief Geronimo and his people were driven from their lands, killed in vast numbers, or forcibly resettled on reservations to make way for the development of the interior by Yankees from the northeast and, in later years, by immigrants from Europe.

It is helpful to think of American capitalism as acting like a large land development agency in addition to its role as an industrial enterprise. During the period of formative growth, entrepreneurs singled out choice locations in the advancing path of expansion and built cities. According to the historian Richard C. Wade (1959), city construction took place in many cases *before* population influx; that is, urbanization in the United States was often land speculation that proceeded with the aid of local governments. In a sense, the establishment of a town as a political entity harnessed land to the control of growth interests. As a consequence of political reforms during the presidency of Andrew Jackson, it was comparatively easy for groups of capitalist land developers to declare their projects incorporated cities. Hence, with the aid of home rule, the expansion westward during the century between 1812 and 1920, when the majority of the U.S. population became city residents, was an urban expansion and simultaneously an explosion in the number of governments at the local level. By founding towns, developers also used local governments to provide a civic or community structure for people who came there to live.

Land Development and Technology

Prior to the 1820s, the U.S. urban population remained relatively stable at around 10 percent of the total. After that time, a sudden burst of urbanization surfaced that did not abate until the 1930s. By the 1920 census, over half of all Americans were already living in cities. In the one hundred years following 1820, the United States was transformed into an urbanized nation.

After the War of 1812, urban development continued in the form of networked cities along the Great Lakes and the Ohio River Valley. At this stage, economic interests located within the large East Coast cities reversed their focus on the mercantilist needs of Europe and began actively pursuing the development of the American interior. In all respects, early westward expansion was highly dependent both on the development of transportation technology and on the protection of white settlers by government from attacks by Native American residents. Land was realized as a capital investment only after transportation and communication infrastructure was put in place. Roads had to be built. Tracks had to be laid. Telegraph lines were installed. In addition, the safety of work crews for all these efforts had to be ensured. Land was being taken from Native Americans, an effort that required organized government activity and military intervention.

The earliest urban rivalry involved local capitalists situated in the important East Coast port cities. Their future fortunes depended on the continuing success of their respective trade routes to the interior, because that region was the source of raw materials needed by local manufacturers and also a market for manufactured goods. Just after the War of 1812, the shortest route to the West lay across either Pennsylvania or Maryland. There were two roads—the "national road" out of Baltimore and the "Pittsburgh Pike" out of Philadelphia—but these links were inadequate for handling the heavy agricultural products of the interior (Rubin, 1970:128). Instead, produce was shipped south on the Mississippi River to New Orleans, making that city the most important export center.

New York entrepreneurs saw their city facing decline as the frontier expanded westward. In 1817, they began construction of a 364-mile canal that linked the Hudson River at Albany with Lake Erie at Buffalo. In a bold stroke, they hoped to create the most efficient link to the hinterland, with Buffalo becoming an inland port for the Great Lakes region of the Midwest. The canal was completed in 1825 and was so successful that it inspired a craze of canal building across the United States. From its inception, New York City competed effectively with New Orleans as an export point for agricultural produce.

As a result of the successful Erie Canal venture, Philadelphia and Baltimore financial interests faced decline, if not extinction. As the historian J. Rubin (1970:131) notes, they responded with their own schemes, aided greatly by government laws and subsidies. Initially, Philadelphia interests demanded that the state proceed with a canal to Ohio. However, construction failed in the Allegheny Mountains, and a rail segment was required. This occurred several times, and Philadelphia ended up with a mixed canal and rail portage system that required several transshipments. The route was hopelessly incapable of competing with New York's Erie Canal.

Baltimore interests viewed Philadelphia's problems with trepidation; they saw the difficulty of crossing the Appalachian Mountains via canal. By the 1830s, the steam locomotive had just been perfected in England, and in a venture as bold as the New York effort, they opted for the construction of a railroad line that would connect Baltimore with the Ohio Valley over the mountains. The line was eventually called the Baltimore and Ohio Railroad, and it was remarkably successful. As a consequence of these improvements, New York and Baltimore prospered while Boston and Philadelphia declined. In addition, the links to the interior forged in the 1830s helped found the Midwestern Great Lakes cities of Chicago, Detroit, and Cleveland, which also prospered because of successful rail and canal traffic to East Coast ports.

In the period between 1830 and 1920, the most significant technological innovation was the joint development of the steel rail and the steam locomotive, which perfected the long haul for commerce, resources, and people. Of the 153 major U.S. cities existing today, 75 percent were established after 1840 when the railroad had matured as an established infrastructure; only 9 percent of today's major cities were built after 1910 (Monkkonen, 1988:75). It would be simple to suggest that transportation technology alone caused the explosion of urbanization. This would be misleading, however. Technology became the means of growth, but inception and execution were the result of both the quest for wealth among entrepreneurs and the ambition of politicians in all levels of government—local, state, and federal—that joined these ventures, accommodating them with political resources. It is precisely this conjuncture of investors, political power mongers, and the dream of wealth that characterizes the second stage of urbanization in the United States. According to the historians Glaab and Brown, for example,

Earlier rivalries had been limited by nature—by the location of rivers and lakes. But railroads were not bound by topography, by the paths of river commerce, or by natural trade patterns. Railroads could be built anywhere, creating cities where they chose. Since the building of railroads was dependent to a considerable extent on subsidies from local communities, railroad leaders were willing to bargain with competing towns to obtain the best possible deal in stock subscriptions, bond issues, and right-of-ways. . . . The "boosterism" associated with the midwest and areas further west is largely a legacy of the late nineteenth century era of urban rivalry. (Glaab and Brown, 1967:112)

As we will see as well in our discussion of the last two stages of urban growth, this pattern of capital investment, coupled with government subsidies and competition among separate places, is repeated countless times and characterizes urban growth and change in the United States and possibly elsewhere. As the sociospatial approach suggests, development was a consequence of a combination of economic, political, and cultural factors— the frontier myth and the American Dream of wealth combined with cooperative government officials and venture capitalists to urbanize the nation.

What exactly were the proportions involved in the lure of wealth that accompanied town building? Consider the Illinois Central Railroad. Its promoters were also prolific city builders. In 1850, 10 towns existed in the vicinity of the railroad's route. After ten years of expansion, there were 47 towns, and by 1870 there were 81. When the Illinois Central entrepreneurs could not reach lucrative subsidy agreements with the politicians of existing towns for their right of way, they just built their own towns nearby. Champaign, Illinois, for example, was constructed by the railroad company, adjacent to the existing town of Urbana.

Another example shows us the size of the profit realized from real estate investment alone. The town of Kankakee, Illinois, was built by this same railroad company in 1855 at a cost of $10,000, and after just one year, the owners had already realized $50,000 in lot sales, or a profit of 500 percent, with more city land remaining. As expansion moved west, a similar pattern recurred involving a host of other promoters and their railroads. In San Francisco, which had developed as the premier city of the West Coast during this period, town lots that could be bought for $1,500 in 1850 were worth from $8,000 to $27,000 just three years later in 1853 (Glaab and Brown, 1967:113, 121).

Manufacturing

So far we have fostered the impression that city building involved exclusively land development schemes combining capital, government, and transport technology. During the period between 1812 and 1920, however, the United States became a world leader in manufacturing. The same forces of industrialization that unleashed such tremendous impacts in England during this time had similar results here. During the period between 1850 and 1900, for example, U.S. production of textiles multiplied sevenfold, iron and steel production increased tenfold, the processing of agricultural products expanded fourteen times, and the production of agricultural implements increased by a factor of twenty-five (Hoover, 1971:180).

The very heart of industrialization was the factory, which was the engine that drove the industrial stage of capitalism. But workers and capitalists were not simply disembodied abstractions. They were people who required places to live, raise families, and spend whatever leisure time they had. Industrialization, therefore, produced the factory town, which contained workers' families and houses, machinery, and energy sources, all within close proximity.

The first American manufacturing city was Lowell, Massachusetts, which was built on the Merrimack River at a site where the water dropped 90 feet, providing the original power source for its factories. Investors chose this place for a complex of cotton mills and struck on the idea of importing a labor force of young women from the neighboring cities, especially Boston, as a plentiful source of compliant, nonunion labor power. The geographer James Vance gives this account of the city:

> In 1845, thirty-three of the large mill buildings ranged along the canals and banks of the Merrimack, making Lowell the largest cotton town in America and one of its few great industrial cities, with a population of thirty thousand. A full third of the population was engaged as operatives in the mills or their workshops, though female employment remained disproportionate with 6,320 females and 2,915 males. (Vance, 1990:347)

Early industrialization in the United States is associated with the names of products perfected by innovative entrepreneurs: Singer sewing machines, Yale locks, canned hams, McCormick reapers, and Remington typewriters are but a few of these novel inventions. In most cases, the descendants of the originators carried on the family name and its business. In the 1860s, the leading industries reflected early development of manufacturing and the persisting importance of the United States as a supplier of natural resources. Cotton goods, lumber, boots and shoes, and flour dominated. By 1910, according to Geruson and McGrath (1977:68), the major industries reflected the maturation of manufacturing and consisted of machinery, iron and steel, lumber, clothing, and railroad cars, among other products.

TABLE 5.2   The Most Populated Urban Areas in the United States, 1890–1950

1890		1920		1950	
New York	1,515,300	New York	5,620,000	New York	7,892,000
Chicago	1,099,900	Chicago	2,701,000	Chicago	3,621,000
Philadelphia	1,047,000	Philadelphia	1,823,800	Philadelphia	2,071,600
Brooklyn	806,300	Detroit	993,100	Los Angeles	1,970,400
St. Louis	451,800	Cleveland	796,800	Detroit	1,849,600
Boston	448,500	St. Louis	772,900	Baltimore	949,700
Baltimore	434,400	Boston	748,000	Cleveland	914,800
San Francisco	299,000	Baltimore	733,800	St. Louis	856,800
Cincinnati	296,900	Pittsburgh	588,300	Washington, D.C.	802,200
Cleveland	262,400	Los Angeles	576,700	Boston	801,400
Buffalo	255,700	Buffalo	506,800	San Francisco	775,400
New Orleans	242,000	San Francisco	506,700	Pittsburgh	676,800
Pittsburgh	238,600	Milwaukee	457,100	Milwaukee	637,400
Washington, D.C.	230,400	Washington, D.C.	437,600	Houston	596,200
Detroit	205,900	Newark	414,500	Buffalo	580,100

SOURCE: Campbel Gibson. *Population of the 100 Largest Cities and Other Urban Places in the United States, 1790–1990.* Washington, D.C.: U.S. Bureau of the Census, Population Division, Working Paper. No. 27, June 1998.

Population Churning and Immigration

We have covered several features associated with urbanization in the United States. One of the most distinctive is the phenomenon of population turnover, or "churning," which for a time was quite pronounced in the United States compared to other countries. From the mid-1800s to the early 1900s, American cities functioned as giant magnets that attracted immigrants from all over the world. Prior to the 1800s, most people came from the British Isles or as slaves brought forcibly from Africa. After 1830, many more arrived from Germany, Scandinavia, Central and Eastern Europe, and China. Between 1800 and 1925, more than 40 million immigrants entered the United States. Seventeen million arrived during the period between 1846 and 1900 alone (Vance, 1990:359).

These figures alone cannot capture the way cities functioned as entry points for people. In effect, cities such as New York, Chicago, Philadelphia, and Boston processed vast numbers of immigrants from Europe and elsewhere, orienting them to life in America before many made their way into the hinterland. At this time, the internal demographic differentiation of cities took on the characteristics commonly associated with their residential patterns, namely, mosaics of ethnic enclaves of immigrants. The robustness of cultural life found there inspired succeeding generations of urban sociologists in their studies.

Population influx had a dramatic effect on the internal configuration of cities. Owners of buildings soon discovered that the voracious demand for housing could be met by converting structures to rental units. Later, new buildings called *tenements* were constructed specifically for rental use. These buildings were designed to squeeze as many families together as possible. The increased density made public health crises common. It also increased the risk of fire. On October 18, 1871, for example, the city of Chicago was almost destroyed by a single fire. Other fires at the turn of the century devastated cities such as Boston and San Francisco. Yet the escalating demand for housing also afforded handsome profits to owners of tenements. According to one estimate, by 1890 as much as 77 percent of all city dwellers were renters, and the annual returns on rentals could be as high as 40 percent (Glaab and Brown, 1967:160). In Chapter 8, we take a closer look at the importance of immigration for American cities.

THE RISE OF THE METROPOLIS: 1920–1960

During the period of urban expansion, economic interests located within cities competed with one another, and land development in the West made people wealthy. This stage ended as individual entrepreneurs and small businesses were gobbled up by large businesses, often located in different cities or even different states. The phase of *competitive capitalism* slowly gave way to a new era, that of *monopoly capitalism.* In turn, cities grew progressively larger.

City building slowed down considerably in the United States in the 1900s following a series of economic recessions that would culminate in the Great Depression. Economic activity and urban growth picked up again in the late 1930s as government reforms aided economic recovery and the United States mobilized for another world war in the early 1940s. During the *metropolitan period,* cities not only grew larger but also spread out beyond the political boundaries of their local governments. New areas of development became, in turn, new cities; in many cases, urbanization simply engulfed the smaller towns adjacent to the large cities through a region-wide process of suburbanization.

In the metropolitan period, it was becoming necessary to think about the urban phenomenon less in terms of the large city and more in terms of a region consisting of a mix of residential, work, recreational, and shopping places. The U.S. Department of the Census introduced the term standard metropolitan statistical area (SMSA—see Chapter 1) to account for the regional nature of development. Large central cities such as New York and Detroit also assumed vast economic importance far beyond their borders because of the businesses that were centered there, in this case finance and cars, respectively. This conjunction of spatial reach and economic might gave the city a new name: the "metropolis," or "mother city." Visions of the immense city outgrowing its boundaries began to appear in many countries. The German film *Metropolis* is one such example. Cities such as Tokyo, London, Paris, Berlin, Rome, Rio de Janeiro, and Calcutta all reached an unprecedented scale of size and population.

The metropolitan pattern of increasing size and geographical territory became characteristic of many cities in the United States. Following the Great Depression, urban scientists became interested in the phenomenon of the metropolitan region, and many studies were carried out to discover its social, political, spatial, and economic characteristics (McKenzie, 1933; Schnore, 1957; Bollens and Schmandt, 1965). Research revealed that two processes contributed most to regional growth: greater differentiation of the system of cities, expressed as changes in spatial, functional, and demographic differentiation; and the process of suburbanization (the topic of Chapter 6).

Metropolitan development and change do not occur because of technological factors alone but are also dependent on political and cultural relations. Economic activities, for example, require a workforce and certain community services, such as adequate schooling and health care, for businesses and their labor pools to survive over time. When there is a proper mesh between the human tissue of family and community life and associated economic activities requiring particular skill levels, both businesses and neighborhoods prosper. The sociospatial perspective emphasizes the fact that the relations among the economy, political structure, and culture are reciprocal.

Accommodations between the social fabric of community life and the needs of business produced the early factory towns, such as Burlington (Vermont) and Birmingham (Alabama), during the early period of family capitalism. One characteristic of this phase was that sources of employment and the labor pool were close together and both were tied to the general fate of the city itself. As the structure of capitalism changed in the 1930s, this equilibrium was shattered, and upheavals in the community paralleled those in business. Neighborhood relations changed when people were thrown out of work after plants closed or businesses altered their skill needs. New demands were placed on school systems, city budgets, and families to aid in the adjustment. In many cases, the success or failure of new ways of doing business depended on how well the community, local government, and families adapted to change. Thus, while economic alterations affect the social fabric, the latter in turn can also affect the well-being of the local economy.

As a result of this interdependency, each time new economic priorities are put in place, they affect the composition of territory and alter community life. The social organization of a particular place—the way it is organized according to locational choices of business, the scale of community, the flows of commuters, definitions of city service districts, the pace and structure of family life, and so on—is affected by the reciprocal relation between the local economy and the social fabric. In this section, we discuss the changes brought about by the economic restructuring that occurred in the 1930s in response to the Great Depression. They involve a process of *horizontal integration* of business activity coupled with metropolitan regional expansion. In Chapter 6, we consider equally important changes that have occurred since 1960.

Changes in Spatial Differentiation

Following the Great Depression, the economic system of the United States changed from a comparatively competitive form of industrial capitalism with a relatively large number of firms in each industry to a concentrated form called "monopoly capitalism" (Baran and Sweezy, 1966) where ownership was consolidated in a few hands. One distinguishing characteristic of the new form was the growth of monopolistic (one firm) or oligopolistic (a select few firms) control of major industries. For example, automobile production prior to the 1930s involved a host of firms such as Studebaker, Hudson, Tucker, and De Soto, along with Ford, Pontiac, and Chrysler. These companies were scattered across much of the United States, and their fates were often intertwined with specific cities and communities. After the 1930s, production of automobiles was essentially in the hands of the Big Four—General Motors, Ford, Chrysler, and American Motors (today it's down to the first three). While these companies also maintained branch plants across the country, their operations were national in scope and their headquarters were no longer tied to the places where they had their major factories. The Detroit area in particular became the headquarters for much of the auto industry, and decisions made there affected towns across the country. This change in the horizontal integration of large businesses to a more dispersed pattern, coupled with greater concentration of ownership, was also repeated in other industries, including steel and the production of consumer durable goods (such as electrical appliances). The trend even extended to retailing outlets, as department stores followed branch-marketing schemes (such as Sears, Roebuck and Montgomery Ward).

The changes in the scale of economic organization had spatial effects, especially on local community life, and several classic sociological studies documented them (Vidich and Bensman, 1968; Lynd and Lynd, 1937).

Concentration of wealth and ownership led to greater horizontal integration of business activities and changes in the spatial relations among community, work, and region. That is, prior to the Depression, most companies had all their functions located together and generally in the same city. These firms were replaced by companies with divisions in any number of locations, which used dispersal in space to cut costs, especially labor costs. For example, a large company that was part of an oligopoly in one industry might have its headquarters in a center such as New York, where it would be close to the headquarters of the other oligopolists in the same industry. It would also be close to banking and related services necessary to the command and control function of business administration. Its specialized needs would stimulate the local community to supply laborers with adequate training for the jobs that were created. This same firm might have a branch plant for production located in Newark, a central distribution facility in Philadelphia, and so on, each with its own impact on the local community and labor force. Such a pattern of related functional differentiation and spatial or horizontal integration was replicated in many industries.

Changes in Functional Differentiation

As a consequence, after 1930, a new, functionally differentiated system of urban places emerged in the United States; that is, different cities were the homes of different aspects of industry or commerce. Instead of competing with one another, as was the case during the previous period of competitive capitalism (discussed in Chapter 3), local capital was now organized and integrated by a national system of concentrated wealth. This pattern was not a product of the city itself but was attributable to the powers of institutions and social actors whose activities were deployed *within* the cities that were linked to the national corporations producing most of the country's wealth. Thus, horizontal integration and functional differentiation were two related outcomes in the restructuring of economic organization after the 1930s. We call this interlinked complex of functionally differentiated activities located within urban places a *system of cities* (McKenzie, 1933; Berry, 1972; Bourne and Simmons, 1978). In studying this system, it is always important to keep in mind that functional differentiation is a feature of the particular complex of economic activities that are located within a city rather than a characteristic of the city itself. Furthermore, the diverse activities across the nation are horizontally integrated by large corporations that possess "command and control" headquarters.

By the 1960s the U.S. urban system consisted of a select group of large cities with populations ranging from several hundred thousand to over 7 million. This pattern represents *balanced urbanization,* which is characteristic of the older industrialized countries such as England (see Chapter 12 for a contrast with less developed countries). Several studies have documented the structure of the urban system in the United States (Pred, 1973; Chase-Dunn, 1985). It is arranged across two different dimensions. On the one hand, cities seem to be distinguished by a concentration of business in either manufacturing or services, with the larger cities less specialized. On the other hand, there is specialization in finances or commerce. Furthermore, from 1950 to 1970, the functional specialization of the cities in the U.S. system remained relatively stable (South and Poston, 1982). Cities such as New York, San Francisco, Chicago, and Atlanta, for example, were diverse areas, whereas cities such as Baltimore, Detroit, and Los Angeles were more concentrated in manufacturing, and Portland, Kansas City, and Minneapolis specialized in financial activities and commerce. These specializations and rankings are somewhat different today. Until the 1970s they showed that important business activity remained concentrated within central cities. That is no longer as true today.

The immense economic changes that brought about the concentration of capital in large cities were only one aspect of the metropolitan era. As central cities prospered, they attracted talented people from all over the nation. Metropolitan areas became centers of culture and political power as well. They were the sites of important museums, universities, and symphony orchestras. They housed art movements and literary revivals. With their immense populations, they also wielded great political power. In many cases, such as Chicago and New York City, carrying the state in a presidential election meant, in effect, carrying the city. Much of this confluence of economic, political, and cultural centrality was to change rapidly beginning with the 1960s.

Recent research by Duranton and Puga (2005) suggests that a transformation in urban structure is taking place, in which sectoral specialization is being replaced by functional specialization. Because of increased costs connected to urban growth and congestion, and because communication costs have been greatly reduced by new computer technologies, many businesses have relocated production facilities in smaller cities. The new functional specialization of cities within the urban system of the United States and other countries is one where headquarters and business services are clustered in larger cities, while manufacturing plants and production facilities are clustered in smaller cities (see Box 5.2 for contemporary examples).

Urban sociologists have long been interested in the functional specialization of metropolitan regions. The specialization of cities within the American

Box 5.2   Functional Specialization of Selected US Cities

Education	Government	Government and Education	Manufacturing	Entertainment / Recreation
Ann Arbor, MI	Albany, NY	Austin, TX	Birmingham, AL	Atlantic City, NJ
Athens, GA	Carson City, NV	Baton Rouge, LA	Buffalo, NY	Branson, MO
Berkeley, CA	Denver, CO	Columbia, SC	Cleveland, OH	Ft. Lauderdale, FL
Bloomington, IN	Harrisburg, PA	Columbus, OH	Detroit, MI	Las Vegas, NV
Boulder, CO	Indianapolis, IN	Des Moines, IA	Evansville, IN	Los Angeles, CA
Champaign, IL	Lansing, MI	Lincoln, NB	Gary, IN	Miami Beach, FL
Gainesville, FL	Raleigh, NC	Madison, WI	Milwaukee, WI	New Orleans, LA
Knoxville, TN	Sacramento, CA	Oklahoma City	Newark, NJ	Santa Fe, NM
Tempe, AZ	Springfield, IL		Pittsburg, PA	Vail, CO
Oxford, MS	Jackson, MS		Toledo, OH	Virginia Beach

urban system is quite different from that of European countries. The location of state capitals in the central part of the new territories resulted in the formation of new cities that even today have small populations—the state capital of Illinois (Springfield) and Michigan (Lansing) are much smaller than Chicago and Detroit—and it often was a conscious decision to locate the state universities outside of both the state capital and largest city (the University of Illinois is located in Champaign-Urbana, and University of Michigan is located in Ann Arbor). This has produced a very interesting pattern of functional specialization of American cities, as shown in Box 5.2.

The extensive changes in urban form that occurred during the metropolitan period spawned new changes. By the early 1960s, the movement of white families from the central city to the suburbs was well underway, and investment in areas outside of the central city paved the way for the creation of the multicentered urban region. A new functional differentiation emerged within the multicentered metro region, as well as among regions nationally. Many central cities developed extensive ethnic and minority communities and by the end of the century would be more diverse than they had been one hundred years earlier. Increasingly, the cities would become the home of ethnic communities and the white working class, while the white middle class would dominate the suburban areas. The crucial factor in all of this is the process of suburbanization, which also is responsible for the creation of the multicentered urban region.

KEY CONCEPTS

mercantile capitalism / industrial capitalism
monopoly capitalism / global capitalism
colonial cities / colonial dependency
mercantile cities
population churning
immigration
economic organization
metropolitanism
spatial differentiation
functional specialization

DISCUSSION QUESTIONS

1. How does urbanization in the United States differ from that of other countries discussed in Chapter 2? Identify three specific differences and explain their significance for urban development in the United States.

2. The legacies of colonialism were important for later urban development in the United States. What are the legacies of colonialism, and how have these influenced the development of American cities?

3. Industrial development led to the rapid growth of cities at the end of the nineteenth century. What are some of the social problems that resulted from this rapid growth? How were these problems dealt with by local governments?

4. What are some of the technological developments that influenced the physical structure of the industrial city at the end of the nineteenth century? How did these technological developments alter the spatial structure of the industrial city?

5. How was metropolitan growth from 1920 to 1960 linked to changes in the nature of U.S. capitalism? How did the urban system in the United States change during this period? Why did metropolitan growth in this period result in increased functional differentiation of cities in the U.S. urban system?

SUBURBANIZATION AND THE CREATION OF THE MULTICENTERED REGION

Although **suburbanization is common across** industrialized countries, the massive scale of this phenomenon in the United States is quite distinctive. To be sure, many societies have experienced growth beyond city borders, but in the United States this has assumed the form of single-family home construction for the middle class on an unprecedented scale. Suburbanization of the white middle class to single-family homes accelerated its pace after the 1930s, and especially after World War II, but it was always an important aspect of settlement patterns. As we learned in Chapter 2, the expansion of cities in the United States was not constrained by medieval walls. Development in the urban fringe accompanied the growth of the city itself. In Europe, the city walls were torn down, converted to boulevards that would ring the city center, or simply were overgrown. Suburbanization would take place in these countries as well, but at a slower pace and with a different, more working-class-oriented mix of population that was housed in multifamily or apartment buildings.

Expansion beyond city borders was a common feature of industrialized societies as early as the nineteenth century. In fact, the desire to live outside the city seems to be as old as the city itself. Although we can point to numerous writers who extol the virtues of city living, there has always been an expressed "anti-urban" bias in every urbanized civilization. The biblical prophets, for example, took to the deserts east of Jerusalem to escape the excess and decadence of the city and to cleanse themselves. Across the centuries, those who could afford to do so always had a country home to balance against time spent at a city residence. The historian Kenneth Jackson offers the following excerpt from a letter written over 2,500 years ago as evidence that suburbanization was a process coextensive with urbanization itself: "Our property seems to me the most beautiful in the world. It is so close to Babylon that we enjoy all the advantages of the city, and yet when we come home we are away from all the noise and dirt" (1985:12).

But the desire for country living or anti-urban bias among city dwellers cannot explain the immense scale of suburbanization characteristic of the United States. The demand-side view of suburbanization is instructive in this regard. By "demand side" we mean the production of a settlement space pattern through the desires of consumers and businesspeople acting in the marketplace. Demand-side theories of urbanization make the assumption that settlement patterns are the result of a large number of individuals interacting competitively in the market to satisfy desires. Often they are simply aided by innovations in transportation technology. Many geographers, such as John Borchert (1967), and urban sociologists, such as Amos Hawley (1981), suggest this approach as an explanation of urban spatial patterns.

To an extent, the demand-side view helps us understand aspects of suburbanization, especially the desire of U.S. residents for a home of their own. Homeownership is a potent cultural symbol in our society. It provides people with their most important social status. Owning a home also links with other aspects of consumerism that express basic values in U.S. culture (Veblen, 1899).

There is also, however, a "supply-side" view to urban patterns. In this approach, what counts in development is less the desires of individuals than the quests of special interests, especially networks of businesspeople aided by allies in government that promote development to acquire profits. Feagin sums up the supply-side view:

> Traditionally most urban analysts and scholars have argued that everybody makes cities, that first and foremost the choices and decisions by large groups of consumers demanding housing and buildings lead to the distinctive ways cities are built. But this is not accurate. Ordinary people often play "second fiddle." In the first instance, capitalist developers, bankers, industrial executives, and their business and political allies build cities, although they often run into conflict with rank-and-file urbanites over their actions. Cities under capitalism are structured and built to maximize the profits of real estate capitalists and industrial corporations, not necessarily to provide decent and livable environments for all urban residents. (1983:8)

The history of suburbanization in the United States is a protracted story of bold quests to acquire wealth through the development of fringe area land and individual or group pursuits of a residential vision that would solve the problems of city living. In other words, an account of this phenomenon must consider supply-side and demand-side factors as intertwined.

In the early 1800s, for example, industrialists who had recently acquired fortunes, such as Leland Stanford in railroads, Andrew Carnegie in steel, and James B. Duke in tobacco (the so-called "nouveaux riches"), sought symbols of their newfound wealth. One practice was to purchase a palatial home with substantial space for manicured lawns and at some distance from the city. According to Thorstein Veblen (1899), who introduced the term *conspicuous consumption,* space in these suburban homes was used as a symbol of "excess" and the ability to afford it. The fronts of houses were given over to large, manicured lawns labored over by a team of hired gardeners, lawns that were used for nothing except the growing of grass. The mansions themselves had many more rooms than were needed to house family and servants. Guests could always be accommodated on the spot with their own individual bedroom; space was simply held vacant. The backyards were devoted to "suburban" leisure—genteel games such as croquet or badminton, lazing in lawn chairs, or simply walking in the garden. Conspicuous consumption, pastoral delights, and the large, single-family house with generous living space became for many Americans the suburban ideal. This cultural value glorifying a particular space fed the economic aspects of demand for homeownership outside the city. In Chapter 9, we will see that other metropolitan lifestyles are also dependent on their own particular spaces for cultural expression.

Traditional explanations for suburbanization stress the importance of transportation technology as its cause (see, for example, Jackson, 1985; Muller, 1981; Hawley, 1981), with each innovation, such as the switch from commuter rail to automobile, signaling a new pattern of land use. Transportation modes, however, served only as the *means* for residential suburban development; they were not the cause. Transport technology was always used to further real estate developer schemes. The demand-side view demonstrates that the desire for the suburban lifestyle may have been active in the minds of urbanites because people emulated the rich and disliked the confines of the large city. But dreams alone did not produce concrete spatial patterns. Rather, suburbanization was generated by the supply-side activities of real estate entrepreneurs and government subsidies responding to and feeding demand-side desires.

Early suburban development leapfrogged over the urban landscape. Suburban housing was built as a separate town removed by several miles from city boundaries. In the late 1800s, Westchester and Tuxedo Park outside New York City, Lake Forest and Riverside outside Chicago, Hillsborough adjacent to San Francisco, Palos Verdes near Los Angeles, Shaker Heights eight miles from Cleveland, and Roland Park outside Baltimore were all private developments built as towns. Most of these places advertised themselves as extolling suburban virtues, which at the time meant racial, ethnic, and class exclusion in addition to low-density residential living. It was not until the late 1940s that suburban development occurred on a mass scale. Hence, the desire for racial, class, and religious exclusion also added to the complex of cultural factors contributing to the desire to suburbanize.

The early deconcentration of industry followed this same pattern. In the 1800s, owners of large businesses often moved all their operations outside the city by developing a separate town. The classic study of such "satellite cities" was done by Graham Taylor in 1915. Gary, Indiana, for example, was built on sand dunes on the southern shore of Lake Michigan by U.S. Steel in the 1880s. At about the same time, George Pullman pulled his railroad car business out of Chicago and built Pullman, Illinois, a few miles away. In 1873, Singer Sewing Machine relocated from Manhattan to an existing city, Elizabeth, New Jersey, but converted it through its presence into a company town, where the factory remained until 1982 when it closed due to foreign competition.

Taylor (1915) gives two main explanations for the creation of satellite cities. First, the new ventures represented an important investment in real estate as well as an industrial relocation. More space was needed for industrialized plants, hence the need to move out of the congested central city. But the need for space was coupled with the acquisition of real estate. Pullman, for example, expected to make as much money from the development of land he owned in the new city as from the factory itself. Second, industrialists pulled their plants out of cities because the latter were hotbeds of union activity. Workers in any one plant were invariably in contact with workers in other plants and other industries. The city concentrated unions as well as people. During the sequential recessions in the United States, beginning in the 1870s, worker activism was widespread and strikes were frequent. The decentralization of industry and employment from the central city to the satellite industrial city was an important tool for minimizing union influence, according to Taylor.

To be sure, transportation technology would eventually play an important role in suburbanization. After the 1920s in particular, the movement of people to the suburbs was aided greatly by the mass production and consumption of the automobile. Prior to that time, regional metropolitan space was organized in a star-shaped form with greatest development situated along the fingers of rail corridors. The private automobile enabled developers to work laterally and fill in the spaces between the mainline tracks. In the 1920s, 23 million cars were registered in the United States, and that figure increased to 33 million within ten years. "By 1940, the U.S. auto registration rate exceeded 200 per 1000 population and the average number of cars per capita (which was 13 in 1920) had fallen to less than 5" (Muller, 1981:39).

Turn-of-the-century suburbanization played a great role in determining the patterns of growth during the years between 1920 and 1960. Trolley lines and tract housing laid down in the previous period provided the material infrastructure, such as right of ways, sewers, and utility lines, for much of the urban growth that was to follow. It is often suggested, for example, that Los Angeles looks the way it does—spread out in a pattern of immense sprawl—because it was built during the age of the automobile. Actually, the formative period of development for Los Angeles took place prior to the invention of the auto. Los Angeles was a product of electrified trolley lines and very active, aggressive real estate speculation schemes that capitalized on the ease of home construction in the region (Crump, 1962). Today's freeways in Los Angeles simply follow the transit routes of the major trolley lines that once existed. The fact that the latter were pollution free should not be lost on the present generation suffering from smog, nor should we forget Spencer Crump's (1962) case study showing how automobile, oil, and highway construction companies colluded to sabotage the trolley car transit business.

The major thrust of suburbanization in the United States took place after 1920, with a profound acceleration of growth after World War II. Truly it can be said that present-day regional patterns of metropolitan development materialized during this time. Prior to the 1920s, a suburban residence could be afforded only by the more affluent; after 1940, suburbanization became a mass phenomenon. So far in this chapter we have mentioned several supply-side factors contributing to decentralization. On the demand side, we have indicated the profound cultural effect that the style of life associated with affluent suburbia had on the tastes of urban individuals and families. Although many Americans may have desired to leave the city, few had the means prior to World War II, especially during the Great Depression. However, the federal government became a crucial factor in creating a mass housing market through its policies promoting single-family homes.

In the 1930s, the Depression was ravishing the home construction industry. Because a principal asset of banks was (and still is) home mortgages, the economic downslide also had a devastating impact on the banking industry. In one estimate, housing values declined by 20 percent between 1926 and 1932, and by 1933 at least half of all home mortgages were in default (Jackson, 1985:191). The Great Depression altered the nature of U.S. capitalism, as the federal government became a direct subsidizer of business rather than the heretofore indirect participant in the economy. In the 1930s, policymakers in Washington, D.C., attempted a rescue of the housing industry in an effort to support the banking industry.

In 1934, Congress passed the National Housing Act, which established the Federal Housing Authority (FHA). Briefly put, for qualified houses, the federal government insured buyers' mortgages. For banks, this took the risk out of private loans. It also pumped needed capital into the housing industry. Foreclosures went from 250,000 in 1932 to 18,000 by 1951 (Jackson, 1985:203). The act also established the Federal National Mortgage Association (Fannie Mae), which facilitated the transfer of funds by banks across geographical and political boundaries in the United States. The Fannie Mae program and later Ginnie Mae, or the Government National Mortgage Association, helped restructure the banking community and subsidized mortgage lending on a mass scale.

Subsequent housing acts were passed in 1937 and 1941. Along with earlier initiatives, they established the homeowner's tax subsidy. Homeowners could now deduct the interest paid on mortgages from their taxes. This subsidy quite literally made it cheaper to own a home than to rent. Along with this tax subsidy, the Serviceman's Readjustment Act of 1944 perhaps had the most direct effect on housing. As the war was ending, Congress pledged to support returning servicemen with a package of welfare measures including subsidized education. One provision of this act established the Veterans Administration (VA) guaranteed loan program. Under the plan, GIs could purchase homes with no money down. The mass exodus to suburbia was now guaranteed.

So we see that mass demand for housing was primed by government programs. Most new construction took place in the suburbs. Over 16 million returning servicemen were eligible for benefits under the 1944 act, and a mass market was created. At this time, and due expressly to the war effort, the United States had perfected mass production assembly line techniques that could manufacture vast quantities of goods. All types of consumer durable goods, including cars, washing machines, vacuum cleaners, toasters, dishwashers, refrigerators, and air conditioners, were being produced on an immense scale after the 1940s. Suburban housing developments featured the new goods, and in the 1950s all aspects of mass production—housing, durable goods, automobiles—combined to create the characteristic view of suburbia as the epitome of the consumer society. This political, economic, and cultural conjuncture that led to a society *domestically* producing and consuming mass quantities of goods with a large population engaged in assembly line factory work and active union membership is called *Fordism,* and it is a characteristic of monopoly capitalism. As we will see in the next chapter, under global capitalism the structure of Fordism broke apart as manufacturing activity drained from the United States to other countries.

The beneficiaries of suburbanization were overwhelmingly white. From 1940 to 1960, in two decades, the majority of the white child-rearing middle class left the central cities for the suburbs. In the previous chapter, we saw that this coincided with a period of mass black migration out of the South. This population transfer of whites and blacks is sometimes referred to as "white flight." Experts on the topic indicate that it is largely a product of the pull factors identified earlier (Frey, 1979). That is, whites did not leave large cities because blacks were moving in or the quality of life was declining; rather, they left because the quality of life was much better in the suburbs and because government programs subsidized them. Racial factors, according to the demographer William Frey (1979), had less impact on the decision to move than the destination of choice; that is, whites preferred to move to exclusively white areas in the suburbs.

Racism played a more overt role in preventing African Americans from moving to the suburbs themselves. Few were able to make that change in status. Those blacks who did suburbanize could find housing only in other black areas outside the city. The color barrier was strictly enforced by suburban developers. Box 6.1, which contains a case study of Levittown, New York, illustrates both the mass phenomenon of suburbanization after World War II and the racial exclusion on which it was based.

A number of factors contributed to the decentralization of people to suburbs prior to the 1960s. On the demand side: city congestion, urban environmental concerns, the popularity of the suburban lifestyle, and effective transportation choices. On the supply side: active real estate development and speculation at the urban fringe, decentralization of industry, government-subsidized programs, and tax incentives.

THE RESTRUCTURING OF SETTLEMENT SPACE: 1960 TO THE PRESENT

In the 1950s, most people still lived in large cities with an economic base grounded in manufacturing. Although suburbanization had commenced decades earlier, this trend could not match the magnitude of central city growth. After 1960, processes of *deindustrialization*—the loss of manufacturing—and *deconcentration*—the movement of people and activities away from the large

BOX 6.1   Profile of 1950s Levittown, Long Island

Prior to the 1940s, most homes were custom built or were renovated farmhouses, and most of this suburban housing remained relatively expensive (Gottdiener, 1977). After the war, voracious demand supported by federal government programs made it possible to build housing in large quantities, but construction techniques had not quite been perfected to build single-family homes that were affordable. Abraham Levitt and Sons was one of the nation's largest builders in the 1940s. Work on many military construction projects had given the company the experience necessary to build inexpensive housing on a mass basis. Levitt built the first large-scale, afford-able suburban housing development on several thousand acres of converted potato farms in the town of Hempstead on Long Island, adjacent to New York City:

> After bulldozing the land and removing the trees, trucks carefully dropped off building materials at precise 60-foot intervals. Each house was built on a concrete slab (no cellar); the floors were of asphalt and the walls of composition rock-board. . . . The construction process itself was divided into 27 distinct steps. . . . Crews were trained to do one job—one day the white-paint men, then the red-paint men, then the tile layers. Every possible part, and especially the most difficult ones, was preassembled in central shops, whereas most builders did it on site. Thus, the Levitts reduced the skilled component to 20–40 percent. . . . More than thirty houses went up each day at the peak of production. (Jackson, 1985:234)

Levitt was not sure that government subsidies and the GI bill would prove effec-tive in supporting homeownership on a mass basis, so the first houses were offered only for rent in 1947. Soon after, in 1949 and in response to overwhelming demand, they were sold outright. The two-bedroom Cape Cod boxes initially cost $6,990. The community, now called Levittown, eventually numbered over 17,000 houses and contained over 80,000 residents. Levitt's organization feared that if they let in blacks, they would run the risk of failing to sell their homes to the white majority. Consequently the developer carefully screened prospective customers for race. Hence, the blue-collar community, which became a symbol for the postwar American Dream, was not integrated.

Unlike large-scale developments of today, early suburban projects were marketed with a full complement of community amenities. Builders were obligated to supply a community quality of life, not just housing. Levittown came with nine swimming pools, sixty playgrounds, ten baseball diamonds, and seven "village greens," or mini-mall centers, within the development (Jackson, 1985).

After Levittown was completed, Levitt and Sons built communities in Pennsylvania and New Jersey. The modular construction process they innovated was duplicated by builders throughout the United States, and the mass construction of suburbia began.

city—transformed the United States, and a new pattern of sociospatial organization emerged. The growth trends of the present are so powerful that they require special attention.

Since 1970, population growth has been greater for metropolitan areas outside city centers than inside them, which reverses the traditional urbanization process of population concentration. This process is known as *population deconcentration*. Commenting on the 1980 census when the trend was first recognized, a demographer noted, "For the first time in well over 100 years, there was virtually no major nationwide population trend in the direction of concentration" (Long, 1981:11). For a brief time in the 1970s, even small incorporated cities lying outside the major metropolitan centers grew faster than the large cities, although by the 1980s that rapid growth had already subsided.

Other demographers were just as astounded by the changes of the past several decades. Most of the trends that characterized the U.S. population prior to the 1960s changed and, in some cases, reversed from 1980 to the present. Although there has always been a progressive drift of people from the East, Midwest, and South to the West, after 1960 this shift accelerated, producing rapid growth in the West. After the 1970s the South gained more than the West, for the first time, in net population growth. By 1980, the Sunbelt region of the West and South together contained the *majority* of the nation's population—a historical shift indeed! Today the Sunbelt still leads the nation in population growth (Perry and Mackun, 2001).

During the industrial and metropolitan period of development, large cities expanded faster than smaller ones. In the post–World War II years this pattern reversed, with the growth rates of smaller Sunbelt cities outstripping those of larger cities. In 1950, for example, Phoenix had a population of 106,000. By 1970 this number increased to 581,000, and by 2000 Phoenix had a population of 1,321,000 and was the sixth largest city in the country. Many other Sunbelt cities experienced similar growth during this period. In contrast, with the exception of New York City, all large Snowbelt cities (those in the Midwest and East Coast) lost population after 1950, including Chicago (a loss of 600,000), Philadelphia (500,000), and perhaps most spectacularly, Detroit, which lost half of its population (900,000). Other older, industrial cities such as Cleveland, St. Louis, and Buffalo experienced similar population losses.

Finally, the shift of metropolitan residents to suburbia accelerated during this time. By 1970, more people lived in suburbia than in central cities. If, in 1920, we could say with truth that the United States had become an urbanized nation, today we can say with equal confidence that the United States is dominated by suburbanization. Between 1960 and 1990, the United States went from a society dominated by large central cities in the Snowbelt to a nation with the bulk of its population living in multinucleated metropolitan regions and in the Sunbelt.

Let us examine these changes according to the sociospatial perspective. Other approaches place too much emphasis on technological changes or the push factors of economic growth. In this chapter we look at these considerations but also discuss the roles of government intervention, real estate activities, and the changed spatial arrangements of businesses and people.

HOW CITIES HAVE CHANGED

In 1950, the proportion of total employment devoted to manufacturing was 26 percent, with the next largest sector, retailing and construction, accounting for 22.6 percent. By the 1980s, the proportion of the latter sector was virtually unchanged, but the proportion of total employment engaged in manufacturing dropped to 22 percent. The largest sector, consisting of 24 percent of total employment, was the so-called *nodal services* sector: transportation, finance, wholesaling, business repair, insurance, and real estate. Within thirty years, cities had shifted from an economy dominated by manufacturing to one that specialized in services (Frey and Speare, 1988). For the largest cities, such as New York and Chicago, there is considerable evidence that the sector of capital involved in the national and global processes of financial investment has taken over the downtown areas (Gottdiener, 1985; Sassen, 1991). Employment in the sector of finance capital alone has increased dramatically for the categories of investment services, management consulting, legal services, accounting services, and the like.

Observers such as Bluestone and Harrison (1982) have referred to the drastic decline of manufacturing in the United States and other advanced countries as *deindustrialization,* or the closing of factories, the rise of manufacturing unemployment, and the relocation of manufacturing to other countries. Between 1970 and 1980 alone, the United States and Western Europe lost 8 million manufacturing jobs, while other countries, such as Japan and Korea, gained over 6 million jobs (Yago et al., 1984). We discuss the political economy of these changes more fully in Chapter 7.

Economic Restructuring

In the 1950s, the typical city was an industrial city. Factories filled the air with the smoke of manufacturing activity. Workers in plants lived nearby in socalled blue-collar neighborhoods. Although predominantly white, this population was made up of many ethnic groups—Italian, Irish, Jewish, Polish,

Hungarian, German, and Scandinavian. Everyday life was circumscribed by the factory routine for both women and men. A coordinated exodus of workers from their homes converged on the plants in the morning, while children ran off to neighborhood schools at about the same time. Schools provided vocational training for most boys and homemaker or secretarial skills for girls as a means of fitting them into a working-class world with limited aspirations that few thought would ever change. Past generations of working-class families had grown to maturity within this milieu, and it was expected to continue.

By the 1980s, this pattern of everyday life had changed. Cities no longer were dominated by manufacturing, and working-class family life based on predictable employment opportunities in manufacturing had largely disappeared, producing attendant changes and crises in education and job training. The city of Pittsburgh, for example, was once synonymous with steel. In 1930, over 32 percent of its workforce was engaged in manufacturing. By 1980, only 14 percent of the labor force was employed in manufacturing, and steel production engaged only 5.5 percent. In contrast, service employment had risen to 38 percent, thereby dominating the economy (Jezierski, 1988). Pittsburgh had been transformed from an industrial to a nodal service city. In the process, however, it lost 24 percent of its jobs and 37 percent of its population between 1940 and 1980. Between 1980 and 1990, it lost an additional 12.8 percent of its people. Cities have shifted from an economy dominated by manufacturing to one that now specializes in services and retailing, but with a smaller employed labor force and, in many cases, a smaller population than in the past (Frey and Speare, 1988:4).

Social Restructuring

Another and equally important change was that most central cities experienced slow population growth beginning in the 1950s, and by the 1970s, many began to experience population loss. The child-rearing middle class virtually abandoned the large city as a place to live, and even today children are greatly under-represented in the city population. However, as with the other shifts, national figures mask the regional nature of this phenomenon, which was most pronounced in the older industrial cities of the Midwest and Northeast. Table 6.1 shows the populations of the largest cities from 1950 to 2000 and illustrates the regional differences in these population shifts, most notably the decline in the Midwest and the growth in the Sunbelt after 1950.

From 1950 to 2000, the population of New York City increased from 7,900,000 to just over 8,000,000 persons despite a 10.4 percent decline in the 1970s. But other Snowbelt cities experienced significant population losses. Chicago lost some 600,000 persons from 1950 to 2000 (even after adding

100,000 residents in the 1990–2000 decade) and fell from second to third in population. The Los Angeles total of 3,695,000 is just slightly larger than Chicago's 1950 population of 3,600,000. Philadelphia declined from 2,072,000 to 1,517,000 (a loss of some 550,000), Baltimore from 950,000 to 650,000 (a loss of some 300,000), and Detroit from 1,850,000 to 951,000 (a loss of 900,000). Other industrial cities lost half or more of their population: Cleveland declined from 914,808 to 461,324; St. Louis from 856,796 to 332,233; Pittsburgh from 676,808 to325,337; and Buffalo from 580,132 to 285,018. (These cities do not appear in Table 6.1 because their 2000 population was less than that of El Paso, even though their 1950 population was much greater than that city's total of 560,000.)

In contrast, cities in the Sunbelt thrived during the same period. Los Angeles increased from 1,970,000 to 3,695 persons and became the second largest city in the country. Dallas increased its population by more than 400 percent (from 434,000 to 1,888,000 persons), and two of the larger Sunbelt cities more than tripled their population: Houston (from 596,000 to 1,954,000 persons) and San Diego (from 334,000 to 1,223,000 persons). The populations of several Sunbelt cities experienced periods of rapid growth in the early post-war period: Phoenix grew more than 400 percent from 1950 to 1970, San Jose grew more than 350 percent, and Jacksonville and El Paso grew about 150 percent. Other Sunbelt cities also experienced significant growth in the last half of the period shown in Table 6.1. The fastest growing city in the United States over the last two decades was Las Vegas (increasing by nearly 90 percent from 1990 to 2000), but it does not appear in the table because the 2000 population total (479,639) is less than that of El Paso. The phenomenal growth of the Sunbelt cities is discussed later in this chapter.

These population trends have been accompanied by profound ethnic and racial change, with minority populations increasing in many cities even before the increased immigration of the 1980s and 1990s. In New York, for example, the black population increased from 21 percent in 1980 to 26.6 percent in 2000, while in Detroit the increase was from 43.7 percent in 1980 to 81.6 percent in 2000. White flight from the central cities, produced largely by the pull of the suburban dream, was a significant factor in these increases in minority population. By 2000, 64.3 percent of the population of Baltimore and 60 percent of the population of Washington were black. The black population is smaller in many Sunbelt cities (11.2 percent in Los Angeles, 7.9 percent in San Diego, and just 5.1 percent in Phoenix), although Dallas (25.9) and Houston (35.8) have sizeable black populations. The growth of the Hispanic population over the last two decades has also been significant; in 2000 Hispanics accounted for 46.5 percent of the population in Los Angeles, 58.7 percent in

TABLE 6.1 Most Populated U.S. Cities, 1950–2000

City	1950	1970	1980	1990	2000	Percentage Change 1950–1970	1970–1980	1980–1990	1990–2000
New York City	7,891,957	7,894,862	7,071,639	7,322,564	8,008,654	0.0	−10.4	3.5	9.4
Los Angeles	1,970,358	2,816,061	2,966,850	3,485,557	3,694,742	42.9	−5.6	17.5	6.0
Chicago	3,620,962	3,366,957	3,005,072	2,783,726	2,896,647	-0.7	−10.1	−7.4	4.1
Houston	596,163	1,232,802	1,595,138	1,630,864	1,953,633	106.7	29.3	2.2	19.8
Philadelphia	2,071,805	1,948,609	1,688,210	1,585,577	1,517,550	-5.9	−13.4	−6.1	-5.8
Phoenix	106,818	581,562	789,704	984,309	1,321,190	444.4	35.3	24.5	34.2
San Diego	334,387	696,769	875,538	1,110,623	1,223,429	108.4	25.7	26.8	10.2
Dallas	434,462	844,401	904,078	1,007,618	1,188,589	94.4	11.3	11.4	23.8
San Antonio	408,442	654,153	785,880	935,393	1,151,305	60.2	20.2	19.1	23.1
Detroit	1,849,568	1,511,482	1,203,339	1,027,974	951,270	-18.3	−20.5	−14.6	-9.1
San Jose	95,280	445,779	629,442	782,224	895,193	367.9	36.7	24.3	14.4
Indianapolis	427,173	744,624	700,807	731,311	781,864	74.3	−4.9	4.4	6.9
San Francisco	775,357	715,674	678,974	723,959	776,733	-7.7	−5.2	6.6	7.3
Jacksonville	204,517	528,865	540,920	635,230	735,617	158.6	21.7	17.4	15.8
Columbus	375,901	539,677	564,871	632,945	711,265	43.6	4.6	12.0	12.4
Austin	132,459	253,539	345,890	465,622	656,562	91.4	36.4	34.6	41.0
Baltimore	949,708	645,153	785,795	736,014	651,154	-32.1	−13.0	−6.3	11.5
Memphis	396,000	623,350	646,356	618,652	650,100	57.4	3.5	−5.6	5.1
Milwaukee	637,392	717,099	636,212	628,088	596,974	12.5	−11.3	−1.3	-5.0
Boston	601,444	641,071	562,944	574,283	589,141	6.6	−12.2	2.0	2.6
Washington, D.C.	802,178	756,510	638,333	606,900	572,059	-5.7	−15.7	−4.9	-5.7
Seattle	467,591	530,831	493,846	516,259	563,376	13.5	−7.0	4.5	8.4
Charlotte	134,042	241,420	315,474	395,934	557,834	80.1	30.7	25.5	40.9
El Paso	130,485	322,261	425,259	515,342	563,657	147.0	32.0	21.2	9.4

SOURCE: U.S. Department of Commerce, Bureau of the Census, ranked by 2000 population.

San Antonio, 37.4 percent in Dallas, and 34.1 percent in Philadelphia. In many cities, the combined black and Hispanic minorities constituted a majority of the total population, thereby changing the racial balance. In 2000, several of the largest cities had combined black and Hispanic populations that constituted majorities, including New York City (53.6 percent), Los Angeles (57.7 percent), Chicago (62.8 percent), Houston (62.7 percent), and Philadelphia (51.7 percent). The National Council of Black Mayors was founded in 1974 and currently represents more than 450 African American mayors from cities across the country—a substantial increase from the 81 black mayors in 1970 and 314 in 1990 (Bositis 2003). Hispanic mayors were elected in San Antonio (1981), Miami (1985), and Los Angeles (2005). In Chapter 10, we discuss issues of minority empowerment and political representation.

At the same time as our largest cities were experiencing population decline and racial shifts, they were also experiencing profound ethnic shifts. The waves of immigration from Europe that gave U.S. cities much of their ethnic character had ceased by World War II. Beginning with the 1970s and accelerating in the 1980s, new waves of immigration flowed through our largest cities, increasing the percentages of foreign-born residents. For example, in the Sunbelt cities, much of the 60 percent population increase from 1970 to the present reflects a large influx of Hispanic residents. Concurrently, metropolitan regions on the West Coast have seen a large increase in the Asian population, often with specific groups settling into suburban counties, such as the Filipino communities in Daly City (San Francisco) and Mira Mesa (San Diego, sometimes referred to as Manila Mesa) and Chinese into Monterey Park (Los Angeles). Metropolitan areas on the East Coast have had an increasing proportion of new immigrants from the Caribbean and Eastern Europe. In Los Angeles, the foreign-born population increased 400 percent between 1970 and 2000—from 14.6 percent of the city population in 1970 (411,000) to 39.6 percent (1,645,000) in 2000. In New York City it more than doubled, from 18.2 percent (1,437,000) in 1970 to 35.9 percent (2,871,000) in 2000, and in Miami it increased from 41.8 percent (140,200) in 1970 to 59.5 percent (215,700) in 2000. In the Midwest, as well, the new wave of immigration has resulted in startling changes. The Chicago metropolitan area, once known for its Polish, Italian, and Bohemian neighborhoods and suburbs, now is home to more than 1 million Hispanics, mostly of Mexican origin, making it the third largest Mexican community in the United States (after Los Angeles and San Antonio). The number of foreign born in Chicago more than doubled, from 11.1 percent (273,900) in 1970 to 21.7 percent (628,900) in 2000 (Singer, 2004).

As immigration in the 1980s and 1990s reached record levels, urban and suburban settlement spaces across the country became more ethnically diverse than at any previous time in the country's history. The development of ethnic communities within metropolitan regions—most new immigrants move into suburban communities, not the central city—is discussed in Chapter 8.

Uneven Development

The final change that took place in cities links economic shifts with changes in the composition of the population and uneven social development. As we have already discussed, employment growth was located principally in the service sector, especially in nodal services that were provided to corporations and banks—legal services, printing, business consulting, financial consulting, and related services in communication and transportation. Early observers of this trend toward specialization in nodal services suggested that they would provide the core industry for economic revitalization of cities following the profound decline in manufacturing (Noyelle and Stanback, 1984; Sassen-Koob, 1984). It is now clear that no real renaissance has taken place. Instead robust activity in advanced services has benefited a relatively small and select group of trained professionals who earn high salaries, while providing modest employment in low-paying service and clerical jobs in activities that aid the work of the highly paid core. The so-called service city actually consists of two layers: a core of nodal services forming the focus of internationally important economic growth that employs highly trained professionals, and a second segment of relatively low-paid service workers who clean the buildings and maintain the landscaped areas around the buildings that contain the new service industries and the relatively affluent professionals they employ.

Manufacturing of a sort has returned to the city. In recent years nonunionized, low-wage factory work has appeared, such as fashion industry sweatshops, which often rely on the use of undocumented workers (Davis, 1987). These industries clash with the glitz of the much touted "command and control" centers that large cities advertise as being their core economic function. This contrast between affluence and poverty, between "yuppie" professionals and the working poor or undocumented laborers, seems to characterize many cities today. This so-called "dual city" has been the subject of some debate (Mollenkopf and Castells, 1991). Social polarization has occurred in the city, but there are more divisions than the class distinctions between wealthy and poor. Moreover, these contrasts have increased significantly within large cities in all areas of the world, not just the United States.

In addition, immense numbers of less affluent, immigrant, and marginalized workers have created within the city a large, *informal economy*. The informal economy is defined as the combination of goods produced in unregulated factories with non-unionized and undocumented laborers, goods and services produced and exchanged for barter (that is, not cash but in-kind), and goods and services sold without regulation on the streets. The informal economy in some countries often rivals the formal sector. Everywhere, this aspect of economic activity has emerged as an increasingly important way for people within urban areas to make a living. One example of the informal economy is the illegal drug industry, which runs into the billions of dollars in sales and is an international operation. And in cities such as New York, illegal factories manufacture "faux" designer fashion items, such as fake Rolex watches, and then use recent or undocumented immigrants to sell them on Manhattan street corners for only a fraction of the genuine article's price. Even discounting the major effect of drug dealing, the informal economy in large cities represents a formidable source of jobs and income (see Mingione, 1988). The informal economy is usually not discussed, and its presence clashes with the legitimated image of large cities as centers for multinational business leaders (Boer, 1990).

In sum, cities have changed significantly since the 1960s. They include a larger minority population, due in part to a growing immigrant population. Except for new immigrants, population growth in metropolitan areas of the United States has been slow, except in the Sunbelt. Today's large cities possess a transformed economy that is more specialized in nodal services and low-wage manufacturing, with a thriving informal economy of drug dealing and illegal factories that employ immigrants. All of these economic and social processes fuel a growing social disparity between the working poor, new immigrants, and street vendors, on the one hand, and affluent professionals, on the other (see Chapter 9).

HOW SUBURBS HAVE CHANGED

In the 1950s and 1960s, suburbs were considered places where urban professionals who worked in the city bought homes to live and raise a family. They were called "bedroom communities" for this reason (Jackson, 1985). We now know that this image merely represented an early view of such places. Since the 1960s, suburbs have matured (Schnore, 1963). Many suburban communities have become diverse culturally, economically, and politically, much like medium-size urban areas (Muller, 1981). Places such as Tysons Corner, Virginia, outside of Washington, D.C.; Costa Mesa, California, beyond the boundaries of Los Angeles; and Dunwoody, Georgia, outside of Atlanta, all are important and developed suburbs.

Researchers have defined suburbs for study purposes as the "outside central cities" portion of the metropolitan statistical area (MSA). But this definition underestimates the expansion that has created new suburbs and regional development outside the MSA since 1970 (Muller, 1981). A compromise definition counts all the "outer rings" of the MSA as suburban, but this definition still underestimates the extent of deconcentration. In addition, the census has come to recognize that some areas of the country are now fully urbanized despite lying outside the MSA and lacking major city centers. Consequently, in the 1970s the census designated the suburban regions of Nassau and Suffolk counties (outside the New York City MSA) and Orange County (outside the Los Angeles–Long Beach MSA) as all-suburban, independent MSAs. In the future it is very likely that other counties, such as those outside the cities of Chicago, San Francisco, and perhaps Houston, will also achieve independent MSA status. Thus, we now recognize that many suburban regions contain a social organization as complex as that of cities.

In 1970, the U.S. census noted for the first time that more people were living in suburbs than in other settlement spaces. At that time, 37.1 percent of the population was suburban, 31.5 percent lived in the central city, and 31.4 percent lived in rural areas. In 1980, 44.8 percent of the U.S. population lived in suburbs, and this increased to 46.2 percent in 1990. By 2000, even more rural areas had been absorbed by suburban growth, and the plurality of that population increased further. According to census figures, 50.0 percent of the 2000 population lived in suburbia, 30.3 percent in central cities, and 19.7 percent in rural areas (Hobbs and Stoops, 2002:33). Whereas virtually all central cities suffered from no or slow growth over the past decades, suburban regions remained the most rapidly growing areas of the country.

Push and Pull Factors in Suburbanization

Massive suburbanization since 1960 has occurred due to a combination of push and pull factors. Government intervention played a significant role in the development of the immense tracts of land outside large cities after World War II. Most instrumental were the tax laws allowing for the deduction of mortgage interest from income taxes. In effect, this subsidized middle-class housing needs, and because most affordable single-family housing was and still is located in the suburbs, this program also subsidized suburbanization. Since the 1940s, it has literally paid to own your own home.

The home mortgage subsidy is equal to or greater than all other government spending on housing (Feagin, 1983). Subsidization of suburbanization, however, did not stop at housing. During the 1950s, pressure was placed on the federal government to construct a national system of highways. The result was the 1956 interstate highway program, which acted in the name of national defense to subsidize the construction of over 40,000 miles of roads. A gasoline tax was imposed to pay for this construction, and at its height the highway fund amounted to $50 billion (Muller, 1981). This system of interstate highways carved up the countryside adjacent to cities, opening up the vast U.S. hinterland to suburbanization.

The combined efforts in promoting single-family housing and automobile transportation created a form of suburbanization in the United States that differs from that of other advanced industrialized countries. In Britain and Sweden, for example, ambitious mass transportation schemes were harnessed to aggressive town planning to produce suburban housing that was accessible and affordable.

In the United States, by contrast, mass transportation systems that had been in place prior to World War II were abandoned and replaced by highways that were the result of the cooperative efforts of automobile companies, highway construction firms, and local politicians (Crump, 1962; Whitt, 1982). The result is a suburban landscape consisting of immense regions of single-family home developments and the hegemony of the automobile culture (Weiss, 1988; Davis, 1986).

Suburban Social Characteristics

There is no typical suburb or, just as understandably, unique suburban lifestyle, although there is a typical suburban everyday life associated with single-home ownership, automobile commutation, and low-density neighborhoods that differs from life in the central city. Through much of the postwar era, it was assumed that people who lived in the suburbs would commute to the downtown areas to work and even to shop. In the 1960s and 1970s, human ecologists studied the employment-to-residence ratio, which compared the number of jobs within a suburban community with the number of persons in the labor force. Leo Schnore (1963) was able to categorize suburban communities as bedroom suburbs (perhaps the stereotypical suburb of the era), service suburbs, mixed residential suburbs, and net-employment suburbs. Since that time, the employment patterns of suburban residents have changed greatly. The majority of people who live in the suburbs are now employed at jobs within the suburban region, not in the city. The commute from the suburb to a downtown office has in many cases been replaced by the commute to a job in a suburban office complex—or manufacturing plant or shopping mall. Although there are important differences among different types of suburban communities, most now represent the mixed residential suburb.

While white households have found suburbs open to them, the uniformity of housing price within each subdivision has resulted in stark income segregation within suburban regions. Wealthier suburbs in particular have been successful in keeping blacks and the less affluent out of their areas through the home rule device of *exclusionary zoning;* that is, local control over land use and building codes enables individual communities to prohibit the building of moderately priced housing. This reinforces the value of higher-priced homes, thereby maintaining exclusivity. Years of such practices have made suburban housing increasingly expensive, thus creating a housing shortage in suburbia for first-time buyers.

Hence, the vast suburban regions are increasingly segregated by class and race. In its own way, this pattern replicates the division of race and class within the central city. Thus, city problems of residential segregation have been duplicated in the suburbs and are now regionwide.

Economic Deconcentration

For the suburbs, economic deconcentration has meant a combined process of both capturing new job growth and decentralizing economic activities from the large central city, as well as the process of their recentralization in mini-centers within the suburban region. Let us consider the separate economic dimensions of deconcentration.

Retailing. The total amount of all retailing in the United States is now dominated by malls located in suburban realms of the metropolis. By the time of the 1970 census, the suburban share of MSA sales passed the 50 percent mark for the fifteen largest MSAs. According to Muller,

> Steadily rising real incomes, fueled by the booming aerospace-led economy of the middle and late sixties, created a virtually insatiable suburban demand for durable consumer goods. With almost no pre-existing retail facilities in the burgeoning outer suburbs, huge capital investments were easily attracted from life insurance companies and other major financial institutions. Not surprisingly, regional shopping centers quickly sprang up at the most accessible highway junction locations as their builders strived to make them the focus of all local development. (1981:123)

Suburban shopping malls were so successful that their numbers increased more than tenfold from approximately 2,000 in 1960 to over 20,000 in 1980. Over time this success threatened central city shopping areas and bypassed them as the important places to consume. Sizes of suburban retailing centers increased over time to malls and supermalls. Houston's Galleria complex, for example, is modeled after the Galeria of Milan, Italy. It is several stories high and is built around an Olympic-size skating rink that is open year-round, a feat of some proportions if you consider the warm, humid climate of Houston. The Galleria has three large department stores, over two hundred smaller shops, four office towers, two hotels, over fifteen restaurants and cinemas, nightclubs, and even a health club. Its seven-level parking facility has room for more than 10,000 cars. Lately, the name *Galleria* has become popular for malls in many other places in the United States, and it usually connotes a large and expansive upscale mall.

This type of spectacular, fully enclosed space for shopping has begun to replace the downtown streets of the central city department store district. As the success of malls has advanced, the scale of their construction has increased. Over the past decade, the phenomenon of "megamalls" has emerged as the new suburban focus of retailing. In the summer of 1992 a new, fully enclosed complex was constructed outside the city of Minneapolis that is so large it has room at its center for a seven-acre miniversion of a famous California theme park, Knotts Berry Farm. This "Mall of America," as it is called, contains 2 million square feet of space and enough parking for thousands of cars. Central cities cannot compete with such family attractions in immense suburban spaces.

Manufacturing.   We have noted the progressive decline of manufacturing in the United States and its devastating impact on central cities. Over the years suburban areas have changed their bedroom image in part by being the recipients of many new manufacturing industries that have remained active. By the 1980s, the percentage share of manufacturing for the suburban rings of most metropolitan areas nationwide exceeded 50 percent. In both Boston and Pittsburgh, for example, more than 70 percent of manufacturing is located in the suburbs; in Los Angeles, Detroit, San Francisco, St. Louis, and Baltimore, more than 60 percent of manufacturing is located in the suburbs.

Suburban developers innovated a form of space called the "industrial park," which is zoned entirely for business, especially manufacturing. Local town or county governments often provide significant tax incentives, infrastructure, and other subsidies to attract manufacturing. The presence of such attractive and inexpensive locations in suburbia is one factor in the progressive deconcentration of manufacturing.

Most recently, suburbs have innovated a new form of local space known as a *high-tech growth pole* or "science park." These are more specialized research and development centers that are often linked with manufacturing and located near university facilities. The most spectacular example is Silicon Valley, adjacent to Stanford University in California. A corridor stretching from the city of

San Jose to Palo Alto makes up the spine of Silicon Valley and contains hundreds of factories that once produced state-of-the-art electronics and computer products, but now have diversified. This complex is intimately connected to the research resources of Stanford University, where the transistor was invented and where the largest electrical engineering department is located.

While Silicon Valley remains the best known of the new spaces created by high-tech industries, other examples of growth are Route 128 outside of Boston, the San Diego–LaJolla complex associated with electronic medical technology innovators, the Research Triangle complex located near the Duke and University of North Carolina campuses, and the Iowa-to-Minnesota corridor of high-tech medical firms anchored at the Mayo Clinic in Rochester, Minnesota. The area around Irvine, California, is very typical of the new spaces created by high-technology industries. It is anchored by the University of California at Irvine campus and stretches for miles across what was once farms and ranches. This region has been the subject of a study (Kling, Olin, and Poster, 1991) arguing that a new social order has developed here that surpasses the stereotype of suburban life and is based on consumerism, professional occupations, and an economic base of knowledge- or information-processing industries. In Chapter 13, we discuss the emergence of similar spaces located in advanced industrial societies around the globe.

The significance of these high-tech growth poles is that they foster industrial development that is completely independent of the central city. Because of their economic success, they often become the principal places in the society that earn money on the global market, thereby leading the country's growth. In the past, models of industrial development have placed the city in a dominant role by referring to it as "the core," with the suburbs described as "the periphery." Development of society meant nurturing city-based industry. In this model, which better describes urban growth in the '60s and '70s, manufacturing was believed to originate in the city and then migrate out to the suburbs. All evidence now invalidates this model.

The city is no longer privileged as the incubator of most industries, although some new manufacturing, such as textiles and light manufacturing, may still start up there. Development begins just as frequently in the suburbs as in the cities, and "suburbia is quickly identified as a major zone of industrial expansion in its own right, in which *self-generated* growth has been primarily responsible for its current eminence" (Muller, 1981:143). Hence, the new patterns challenge the way people once thought about economic development. The central city has lost its role as the dominating node of a regional economy. In many industries, important businesses are likely to locate in the suburbs, and economic development is now a metropolitan regional affair.

Office and Administrative Headquarters. Perhaps the most significant example of the increasing importance of mature suburbs and, simultaneously, the decline of the central city is the progressive relocation of corporate headquarters to fringe areas. In the past, such headquarters were almost exclusively located in the central city. Today this is much less the case, although many headquarters remain in city centers. During the 1960s, New York City, for example, was host to more than 130 of the Fortune 500 companies. By the 1980s, the number was down to 73, and it is now fewer than 60, or a loss of more than 70 corporate headquarters in thirty years.

According to some researchers, large cities have emerged as the "command and control" centers for the global economy (Sassen, 1991). This overstates the case for the economy in general and ignores decentralization to areas outside the city but within the metropolitan region. As indicated above, the largest cities have become the centers for finance capital activities, while other aspects of capitalism, such as producer services, marketing, and manufacturing, have decentralized. One indicator of this more complex spatial differentiation of functions is the phenomenal thirty-year decline in the number of corporate headquarters located in New York City.

We have seen that the city can no longer be regarded as the dominant location choice for manufacturing or corporate headquarters. But the maturation of suburban areas with regard to administrative employment is even more significant. Despite some predictions that, as metropolitan regions grew, central cities would retain their command and control functions (Hawley, 1981), this has not proven to be the case.

In a study of the twenty-one largest MSAs, Ruth Armstrong (1972, 1979) found that, leaving the special case of New York City aside, administrative functions were evenly distributed between large cities and their suburbs in 1960. During the decades following her study, administrative and headquarter employment decentralized in favor of the suburbs as companies such as Pepsico and General Electric abandoned centers such as Manhattan for the adjacent suburban towns of Purchase, New York, and Fairfield, Connecticut, respectively. Several other studies have verified that this trend is continuing and that command and control centers are growing in the suburbs (Quante, 1976; Pye, 1977). In short, administrative functions, like all other economic activities, have been deconcentrating since the 1960s.

Over the years, then, suburbs have matured, becoming more and more like the diversified urban space of the past. They are autonomous employing regions with diverse populations (except for minority representation). Given this shift, we can no longer talk of a city-suburb hierarchy with a privileged city as the dominating center. In fact, for many metropolitan regions, such as the St. Louis and Philadelphia areas, the power of the suburbs outweighs the central city itself.

BEYOND SUBURBIA: THE MULTINUCLEATED REGION

By the 1990s, suburban regions in many areas of the United States had so matured that development was occurring in peripheral areas independently of major urban centers. This special and independent mode of regional, multinucleated growth was manifested as the *fully urbanized county,* such as Orange County, California, which is a net employing region with a labor force of more than 1 million people (Kling, Olin, and Poster, 1991). The most important characteristic of the fully urbanized county is that it does not contain any large cities, yet it functions much like a city by providing jobs as well as housing for its residents.

First studied by Gottdiener and Kephart (1991), fully urbanized counties appeared in number during the 1980s, although two regions, Orange County in California and Nassau–Suffolk Counties in New York, had already achieved independent MSA status by 1980. Other multinucleated counties lie outside of MSAs. Oakland County, just outside but adjacent to the Detroit MSA in Michigan, is typical. In 1980, it had a population of more than 1 million people, but its largest city contained only 76,715. The region had grown by 11 percent in the previous decade (a rapid rate considering that Detroit itself declined in population). It employed virtually all of the people who lived there, achieving an employment-to-residence ratio of 0.93 in 1980. Oakland County possessed a balanced, diversified economy, with 26 percent of the labor force engaged in manufacturing, 30 percent in retailing and wholesaling, and 25 percent in services, as well as in other industries. Finally, in 1980 Oakland County had a median family income of $28,407—above the national average—and was 93 percent white.

Oakland County in Michigan was very much like at least twenty other multinucleated metropolitan regions in the country that were identified as a new form of space because of their urban character and their deconcentrated form (Gottdiener and Kephart, 1991). In sum, our notion of suburbia was completely transformed from the early designation of the "bedroom community" to the fully urbanized but multicentered region.

THE SHIFT TO THE SUNBELT

Without question the population and economic shift to the Sunbelt is the most important demographic event of the last half of the American twentieth century. The scale of change is quite spectacular. Although variations exist, most analysts define the Sunbelt as thirteen southern states—Alabama, Arizona, Arkansas, Florida, Georgia, Louisiana, Mississippi, New Mexico, North Carolina, Oklahoma, South Carolina, Tennessee, and Texas—plus parts of two western states: southern California (counties south of San Luis Obispo) and southern Nevada (Las Vegas, SMSA) (see Bernard and Rice, 1983). Between 1945 and 1975, the Sunbelt region doubled its population. In the decade between 1960 and 1970, Sunbelt MSAs accounted for 63.8 percent of the total population increase for *all* MSAs (Berry and Kasarda, 1977:168). Between 1970 and 1980, the Northeast lost 1.5 percent of its population, the Midwest gained only 2.6 percent, but the South grew by 21.5 percent and the West by 22.6 percent, including a natural increase for all regions (Frey and Speare, 1988:50).

Table 6.2 shows population growth for selected Sunbelt cities from 1950 to 2000 (this table includes several cities not shown in Table 6.1). As described earlier, even the largest of the Sunbelt cities—those that had a population of 400,000 or more in 1950—experienced high rates of growth during this period. Dallas increased its population by more than 400 percent, and San Antonio and Houston grew by more than 300 percent. The growth for many of the other Sunbelt cities that had relatively small populations in 1950 is even more phenomenal: Phoenix grew from 106,000 in 1950 to more than 1,300,000 in 2000—an increase of more than 1200 percent; San Jose grew from 95,000 to 895,000, an increase of more than 800 percent; Charlotte, El Paso, and Austin, all of which started out with populations around 130,000 in 1950 now are between 557,000 and 656,000. The most astonishing growth of all has been the emergence of Las Vegas as a major city. In 1950 the desert community had a population of less than 25,000; this increased by a factor of ten to more than 250,000 in 1990 and then nearly doubled to 480,000 in 2000. Las Vegas has been the fastest growing major city in the United States for each of the past two decades and also has been the fastest growing metropolitan region. As in other cities across the country, the suburban population of Las Vegas is much larger than that of the city itself. It is important to remember that all of this growth took place while Snowbelt cities stagnated with population decline or limited growth.

The growth of the Sunbelt is even better illustrated by the regional perspective of Table 6.3, which shows metropolitan regional growth for selected Sunbelt cities from 1970 to 2000. Although all metropolitan regions of the country grew during this period, the rate of growth was much larger in the Sunbelt. The pattern of growth is similar to that of the Sunbelt cities (but over a shorter period of time): the population of the Los Angeles–Anaheim–Riverside region

TABLE 6.2 Population Growth for Selected Sunbelt Cities, 1950–2000

| City | 1950 | 1970 | 1980 | 1990 | 2000 | Rate of Growth | | | |
						1950–1970	1970–1980	1980–1990	1990–2000
Los Angeles	1,970,358	2,816,061	2,966,850	3,348,557	3,694,742	42.9	5.6	17.5	10.3
Houston	596,163	1,232,802	1,595,138	1,630,864	1,953,633	106.7	29.3	2.2	19.8
Phoenix	106,818	581,562	789,704	984,309	1,321,190	444.4	35.3	24.5	34.2
San Diego	334,387	696,769	875,538	1,110,623	1,223,429	108.4	25.7	26.8	10.2
Dallas	434,462	844,401	904,078	1,007,618	1,188,589	94.4	11.3	11.4	18.0
San Antonio	408,442	654,153	785,880	935,393	1,151,305	60.2	20.2	19.1	23.1
San Jose	95,280	445,779	629,442	782,224	895,193	367.9	36.7	24.3	14.0
Jacksonville	204,517	528,865	540,920	635,230	735,617	158.6	21.7	17.4	15.8
Charlotte	134,042	241,420	315,474	395,934	557,834	80.1	30.7	25.5	40.9
El Paso	130,485	322,261	425,259	515,342	563,657	147.0	32.0	21.2	9.3
Austin	132,459	253,539	345,890	465,622	656,562	91.4	36.4	34.6	41.0
Las Vegas	24,624	125,787	164,674	258,295	479,639	410.8	30.9	56.9	85.7

SOURCE: U.S. Department of Commerce, Bureau of the Census, ranked by 2000 population.

TABLE 6.3 Metropolitan Regional Growth for Selected Sunbelt Cities, 1970–2000

City	1970	1980	1990	2000	Rate of Growth		
					1970–1980	1980–1990	1990–2000
Los Angeles–Anaheim–Riverside CMSA	9,981,000	11,498,000	14,532,000	21,200,000	15.2	26.4	12.7
San Francisco–Oakland–San Jose CMSA	4,754,000	5,368,000	6,250,000	7,039,000	12.9	16.5	12.6
Dallas–Fort Worth CMSA	2,352,000	2,931,000	4,037,000	5,222,000	24.6	32.6	29.4
Houston–Galveston–Brazoria NECMA	2,169,000	3,100,000	3,731,000	4,670,000	42.9	19.7	25.2
Atlanta MSA	1,684,000	2,138,000	2,959,500	4,122,000	27.0	32.5	39.3
Miami–Ft. Lauderdale CMSA	1,889,000	2,644,000	4,056,000	3,876,000	40.0	20.8	23.5
Phoenix MSA	971,000	1,509,000	2,238,000	3,252,000	55.4	40.6	45.3
San Diego MSA	1,358,000	1,862,000	2,498,000	2,814,000	37.4	34.2	12.7
Tampa–St Petersburg–Clearwater CMSA	1,105,552	1,613,600	2,067,959	2,396,000	46.0	28.2	15.9
San Antonio MSA	901,220	1,088,881	1,324,749	1,592,000	20.8	21.7	20.2
Las Vegas MSA	304,744	528,000	741,000	1,563,000	73.3	40.3	115.6
Charlotte MSA	840,346	971,447	1,161,546	1,499,000	15.6	19.6	22.5
Austin MSA	398,938	585,051	846,227	1,250,000	46.7	44.6	47.6

SOURCE: U.S. Department of Commerce, Bureau of the Census, ranked by 2000 population.

increased 64.1 percent (from 9,900,000 to 16,300,000); the San Francisco–Oakland–San Jose region increased 48.1 percent (from 4,700,000 to 7,000,000); while the Houston–Galveston–Brazoria and Dallas–Fort Worth regions increased 122.0 and 115.3 percent respectively. The populations of two large Florida metropolitan regions (Miami–Fort Lauderdale and Tampa–St. Petersburg–Clearwater) more than doubled. The metropolitan regions that developed around the smaller Sunbelt cities in the Southwest (Austin, for example, had a population of less than 150,000 in 1950, and Phoenix a population of less than 110,000) have experienced even higher rates of growth; the populations of both the Austin and Phoenix metropolitan regions increased more than 300 percent from 1970 to 2000. The more than 500 percent increase in the population of the Las Vegas metropolitan region—from 304,000 to more than 1,500,000 persons—is the largest in the country.

Rapid demographic growth has been matched by rapid employment growth in the Sunbelt. Between 1970 and 1980, manufacturing expanded by 12 percent in the North but more than double that, or 24.4 percent, in the South. While service employment grew by 11.5 percent in the North, it increased by 44 percent in the South and 47 percent in the West (Frey and Speare, 1988:92). According to one observer, "never in the history of the world has a region of such size developed at such a rate for so long a time" (Sale, 1975:166).

The movement westward and southward has been evident for some time. Sunbelt states have been receiving a greater share of MSA population than the Snowbelt since the 1920s (Berry and Kasarda, 1977:168). Indeed, the movement of people westward has been a trend in the United States since the 1800s. The shift to the Sunbelt, however, displaces the economic center of gravity in the United States toward the West from the East Coast, and also obliterates what was once a core-periphery relation between a formerly agrarian South and West and an industrialized North and Midwest. Today the Sunbelt is more formidable economically than other areas of the country. Between 1970 and 1980, almost three-fourths of all job growth took place in the Sunbelt. By the 1990s, however, the economic recession had hit Sunbelt areas especially hard. California, for example, suffered major job losses, as did Texas. Hence, current patterns of Sunbelt growth reflect a cycle of boom and bust.

Push and Pull Factors in Sunbelt Development

As we have seen, the Sunbelt had an advantage over other parts of the United States because of its comparative economic potential. This represents a potent pull factor. The region has other advantages as well. Energy and tourism are also exploitable industries. Cheap energy in particular and the warmth of the Sunbelt climate cut home maintenance costs drastically compared to the Snowbelt. Low energy costs are a major locational incentive for business, both now and in the future. Lower home maintenance costs and comparatively lower homeowner tax rates also provide considerable incentives for people to move to the region.

A comparison between Snowbelt and Sunbelt locations reveals advantages for the latter regarding labor costs. The Sunbelt does not have a past history of union organizing, and wages there are comparatively lower for manufacturing industries (although higher for many professional services). Sunbelt cities flaunt what they call a "good business climate." This usually means the absence of unions, tax breaks to business, and a general "hands-off" policy of minimal government regulation.

As in the case of suburbanization, one of the most potent supply-side forces that has led to the development of the Sunbelt as a place to live and work is government intervention. To the extent that government subsidization of real estate development aided growth, it was instrumental in the population shift to the Sunbelt, where real estate is a major industry. But government involvement goes way beyond this obvious observation. Most of the heavily subsidized government industries in the United States, including agribusiness, energy, and military spending, are pillars of the Sunbelt economy.

Over the years, the heavily subsidized agriculture industry has witnessed an immense shift of population out of farm residence, from over 30 percent in 1920 to around 3 percent today. At the same time, the family farm involved in agriculture has given way to the large landholdings of corporations engaged in agribusiness. Farm production has become more specialized and a part of a total conglomerate structure involving the growing, processing, and marketing of food by giant corporations linked to the multinational system of capital (Shover, 1976; Hightower, 1975; Berry, 1972).

An important consequence of the rise to hegemony of agribusiness has been the shift of food production away from the Northeast and Midwest and to the Sunbelt (Sale, 1975; Coughlin, 1979), where large, open tracts of land are being put into production. According to Sale (1975), the shift to agribusiness in the Sunbelt has made the family farm uneconomical, causing many small farmers to sell their land to suburban developers. Finally, agribusiness remains subsidized on a grand scale by the federal government, whose Department of Agriculture is the second largest bureaucracy after the Department of Defense (Shover, 1976).

A second pillar of Sunbelt growth is the energy industry, which is also subsidized by the government. The Atomic Energy Commission and its government affiliates are among the largest employers in the state of New Mexico. In a case study of Houston, Texas, Joe R. Feagin (1988) shows how state supports underpin the energy industry, while at the same time business leaders espouse the virtues of "free enterprise." Feagin observes that when discussing government involvement, a distinction is made between state forms of regulation, which are opposed by business, and state promotion and subsidization of economic activity, which is supported wholeheartedly.

In the case of the alleged "free enterprise" city of Houston, development was aided over the years by active government promotion of projects, while regulation was kept at a minimum. Contrary to the prevailing view of Sunbelt cities as economically backward until recent times, Houston was already a major agricultural center for the Texas cotton industry prior to the growth of the petroleum business. As the latter became the new focus of the local economy, government subsidization went hand in hand with the development of the city through private ventures. The federal government provided funds for the dredging of the Houston ship channel and periodically cleared the important port facility for ship traffic. In addition, oil refining and new petrochemical industries during the 1940s were supported directly by the federal government, ranking sixth in receipt of national government plant investment (Feagin, 1988:68). Local businesses were the beneficiaries of these subsidies. As a consequence, Houston developed into the energy capital of the United States, only to be hit by a downturn and restructuring in the 1980s.

The third government-subsidized pillar of Sunbelt growth is military spending. During World War II, 60 percent of the total $74 billion spending effort went to the fifteen states of the Sunbelt (Sale, 1975:170). Major industries in Sunbelt states were established during this time. Los Angeles became an aircraft and shipbuilding center. Kaiser Steel was formed in southern California, importing many workers from the East. Petrochemical and energy-related efforts were also subsidized, as we have already seen. Armaments industries and arsenals were expanded in the South and West. Huge military bases were constructed in California, Texas, Georgia, Florida, Alabama, and the Carolinas, among other Sunbelt states.

By the 1970s, the fifteen Sunbelt states were receiving 44 percent of all military spending, including over 50 percent of the Defense Department payroll; had the majority of all military installations (60 percent); were employing more scientists and technicians than all the rest of the United States; and received 49 percent of "Pentagon research and development funds—the seed money that creates new technologies and industries" (Sale, 1975:171). All of this effort and money created a new industrial core in the Sunbelt that continues to be supported by government spending. Because taxes are collected across the United States but differentially spent on military-related activities, the federal government has for decades transferred wealth from all other regions of the United States to the Sunbelt.

Military spending in the Sunbelt region has continued to grow throughout the 1980s on an immense scale. In 1975, military spending was approximately $90 billion. By 1987, it had increased to $390 billion, a fourfold change that took place after the Vietnam War (Gottdiener, 1990). Arms sales in particular became a key U.S. industry in the 1980s, prompting one observer to suggest that the nation had switched to a permanent war economy (Mandel, 1975; see also Melman, 1983; Stubbing and Mendel, 1986). Now, with the war in Iraq entering its third year, this prediction seems chillingly accurate.

Recent Sunbelt Trends

The shift to the Sunbelt is a spectacular example of regional realignment experienced by an advanced industrial country. As we will see in Chapter 12, there are parallels to the U.S. case in such countries as England, France, and particularly Germany, which have also undergone regional shifts as a consequence of high-technology industrial restructuring. Yet despite these changes, it is possible to overstate the case of Sunbelt prominence. There are at least three reasons to temper the notion that this region is gaining in autonomy and power at the expense of areas elsewhere: the need to place Sunbelt economic activities within a national and global context, the boom and bust cycle of development, and the enormous environmental costs of growth.

Economic Differentiation and the Global Economy.   Because the U.S. economy has become more functionally specialized, many of the rapidly growing Sunbelt industries are tied administratively and economically to Snowbelt centers. The latter still retain the majority of corporate headquarters, for example. Banking and finance are still controlled by Snowbelt interests (Gottdiener, 1985). In addition, since the 1970s many U.S. firms have been either bought out or heavily invested in by multinational corporations that have headquarters in other countries. Sunbelt factories, no matter how stable in employment, may be only a part of some larger corporation that also includes Snowbelt command and control centers or foreign operations. Hence, splits between the regions are *not* autonomous. They reflect instead a growing regional specialization in the United States and the entire world as multinational interests utilize space and place to improve economic performance.

The Cycles of Growth and Decline.   As we have seen, the best way to describe Sunbelt development is in terms of boom and bust cycles that fluctuate relatively rapidly. Sunbelt residents who have been attracted to the region by visions of affluence may have to tolerate a life of feast or famine. In the 1990s, the national recession hit many Sunbelt areas especially hard. The powerful states of Texas and California, once thought immune to downturns, have been in the doldrums since the late 1980s. Unemployment was above the national average for a time. California experienced two straight years of fiscal crisis in the early 1990s that required cuts in spending, wage freezes, and a reassessment of the state's credit rating. Today it struggles with a major debt crisis once again. Social services such as education are now besieged due to lack of funds, and the quality of life has deteriorated accordingly.

The Environmental Costs of Rapid Growth. Because it has been the site of rapid and largely minimally planned growth, the Sunbelt region has also encountered monumental environmental problems. In fact, we may be poised at a point of immense growth difficulties for many areas of the Sunbelt. The environment has long suffered the initial impact of development. Unique and pristine formations, such as the Tampa and San Francisco bays, have been almost destroyed biologically in the wake of change. Clear cutting of virgin forests, pollution of lakes and streams, fouling of beaches with oil or sewage, and emissions of choking smog are but some of the environmental problems already well established in the South and West. After years of uncertainty regarding published accounts of the effects of smog, for example, it was reported that constant exposure produces permanent lung damage in both children and adults (*Press Enterprise,* May 17, 1992: AA–1). The population of Los Angeles lives in just such an environment, yet the presence of damaging smog has done little to stem the otherwise constant stream of new arrivals to the region (see Chapter 14 for a more detailed discussion of the environment and the sociospatial perspective).

In more recent years, other effects of population growth have emerged. Crime is a serious problem, for example. New York was often stereotyped as an unsafe city (Mercer, 1991) both before and after Mayor Giuliani's crackdown on crime in the 1990s. Its murder rate was 7.3 per 100,000 persons in 2002. But the murder rate in Phoenix was 12.6; in Dallas, 15.8; and in Los Angeles, 17.1. The rate of forcible rape in New York was 20.9 per 100,000; the rate for Phoenix was 29.2; for Dallas, 52.8; and for Los Angeles, 36.9. Although some Sunbelt cities have had relatively low rates of violent crime, many cities have had higher rates of violent crime than New York, as the above statistics attest. Sunbelt cities have also had very high rates of property crime. Continuing the New York City comparison, New York had a burglary rate of 372.3 per 1,000 persons in 2002. The figure for Los Angeles was 662.4; for Phoenix, 1,199.7;

and for Dallas, 1,639.3. There is great variance in both violent crime and property crime across Sunbelt cities, but it is clear that crime is a serious problem for many of these urban areas. Patterns of crime and the costs of crime are discussed in detail in Chapter 10.

In addition to crime, overcrowding in schools and declining educational quality are a common problem across the Sunbelt. These conditions are expected to get worse as the western and southern states encounter intractable budget crises such as the current one in California.

In rapidly growing areas, traffic congestion is so bad that it is fast approaching gridlock. It's not uncommon for commuters in parts of California to travel four hours both ways by car, especially when no other alternatives to commuting are available. Finally, housing prices have soared in the best locations, making first-home purchasing progressively out of reach. But despite these and other constraints, life in the Sunbelt continues to attract new people, especially highly trained professionals who have the ability to find well-paying jobs (Kephart, 1991). It is expected that the fifteen states of the Sunbelt will continue to grow in the future. This region already contains half the nation's population.

Since the 1960s, the relationships among people, spatial living, and working arrangements have profoundly changed. Gone is the highly compact industrial city with a working-class culture and labor-influenced politics. In its place, everyday life now transpires in multinucleated metropolitan regions across the country. Development is dominated by the population shifts to the suburbs and the Sunbelt, while the vision of unending growth and affluence has been tempered by the experience of living through rapid cycles of boom and bust. These changes can be explained by the sociospatial perspective, which emphasizes the pull factors of economic and technological change (as do other approaches) but also the importance of government intervention, real estate development, and the restructuring of sociospatial arrangements in business and residential activities.

KEY CONCEPTS

metropolitan region
federal subsidies for home ownership
Levittown (Long Island)
Fordism
conspicuous consumption
demand-side / supply-side explanations
deindustrialization

population deconcentration
nodal services
uneven development
dual city
informal economy
exclusionary zoning
corporate headquarters
industrial park
fully urbanized county
Sunbelt / Snowbelt
military spending
regional realignment
Los Angeles School of urban studies

DISCUSSION QUESTIONS

1. What are some of the explanations for the extensive suburban development that occurred from 1920 to 1960? What are some of the demand-side factors that might be responsible for this development? What are some of the supply-side factors that might be responsible? Explain how the roles of real estate development, government programs, and cultural factors fit into these supply-side and demand-side explanations for suburban growth.

2. Describe and discuss two factors responsible for the shift in population from the Northeast and Midwest (the Snowbelt) to the South and West (the Sunbelt). How do these factors affect cities in both the Snowbelt and Sunbelt?

3. Discuss the changes in large central cities that have accompanied the restructuring of settlement space over the past four decades. Pick two changes that you consider to be representative and explain the causal factors responsible for these changes.

4. Profound changes have occurred in the ethnic and racial composition of cities and suburbs over the past four decades. Discuss these changes and explain them by focusing on two factors.

5. Suburban settlement spaces have changed greatly since the 1960s. What are some of the most important changes that have occurred in your metropolitan region? Pick two factors responsible for those changes and discuss their significance and their effects on suburban life.

PEOPLE AND LIFESTYLES IN
THE METROPOLIS

In previous chapters, we studied the growth and development of metropolitan regions in the United States. This chapter and the one that follows concern the people of the metropolis and explore the relationship between everyday life and local territory. The sociospatial approach to metropolitan life asserts that diversity in lifestyles and subcultures exists not just within the city but throughout the metropolitan region. This is especially the case since 1980 as suburban settlement spaces have matured. In this chapter we consider the interplay between the social factors of income, gender, age, and race and the spatial patterns of population concentration or dispersal across the metropolitan region.

A basic tenet of the sociospatial approach is that social factors determining the patterns of population dispersal are also linked to particular spaces. Class or gender relations, for example, are conducted through spatial as well as social means. Lifestyle differences are externalized in a specific environment: the ghetto, the street corner, the mall, the golf course. Furthermore, these places are always meaningful. Interaction is shaped through the signs and symbols of sociospatial context. In this chapter we consider the effect of class standing on lifestyles, gender differences and everyday life, racial and minority distinctions, and new patterns of ethnic formation and immigration. The effects of class, gender, and race are so powerful in our society that we will also consider them in Chapter 10 when we discuss social problems. We will see how differences in sociospatial factors affect the way people live, their interactions with others, and their use of space.

CLASS STRATIFICATION AND SPATIAL LOCATION

Max Weber believed that an individual's class position is important because it helps determine the possible opportunities or constraints for future achievement open to any individual. Weber also suggested that economic factors of class status, such as the type of occupation or monetary resources that an individual possesses, are not the only determining factors of overall social status. One's social standing in the society's hierarchy also depends on particular cultural attributes, such as religion, ethnicity, or symbolic differences, and on the possession of political power. Thus, life chances differ according to economic, political, and cultural factors, but material wealth, as Karl Marx maintained, clearly is the most important of all social variables.

The United States is a stratified society. This means that individuals and households are located within a social hierarchy that determines their access to resources. Stratification is often pictured as a pyramid of social standing. Those at the very top control most of society's resources; they also enjoy the most symbolic prestige and political influence. Those below are the most numerous and have the least power. The United States, despite an active ideology that preaches equality, has the most unequal distribution of wealth of any industrialized nation (Philips, 1990). The top 1 percent of the population controls more than 70 percent of the wealth, and the top 5 percent controls more than 90 percent. Status considerations such as driving an expensive car, living in a large home, taking fabulous vacations, and wearing expensive clothing are greatly influenced by the media images of affluence and what life is supposed to be like at the top of the stratification diamond.

American culture and the lifestyles it supports connect the financial resources of individuals and families, expressed in our hierarchy of social stratification, to patterns of consumption. For this reason, sociologists often study how class differences in our society are expressed by different styles of consumption. Consumption patterns are also supported by credit card debt, housing loans, car loans, educational loans, buying through financing, and other arrangements that enable people to spend more than they earn. As we move through different local spaces within the metropolitan environment, we encounter a tremendous diversity in lifestyles. These differences are a function of relative class standing and, in turn, are expressed through the activity of consumption. While many persons in our society consume at a high level by incurring debt, they do so in distinct ways, thereby enabling us to observe lifestyle differences in the metropolitan region.

Research on the American class structure divides our society into a number of different groups based on what social scientists call *socioeconomic sta-*

tus, or SES, which is a particular combination of wealth, occupation, education, gender, and race, among other factors (see Robertson, 1987). Many studies divide the population into five groups: the lower class, the working class, the lower middle class, the upper middle class, and the ruling class. Only the ruling class controls enough wealth to be considered independent from economic needs; many persons in the lower class do not have access to regular sources of income because of a lack of jobs in the inner city, while many working-class households have discovered that it is necessary for both husband and wife to work to support their families, and middle-class families find it increasingly difficult to maintain their standard of living due to stagnant wages and the declining dollar in the world economy.

Socioeconomic standing also involves the ability of the household to establish residence in a particular place. Thus, a significant component of socioeconomic status is determined by one's address and the symbolic reputation of particular neighborhoods within the metropolitan neighborhoods. It means something very different to live in the North Shore suburb or oceanfront town than it does to be from the "'hood" or to have grown up in the projects. In our society, due to stratification differences, the choice of residential location is not always voluntary. Restrictions of wealth, race, and gender are particularly potent sifters of population across the metropolitan regions. Socioeconomic difference and the system of social stratification therefore manifest themselves both as differences in individual lifestyles and as differences in residential neighborhood or local space. Let us consider some of the distinct ways stratification is reflected in this interaction between social relations and territorial practice, as the sociospatial perspective suggests.

The Wealthy

Members of the upper classes often have the advantage of owning several homes because they are able to afford them. Former President George Herbert Walker Bush, for example, for many years maintained residences in Houston, Texas; Washington, D.C.; and Kennebunkport, Maine. Many wealthy people alternate among townhouse, suburban estate, and rural recreational home. Obviously, at any given time the family can occupy just one of these residences, so multiple home ownership is a symbol of wealth and power that has some meaning and prestige in our society. In the city, the wealthy are associated with the more fashionable urban districts such as Nob Hill in San Francisco, Beverly Hills in Los Angeles, the Gold Coast near Lake Michigan in Chicago, Beacon Hill in Boston, and Park Avenue in New York City. Their activities take place within certain spaces that are allocated to the particular mix of restaurants, boutiques, and social clubs reserved for the upper class.

One important way the wealthy manifest their power and status is by isolating themselves as much as possible from the rest of the population. This type of segregation is voluntary. In the city, voluntary segregation may be accomplished by living in ultra-expensive housing with security guards and controlled entrances. Even though public transportation and taxis are available, the wealthy often utilize private, door-to-door limousine services. Shopping and recreation are all located in heavily policed areas. Maintaining this level of isolation remains somewhat of a constant chore that taxes the resources of surveillance and control, requiring private security guards, apartment buildings with 24-hour doormen, and private schools or academies for children. In the suburbs or at country homes, however, the benefits of isolation are more readily enjoyed in gated communities and exclusive country clubs.

The upper class is not confined to city residence. One of the earliest studies of the affluent in suburbia was Thorsten Veblen's *Theory of the Leisure Class* (1899). Although their wealth was evident in their behavior, the most important characteristics of the lifestyle were symbolic or cultural. Veblen coined the term conspicuous consumption to refer to this particular aspect of the affluent style of suburban life. This concept refers to an outward display of consumption that demonstrates wealth and power through the wasting of resources and the symbols of upper-class membership. The suburban homes of the wealthy, for example, were endowed with excess. Houses were huge, over 5,000 square feet or more, with many more rooms than were necessary to service the immediate family. Estates had large front and rear lawns that were landscaped and maintained by a staff of gardeners. Conspicuous consumption was symbolized by the landscaping of yards precisely because the land was allowed to lie uncultivated as a resource—the lawn was just for show.

The suburban lifestyle of the wealthy is focused on leisure activity as a sign of conspicuous consumption. This is particularly significant because symbols of leisure mean that people do not have to work. The suburban country club, costly to belong to and restrictive in its membership, is an essential component for the exclusive set. The fees usually run into the tens of thousands of dollars, thereby automatically keeping the working class out. In many parts of the country, clubs such as the Everglades Country Club in Florida prevented African Americans and Jews from belonging even if they could afford membership fees. The leisure activity of choice for the affluent is golf, and in recent years this game has come to symbolize suburban wealth and leisure itself, because golf is most often played at country clubs, and they require immense amounts of water and daily care. For the most affluent families in the largest cities and most exclusive suburbs, membership in the local polo club may be the most significant indication that the family has reached the top of the stratification pyramid.

Wealthy suburbanites maintain their isolation through mechanisms similar to those utilized in the city, such as the high price of homes, surveillance and control by private security forces, gate-guarded and enclosed communities, and the separation that comes from spatial dispersal itself. Whether we are dealing with the city or the suburbs, the wealthy tend to use topography to their advantage. Their homes are located at the greatest heights. In the suburbs, this often means that estates are built on the high ground, on hillsides or escarpments. In the city, this "God's eye view" is acquired with an apartment at the top of a luxury high-rise, and there is intense competition for the condominium that has the best view of the city.

In short, the wealthy possess a distinct lifestyle founded on class privilege and symbols of high social status. Their daily life manifests itself in space through unique molding of the environment to create isolation and exclusion. The wealthy also overcome the limitations of space by owning several residences, each with its own locational advantages. Whether living in the city or the country, their lifestyle, like any other, is sociospatial; that is, it is organized around expressive symbols (Fussell, 1983) and particular spaces.

Yuppies, Buppies, Dinks, and the Suburban Middle Class

A large proportion of central city residents are not members of the upper class but do have significant discretionary income because of monetary rewards associated with their chosen field of work. Since the 1970s, as manufacturing has declined in the city, there has been a phenomenal increase in service-related jobs (see Chapters 6 and 10). Many of these are professional positions created by the information-processing economy of the city, such as the financial and legal institutions associated with corporate headquarters. In previous chapters, we discussed how certain kinds of economic activity create or help reinforce lifestyles, community relations, and expressive symbols. The shift to information-processing professional services has also affected metropolitan settlement space by reinforcing certain upper-middle-class patterns of behavior. As with all other lifestyles in our society, socioeconomic standing and the financial resources of these groups are expressed through particular consumption patterns.

The term yuppy, or *young urban professional*, has acquired a derogatory connotation, but it is a very useful way to describe relatively young (late 20s to early 40s) middle-class professionals who live in the city. The same can be said for the term dink—double income, no kids—which describes yuppie couples without children. We should note that yuppies and dinks represent urban subpopulations characterized by their income, occupation, and lifestyle; they are not identified by ethnicity or race. As large numbers of African American college graduates entered the labor force in the 1980s, the term buppy was used to identify the *black urban professional.* Only recently have such components of the middle class achieved the kind of numbers that have attracted attention. According to Zukin (1991), yuppies were responsible for gentrification and the upgraded housing and renovation of older loft buildings in New York and other cities; their culinary demands spurred the opening of many new and often exotic restaurants; and their more specialized everyday needs, such as last-minute food shopping, health and fitness requirements, and reading and cinema tastes, have opened up new sectors of employment for a host of immigrant groups and working-class urban residents looking for entry-level service positions.

In the early 1980s, the leaders of many cities believed that the two-pronged explosion of jobs and spending related to the expansion of the business service sector would replace manufacturing as the key growth industry of urban areas. Indeed, places such as Pittsburgh (Jezierski, 1988) managed to change from centers of industry to focal points for global banking and investment. Restructuring of the financial and corporate business sectors with a consequent decline in the growth of jobs, however, occurred in the mid-1980s, cutting short this expansion. Especially significant were the changes occurring after the October 1987 "crash" of the New York stock market, which led to greater computerization of financial transactions, the reining in of risky ventures such as junk bonds, and the failure of several investment firms (Minsky, 1989). Throughout the 1990s, corporate downsizing led to the loss of tens of thousands of white-collar jobs in cities across the country. Hence, despite what was once believed, the place of yuppies in the revitalization of central cities may be overrated.

Most households that we would identify as part of the middle class do not live in the city. Decades of white flight for those who could afford to move to the ever-expanding suburbs have emptied the central city of much of the middle class (Egan, 2005). The majority of middle-class Americans have spread out and prospered across the vast expanses of developed housing tracts located in suburban settlement space throughout the metropolitan region. Middle-class suburban living might be thought of as the upper-class lifestyle within a more modest budget. Symbols of status abound in this kind of environment as well. The typical suburban home is a scaled-down replica of the upper-class estate. It consists of a front yard that is strictly ornamental and a backyard reserved for leisure. In the warmer parts of the country, the desirable backyard may contain a built-in swimming pool, which usually is no more than thirty

BOX 7.1   The Middle-Class Suburban Lifestyle

A picture of middle-class suburban life was drawn by the geographer Peter Muller:

> The needs and preferences of the nuclear family unit shape modes of social inter-action in middle-income residential areas. The management of children is a cen-tral group-level concern, and most local social contact occurs through such family-oriented formal organizations as the school PTA, Little League, and the Scouts. However, despite the closer spacing of homes and these integrating activ-ities, middle-class suburbanites . . . are not communally cohesive to any great de-gree. Emphasis on family privacy and freedom to aggressively pursue its own upwardly mobile aspirations does not encourage the development of extensive local social ties. Neighboring (mostly child-related) is limited and selective, and even socializing with relatives is infrequent. Most social interaction revolves around a nonlocal network of self-selected friends widely distributed in suburban space (1981:72).

This relative isolation of individuals in suburbia and the exclusive auto depen-dency of the spatial arrangements are particularly hard on teenagers. Ralph Larkin makes these observations about suburban teenagers in a place he calls Utopia:

> The most serious complaint among Utopia High School students is boredom. They are restless. Many complain of having nothing to do. They are forced to compete with each other for grades, sexual attractiveness, hipness, and all the other minu-tiae that are involved in the status race. Since everyone else is struggling for the same, somehow scarcer rewards, friendship has a hollow quality to it. It is a gloss on a relationship in which vulnerabilities are hidden so they won't be capitalized on by others. (1979:60)

feet long. The 1990s may be known as the decade of the backyard deck; most new middle-class homes have decks in the backyard where children play and adults cook on the gas barbecue, and home improvement chain stores have spread across the suburban landscape. While the upper-class estate requires a team of gardening and maintenance people to take care of the yard, the middle-class homeowner is a "do-it-yourselfer." Indeed, the stereotyped ac-tivities of the suburban male invariably involve fighting crabgrass in the lawn, repairing the roof, and maintaining home appliances. Women in suburbia also have a unique lifestyle, as we discuss more fully when we consider the relationship between gender and space.

For suburbanites, leisure activities are confined to the weekend, when there is some free time from work—at least for those households where parents do not have to work overtime or stagger their work schedules during the week so that one parent can stay home with the kids. In many municipalities, tax monies have been used to acquire the kind of public facilities that the affluent enjoy in private. These include public golf courses, swimming pools, tennis courts, and parks. In areas close to the ocean or a lake, suburban municipalities often build and service public marinas for boating and other water sports. Suburban life is family life.

The Working Class and the Working Poor

In the nineteenth century, life in the city was dominated by factories. Modest working-class housing was constructed in grid-pattern rows nearby. Weekly routines were centered in this space, which included the few amenities available to the working class—the pub, the association football park (soccer) or the local baseball diamond, and the streets themselves, which served as playgrounds for children (Hareven, 1982). In the period immediately after World War II, U.S. cities contained a prodigious density of such working-class districts. Since the 1960s, however, this pattern has been in decline. One reason is that many factory workers attained middle-class status with the ability to purchase single-family homes in the suburbs (Berger, 1960), often with liberal government-sponsored veterans' benefits. A second, more direct cause was the decline in manufacturing itself. When the factories closed, working-class life became all the more precarious.

Although working-class families have suburbanized in large numbers since the 1960s, many still remain residents of large cities. They are often referred to as the "working poor" because their standard of living is declining as cities themselves have become expensive places in which to reside. The decline of the minimum wage and of household incomes (in real dollars over time) has made it difficult to maintain a standard of living comparable to that of working-class families just a generation ago. The quality of life of the working class is dependent on the public services provided by local government. They require mass transportation, for example, which is becoming increasingly expensive. The level of medical care for this less affluent group is precarious and dependent on city-supported hospitals because they work at jobs that do not provide adequate, if any, health insurance. In fact, the Health and Hospitals Administration of New York City, which runs that city's medical facilities, has a yearly budget of about $1.5 billion, as much as the entire budget of several small countries.

Because so much of their standard of living depends on city services, the working poor are often at odds with public administrators. City politics involves clashes between this public and the municipal administration over the quality of services. Since the latter 1970s, the declining fiscal health of cities has made this political conflict worse because of budget crises and cutbacks (as we will see in Chapter 10). The working poor and their advocates in the city fight a running battle with the mayor over the declines in education, fire and police protection, sanitation, highway maintenance, health care, and recreational amenities.

The Underclass

The *underclass* consists of the most isolated elements of the poor who have little prospect of employment and are residents of husbandless households, and whose lives are besieged by crime and drugs. This segment of the population was first called to our attention by Ken Auletta's (1983) journalistic account and later analyzed by William J. Wilson (1987). In recent years, the term underclass has become tainted, as it was appropriated by conservative pundits who fault the victims of racial and economic deprivation. The term was originally introduced within the context of identifying the causes of extreme poverty and isolation. To avoid the negative connotations of this term, we will use the term ghettoized poor when referring to lower-income groups in the inner city (see Chapter 9 for further discussion of these issues).

The plight of the ghettoized urban poor arises from the loss of jobs in the inner city. They have become so isolated and concentrated in specific areas of the city that their needs fundamentally outstrip the available municipal resources aimed at alleviating the condition of poverty. As a result, they are doomed to raise children with few prospects for a better life unless they turn to criminal activity. Box 7.2 details aspects of life in the central city in those neighborhoods of extreme poverty and isolation studied by Wilson. The so-called "underclass" phenomenon is really caused by a combination of sociospatial factors—such as poverty and racial exclusion—and by the spatial concentration of large numbers of poor people within specific areas of cities and suburbs, rather than by individual failings (see Chapter 10).

Living in the worst areas of the central city means that the ghettoized poor are subjected to an almost unending list of pathological consequences of city living, including public health crises such as AIDS, child abuse, tuberculosis, substandard schools, juvenile crime, drug addiction and the bearing of addicted babies, juvenile motherhood, murder, rape, and robbery. The crime and pathology associated with poverty-stricken ghettos make city living difficult for everyone and are largely responsible for the continuing levels of violence associated with the inner city.

BOX 7.2   The Ghettoized Poor

Sociologists Terry Williams and William Kornblum studied poor inner-city areas in four cities: Cleveland, Ohio; Louisville, Kentucky; Meridian, Mississippi; and New York City, New York. A common stereotype is that all members of the underclass are poor. Although many are, others have made fortunes in the drug-centered economy within ghetto areas. Williams and Kornblum contrast two individuals living in the same place. Much of daily life revolves around a particular space, the local "candy store" and the street corner on which it is situated. As they observed:

> The neighborhood once was flooded with junkies, but it is changing slowly. The candy store is one of the last institutions in the area to serve this particular consumer group. In fact, the store operates on several levels. It's a hangout for kids, number runners, drug dealers, and winos. The kids can buy reefer; adults can buy wine under the counter; boosters (sellers of stolen goods) sell their wares to customers and managers alike. . . . Seventh was the avenue of the big-time hustlers. There they sported their fine cars and pretty women. . . . The names of infamous street hustlers who made it into big time are given legendary status. (1985:48–49)

WOMEN, GENDER ROLES, AND SPACE

The issue of gender and urban space is a topic on which urban sociologists have largely been silent. As recently as the 1970s, one well-known geographer wrote a book titled *This Scene of Man* (Vance, 1977) and, not to be outdone, more than a decade later an equally famous urban sociologist published a study of Chicago titled *The Man Made City* (Suttles, 1990). Feminist scholars would indeed agree that the city is man-made because women had little to do with its planning, less to do with its construction, and received few benefits from being confined within a man-made environment. The built environment reflects men's activities, men's values, and men's attitudes toward settlement space. Yet the lives of women are a critical component of urban and suburban activities. Increasingly, with the prodding of feminist observers, urban sociology is gaining greater insight into the role of women, and their needs, in everyday metropolitan life (Hayden, 1981).

Women and the Urban Political Economy

During the nineteenth century, in the early stages of industrial manufacturing, home life was second to the needs of the factory, and even children were pressed into the service of wage labor in textile mills and other industries (Hareven, 1982). It was not uncommon for entire families to work in the factory; a six-day work week of ten- to twelve-hour days was the norm. Over the years, conditions in these "Satanic mills," as Karl Marx (1967) called them, changed. Child labor laws were passed at the turn of the century in the United States prohibiting school-age youth from full-time employment. Many women continued to work, but as more families joined the ranks of the middle-class during the economic boom of the 1920s, people began to copy the upper-class lifestyle, and more married women chose not to work. As a result of this class mobility, which occurred because of sustained economic growth during the early part of the twentieth century, the middle-class woman's role was redefined as housewife (Spain, 1992).

Over the years, other changes would alter the relationship of women to both the family and the larger society. Status differences were the result of not only male social dominance, which dictated women's roles, but also the economy. For example, during the prosperous 1920s, middle-class women were expected to be housewives. During World War II, however, many women assumed the full-time jobs of men sent overseas as soldiers. The critical role of women in the wartime economy was symbolized by the image of "Rosie the Riveter." After the war, and especially during the suburbanization of the 1950s, middle-class women were expected to resume their role as housewives. By the 1970s, however, as real wages in the United States began to decline and participation in the middle-class lifestyle grew increasingly expensive, many women returned to the workplace. Today, buying a home in the suburbs typically requires more than one income, and it is common for both spouses to pursue full-time employment. A majority of all adult women now work outside the home, whether single or married.

The participation of middle-class women in the formal economy has been cyclical but has increased significantly in recent decades. Since the 1970s, women have entered the paid labor force in record numbers. As a result of economic restructuring—that is, with the decline in manufacturing and the rise of service industries (see Chapter 6)—new opportunities have been created for women. Women have responded by returning to college and moving into the professional service sector. One consequence of this shift has been a change in the way both men and women view household tasks, with a greater willingness among middle-class men to share in domestic labor, especially a growing percentage of men who "parent" (Lamb, 1986; Grief, 1985). Another consequence has been the multiplication of service-related jobs created by working mothers. Many of the pressing household tasks have been farmed out to specialized service workers for a fee. Child care, housecleaning, shopping assistance, and lawn care are but some of the services that have taken the place of unpaid domestic labor. In addition, fast-foods, restaurants, and take-out shops have expanded their operations greatly over the past twenty-five years. All of these new economic activities have changed the texture of space in both cities and suburbs. Specialty shops and services spring up everywhere to cater to those families with double incomes. Supermarket and giant merchandising stores such as Wal-Mart make shopping more efficient for the consumer although they have negative consequences for local business. In the process of providing these services, retailers have redefined metropolitan space through the construction of malls and minicenters across the region.

The sociospatial relations of the modern, global economy have much to do with gender roles and patriarchy, but they also are a consequence of economic and political factors. When women stayed at home and engaged in full-time but unpaid labor, they were responsible for keeping up the appearance of the neighborhood. When middle-class women in the United States began to enter the workforce in great numbers, many were still expected to do a "double shift." As a result, service industries that catered to domestic needs surged, and neighborhoods changed to accommodate fast-food restaurants and take-out places, laundries and dry cleaners, and supermarkets and malls (see Box 7.3).

Houses in the suburbs required at least two-car garages because both spouses commuted to work, and teenagers required their own vehicles for work, school, and leisure activities. In both urban and suburban settlement spaces, day care and extended child-care programs changed the place where children went to play—from city streets supervised by mothers to indoor group play areas supervised by paid day-care specialists. Elsewhere in the global economy, young girls make up the bulk of the manufacturing labor force in electronics and garment industries because patriarchal relations make them docile and low-paid workers. The control of women's bodies is as essential to the sustenance of Third World countries as it is to the "First World" patriarchal societies. Everywhere, then, the nature of gender roles has a direct effect on sociospatial relations.

Women and the Environment

The relation between settlement space and gender extends from the home to the community to the larger metropolitan region. The home, for example, is the one space in the environment where people can be themselves. It is the most private and intimate space. Due to the family division of labor, women have been assigned the main task of decorating the home. Through this activity they express their own individuality (Matrix Collective, 1984). Of course, housing has several meanings, as we will see, and it is a signifier of class status. But for women, their control over the environmental space of the home

BOX 7.3   Gendered Space in the Built Environment

The sociospatial approach asserts that urban and suburban settlement spaces influence individual behavior; however, this influence is mediated by gender, class, and other individual characteristics. In this way, the meaning of space and the built environment may differ for men and women. Consider the ways in which the structure of settlement space in Sweden and that in the United States have very different consequences for the daily activity and well-being of women.

Suburban developments in the United States usually consist of single-family homes located some distance from the urban center. Local zoning restrictions require that suburban settlement space be low-density (not simply single-family homes instead of apartments, but also lot sizes of between one and three acres). Land-use plans also require physical separation of residential areas from business and commercial development. The federal government has spent billions of dollars constructing a highway system for private automobiles, and public transportation is limited.

In Sweden, suburban developments are of moderate density, usually garden-type apartments located in mixed-use districts where stores and businesses are located within walking distance. Extensive public transportation connects suburban settlement space to the city core, and child care and other services (provided through the public sector) are available within the local community (Popenoe, 1977).

The effects of these two very different built environments on women's lives could not be more dramatic. In the United States, women who live in suburban housing developments are comparatively isolated from friends, relatives, their place of employment, and health and other public services. A second family automobile is needed for women to take their children to day care, go grocery shopping, or travel to their jobs. Then there is the cost of travel time to and from each of these destinations (separated from one another by zoning). In Sweden and other Scandinavian countries with similar welfare state structures and urban planning, women in suburban developments are more likely to live near friends, relatives, and their place of employment. If they do not, public transportation is available, eliminating the need for a second automobile. Because day care and other family services are funded by the state and located in the new planned suburban communities, they are readily available. And because friends and even relatives may live within walking distance, it is easier to pool resources to arrange for other family needs (Popenoe, 1980).

The arrangement of suburban settlement space in Scandinavian countries encourages women to become fully integrated into the metropolitan community and to build strong social networks with others in the community. In contrast, the structure of suburban settlement space in the United States—where homes, workplaces, schools, and shopping areas are separated from one another in everyday life and imagination—places a significant burden on the time needs of suburban women and isolates them from employment opportunities and social interaction with others within the metropolitan region.

has meant an opportunity for self-expression. For the middle class, it also has developed into a restricted domain within which women are allowed to influence their environment.

If the home space can be viewed in this way, it is partly because women have been socialized to take on responsibility for shelter maintenance. Spatial relations therefore play a great role in the perpetuation of female socialized roles in our society. However, if the female gender role assigns a certain power to women through control of the home environment, the opposite is the case for the larger physical environment of the city and metropolis. Once out in public space, women have to beware. They are subject to harassment and, quite often, danger. Women living in large cities must acquire "street smarts" early if they are to successfully negotiate public space. As one commentary noted:

> Whether you wear a slit skirt or are covered from head to foot in a black chador, the message is not that you are attractive enough to make a man lose his self-control, but that the public realm belongs to him and you are there by his permission as long as you follow his rules and as long as you remember your place. (Benard and Schlaffer, 1993:390)

In contrast to men, women are situated in a constrained space and do not enjoy the same freedom of movement. For example, women are cautioned not to go out alone at night, and with good reason. If they walk or jog around the neighborhood, they usually do so only in secure places. The women's movement has been particularly attentive to the needs of females for safe places; witness such events as "Take Back the Night" rallies. The constricted and confined safe places for women in our society are another form of oppression. By patterning what activities are allowed, what are isolated, what are considered safe or dangerous, and what are connected to other activities, such as the combination of child care and shopping found in the mall or the gender segregation of children in elementary schools (Thorne, 1993), space plays a role in gender socialization.

The secondary status of women is reinforced through spatial design. Community planning invariably assigns the major portion of open space to traditionally male-dominated activities, such as sports. Places for mothering are rarely considered at all and often are restricted to playgrounds. Creating safe environments for children and mothers requires some planning. In Columbia, Maryland, one of the totally planned New Towns in the United States, pedestrian and automobile traffic are separated by space. This feature of Columbia makes it easier for mothers to protect children at play. It is not so easy to suggest ways the home and community environments can be improved by taking the needs of women into account, although some progress through feminist activism has been made in sensitizing planners and architects to the specific needs of women (see Matrix Collective, 1984). Change in the accepted gender roles and the new demands placed upon family life may affect our environment in the years to come (see Chapter 14 for an extended discussion on environmental and planning concerns).

KEY CONCEPTS

class stratification
socioeconomic status
conspicuous consumption
working poor
underclass
ghettoized poor
double shift
social reproduction
gendered space

DISCUSSION QUESTIONS

1. What is the difference between the terms underclass and ghettoized poor? Which term do the authors suggest be used by urban sociologists? Why?

2. The sociospatial approach emphasizes the relationship between class differences and spatial location. What areas of the region where you live can be identified as being upper class, middle class, etc.? What differences in lifestyle can you identify among these residential spaces?

3. What is meant by the phenomenon of gendered space? What are some examples of gendered spaces within your community? How does the physical structure of the built environment within your community influence the everyday life of women? Is this different from the way in which the physical structure of the built environment influences the everyday life of men within your community?

ETHNICITY AND RACE
IN THE METROPOLIS

The United States is more diverse today in its ethnic and racial makeup than at any other time in its history. This is particularly true of U.S. cities and metropolitan regions. Because of changes in immigration law, immigrants are now coming from areas of the world that were previously restricted. The number of immigrants over the past decade matches that of the peak years of the "great migration" at the beginning of the twentieth century. In 2002, there was an all-time high of 32.5 million foreign-born persons living within the United States, more than 11 percent of the total population (Schmidley, 2003). For the country as a whole, these developments have resulted in substantial increases among many groups that were relatively unknown in the past: while the Chinese population has increased from 435,000 persons in 1970 to 2,730,000 in 2000, and the Filipino population increased from 343,000 to 2,360,000 during the same period, the Korean population grew from 69,000 to 1,200,000 persons, and the Laotian (largely Hmong) population, not included in the 1970 census, numbered some 1,230,000 persons in 2000. Similarly, the Mexican-origin population has nearly doubled each decade since 1960, and Hispanics now constitute the largest minority population, surpassing the African American population shortly after the 2000 census.

As was true of the earlier period of great immigration (1895–1915), the majority of recent immigrants have settled in urban areas. In 2000 there were some 29 million immigrants living in metropolitan areas across the country, an increase of 10 million immigrants from just ten years earlier (Logan, 2003). More than half of the foreign-born population in the United States is found in just thirteen metropolitan areas, and this increase is not bounded by the geography of earlier immigrant neighborhoods. Immigrant growth in the suburbs (an increase of 4.8 million from 1990 to 2000) greatly outnumbered that in the central cities (an increase of 3.5 million). By 2000 fully 25 percent of the suburban population consisted of minority populations, due in large part to the movement of immigrants into suburban communities and, in some cases, into suburban ethnic enclaves. Many cities—and suburbs—have undergone visible change in ethnic populations and neighborhoods. In Chicago, for example, the Hispanic and Asian populations have doubled each decade since 1950. In the 1960s, Chicago was primarily a white and black city; in the 1970s, Chicago became a white, black, and Hispanic (largely Mexican) city. Since 1990, however, Chicago has become a multicultural city with distinct white, black, Hispanic, Asian, and European immigrant communities across the metropolitan area.

Table 8.1 shows the metropolitan areas with the largest immigrant populations in 2000. For the most part, these areas are the largest metropolitan areas in the country (New York, Los Angeles, and Chicago) as well as other large cities and their suburban regions. The table indicates that in the largest metropolitan areas a significant number of persons are very recent arrivals in the United States (more than 10 percent of persons living in the Los Angeles and New York PMSAs). In these areas, more than 40 percent of the foreign-born population speaks a language other than English; in the metropolitan areas of Chicago, Washington, Houston, and Dallas, more than 20 percent of the foreign-born population speaks a language other than English. In each of these areas, the original barrios and Chinatowns have been eclipsed by the growing suburbanization of many different ethnic subgroups.

Ethnic and racial formation in the United States is the consequence of government policy and intergroup competition within an ethnically diverse society (Omi and Winant, 1992). In relatively homogeneous societies, lifestyle differences may exist, but they usually are not expressed as ethnicity; class, gender, religious, subcultural, and age differences may be more important. When indigenous people, such as mainland Chinese, immigrate to another country that contains people from many different origins, such as the United States, subcultural differences may take on the dimensions of ethnic differences. These are almost wholly "semiotic" or symbolic in nature (see Chapter 7). In particular, ascribed characteristics and inherited beliefs may make individuals with foreign heritages uniquely different. What counts for the dynamics of ethnicity is the extent to which those symbolic differences clash with those of the dominant society or of other ethnic groups in a diverse society.

In the United States, ethnic lifestyles are closely connected to the waves of immigration from abroad. Our understanding of immigration should in-

TABLE 8.1 Metropolitan Regions with Largest Immigrant Populations, 2000

Metropolitan	Total Population	Foreign born	Immigrated before 1995	Immigrated 1995–2000	Speak Other Language
L.A.-Long Beach, PMSA	9,519,338	36.2	12.6	23.6	54.1
New York, PMSA	9,314,235	33.7	14.2	19.5	44.8
Chicago, PMSA	8,272,768	17.2	7.7	9.5	26.5
Philadelphia, PMSA	5,100,931	7.0	2.9	4.1	12.3
Washington, DC, PMSA	4,923,153	16.9	8.0	8.9	20.8
Detroit, PMSA	4,441,551	7.5	3.3	4.3	11.0
Houston, PMSA	4,177,646	20.5	9.9	10.5	33.4
Atlanta, MSA	4,112,198	10.3	6.2	4.0	13.3
Dallas, PMSA	3,519,176	16.8	9.4	7.4	26.3
Boston, PMSA	3,406,835	14.9	6.5	8.4	19.8
Riverside-S. Bernardino, PMSA	3,254,821	18.8	5.8	13.0	33.5
Phoenix-Mesa, MSA	3,251,876	14.1	7.5	6.5	24.2
Minneapolis-St. Paul, MSA	2,968,806	7.1	3.9	3.2	10.2
Orange County, PMSA	2,846,289	29.9	11.7	18.2	41.4
San Diego, MSA	2,813,833	21.5	7.7	13.9	33.0
Nassau-Suffolk, PMSA	2,753,913	14.4	4.4	10.0	20.0
St. Louis, MSA	2,603,607	3.1	1.6	1.5	5.3
Baltimore, PMSA	2,552,994	5.7	2.4	3.3	8.4
Seattle-Bellevue, PMSA	2,414,616	13.7	6.6	7.2	16.5
Tampa-St. Petersburg, MSA	2,395,997	9.8	3.8	6.0	15.3

SOURCE: Adapted from Lewis Mumford Center for Comparative Urban and Regional Research, Metropolitan Ethnic and Racial Change, Census 2000.

clude a spatial perspective that acknowledges the important role of the globalization of capital as well as the push and pull factors that most often are used to explain why people left their land of origin in the first place. Three distinct waves of immigration to the United States have occurred. We discuss the first two waves and then survey the theories of immigrant adjustment, before exploring the third wave, or "new immigration," which is still ongoing.

THE FIRST WAVE

Many thousands of years ago, persons from Central Asia immigrated to the Western Hemisphere over a land bridge to Alaska. Beginning with Columbus's fateful voyage in 1492, Western European settlers from the British Isles, Spain, Holland, and France confronted the Native Americans. These European settlers arrived as a consequence of official state policy. Some were convicts taking advantage of an alternative sentence to debtors' prison in their homeland. Others signed on with the promise of free land and other resources. Still others, such as the Puritans who founded the Massachusetts Bay

Colony and William Penn and his Quaker community, came in search of religious freedom. At the time of the American Revolution, some 95 percent of the white population immigrating to the United States was Northern European, and nearly 70 percent came from Great Britain (Steinberg, 1996).

During the 1840s, the potato famine in Ireland forced many people from that country to immigrate. The Irish people were the first large group of immigrants to the United States who were not Anglo-Saxon Protestants, and they confronted extensive discrimination because they were Catholic (Higham, 1977). By the time they arrived, the earlier groups had entrenched themselves as the ruling class. Many of them, such as John Astor (from England) and Cornelius Vanderbilt (whose family had come from Holland), had made fortunes in the burgeoning industrial economy of the United States. The Irish were considered less valuable than the African slaves of the South, and they were used for dangerous tasks, such as the building of the railroads, or as the first proletarian factory workers in the northern cities where slavery was not allowed.

THE SECOND WAVE

By the last decades of the 1800s, industrialization was in full swing, and the cities of the United States were expanding. A second substantial wave of new immigrants arrived here from the countries of Central and Eastern Europe. Most second-wave immigrants made their homes in the city. Many had come from rural backgrounds and had to make adjustments to the urban way of life (Handlin, 1951). As we noted in Chapter 5, the cities of the time were overcrowded. Housing for most immigrants lacked the basic necessities of sanitation and sewage. Public health crises and crime waves were quite common (Monkkonen, 1986). The quality of urban life went into decline. In addition, most of the jobs open to immigrants were in the factories of the largest cities, and immigrants had to accommodate themselves to the industrial daily schedule.

It wasn't long before antagonisms developed between immigrant groups—now organized as workers—and factory owners, with the backing of city officials. Both the Irish, who had arrived somewhat earlier, and the second wave of Central and Eastern Europeans were viewed by established residents as threatening to the American way of life. Some second-wave immigrants had already been exposed to radical labor movements in Europe, and these groups, such as the Industrial Workers of the World (IWW), started up in the United States. Because of the large majority of Catholics among the foreigners, particularly the Irish, Italians, and Poles, a popular anti-urban sentiment was that large cities were centers of "rum, Romanism, and rebellion."

It may be difficult for us to imagine today, but the older, first-wave immigrants, especially those among the elite of the country, propagated racist ideas about the Irish, Italians, Poles, and Jews in the late 1880s. Among the books published was Josiah Strong's (1891) racist diatribe that blamed the white foreigners for diluting the "American Race" and for spawning the crises of the city. In another case, during the 1920s, many outspoken anti-Semites operated in the open, including Henry Ford, who would not allow Jewish workers in his factories and financed a successful reprinting of the virulently anti-Semitic forgery, *The Protocols of the Elders of Zion*—a racist book that still circulates today.

To a great extent, such racist and anti-Semitic attacks appeared alongside others accusing the new immigrants of harboring communist and anarchist or anti-capitalist ideas. Thus, anti-immigrant racism was a strong weapon calling immigration itself into question. Around the turn of the century, reaction to the second wave of arrivals was so strong that it eventually led to a restriction of immigration from Eastern and Southern Europe. This was accomplished in a succession of federal acts that established quotas favoring first-wave, Western European, and Northern European countries. These quotas remained in force until the immigration reform bill of 1965.

The struggle between employers and workers was not the only conflict of the time; conflict also took on a spatial manifestation. Areas in the city were marked off by ethnicity, class, race, and religion. For example, most large American cities historically have had two separate Irish neighborhoods—one for Irish Catholics, the other for Irish Protestants. These groups competed with each other over territory and access to public resources. Employers would also pit workers from different ethnic groups against one another in a largely successful effort to prevent union organizing and keep workers' wages low. Thrasher's study of Chicago gangs (1927), discussed in Chapter 3, provides an excellent example of how these "defended neighborhoods," which are a sociospatial phenomenon of ethnicity, came into being.

THEORIES OF IMMIGRANT ADJUSTMENT

The image of the American city as a mosaic of ethnic neighborhoods emerged at the turn of the century as a consequence of competition for settlement space within the industrial city. Early studies described the adjustment of ethnic groups in terms of Robert Park's race relations cycle, which included stages of contact, conflict, accommodation, and assimilation. And in keeping with the analogy of a biological model from the natural sciences, Park, and later Roderick McKenzie, would describe population change within urban neighborhoods as part of a cycle of invasion–succession (McKenzie, 1944). This "ecological" model was criticized early on as being too mechanical for the complicated process of neighborhood change (Alihan, 1938).

Today we know that the turmoil of population turnover in the city had more to do with competition for jobs within a labor market segmented by race and ethnicity and the competition for housing among large numbers of immigrants than it did with some innate biological contest over territory among separate ethnic groups. However, this now outdated "ecological" model was notable for its appreciation of the role of space in the actions of social groups. That is, in the conflict among different economic, residential, and commercial interests, control of space was one very important feature, especially for cultural reasons.

The most powerful theory of immigrant conflict and accommodation in the United States was the "melting pot" view. It was believed that change would occur gradually and, in some cases, over successive generations, as the children of arrivals eventually assimilated into the American way of life. Immigrants might find the United States a strange country and would experience certain difficulties upon arrival, such as having to learn English. As a consequence, they would invariably seek out enclaves of their own kind within the city, thus perpetuating the ethnic character of the neighborhood. Over time, however, the melting pot theory suggested, their children would become familiar with U.S. culture and language. They would leave the enclave and mix, or "melt," with the children of others. Those adhering to the melting pot theory asserted that the forces operating to bring about such changes were the free-market economy, the public schools, and the institution of democratic politics, all of which allowed for active participation in public life. Adjustment to the United States would occur, according to this view, over several generations with assimilation the end result (Glazer and Moynihan, 1963; Gordon, 1964; Sowell, 1981; Lieberson and Walters, 1988). Implicit in this view was the notion that the United States was a land of unbridled opportunity and mobility. The widely believed "American Dream" fostered the idea that any immigrant who worked hard and lived a responsible life could become a successful U.S. citizen. Beyond this variant of the American Dream was the belief that success in the United States depended principally on individual self-worth, or human capital. That is, skill and hard work (human capital) were all that was needed for success, because the opportunities were there for the taking.

Lieberson (1980) and Morawska (1990), among others, have challenged this melting pot theory. They have suggested that although individual attributes are important to future success, there are also institutional impediments that may prevent immigrants from realizing their full potential, such as economic and political constraints. In particular, mobility and success are often a function of business cycles. When economic times are rough, the task of self-improvement is extremely difficult for newly arrived residents. However, when the economy is expanding, as it was for much of the period between 1840 and 1920, immigrants may indeed find golden opportunities.

THE THIRD WAVE

Earlier ideas about race and ethnicity and the immigrant experience are being challenged by the newest, third wave of immigrants that has arrived since the 1970s. Changes to immigration laws enacted in 1965 replaced the earlier quota system (which had been designed to keep Asians and other non-European groups out of the country) with a preference system based on occupational characteristics. Supporters of the immigration reform legislation could not have anticipated the unprecedented response across the globe. Between 1968 and 1990, some 10 million people immigrated to the United States. Further reforms passed by the George W. Bush administration limited immigration to some 540,000 persons each year. But after intense lobbying from the U.S. Chamber of Commerce and other business groups, this number was increased to 650,000 legal immigrants each year. This rate has not been observed here since the last great wave of immigration at the beginning of the twentieth century. And just as in this earlier period in our history, increased immigration is supported by business as a way to increase the labor pool—and thereby keep wages from increasing.

The composition of the third wave of immigrant groups is very different from that of earlier periods. During the first and second waves, 75 percent of the arrivals were from countries in Europe. Today a similar percentage of arrivals are from Latin America and Asia. Each year since 1970, more than 55,000 Mexicans and 50,000 Filipinos have immigrated to the United States. During the 1970s in California, for example, 22 percent of new immigrants came from Asia and 43 percent from Mexico (Espiritu and Light, 1991). Also striking is the fact that the majority of new immigrants to the United States are female—and this is true even from countries such as Mexico and the Philippines, where women are often thought to be less independent. As a consequence of this new immigration, the United States of the twenty-first century will be more culturally diverse—and more Asian and Hispanic—than at any time in its history. To understand just how significant these changes are, consider the fact that Hispanics now outnumber African Americans and have become the largest minority group in the United States. Furthermore, even if immigration were halted completely, the U.S. Hispanic population would still double within the next twenty years, from some 14 million to more than 30 million.

A third distinct characteristic of the new immigration is that it is economically diverse. Many recent immigrants exhibit the classic characteristics of the past: limited education, rural backgrounds, and limited resources. A large number, however, are the exact opposite. These well-endowed immigrants are educated—many have college degrees—they are former city dwellers, and they often come with enough personal financial resources to start their own businesses. In their home countries of India, Korea, the Philippines, and elsewhere, this loss of a young and highly educated population is referred to as the "brain drain." Thus, many third-wave arrivals have achieved success in the United States in a relatively short time. According to Portes and Rumbaut (1990), in the decade between 1980 and 1990, professionals and technicians accounted for only 18 percent of the U.S. labor force but represented 25 percent of the immigrant population.

This "bimodal" distribution—that is, having two peaks: one high income, one low income—of immigration is a consequence of uneven development within the global system of capitalism. In the 1960s and 1970s, many countries underwent crash modernization programs that were not entirely successful. On the one hand, large numbers of the middle and working classes received technical and professional training, but upon graduation, their economies had not expanded fast enough to offer them work. On the other hand, agricultural reform programs and development of interior places forced many impoverished and uneducated rural residents into the cities. They too took the chance on immigrating rather than waiting around in their home countries for work (Espiritu and Light, 1991).

Audrey Singer's (2004) analysis of immigration to metropolitan regions during the twentieth century suggests that the combination of recent immigration and historical settlement patterns of earlier ethnic groups has produced six types of *immigrant gateway cities*. Singer defines the six types in the following manner (see Box 8.1):

> **Former gateway cities:** Above the national average in the percentage of immigrants during 1900–1930, followed by percentages below the national average in every decade through 2000. This category includes cities like Cleveland and Buffalo, which were destinations for large numbers of immigrants in the early 1900s but no longer receive immigrants. Many of these older industrial cities are located in the Snowbelt.
>
> **Continuous gateway cities:** Above-average percentage of immigrants in every decade of the twentieth century. Includes cities like Chicago and New

York, which are long-established destinations for immigrants that continue to attract large numbers of foreign born. Many of these cities are located in the larger New York metropolitan region.

Post–World War II gateway cities: Low percentage of immigrants until after 1950, followed by percentages higher than the national average for the remainder of the century. Includes cities like Los Angeles and Miami, which were relatively small at the time of the Great Migration but have served as destinations for new immigrants in the past fifty years. Many of these cities are located in the Sunbelt.

Emerging gateway cities: Very low percentage of immigrants until 1970, followed by high proportions in the post–1980 period. Includes cities like Atlanta and Washington, which are located in metropolitan areas that nearly doubled in the 1980s and 1990s. They have experienced rapid immigrant growth in the past twenty years, and the total number of foreign born has increased five times during that period. With the exception of Washington, all are located in the Sunbelt.

Re-emerging gateway cities: Above-average percentage of immigrants during 1900–1930, below average until 1980, followed by rapid increases in post–1980 period. This category includes cities such as Seattle and Minneapolis–St. Paul, which were destinations for immigrants in the early twentieth century and now receive large numbers of immigrants. With the exception of the Twin Cities, all are located in the Sunbelt or in the West.

Pre-emerging gateway cities: Very low percentage of immigrants for the entire twentieth century. This category includes cities such as Salt Lake City and Raleigh-Durham, which experienced rapid growth of both foreign-born and native-born populations between 1980 and 2000. They attracted significant numbers of immigrants in the 1990s and appear to be emerging as new immigrant gateway cities for the twenty-first century. With the exception of Salt Lake City, all are Sunbelt cities, and most are located in the Southeast.

There are important differences in demographics and settlement patterns among these six types of immigrant gateway cities. Some are located in fast-growing metropolitan regions in the Sunbelt, while others are located in older and larger metropolitan regions of the Midwest and East Coast that have experienced slower overall population growth. Some of the cities have become multicultural melting pots, while others are dominated by a relatively smaller number of ethnic groups. Singer notes that in the fast-growing emerging gateway cities such as Atlanta and St. Louis, immigrants are settling in communities that are greatly stressed by rapid population growth—a situation different

BOX 8.1　Six Immigrant Gateway Types

Former	Continuous	Post–World War II
Baltimore	Bergen-Passaic	Fort Lauderdale
Buffalo	Boston	Houston
Cleveland	Chicago	Los Angeles
Detroit	Jersey City	Miami
Milwaukee	Nassau-Suffolk	Riverside-San Bernadino
Philadelphia	Newark	San Diego
Pittsburgh	New York	Orange
St. Louis	San Francisco	

Emerging	Re-emerging	Pre-emerging
Atlanta	Denver	Austin
Dallas	Minneapolis-St. Paul	Charlotte
Fort Worth	Oakland	Greensboro-Winston
Las Vegas	Phoenix	Raleigh-Durham
Orlando	Portland	Salt Lake City
Washington, D.C.	Sacramento	
West Palm Beach	San Jose	
	Seattle	
	Tampa	

SOURCE: Adapted from Table 1 in A. Singer, 2004. *The Rise of New Immigrant Gateways* (Washington, D.C.: The Brookings Institution, Center on Urban and Metropolitan Policy).

from that of those who have moved to cities with a long history of immigrant settlement (2004:18).

Singer's study of the immigrant gateway cities is important for our understanding of the effects of the new immigration on metropolitan regions across the country. One problem with the analysis—something that is discussed in the report—is the focus on the gateway city, because most of the new immigrants live in suburban towns within the metropolitan region, not in the central city. Our focus on the sociospatial perspective will help us to understand the importance of moving beyond the city and looking at the metropolitan region more broadly when we study immigration and other demographic trends that affect our communities.

Although it is common to speak of ethnic neighborhoods in American cities— and most of us are familiar with Chinatowns, Mexican neighborhoods, Greektowns, and the like—urban sociologists are more likely to talk about the ethnic enclave, a concept that emphasizes the ways in which work, residence, and other

BOX 8.2   The Ethnic Enclave

Ethnic neighborhoods have a long history in the United States, from the Chinatowns and Irish communities of the mid-nineteenth century to the "Little Italies" and Poletowns of the twentieth century. Within the ethnic ghettos, new immigrants could live alongside others from their home countries and quickly build social networks that allowed them to find housing and employment. In the post–World War II period, many older European ethnic neighborhoods began to disappear as the third- and fourth-generation families moved out to the suburbs. In many cities, urban settlement spaces occupied by older ethnic groups have been replaced by new immigrants.

As the new immigrant communities in Chicago, Los Angeles, Miami, New York, and many other cities have continued to expand, ethnic entrepreneurs have started businesses that employ other community residents. These include food stores, restaurants, clothing and textile stores, and other retail stores, as well as repair (auto, plumbing, electrical) and personal services (travel agencies, legal services). Urban sociologists have been studying these ethnic enclaves for many years. We know that the ethnic enclave provides an important service for new immigrants—a place where they can find housing and employment opportunities with others from their home countries. Min Zhou (1992) reports that new immigrants in New York City's Chinatown found access to inexpensive housing and employment opportunities that allowed them to become upwardly mobile.

But others are concerned that ethnic enclaves may have negative consequences for new immigrants. Because most ethnic business enterprises are small, family-run stores, wages are lower than in other companies, and opportunities for advancement are few. Although new immigrants may be able to get by within the ethnic enclave simply by speaking their home language, their lack of English-language proficiency will limit their ability to interact with others outside the community and their opportunities for higher-paying jobs in stores and businesses outside the ethnic enclave economy. Also, new immigrants, especially illegal immigrants, are sometimes exploited within the ethnic enclave by their own compatriots (see Lin, 1998). Undocumented (or illegal) immigrants have been found working in unsafe conditions and being paid below the minimum legal wage at restaurants and factories in the Chinatowns in New York and Los Angeles and in the large Mexican enclaves in Chicago and Los Angeles.

forms of social interaction overlap in urban space. Much of this research focuses on the paradox of the ethnic enclave: the positive effects that social networks can provide for new immigrants, and the negative effects of concentration and isolation within the enclave. Increasingly, we must think of ethnic enclaves not as simply ethnic settlements in the central city, as a majority of new immigrants now reside in suburban communities of the metropolitan region (Gorre, 1991).

Current immigration to the United States (and other developed nations) reflects changes in the global system of capitalism in another respect. Following the breakup of colonial systems after World War II, many European countries saw an increase in immigration from their former colonies—Caribbean blacks and Muslim and Hindu Indians in England, Indonesian and other groups in the Netherlands. At the end of the Second Indo-Chinese War, the United States admitted 300,000 Southeast Asian refugees, and the death squads and political conflicts in Central America in the 1980s brought another 500,000 refugees, despite efforts of the Reagan administration and the Immigration and Naturalization Service to prevent them from entering the country. And as noted earlier, each year some 50,000 people immigrate to the United States from the Philippines, our former colonial outpost in the South Pacific.

The new immigration already has had a profound effect on settlement space within metropolitan regions across the country (Suro and Singer, 2003). Some groups have moved into older ethnic neighborhoods, greatly expanding their numbers and size. In southwest Chicago, for example, the Mexican neighborhood in 18th Street/Pilsen has expanded across the 26th Street/Little Village community into suburban communities beyond the city limits, while the older Chinatown area near the Loop has seen extensive redevelopment that has doubled the number of business establishments and dwelling units. In these and other ethnic communities across the metropolitan region, local residents have constructed new settlement spaces rich with symbolic meanings—from Mexican storefronts identical to those found in Monterrey and Aguascalientes, the primary origins in Mexico for immigrants to Chicago and the Midwest, now reproduced in suburban settlement space, to a new riverfront park in the second Chinatown, designed by a Chinese American landscape architect, which reproduces traditional Chinese design elements in this new urban settlement space.

ETHNIC SETTLEMENT SPACE IN CITIES AND SUBURBS

The multicentered metropolitan region contains a diversity of settlement spaces. Although it is common to speak of differences between cities and suburbs, such differences have largely disappeared (if in fact they ever existed). For many years, sociologists spoke of ethnic communities and racial ghettos in the central city as if ethnic and racial groups lived only in these types of urban neighborhoods. But the history of ethnic settlement has long been one of diverse neighborhoods within the city and constant movement to the suburbs. Although many American cities have had notable German, Polish, Italian, and other ethnic neighborhoods—such as Irish neighborhoods in Boston,

TABLE 8.2 Destinations of Major Immigrant Groups, 1979 to 2003

Nationality	Year	Number	Percent of All Immigrants	Percent in Top 3 Destinations	Top Three Destinations First	Second	Third
Mexican	1979	52,096	11.3	17.3	El Paso	Los Angeles	Houston
	1984	57,557	10.6	27.9	Los Angeles	Chicago	El Paso
	1987	72,351	12.0	33.0	Los Angeles	El Paso	San Diego
	1993	126,561	14.0	31.4	Los Angeles	Chicago	Houston
	1998	131,575	19.9	26.8	Los Angeles	Chicago	Riverside
	2003	115,864	16.4	23.8	Los Angeles	Chicago	Riverside
Cuban	1979	15,585	3.4	59.1	Miami	New York	San Juan
	1984	10,599	1.9	51.8	Miami	Jersey City	New York
	1987	28,916	4.8	86.0	Miami	New York	Tampa
	1993	13,666	1.5	81.5	Miami	Jersey City	Tampa
	1998	17,375	2.6	76.2	Miami	Tampa	Ft. Lauderdale
	2003	9,304	1.3	62.8	Miami	Tampa	Las Vegas
Dominican	1979	17,519	3.8	80.6	New York	San Juan	Bergen-Passaic
	1984	23,147	4.3	78.7	New York	San Juan	Bergen-Passaic
	1987	24,858	4.1	76.0	New York	San Juan	Bergen-Passaic
	1993	45,420	5.0	71.1	New York	San Juan	Boston
	1998	20,387	3.1	59.8	New York	San Juan	Boston
	2003	26,205	3.7	66.1	New York	San Juan	Bergen-Passaic
Filipino	1979	41,300	9.0	17.8	San Francisco	Los Angeles	Honolulu
	1984	42,768	7.9	28.1	Los Angeles	San Francisco	Honolulu
	1987	50,060	8.3	30.0	Los Angeles	San Francisco	San Diego
	1993	53,457	7.0	26.0	Los Angeles	New York	San Diego
	1998	34,466	5.2	27.4	Los Angeles	Honolulu	San Francisco
	2003	45,397	6.4	21.6	Los Angeles	Honolulu	San Diego
Total	1979	460,348		25.5	New York	Los Angeles	Miami
	1984	543,903		29.8	New York	Los Angeles	Chicago
	1987	601,516		33.2	New York	Los Angeles	Miami
	1993	904,292		30.9	New York	Los Angeles	Chicago
	1998	660,477		26.1	New York	Los Angeles	Chicago
	2003	705,827		45.3	New York	Los Angeles	Chicago

SOURCE: U.S. Immigration and Naturalization Service, *Statistical Yearbook* (Washington, D.C.: U.S. Government Printing Office, 1985, 1988, 1994); U.S. Immigration and Naturalization Service, *Yearbook of Immigration Statistics* (Washington, D.C.: U.S. Government Printing Office, 1988, 1994, 2003).

German neighborhoods in St. Louis, and Polish neighborhoods in Buffalo—
the ethnic ghetto typically contained only a small proportion of all immigrants
from each group. Most Germans, Poles, and Italians lived in other neighborhoods across the city and early on began to make their way into suburban
communities. In contrast, blacks, and to a lesser extent Hispanics, have not
enjoyed mobility. We will discuss the persistence of racial segregation in U.S.
society in Chapter 10.

African Americans

African Americans were forcibly removed from their home countries and
brought to the United States as slaves during the 1700s. In 1990, their descendants constituted 12.4 percent of the total population. Until the twentieth century, the overwhelming majority of blacks, more than 90 percent, lived
in the South, and most resided in rural areas. Since 1900, however, there has
been a steady movement of African Americans to the North in general and to
cities in particular (Lemann, 1991b).

In the 1800s, many slaves fled the South for freedom. Using such routes as
the "underground railroad," they arrived in the cities of the North, and some
even made it as far as Canada. By the end of the Civil War, several communities of African Americans were already established in northern cities. As a result of discrimination against blacks, however, these areas soon became
segregated. A similar pattern of ghettoization occurred in the making of black
communities in Chicago (Spear, 1967), Philadelphia (W.E.B. DuBois, 1899),
and New York (Drake and Cayton, 1945).

At the turn of the century, the mechanization of agriculture, coupled with
the job opportunities created by widespread industrialization, pushed blacks
off southern farms and pulled them into northern factories. This process accelerated during World War I, fell off during the Great Depression, and re-
sumed with full intensity during World War II. As a result, by the 1950s
African Americans were almost as urbanized as whites, with more than 60
percent of their total population living in cities. After 1950 a significant number of whites began an exodus from the cities to the suburbs, which at the
time were nearly all closed to black migration. As a result, the percentage of
African Americans living in central cities rose. By the 1980s, cities such as Los
Angeles, Chicago, Atlanta, and Detroit had black mayors, and in the 1990s
the list grew to include New York and others.

Racial discrimination is still a potent force that prevents African Americans
from integrating into society. For blacks, segregation into distinct ghetto areas
of most cities still persists despite their large urban numbers. During the past
four decades, a growing number of blacks have achieved middle-class status

TABLE 8.3 Ethnic and Racial Composition of the Largest Metropolitan Regions in 2000

Area Name	Total	White	Black	Hispanic	Asian
Chicago, PMSA	8,272,768	4,798,533	1,575,173	1,416,584	415,244
L.A.-Long Beach, PMSA	9,519,338	2,959,614	950,765	4,242,213	1,232,085
New York, PMSA	9,314,235	3,684,669	2,217,680	2,339,836	913,199
Philadelphia, PMSA	5,100,931	3,583,090	1,040,144	258,606	188,414
Washington, DC, PMSA	4,923,153	2,762,241	1,312,419	432,003	366,991
Detroit, PMSA	4,441,551	3,096,900	1,037,674	128,075	118,464
Houston, PMSA	4,177,646	1,923,990	734,732	1,248,586	235,970
Atlanta, MSA	4,112,198	2,460,740	1,202,260	268,851	149,252
Dallas, PMSA	3,519,176	1,979,218	537,789	810,499	155,492
Boston, PMSA	3,405,985	2,725,194	247,675	202,510	181,984
Phoenix-Mesa, MSA	3,251,876	2,140,171	127,227	817,012	84,126
Minneapolis-St. Paul, MSA	2,968,806	2,514,494	180,006	99,121	138,066
Nassau-Suffolk, PMSA	2,753,913	2,105,352	238,293	282,693	108,249
St. Louis, MSA	2,603,607	2,014,776	486,602	39,677	44,167
Baltimore, PMSA	2,552,994	1,692,851	712,002	51,329	77,932
Seattle-Bellevue, PMSA	2,414,616	1,841,254	124,410	126,675	270,728
Tampa-St. Petersburg, MSA	2,395,997	1,821,955	248,058	248,642	53,724
Pittsburgh, MSA	2,358,695	2,100,501	200,229	17,100	30,192
Cleveland-Lorain, PMSA	2,250,871	1,697,660	425,722	74,862	35,914
Portland-Vancouver, PMSA	1,918,009	1,564,685	61,373	142,444	111,732

SOURCE: Adapted from Lewis Mumford Center for Comparative Urban and Regional Research, *Metropolitan Ethnic and Racial Change, Census 2000.*

and now live alongside white families in downtown high-rise apartment buildings, upscale city neighborhoods, and a wide range of suburban communities across the metropolitan area. However, much of the African American population remains highly segregated; in Chapter 10, we discuss the immense problems this segregation poses for the quality of urban life. The sights and sounds of poverty and discrimination and the symbols of political struggle mark racial ghettos from other urban settlement spaces.

Hispanics

Much of the American Southwest, including parts of California, Arizona, New Mexico, and Texas, once belonged to the country of Mexico. Over time these lands were taken over by the United States. As a result, a significant Mexican population was included within our borders and for many decades suffered discrimination at the hands of the "Anglos," or non-Hispanic Americans. Due to the language barrier, they also found it difficult to achieve mobility. Settlement in much of the Southwest was confined to specific ghettos or barrios, which literally means "neighborhood" (Moore, 1976).

In 2000, there were more than 35.3 million Hispanics in the United States—some 12.5 percent of the total population. Mexicans constituted roughly 67 percent of all Hispanics (U.S. Bureau of the Census, 2000). Between 1990 and 2000, the Hispanic population as a whole increased by more than 57 percent. This figure underestimates the total number of Hispanics, because many are illegal aliens. Mexicans continue to cross over to the United States in record numbers, and the community will retain its rapid growth rate in the future. Most settle in the border states of California and Texas. Often overlooked are the longtime urban populations of Midwestern cities such as Chicago and Detroit, where Mexican and Mexican American workers were recruited to work in the steel mills, auto assembly plants, and meatpacking houses in the 1920s. Chicago's Mexican neighborhoods now contain the third-largest Mexican population in the United States (Hutchison, 1998), and the Chicago metropolitan region includes spillover suburban communities adjacent to the city and new barrios in the manufacturing suburbs, as well as third- and fourth-generation suburban families in the northern Indiana area.

In the Southwest, some barrio areas are known for gang-related activities and a high rate of murder, principally caused by gang violence (Moore, 1978; Vigil, 1988); others are simply areas where Mexican American families can find housing. Recently, however, Mexican Americans have achieved a certain level of mobility and have entered the ranks of the professional middle class. For example, Denver and Los Angeles elected their first Mexican American mayor; Tomas Rivera served as a chancellor of the University of California; and several Mexican Americans are now members of Congress and the president's cabinet. As language barriers are overcome, and with their increasing numbers, this group is expected to play a greater role in U.S. society.

Puerto Ricans

In 1898, the United States defeated Spain in a war of "manifest destiny" and acquired the former Spanish colonies of Cuba, Puerto Rico, Hawaii, and the Philippines. Since that time, Puerto Rico has been governed as a trust, or dependent territory, of the United States. Although the island does not have statehood, Puerto Ricans are citizens of the United States and vote for a representative in the House of Representatives. Like other Caribbean countries, most of the population of Puerto Rico is mestizo—a racial mixture of various European and African ethnic populations—but it has large white and black populations as well. For many years there was a small Puerto Rican presence in the United States, largely limited to Miami and New York, but in the decades after World War II this changed dramatically.

In the 1950s, labor shortages led the U.S. government to recruit workers from Mexico and the Caribbean. The Puerto Rican communities in Chicago, Philadelphia, and other cities were formed around this migration of laborers

TABLE 8.4 Cities with Largest Hispanic Populations, 2000

Total Hispanic		Mexican		Puerto Rican	
Los Angeles-Long Beach, CA	4,242,213	Los Angeles-Long Beach, CA	3,041,974	New York, NY	837,073
New York, NY	2,339,836	Chicago, IL	1,062,264	Philadelphia, PA-NJ	160,076
Chicago, IL	1,416,584	Riverside-San Bernardino, CA	995,651	Chicago, IL	152,045
Miami, FL	1,291,737	Houston, TX	908,105	Orlando, FL	139,898
Houston, TX	1,248,586	Orange County, CA	712,496	Newark, NJ	86,208
Riverside-San Bernardino, CA	1,228,962	San Antonio, TX	572,323	Hartford, CT	82,992
Orange County, CA	875,579	Phoenix-Mesa, AZ	667,747	Miami, FL	80,327
Phoenix-Mesa, AZ	817,012	Dallas, TX	642,800	Tampa-St. Petersburg, FL	75,621
San Antonio, TX	816,037	San Diego, CA	628,460	Nassau-Suffolk, NY	74,796
Dallas, TX	810,499	El Paso, TX	447,065	Springfield, MA	61,310
San Diego, CA	750,965	McAllen-Edinburg, TX	433,198	Boston, MA-NH	58,178
El Paso, TX	531,654	Fresno, CA	349,109	Bergen-Passaic, NJ	58,614
McAllen-Edinburg, TX	503,100	San Jose, CA	323,489	Jersey City, NJ	58,312
Oakland, CA	441,686	Oakland, CA	305,256	Fort Lauderdale, FL	54,938
Washington, DC	432,003	Austin-San Marcos, TX	248,855	Cleveland-Lorain, OH	46,117
Fresno, CA	406,151	Denver, CO	254,986	Middlesex-Somerset, NJ	40,295
San Jose, CA	403,401	Fort Worth-Arlington, TX	247,079	Los Angeles-Long Beach, CA	37,862
Denver, CO	397,236	Brownsville-Harlingen, TX	226,680	Bridgeport, CT	38,307
Austin-San Marcos, TX	327,760	Las Vegas, NV-AZ	232,145	New Haven-Meriden, CT	34,509
Las Vegas, NV-AZ	322,038	Bakersfield, CA	210,828	Allentown-Bethlehem, PA	33,528

SOURCE: Adapted from Lewis Mumford Center for Comparative Urban and Regional Research, *Metropolitan Ethnic and Racial Change, Census 2000.*

from the island. Although Spanish Harlem in Manhattan (New York City) may be the best-known area of Puerto Rican settlement in the country, in the 1960s there was a large increase in Puerto Rican populations in many cities, especially in the Northeast. Like other ethnic groups, Puerto Ricans often settled into older neighborhoods in the central city. Because most Puerto Ricans are part black, some believe they confront greater discrimination in employment and housing than other Hispanic groups; in fact, Puerto Ricans rank alongside African Americans on many measures of poverty, unemployment, and family disruption.

In the 1980s, sociologists began to study the return migration of Puerto Ricans from the urban centers of the North to the home communities of their parents on the island (Alicea, 1990). Although the Puerto Rican population on the mainland has continued to grow from both natural increase and migration, many households and individuals have chosen to return to the island (a decision prompted by both a loss of basic employment in American cities and the discrimination that darker-skinned Puerto Ricans may confront). While we often read of the "problems" of immigrant adjustment for ethnic groups arriving in the United States (as discussed earlier in this chapter), researchers have studied the adjustment of people returning to the island. Just as bilingual programs are required to teach immigrant children to speak English in public schools across the country, bilingual programs in Puerto Rico teach children coming from the United States to speak Spanish so that they can complete their education and find employment on the island.

Asian Americans

The Asian American population has increased dramatically over the past several decades; it is concentrated in large metropolitan areas and in the Pacific coast states (see Table 8.5). The Asian population represents a number of very diverse ethnic populations, groups that have distinctive cultural differences (they speak different languages, they practice different religions, and they eat different foods) and residential patterns. Most large cities in the United States have an older Chinatown, reflecting the early immigration of Chinese laborers to the United States to work in mining and to build the railroads. There were significant Japanese communities in the Pacific states before World War II; these communities were forcibly relocated by the government during the war, and many Japanese families moved to other cities at the end of the war. The more recent immigration of Asian Americans in large numbers has resulted in new Chinese and Japanese settlements, usually in the suburbs of the larger metropolitan areas. Korean immigrants have established an ethnic niche in small business in the inner city and often are concentrated in new Koreatowns in the outer city and suburbs. The cities with the largest Asian populations are shown in Table 8.5.

Filipinos are likely the most Americanized of the Asian immigrants (the Philippine Islands became an American colony following the Spanish American War of 1898 and did not become an independent country until after World War II). Most of the Filipino immigrants to the United States are Catholic and speak English, which facilitates their integration into older urban neighborhoods as well as newer suburban communities. Although there are regional differences, in many cities Filipinos are dispersed across the metropolitan region with no identifiable ethnic center, whereas smaller communities of Vietnamese and other refugee populations, such as Laotians and Hmong, are the most concentrated in distinct residential communities (such as Uptown in Chicago and the Midway neighborhood in St. Paul-Minneapolis).

One suburban Asian community that has been studied in some detail is Monterey Park, a suburb outside Los Angeles that became a focal point for new Chinese immigration. In 1960, the population was 85 percent white. By 2000, more than 234,000 Asian persons were counted in the census, and the population was 43.0 percent Asian, 35.3 percent Hispanic, and just 21.6 percent white. Chinese accounted for 140,000 or 25.8 percent of the total, Vietnamese for 28,000 or 5.1 percent of the total, and Filipinos and Japanese for another 27,000 or 6.2 percent of the total. Much of the Chinese population consisted of new immigrants from China (Logan and Mollenkopf, 2003:67). By 1991, recent arrivals to the United States had invested over $1 billion of their own money in the suburb, and it was estimated that Chinese owned at least 66 percent of all business and property in the suburb (Espiritu and Light, 1991:43). For a time, the city was known as the Chinese Beverly Hills, and it later was referred to as the first suburban Chinatown (Arax, 1987).

Timothy P. Fong (1994) studied the growth of the Chinese population in Monterey Park during the 1980s and 1990s. He identified three prominent changes that accompanied the development of this multicultural suburb from the early 1970s to the early 1990s. The first involved the economic transformation of the community that accompanied the influx of Chinese immigrants and capital. Pro-growth advocates welcomed the first groups of Chinese professionals who moved to the community, as well as overseas Chinese investors. This led to land speculation, uncontrolled construction, and increased commercial and home property values. This in turn led to the relocation of many long-time merchants to other communities, the development of strip malls as commercial properties were subdivided, and the replacement of single-family homes with multi-unit apartment complexes. The end result

TABLE 8.5   Cities/Regions with Largest Asian Population, 2000

Total Asian		Chinese		Filipino		Japanese	
L.A.-Long Beach, CA	1,284,112	New York, NY	386,313	L.A.-Long Beach, CA	296,708	Honolulu, HI	230,044
New York, NY	956,071	L.A.-Long Beach, CA	334,764	Honolulu, HI	191,393	L.A.-Long Beach, CA	138,080
Honolulu, HI	619,253	San Francisco, CA	218,469	San Diego, CA	145,132	Orange County, CA	41,767
San Jose, CA	472,530	Oakland, CA	152,439	Oakland, CA	123,705	Seattle-Bellevue, WA	35,288
Oakland, CA	461,028	Honolulu, HI	135,464	San Francisco, CA	114,433	San Jose, CA	35,124
San Francisco, CA	435,082	San Jose, CA	122,790	Chicago, IL	93,033	New York, NY	34,350
Orange County, CA	434,778	Boston, MA-NH	74,744	San Jose, CA	87,806	Oakland, CA	30,516
Chicago, IL	429,533	Chicago, IL	72,512	New York, NY	72,352	San Francisco, CA	30,243
Washington, DC	379,949	Washington, DC	68,227	Orange County, CA	60,000	San Diego, CA	29,028
San Diego, CA	303,204	Orange County, CA	61,174	Riverside-S. Bernardino, CA	59,093	Chicago, IL	23,395
Seattle-Bellevue, WA	272,961	Seattle-Bellevue, WA	56,111	Seattle-Bellevue, WA	57,015	Sacramento, CA	20,904
Houston, TX	245,418	Houston, TX	48,294	Washington, DC	47,350	Washington, DC	15,714
Philadelphia, PA-NJ	196,054	Philadelphia, PA-NJ	41,940	Vallejo-Fairfield, CA	45,345	Riverside-S. Bernardino, CA	15,258
Boston, MA-NH	186,783	Sacramento, CA	37,818	Las Vegas, NV-AZ	42,596	Portland-Vancouver, OR-WA	13,730
Sacramento, CA	178,894	San Diego, CA	36,660	Sacramento, CA	37,317	Las Vegas, NV-AZ	10,868
Riverside-S. Bernardino, CA	174,117	Middlesex-Somerset, NJ	30,915	Norfolk-Virginia Beach, VA	29,550	Boston, MA-NH	10,827
Dallas, TX	160,971	Dallas, TX	29,057	Stockton-Lodi, CA	28,214	Denver, CO	10,541
Atlanta, GA	155,117	Nassau-Suffolk, NY	28,275	Houston, TX	24,692	Bergen-Passaic, NJ	8,824
Minneapolis-St. Paul, MN	142,322	Atlanta, GA	24,078	Jersey City, NJ	20,066	Detroit, MI	8,621
Middlesex-Somerset, NJ	140,599	Riverside-S. Bernardino, CA	22,600	Bergen-Passaic, NJ	19,908	Phoenix-Mesa, AZ	8,500

SOURCE: Adapted from Lewis Mumford Center for Comparative Urban and Regional Research, *Metropolitan Ethnic and Racial Change, Census 2000.*

was greater density, increased traffic congestion, a loss of open space, and decreased parking. Fong notes that the new economic investment in Monterey Park included small-scale, low-profit, family-run businesses such as small restaurants, curio shops, and specialty stores owned by Chinese immigrant families with few English language skills; professional services such as medical, legal, accounting, and real estate offices run by college-educated Chinese Americans; and Chinese-owned and operated financial institutions, including banks and savings and loans. The economic transformation of the community led to a backlash in the larger community and to comments such as, "This feels like a foreign country!"

The second stage in the development of Monterey Park involved the community's response to the challenge that the new Chinese immigrants presented to the dominant cultural values and to community identity more generally. Older residents looked back at what they recalled as the small-town lifestyle of the suburb and felt threatened by the social changes that accompanied economic development and the influx of Chinese immigrants. Other minority populations in the community, including many Hispanic and Asian American households, also felt threatened by the new immigrants. These sentiments were exploited by some in the community through a variety of anti-immigrant, anti-Asian, and English-only movements that were common across the United States in the 1970s. The economic transformation brought about by the new immigrant community was viewed by some in negative terms as the immigrant institutions began to compete for social and political recognition within the established culture of the older suburban community. When a group of progressive Asian, Hispanic, and white activists joined with pro-growth businessmen to promote multicultural issues, many in the community viewed the group as a political cover for developers and speculators. As Fong noted, race and ethnicity were now used as tools for political organizing (1994:175–176).

The third stage involves continuing efforts to deal with complex controversies resulting from racial, ethnic, and class conflict within the community. Older divisions of white against black, majority against minority, and the like are no longer sufficient to encompass the inter- and intra-ethnic differences among long-term residents (many of them minority) and new immigrants, Chinese Americans and immigrant Chinese, Chinese and other Asian American groups, and other divisions. Although Fong described these as "prominent changes" that have taken place in the community, we have referred to these changes as "stages of development" because they describe the experience of many other suburban communities where new immigrant communities have become established. The process is also described by Logan and Mollenkopf (2003) in their study of political representation in

New York and Los Angeles in association with the demographic changes brought about by new immigration. In the first stage, native blacks and Hispanics become the majority or near majority in urban neighborhoods and then in entire cities. In the second stage, new immigrant groups replace native-born blacks and Hispanics to become the majority or near majority in urban neighborhoods. This results in a new, multicultural city where older racial cleavages have been "blurred and transformed" and where new multi-ethnic coalitions must be formed around common issues that unite rather than divide ethnic groups, classes, and immigrant generations within urban and suburban communities and across the metropolitan region.

Native Americans

The residential settlement patterns of Native Americans are especially interesting. Some Indian tribes continue to live in the same communities first visited by Spanish explorers in the 1500s; indeed, the twelve Pueblo communities outside of Albuquerque, New Mexico, are the oldest continuously inhabited towns in the United States. Other Indian tribes were forced from their homelands by the Indian Removal Act of 1830. The Cherokees had by that time established permanent towns and schools but were forcibly removed from their homes in Georgia, Alabama, and Tennessee and relocated to reservation land in Oklahoma. During the 1870s, the United States ceased to recognize these people as belonging to independent nations, and they came under the administration of the Bureau of Indian Affairs. In the 1950s, the federal government passed the Indian Relocation Act, which gave incentives to American Indians to leave reservations and move to urban centers. More recently, economic development on many reservations has led to a reverse migration as many individuals and families have returned to the reservations that they may only have visited as children.

In the 2000 census some 2.5 million persons identified themselves as American Indian, an increase of 517,000 persons (26 percent) from the 1980 census. The increase is due in part to demographic structure (the population is relatively young and there is a high birthrate), but also because more persons are identifying their American Indian heritage. (Indeed, another 1.6 million persons indicated that they were part American Indian in the 2000 census.) There are more than 520 tribes that are recognized by the federal government; the largest are the Cherokee (729,000), Navaho (298,000), Choctaw (158,000), Sioux (153,000) and Chippewa (150,000) (Ogunwole, 2002).

While we often think of Native Americans as an isolated group living on rural reservations, they also represent an urban population. More than half (57 percent in 2000) of the American Indian population lives in urban areas with especially large concentrations in Los Angeles, Phoenix, and other metropoli-

TABLE 8.6   Cities with Largest Native American Population, 2000

New York City	41,289
Los Angeles	29,412
Phoenix	26,696
Chicago	10,290
Tulsa	18,551
Albuquerque	17,444
San Antonio	9,584
Houston	8,583
San Diego	7,543
Dallas	6,742
Philadelphia	4,073
Detroit	3,140

SOURCE: U.S. Bureau of the Census. 2003. *The American Indian and Alaska Native Population, 2000.*

tan regions, as shown in Table 8.6. The Indian Relocation Act greatly increased the number of Indians living in cities in the post-war period (between 1952 and 1970 nearly 100,000 Indians were relocated to urban areas by the Bureau of Indian Affairs; Champagne et al., 1996). But the recent growth of Indian populations in urbanized areas is also connected with the fact that in several areas of the country Indian reservations are located in metropolitan areas of large cities (such as the Salt River and Gila River reservations outside of Phoenix and the Shakopee Mdewakanton Sioux reservation outside of Minneapolis) or even within the boundaries of cities (such as the Oneida reservation in Green Bay, Wisconsin). For many years, Native Americans suffered extreme poverty regardless of their residence in cities or reservations, and to some degree this is still true. But over the last two decades, many Indian tribes have prospered from economic development associated with casino gambling, although in many ways the patterns of uneven development endemic in the larger economic system have been replicated among Indian tribes across the country.

As we learned earlier, the federal government began cutting funding to states and cities in the 1970s. Instead of raising taxes to cover the additional expense of social programs, politicians in many states passed amendments to their state constitutions that allowed state lotteries. As a consequence of this action, a series of court cases established that Indian tribes (sovereign nations with legal rights comparable to those of states) may run the same type of gambling enterprises (such as lotteries and, by extension, games of chance) as state governments. The rise of the Native American casino industry is a direct consequence of the fiscal crises of the federal and state governments. Indian reservations located close to urban centers have been able to generate substantial revenues from casinos. The actual development strategies used vary greatly from tribe to tribe. In Phoenix, the Salt River Reservation has leased land to a development company that built and manages the largest shopping mall in the metropolitan area, while in Green Bay the Oneida Indian Nation has used profits from gaming to fund new health clinics and elder housing, to purchase land within reservation boundaries lost in previous generations, and to diversify into retail businesses and manufacturing companies. Many of these reservations have seen a population increase as tribal members living in cities across the country have returned to employment opportunities that did not exist two decades earlier. Yet uneven development may still be the rule; while tribes near urban areas have prospered, those in remote areas of the country have been unable to generate revenue from gaming and remain very poor. And within individual tribes, there remains substantial concern over high levels of poverty, family disruption, and low rates of high school completion.

It is often said that the urban Indian population is largely invisible. Lobo (2005:1) notes that "this invisibility or perceived elusiveness is tied directly to urban Indian community characteristics, including a dispersed, rather than a residentially clustered, population and individual mobility." While there are American Indian cultural centers in most large cities that serve as focal points for community activities, these centers serve households representing many different Indian tribes—groups that often are culturally distinct from one another. Over the last two decades, Indian populations have moved into many different areas of the city and for the most part do not form visible ethnic neighborhoods. For many families there is frequent travel back to Indian reservations to visit or care for relatives. Lobo (2003:8) concludes that "Urban Indian communities may, because they are dispersed and based on a network of relations, for the most part be invisible or misunderstood from the outside and to outsiders, but they are anything but invisible to those who participate in them. They are viable communities, but structured on an American Indian-derived model of community or tribe rather than a European-derived one."

CONCLUSION: ETHNIC AND RACIAL DIVERSITY ACROSS THE METROPOLIS

As this summary of settlement patterns for ethnic groups demonstrates, sociospatial relations continue to play a significant role in the lives of minority groups in the United States. Some groups have been able to move into the mainstream of American society and have gained access to employment, housing, and the quality of life that we believe all Americans should have. Others remain in segregated social spaces—ghettos, barrios, or reservations—where they are isolated from opportunities in the larger society.

In the years to come, these new sources of ethnic formation and ethnic identity will influence U.S. culture in ways we have yet to anticipate, just as the formidable influx of Eastern Europeans did some one hundred years ago. At the beginning of the twentieth century, many people feared that foreign workers would take away the jobs of American workers and dilute or destroy American institutions; yet those foreigners are now a permanent part of the American mosaic. In the 1990s, the United States experienced the lowest level of unemployment in nearly half a century at the same time that immigration reached near-record levels, suggesting that immigrant workers may not jeopardize the jobs of American workers. Immigration was not a political issue.

However, in the first decade of the twenty-first century, a group calling itself the Minutemen has organized to patrol the border with Mexico, claiming that high levels of illegal immigration are responsible for the loss of American jobs and the increased costs for public services. Under pressure from large and small businesses, the Bush administration has responded with a proposal to register illegal immigrants as guest workers (this designation is used in many European countries), which would increase the supply of labor, keep wages low, and increase profits. Immigration has once again become a political issue, an issue that has great importance for the future of metropolitan areas across the country.

In a few short decades, the new immigrants of today will become part of an even greater American mosaic, living in ethnic neighborhoods if they choose or do so or living alongside other groups across the metropolitan region. As we will see in Chapter 10, new immigrants have changed the complexion of metropolitan politics. Only time will tell what form this influence will take, but immigration from Asia and Latin America to the United States will likely continue at its active pace well into the twenty-first century.

Years ago it was proper to speak of an "urban mosaic" (a term used extensively by Robert Park) to capture the diversity of people and lifestyles in the city. Today the term is appropriate for the entire metropolitan region, both central cities and suburbs. As we have seen, urban and suburban settlement space is stratified by class, race, and gender. Settlement space is also differentiated according to ethnicity, age, and family status. Each lifestyle manifests its own daily rhythm within the settlement spaces each group has created within the metropolitan region. The built environment displays the expressive symbols of this interaction between social factors and local territory. But settlement space also directs behavior in certain ways. In contemporary societies, sociospatial relations among groups and individuals are conditioned by class and race distinctions ranging from inclusion in neighborhoods of shared interests to the extreme case of ghetto segregation.

Economic and political forces influence sociospatial patterns by planning and regulating the built environment. But so do cultural features. Class, racial, gender, and ethnic differences are expressed as symbols that imply difference. Images of a large home, an expensive car, certain styles of clothing—all patterns of everyday consumption—are potent signs of status. Racial interaction operates largely through the regulation of appearance and of segregated social space. This semiotic dimension of the sociospatial perspective will be discussed more fully in the next chapter. The diversity of metropolitan life has been studied in great detail. In fact, such explorations of the everyday texture of urban and suburban life have formed a central focus for the work of urban sociologists since the early days of the Chicago School. A variety of methodological perspectives are employed in the study of everyday life in urban and suburban settlement spaces, including participant observation, interviews, network analysis, and semiotics. We discuss each of these approaches in the next chapter.

KEY CONCEPTS

race relations cycle
new immigration
ethnic enclaves

DISCUSSION QUESTIONS

1. What is meant by the term immigrant gateway city? Is your city included in this list? If so, what are some of the new immigrant groups in your community? If not, among what kind of immigrant gateway would your city be classified?

2. Immigration to the United States has increased substantially over the past four decades and now is at the highest level in nearly one hundred years. Why has this occurred? What groups are likely to favor this high level of immigration? What groups are likely to oppose it? How do you think immigration will change in the next decade?

3. What are the major ethnic populations in the community that you grew up in? In the metropolitan region where you grew up? Do these groups represent the older waves of immigration or the more recent third wave of immigration to the United States?

4. The chapter describes very different settlement patterns for various ethnic and racial groups in the United States. How does the process of segregation influence the spatial location of different ethnic and racial groups? How do the different theories of immigrant adjustment account for the spatial location of different groups?

5. Compare the advantages and disadvantages of ethnic enclaves for recent immigrants. Do you think that the government should provide home-ownership subsidies to encourage persons living in ethnic enclaves to purchase homes in other areas of a metropolitan region? Do you think that the government should provide small-business loans to entrepreneurs who wish to open or expand their businesses within ethnic enclaves?

NEIGHBORHOODS, THE PUBLIC ENVIRONMENT, AND THEORIES OF URBAN LIFE

Film directors usually establish a Manhattan location by filming a long shot of some busy street in midtown or the financial district. In it we see a crowd of people pressed together—a sea of bobbing heads hurrying on their way to and from business. To establish the location of Los Angeles, in contrast, film-makers often take to the air and provide a helicopter shot of clogged freeways, or at other times, shoot from a car moving slowly on palm tree–lined streets.

Every place possesses some distinguishing feature that can be enjoyed, whether it is the picturesque quality and friendly people of the small town, the quiet and spaciousness of the suburbs, or the hustle and bustle of the large city. A resident of the metropolitan region has a choice on any given day of whether to experience the cultural amenities of urban or suburban life. These opportunities are a function of the activities or features found in particular places, such as cities or suburbs, rather than arising from the particular environment of a city or suburb itself. But many urban sociologists insist that the nature of space does produce differences in behavior on its own so that the city—any city—would influence behavior in specific ways.

The arguments, both pro and con, regarding whether urban and suburban settlement spaces have the ability to change behavior constitute the focus for the study of metropolitan culture. Investigations of urban and suburban ways of life constitute a large part of research by urban sociologists. In Chapter 3 we studied the early contributions of sociologists to the study of urbanism, particularly those associated with the Chicago School, which focused exclusively on the city. In this chapter we consider more contemporary studies exploring the relationship between spatial location and social interaction for all communities in the metropolitan region, including suburbs and cities.

DOES SPACE AFFECT BEHAVIOR? THE SEARCH FOR COMMUNITY

Early urban sociologists in the 1920s and 1930s were preoccupied with whether urban settlement space produced differences in behavior, specifically when contrasted with the rural way of life. Hundreds of thousands of people left the farms and small towns of America and moved to the large industrial cities looking for work. At that time, sociologists worked with an idealized image of small-town life and were suspicious of the city. They believed that small towns offered people a sense of community resulting from primary or intimate ties in social relationships. In contrast, early researchers viewed cities as destroyers of intimacy, forcing secondary or anonymous relations on individuals, with a consequent loss of community feeling. In contrast to the "friendly" rural town, city people were believed to be unfriendly, rushed, uncaring, suspicious, and hard to get to know.

As we also saw in Chapter 3, Louis Wirth, of the Chicago School, believed that living in large cities resulted in forms of social disorganization such as increased crime, divorce, and mental illness because of the decline of close community ties. For Wirth it was the city itself, operating through demographic factors such as size and density of population, that produced urban behavior. When we go to a store in a city, we do not have, nor do we seek, a close relationship with the salesperson. We simply want service and wish to make our purchases as quickly as possible. Rural area residents, in contrast, are likely to already have established primary relationships with the employees and even the owners of local businesses. The same contrast applies to relations with neighbors in the city and rural areas. The domination of secondary relations in the city, Wirth believed, would result in negative effects such as crime and other problems. This assertion is known as the social disorganization thesis of urban life.

Field Research on Community

Following World War II, a number of sociologists decided to challenge Wirth's theory. Studying local neighborhoods within the larger cities, these sociologists discovered communities with strong primary relations among the residents (Whyte, 1955; Gans, 1962). In the 1960s and 1970s, a series of community studies contradicted the social disorganization thesis of the early Chicago School. Researchers discovered evidence of vital, healthy primary relations and an active community life in urban neighborhoods. Ulf Hannerz's (1969) remarkable study of an inner-city ghetto area in Washington, D.C., exemplifies the case study approach to community. This fine-grained analysis depicts ghetto residents as multidimensional human beings, trapped in the ghetto by racism and poverty. Hannerz could not find a single "characteristic" ghetto resident. Rather, he discovered a typology of behavioral patterns reflecting differences in individual character and family organization as each person dealt with racial and economic adversity in his or her own way. These results have been replicated in Elijah Anderson's (1978) ethnographic account of a black neighborhood on Chicago's South Side titled *A Place on the Corner.*

To the outside observer, densely populated inner-city neighborhoods seem chaotic. One sterling accomplishment of field research has been to document the order created out of urban chaos by city residents. Herbert Gans's (1962) classic field study of Boston's East End challenged the view that the area was a "slum" and discovered that life in this working-class community was highly organized around peer groups. Adult males spent leisure time with other males, adult females with their female friends, and so on. Once the form of social organization of the community was understood, it became a familiar place.

Field research carried out in the 1950s and 1960s showed that primary relations and an intimate community life could be found in suburban settlement space. One of the earliest studies of suburban communities was William H. Whyte's *The Organization Man* (1956). Whyte studied the development of Park Forest South, a new planned suburban community located some twenty-five miles south of the Chicago Loop. His research depicts the classic suburb of the early post-war period as a place where nuclear families were housed in single-family, detached homes, where women did not work but spent their time in housekeeping chores and chats over coffee with neighbors, and where men commuted into the city to corporate, professional jobs. For more recent examples, see Baumgartner (1988), Jackson (1985), and Fishman (1987).

While city-based analyses tended to focus on the working classes or "ethnics" with extended familial ties to kin and neighbors who lived in close proximity, suburban studies concentrated on the middle-class nuclear family and its communal relations among friends. This division of labor, which follows from Burgess's model of urban growth as well as Wirth's description of urban life, gave the false impression that social classes had become stratified within urban and suburban settlement spaces. Bennett Berger's (1960) study of working-class households in suburban Richmond, California, was an important milestone, arguing that working-class individuals who moved to the suburbs did not automatically change their behavior and attitudes and become middle class; instead, they preserved their working-class way of life in this new environment. Throughout the 1970s and 1980s, urban ecologists were busy discovering the diversity of social classes and ethnic groups in the suburbs. They concluded that while individual suburbs were internally homogeneous, the suburban region was heterogeneous. We know now that the entire metropolitan region is in fact quite diverse, and this is true not just of urban settlement space but also within and between suburban settlement spaces, as discussed in Chapter 6.

The sociospatial perspective suggests that there are no unique differences in social life between urban and suburban settlement spaces. After several decades of comparative field work, it is clear that cities and suburbs are home to a variety of lifestyles, which are more a function of the complex interplay among class, ethnicity, race, and gender than a result of living in a particular environment. Does this conclusion mean that location has no effect whatsoever on personal behavior? Field research tended to debunk the social disorganization thesis of urban life, but another method, network analysis, discovered conditions under which location did play a specific role in people's lives. Let us consider this research tradition next.

Network Analysis: Does Location Matter?

In the 1970s, Claude Fischer (1975) claimed that while most of the differences among individuals in the metropolis were caused by background factors such as class and race, certain attributes of behavior differed among people according to their location. Because of the size of urban populations, residents of the large city had the opportunity to act in ways that rural residents would ordinarily find more difficult. According to this subcultural perspective on urban life, city dwellers have a greater opportunity to establish relations with a greater variety of people than do persons in places with smaller populations. It is these relationships, or networks, that sustain differences in lifestyles observed between city and rural dwellers. Hence, according to Fischer, the subcultural diversity of cities created by large population size does produce differences between urban and rural behaviors.

Following the subcultural perspective, Fischer (1982) documented the effect of location on the quality and structure of personal networks. He found that individuals in the city differed from rural counterparts in that they had fewer kin or more unrelated intimates in their personal networks. However, Fischer also discovered that the effect of place alone, when controlling for all other factors, was quite small. The single most important predictor of nonkin networks was education: the more years of education, the more nonrelatives

BOX 9.1   Social Network Analysis

The study of social networks in urban sociology originates in the work of two British social anthropologists. J. A. Barnes described social networks as groups of persons interconnected by friendship and kinship relations (Barnes, 1954). Elizabeth Bott's (1957) study of working-class and middle-class households in London was the first study to apply the ideas presented in Barnes's work. She found that the working-class households had overlapping and densely connected family and social networks, whereas the middle-class households had less dense networks. Network analysis uses personal interviews to discover the links among people—whom they interact with on a daily or weekly basis, how many people an individual knows, and so on.

Barry Wellman, a sociologist at the University of Toronto, interviewed urban and suburban residents of the Toronto metropolitan area to determine where their friends and relatives lived and how frequently they visited with each of them. This information allowed Wellman and his colleagues to discover systematic differences in the social networks of urban and suburban residents, and of male and female respondents in both settlement spaces. Wellman (1988) noted that social networks need not be confined to the local neighborhood. In fact, for many urbanites, social networks reach far beyond local settlement space to include friends and coworkers from across the metropolitan area—evidence of the existence of "community without propinquity." With the advent of Internet mail lists and the ubiquitous use of cell phones, social network analysts have expanded upon this earlier work to examine how neighborhood and social networks are constructed across cyberspace.

in an individual's personal network. A second important factor was income, which also contributed to independence from relatives. Thus, although location within urban and suburban settlement space does influence behavior, it is not as powerful as the compositional factors related to education, income, and other social considerations that we discussed in Chapter 7. Box 9.1 examines the network methodology used by Fischer and others to show the differences location makes in lifestyle patterns.

Network analysis has uncovered a second important aspect of urban community relations. As the metropolitan environment of cities and suburbs has matured, people now organize their lives across a greater spatial distance than in the past. Among other things, this means that one's intimate relations may involve people at some distance. Network researchers who have studied this more mature phenomenon of U.S. settlement spaces therefore have redefined our understanding of community, because in the past, people assumed that an individual was most friendly with those who lived nearby as neighbors.

According to Wellman (1979, 1988), the concept of community must be rethought to emphasize the *non*-neighborhood basis of personal ties. People's communities consist of networks that are not spatially distinct but are dispersed across the metropolis and the country.

In the urban literature, this phenomenon is referred to as "community without locality." Among other things, it has been cell phones, Blackberries, and e-mail, that is, new modes of electronic telecommunication, that have contributed to the ability of people to form networks of intimates without regard for spatial location. As discussed in a separate section below, the classical concepts of both "community" and "neighborhood" must be redefined because people today form primary relations through networking at a distance, rather than through intimate contact with local neighbors.

Current research using network analysis on community relations suggests that although spatial location matters, its effects are not large. Other factors, such as class, education, gender, and race, are more important when explaining urban behavior, as we saw in Chapter 6. Because network researchers look at the role of space in only a very specific way, they miss important influences of the built environment. The sociospatial perspective conceives of the influence of space in a broader, more general way while acknowledging the central role played by social factors. In the following section, we consider the role of space in social interaction to highlight how urban and suburban settlement spaces interact with compositional factors. We discuss the new theory of urbanism and look at several issues in which spatial or contextual factors count heavily in our understanding of urban and suburban behavior.

DOES SPACE AFFECT BEHAVIOR?
A NEW THEORY OF URBANISM

The Sociospatial Approach to Metropolitan Culture

Today all areas of the metropolitan region exhibit tremendous diversity. Instead of discussing lifestyle differences as a function of urbanism, it makes increasingly more sense to adopt a metropolitan perspective and relate social differences to locational differences in the region. We suggest that lifestyles within the metropolitan region are explained best by a combination of compositional or social factors and the action of the environment. Although population size and density of the city do play a role in producing distinctive lifestyles, these factors affect settlement space as well as demographic characteristics. The quality of the environment conditions the opportunities available for distinctive lifestyles.

For example, Manhattan in New York City is known for its active street culture. Over 1 million inhabitants are squeezed onto an island that is less than 20 square miles in area. One aspect of Manhattan street behavior involves a strong emphasis on fashion and appearance as a way of judging other people (we will discuss the phenomenon of fashion later). Consequently, New York subcultures possess a highly developed sense of clothing differences. In contrast, Los Angeles dress is notoriously casual. It is not uncommon to see people appearing at fancy restaurants in the least formal attire. Los Angelenos stress the importance of cars in everyday life, and several subcultures have developed around the use of the automobile as an expressive symbol, such as the Chicano low-rider clubs. The city of Los Angeles encompasses almost 1,000 square miles, and public transportation is limited. Consequently, it is understandable to find cars playing so important a role in daily life. Manhattan is a pedestrian town, whereas Los Angeles is notorious for its reliance on the automobile, and this helps to explain some of the cultural differences between the two places, although there are also other reasons, such as historical and demographic differences.

Second, in addition to the influence of the spatial environment on behavior, people's actions are organized according to how they view particular places. Urban and suburban settlement spaces, like other objects in society, possess a social meaning; that is, place or location has a symbolic value that helps to determine behavior. For example, Hummon's (1986) comparative study of big-city, suburban, and small-town residents, using a questionnaire and interview method, found that individuals in each location possessed different imagery by which they reinforced their own positive feelings about where they lived and negative feelings about alternative locations. For the most part, residents of big cities, suburbs, and small towns each participated in the construction of positive images of place rather than all subscribing to some anti-urban bias or some universal desire to escape the city for either the suburbs or a small town.

Third, while all individuals possess a distinctive lifestyle that is based in part on their collectively held symbolic values, they are also constrained by material factors, such as income, in choosing where to live or locate economic activity. People in cities and suburbs selectively locate in different areas of the metropolitan region according to both their symbolic and material needs. Although some portion of their decision is voluntary, where they choose to live may be determined by where they can afford to live or even where they are allowed to live. As we saw in Chapter 6, residential location may also be the consequence of involuntary choice dictated by ethnic or racial factors.

In Chapter 7, we demonstrated the importance of symbolic factors to the patterns of metropolitan life. Let us analyze in more detail how symbolic processes and the sense of place are related to people's behavior in cities and suburbs. In the following section, we examine three aspects of the semiotics of place: mental maps, the spatial context and behavior in public, and the sense of community.

Mental Maps

Cities and suburbs are not simply spaces where people organize their lives; they are also physical environments that are meaningful in different ways to different persons. People assign distinct meanings and associate specific emotions with places. Often a single space, such as the New York City skyline, can invoke an incredible variety of such meaningful associations from individuals. The signifier home, for example, is attached to your place of residence, but it can also signify the block where you live, your neighborhood, or a section of the metropolitan region where your particular living space is located. The feelings of comfort, security, and familiarity associated with your house or apartment may be experienced by returning from a trip outside the neighborhood and glimpsing the familiar objects of the local environment. Sociologists and other urbanists who study the role of meaning and cognition in space often use the method of mental mapping to determine how individuals perceive their physical environment. Box 9.2 provides an example of mental mapping.

People negotiate a metropolitan space of familiar neighborhoods, known workplaces, leisure and consumption places, and unfamiliar areas of little specific meaning. Known places are pictured in great detail by the mind's eye; in between them are areas that are not distinctly detailed. These gray areas are negotiated by direct travel routes so that residents pass through them in the least amount of time possible. Consequently, these zones remain undistinguished. All people, in short, carry with them a "mental map" of their daily routines that varies in its detailed knowledge of space. We use these maps to negotiate space and to assign meanings to different places. Often these maps are a function of power and class differences, or social stratification.

The study of mental maps augments our understanding of how individuals relate to metropolitan environments containing large numbers of people and differentiated activities. Kevin Lynch (1964), an urban planner, discovered not only that variation exists among individuals regarding how they depict a space but also that places themselves vary in their ability to invoke detailed mental images. Thus, a city with an impressive skyline or distinguishing statues and buildings produces an image that is remembered by visitors and residents

BOX 9.2 Mental Mapping

The technique of mental mapping is used to discover how residents of any given place conceive of their environment. They are asked to draw their own local neighborhoods and fill the picture in with as many details as possible. Studies are done by obtaining mental maps from a sample of residents. In all cases, the conception of place will vary from person to person. Researchers then study the causes of such variation by comparing individuals and groups with one another. We know, for example, that the way children draw mental maps of their environment differs from adult maps.

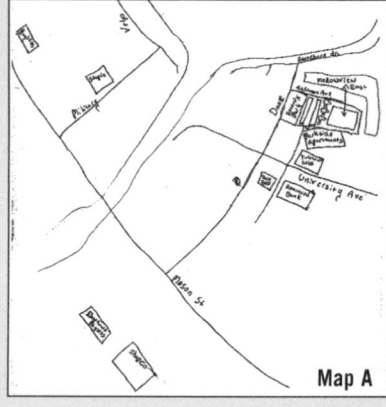

Map A

One of the more common results from mental map research is the discovery that differences in both the conception and meaning of a local place are correlated with differences in class status (Golledge and Rushton, 1976). In general, differences in the conception of space reflect social stratification or the perceived differences regarding power and class in society. Researchers have uncovered racial differences in the way people conceive their local settlement space. One study of the Mission Hill area of Boston, which contains a housing project inhabited primarily by low-income African Americans surrounded by a white community, discovered that the black residents' view of their environment was greatly restricted, while comparable white residents held a much more expansive image of their surroundings (LaGory and Pipkin, 1981:119).

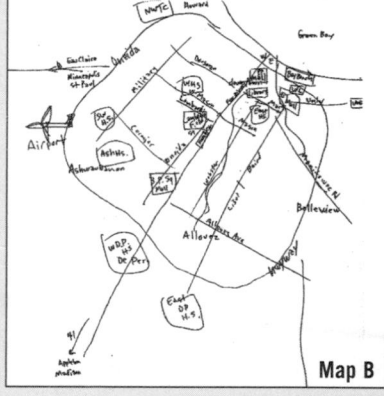

Map B

College students attending the University of Wisconsin–Green Bay drew the two maps shown here. A student who had attended the university for several years but lived in a dorm on campus drew Map A. A student who grew up in the city and commuted to campus to attend class drew Map B. The maps suggest that for the on-campus student, activity was largely centered on shopping areas close to the university, and there was little knowledge of the larger city. The student who lived off campus included a wider range of locations and activities spread across many different neighborhoods in the city. Urban sociologists are interested in the ways in which different groups in the metropolis interact with their environment, and mental mapping gives us some important insights into this question.

alike. In contrast, many places seem so ordinary that their physical appearance is hard to recall even after repeated visits.

Lynch's discovery of the importance of imageability implied that some spaces were better designed than others because they were more legible; that is, they were easier to understand as built environments. Imageability therefore facilitated movement or use. For example, Lynch contrasted the mental maps of residents in two cities—Jersey City, New Jersey; and Boston, Massachusetts. He found that residents of Jersey City had a much less detailed mental image of their space. It was more difficult for them to visualize the features of places they often passed through or went to during the week's routines. Lynch's discovery has important consequences for city planners, architects, and landscapers, as we will see in Chapter 14.

The Semiotics of Place

Mental maps assign meaning to space. But the meanings of objects also come from the various ways we use them as symbols. Material forms, such as particular buildings and constructed spaces like plazas and freeways, all possess meanings that are ascribed to them by social use. They are known to us by their functions, as the study of spatial semiotics suggests (Barthes, 1986). Hence, the phenomenon of the mental map is but a special case of the more general semiotics of settlement space. Malls, theme parks, architectural forms, and neighborhood places all work to orient our behavior and provide us with a sense of place by conveying certain meanings through objects that act as signs of their function as places of business, recreation, amusement, shopping, and the like. Instead of strangeness and disorientation, the signs of space create order and familiarity, which is helpful both in reducing the stress of daily living within giant, metropolitan regions and in enabling residents to use the built environment effectively.

For example, the suburban shopping mall is a successful adaptation of architectural form to the needs of commercial interests. Malls are the counterpart in low-density suburbia of the higher-density city center shopping district. The mall works because of its skillful use of symbols and signs coupled with environmental forms. Malls are designed with large parking lots and blank external façades that make customers respond to the overarching meaning: "For shopping-related activities, enter here." This technique, known as introversion, is meant to discourage prospective customers from dawdling in the mall parking lot. Additional semiotic devices control shoppers once they are inside. Shopping malls feature atriums, "food courts," and even amusement rides for children. Often they are designed with images that invoke city living—avenues with artificial street lamps and small, neatly spaced trees and benches. And because all shoppers are on foot, they provide shoppers with a taste of the typical urban street crowd.

Corporate product signs, or "logos," are also important in the mall. Each store has its own symbolic and functional associations that are the consequence of advertising and of what customers know about its price range. Product signs, or brand-name logos, also take advantage of the fact that people have already been conditioned by advertising to associate certain products with store signs. These internalized associations are then used to advantage in the mall by directing people's attention to specific stores or products. They hold such power only because consumers have already become familiar with them in their daily lives, so they respond to their stimulus and are oriented in their journey through the mall. Customers are able to "read" the space of the mall and make their way through it with ease so that shopping is as stressless as possible. But shopping malls are not public spaces, and they may not be open to all persons.

Behavior in Public Space

For many years, urban sociologists have been aware that the large city with its dense crowds offers special challenges to residents. They have studied the way people negotiate this particular environment and have found that the techniques of accommodation that are used constitute much of what we might identify as uniquely urban behavior. Yet this interaction, which takes place in public space where strangers as pedestrians encounter others in places such as malls, department stores, and bars, also occurs in suburbia. For this reason, the study of behavior in public space can take place throughout the metropolitan region and can involve the interaction of people as pedestrians or as drivers or passengers in cars.

Behavior in public depends on the proper expression, interpretation, and negotiation of signs between people interacting with one another and with the built environment. This semiotic aspect of city and suburban living is quite essential to daily life, as the sociospatial perspective suggests. Elijah Anderson is the author of two classic works in urban sociology, *Streetwise: Race, Class, and Change in an Urban Community* (1990) and *Code of the Street: Decency, Violence, and the Moral Life of the Inner City* (1999). In *Streetwise*, he describes how social interaction in the public space of a large city requires "street smarts":

> One gains street wisdom through a long and sometimes arduous process that begins with a certain "uptightness" about the urban environment, with decisions based on stereotypes and simple rules of public etiquette. Given time

and experience, the nervousness and fear give way to a recognition that street life involves situations that require selective and individualized responses—in this complicated environment, applying broad stereotypes simply will not do. (1990:6)

Social psychologists who have studied this interaction in public insist that all behavior is interpreted according to the particular spatial context; that is, we interpret someone's action based on the space where it occurred (Karp, Stone, and Yoels, 1977). Hence, behavior is a combination of social and spatial factors. If we saw two men fighting each other in a park, we would be concerned and might call the police. The very same action placed inside a boxing arena would be considered entertainment. Thus, we decide how to interpret the behavior of others, which is essential to determining our own behavior, in part by interpreting space as a context for action. In short, spatial context has a very powerful role in the patterning of behavior in public.

Spatial context also determines how individuals behave toward one another. In a classic study, the sociologist Erving Goffman (1963:36) observed that when ordinary situations become extraordinary, interaction rules among complete strangers in the city change, and they might begin to act intimately. Thus, if a subway train gets stalled, the normally silent passengers might suddenly talk to those strangers sitting next to them about the incident. A study on bystanders (Darley and Latane, 1970) discovered that urbanites are not by nature blasé about other people's troubles on the street. But when an incident occurs, the more bystanders who witness it, the less the likelihood that any single one will intervene. Because of the density of city crowds, social responsibility is spread so thin that bystanders may choose not to get involved even when they witness a serious breach of behavior. This phenomenon sometimes makes us wonder about the perceived weakness of social links among people living in large cities. It also suggests that the social disorganization perceived by Chicago School researchers may have been a temporary or short-term product of spatial context rather than an innate or permanent change in people's behavior produced by the move to the city.

The most distinctive aspect of city life involves interaction with large numbers of strangers. Whom to trust and whom not to trust, how to act in a crowd, how to react to people you do not know, and how to interact with strangers in shops, restaurants, museums, and on the street constitute a major aspect of the metropolitan resident's set of behaviors, whether living in the city or the suburbs. As in other cases, signs and meaningful clues make a difference in the way people feel about and act in public space. Some researchers, for example, have studied interaction with strangers as a problem that can bring unattractive consequences from poor judgment in "reading" the sociospatial context. For example, J. Henslin (1972) studied cab drivers in a big city and discovered that their lives might depend on the way they size up a prospective fare. They do not stop for everyone. As a result of this behavior, many African Americans find it difficult to get cabs at night regardless of how wealthy they may be. Also, because many taxi drivers will not travel to ghetto areas or accept fares that do not possess the proper appearance, unlicensed or "gypsy" cabs have appeared as an alternative industry that has become the ghetto resident's taxi of last resort. Gypsy cabs are part of the informal economy of the city (see Chapter 10), and they involve some risks because they usually have no insurance and do not comply with industry regulations.

Appearance and fashion have always figured prominently in the types of judgments people make when dealing with strangers, especially in public space. Goffman (1963) regards the way we look as providing the most concise and meaningful cues to guide the interaction of others in the city (but we can add the suburbs, too). In dealing with strangers, fashion provides us with a way to "read" such things as class standing, lifestyle interests, and even whether or not an individual poses a threat to us. As discussed earlier, in large cities with dense pedestrian environments, people are more attuned to fashion than in places where automobiles dominate, such as Los Angeles, although there may be several reasons why this is true.

The spatial context is just as important in the organization of life within suburban settlement space as it is in the city. Instead of subways or buses, suburbanites contend with cars and carpools, which involve people who are acquaintances who share driving to work, shopping, school, and recreational activities. Unlike individuals riding in city mass transportation, people in carpools feel compelled to be friendly. It is the sociospatial context and not the proximity of one commuter to another that makes the difference. Yet for carpoolers, being friendly at 6:00 A.M. with little sleep and a full day of work ahead may be a difficult chore. Consequently, carpools have never been as popular as they could be. A novelist described the hell suburban mothers go through while chauffeuring children around town to and from schools, doctors, shopping, and friends: "With three children in three different schools, she [the heroine of the novel] lives most of her life now in her Honda hatchback. There is no one to talk to but her slobbering dog, which resides in the back seat, and she longs for a drive-in window at the local psychiatric hospital" (Lawson, 1991:C–1).

NEIGHBORING AND COMMUNITY

Neighboring is often said to be the most characteristic behavior of suburbia. Yet this is a phenomenon of the city as well. Only when we speak in generalities can we say that dwellers in large cities know fewer of their neighbors than do residents of smaller places. Neighboring and community involvement are strongly related to life cycle—whether individuals are single or married, childless or with children. Most neighboring tends to be done by people raising families. The stereotypical image of suburbia as a place of neighboring may be the result of the fact that families with small children prefer to live there. But the spatial separation of families in suburban housing developments may be less conducive to visiting with neighbors, whereas medium-density city neighborhoods with local businesses may facilitate social interaction among community residents. When we look more closely at the city, we can find instances of intense neighboring, such as in the ethnic communities studied by Herbert Gans (1962) and others.

Neighboring/The Neighborhood

Neighboring studies are related to the issue of community and territory. There is a conception of everyday life that places individuals within a nurturing neighborhood of friends and relatives. This conjunction of a certain space with an intimate circle of primary relations became the classic image of the community. Yet the terms "neighborhood" and "community" refer to different concepts. A neighborhood can be defined as any sociospatial environment where primary relations among residents prevail. Generally, suburban areas populated with families raising children conform best to this definition. In contrast, large, densely populated tracts of the inner city, where people live in apartment high-rises and barely know their neighbors, but have their own individual social networks, can hardly be called "neighborhoods." On the other hand, the concept of community can best be defined as a sociospatial environment that possesses an organized social institution that deals specifically with local matters (see below).

In a previous section, we saw that network researchers such as Wellman (1988) and Fischer discovered the important role of social contacts that are spread out across space. As we discussed, there is variation in the extent to which local or dispersed networks exist for residents of cities, and this is best explained by socioeconomic status, or class. The approach of network analysts, like Fischer and Wellman, pinpoints how choice of location affects individual network ties, but it is also remarkable for the way it de-emphasizes the effects of class, age, and gender as they are deployed in space—a relationship that is important to the sociospatial perspective. For example, elderly people living in the city are not physically capable of traveling long distances for companionship or help. They are dependent on their local community, but they may also prefer things that way. Not everyone assertively seeks the most compatible network of people across the metropolitan region. In other cases, people may have an extensive network but may also need a local neighborhood circle of friends. For example, single career women living in a large city may possess a robust network of friends living throughout the metropolis, but they find it uncomfortable to travel or dine alone. They, along with others, may need a close-at-hand network of neighbors.

In reevaluating neighboring studies according to the sociospatial perspective, it is clear that middle-class males are more likely than others to be involved in social networks that are not grounded in settlement space—the "community without locality." In contrast, the poor, the elderly, some women, and most certainly segregated minorities have closer ties to their immediate neighbors. These groups rely more on community and the local territory of friendship relations.

Other neighborhood researchers have remarked on the factors neglected by the network perspective. Susanne Keller (1968) indicated that community relations can be a function of class. She found that middle-class people have more casual acquaintances, whereas working-class individuals are more dependent on their neighbors. Another observer, Ida Susser (1982), carried out an important field study that clearly indicates the differential roles of class, race, and gender in fostering neighborhood ties. As the sociospatial perspective suggests, these factors operate symbolically and within a specific territory to make behavior meaningful. Furthermore, Susser's study also indicated the important role that communities play in inner-city life. That is, when a local area possesses an organized social presence, such as a block association, homeowner association, political ward, or similar organization, residents are better able to deal with the issues and problems of metropolitan living. This organized presence is the basis for what we call "community." Without it, a sense of place beyond the local neighborhood simply does not exist, and residents of such areas are left to fend for themselves when faced with environmental problems.

The Difference Between Neighborhood and Community

It is important to note that although the terms neighborhood and community are often used interchangeably, the concepts are really not the same. As we have already seen, you do not have to be neighborly to belong to a neighborhood. Research on neighborhoods may describe local residential life but neglect connections to community organizations. In contrast, community studies provide evidence of specific links to sociospatial organizations in the area, an approach very much in keeping with the perspective of this text. For example, because of the importance of child rearing in suburban developments, most people living there belong to neighborhoods that they themselves can identify, and they engage in frequent visits to neighbors. On the other hand, very few suburbanites can identify the "community" within which they live. Instead, they usually mention either their immediate housing development name or the section of the metropolitan area as designated by the county. In contrast, people living in the inner city possess a different connection to their location. On the one hand, they may rely on a spatially dispersed network of intimates and probably do not know their neighbors on an intimate basis. On the other hand, areas of the inner city are invariably provided with a community structure by urban planners and government officials. These parts of the city contain block associations, local planning agencies, political districts, and strong religious institutions. All of these elements contribute to the creation of a community with a name and political influence that local residents acknowledge.

SUMMARY

Space affects behavior in many ways. We orient ourselves in particular places by assigning meaning to space. Objects in our environment are meaningful to us. The meanings of space and the objects of the built environment help us organize our everyday lives. This sociospatial process utilizes particular mechanisms in ordering public interaction. We recognize the cues of behavior and acquire street wisdom by repeated use of public space. Our interpretations of behavior require an understanding of spatial context. Spatial context, in short, is a principal component of meaning.

Finally, we have discussed how the metropolitan region is diversified not only with regard to the individuals who live there but also with regard to the types of neighborhood ties and commitments to community found in particular settings. Sociologists have produced a long list of studies that document the diversity of neighborhood types and community relations in both urban and suburban settlement spaces. An understanding of such differences helps us overcome stereotypical thinking about the people of cities and suburbs.

In the last two chapters, the richness of social life across the multicentered metropolitan region was examined in some detail, but metropolitan life also has its problems and challenges. The next chapter considers how metropolitan problems result from the intersection of social, cultural, and spatial factors both within and beyond the metropolis.

KEY CONCEPTS

research methodology
field research
social networks
network analysis
questionnaire and interview method
subcultural perspective
mental maps
neighborhood interaction

IMPORTANT NAMES

Elijah Anderson
Herbert Gans
Claude Fischer
Barry Wellman

DISCUSSION QUESTIONS

1. What are the important differences among the Wirthian perspective, the compositional view, and the subcultural approach toward understanding urban life? How does the sociospatial approach differ from these approaches?

2. Compare and contrast the method of field research and network analysis. What are the respective advantages of each method?

3. What is the relationship between neighboring and community? What does research on this topic tell us about how changing spatial structures in American cities might affect neighboring and community?

4. If you wanted to conduct a research project on your community, what method (field analysis, network analysis, or mental mapping) would you use? What are the reasons for your choice? Describe how you would conduct your study.

METROPOLITAN PROBLEMS

Poverty, Racism, Crime, Housing, and Fiscal Crisis

Early photographic images of American cities feature overcrowding: immense traffic jams of primitive Model T automobiles mixed in with horse-drawn carts, tenements teeming with immigrants, and crowds of children swarming across city streets. For almost a century, city life in this country was plagued by frequent public health crises such as cholera outbreaks, high infant mortality rates, alcoholism, family violence, street gang activity, and crime. At around the turn of the twentieth century, a wave of murders set an all-time record that was not broken until quite recently. For much of our history, then, city life has virtually been synonymous with social problems. Yet we know that these same problems—crime, disease, family breakup—are experienced everywhere, not just in large cities.

The early sociologists of the Chicago School believed that the move to the city was accompanied by social disorganization. Although subsequent research showed that this perception was inaccurate, people in the United States still rank small and middle-size cities as providing the highest quality of life. The negative perception of the large city provides the basis for varying mental images of place (see Chapter 9). Yet we have also seen that there are a good many positive aspects of urban living and that the early belief that migrants to the city lacked a sense of community was unfounded.

This chapter applies the sociospatial approach to metropolitan problems. One purpose of our discussion is to explore whether large cities in particular and metropolitan regions in general possess unique features that propagate specifically "urban" problems.

THEORIES OF URBAN PROBLEMS

Early observers of city life saw immigrants from rural areas with stable family traditions turning to alcoholism, robbery, child abuse, and prostitution. Something about living in a large city, it was suggested, created social disorganization—broken families and broken lives—and this in turn led to all sorts of urban problems.

Several theories explaining the link between urban living and social disorganization have been proposed over the years, including the breakdown of primary group relations, the compositional approach, and subcultural theory. All these theories are derived from Louis Wirth's essay "Urbanism as a Way of Life" and subsequent interpretations of this classic work from the Chicago School of urban sociology. As discussed in Chapter 3, Wirth believed that primary group relationships (among family and kin, for example) are replaced by secondary group relationships (among neighbors and coworkers) in urban society. Secondary relationships are based on temporary, superficial, and impersonal social interactions. As a consequence, urban life produces anonymity and distance among urban dwellers, who rarely get to know even those people with whom they interact daily, such as shopkeepers, fellow commuters, coworkers, and even neighbors. Wirth believed that secondary relations eventually lead to family breakup, alcoholism, crime, and other negative aspects of urban life (Wirth, 1938).

Herbert Gans (1968) argued that the urban environment does not have a major effect on people's lives. Instead, differences between city and suburban behavior can be explained by differences in class background, age, and lifestyle orientations of city and suburban residents. So-called urban problems are really the consequence of the demographic characteristics—the social composition—of the population, such as class, marital status, age, income, race, and educational attainment. Gans referred to these demographic characteristics of the urban population as *compositional factors*. There are no innate qualities of urban life that cause specific problems such as divorce or drug use.

Claude Fischer (1975) claimed that the compositional view neglected the special role cities play in social interaction. Life in the city intensifies local cultures and subcultures (as we saw in Chapter 8). Although there is no intrinsic reason that urban life should produce social problems, cities might have a negative effect on individual behavior. All forms of deviance flourish within urban environments because there are more individuals who support these subcultures. Urban life does not automatically lead to social disorganization, but it does increase the opportunities to be exposed to deviance and negative effects on one's behavior.

THE SOCIOSPATIAL PERSPECTIVE

Social problems are ubiquitous across the metropolitan areas of the United States. Cities do not have an exclusive hold on divorce or family violence, and suburbs are now almost as likely as cities to be afflicted with family disorganization, deviant subcultures, drug use, and gang activity (Barbanel, 1992). Many suburban areas have crime rates comparable to those of the central city. As the suburban settlement spaces have matured, differences in poverty levels, crime rates, and other measures of social disorganization have become more similar.

We know from our earlier explorations of the sociospatial approach that the spatial environment plays an important role in human interaction. Social problems in particular are caused by poverty, racial exclusion, gender differences, and the patterns of uneven development within settlement space that result in differential access to resources and determine one's life chances. Spatial forms are nonetheless important. Environments intensify or diminish these social effects of uneven development. In short, ways of life result from an interaction between social factors and spatial organization.

Cities are not unique in having acute social problems, but the spatial nature of large cities and densely populated suburbs makes the uneven development resulting from the inequities of race, class, gender, and age particularly severe. According to the sociospatial approach, the following factors are the most significant.

First, the principal effect of the city as a built environment is that it concentrates people and resources (Lefebvre, 1991; Engels, 1973). Thus, social problems such as drugs and poverty have a greater impact in large central cities and densely populated suburbs than in less dense areas. In confined urban space under the jurisdiction of a single municipal government, it is the sheer numbers that tend to be involved, such as the frequency of murders and rapes or the number of "crack babies," that make social problems grave concerns.

Second, over the years urban populations have been disproportionately affected by the internationalization of the capitalist economies. For example, large metropolitan regions such as Los Angeles or New York are the destinations of choice for most immigrants from poorer nations who have left their own countries in search of a better life. With the flow of immigrants comes related problems, such as the need for bilingual education, that affect these areas more than other places.

Changes in the global cycles of economic investment also affect metropolitan regions because of the scale of activities in the largest places. For example, after 9/11, Wall Street stocks took a plunge, thousands of trained professionals were laid off from brokerage and financial service firms in Manhattan alone, and prior to that, throughout the 1990s staggering job losses occurred in many areas due to economic restructuring as U.S. companies sought to increase their profits and earnings. Job loss on this scale presents a particularly acute problem for cities.

Finally, social problems are caused by the unequal allocation of resources, which may be accentuated in dense, built environments. For example, large cities are major centers of the global economy. Extreme wealth is created within their boundaries, and the signs of that money are highly visible in the city, such as expensive restaurants, upscale department stores, luxury housing, and limousines. Close by, in the concentrated space of the city, are also people who suffer the most terrible consequences of abject poverty, such as homelessness, malnutrition, and chronic unemployment. Because this contrast is so visible, the issue of uneven development is particularly oppressive to inhabitants of cities.

In summary, social problems that can be considered uniquely urban derive from the concentrated nature of metropolitan space and the scale of changes in compositional factors. In this chapter, we consider a number of problems often associated with urban life, including racism and poverty, crime and drugs, fiscal problems such as declines in educational quality and infrastructure problems, and finally, housing inequities and homelessness.

RACISM

The most extreme and continuing effects of racism have been felt by African Americans, who have been systematically discriminated against in employment and in the housing market. As a consequence, their social mobility has been severely constrained. The most powerful indicator of continuing institutional racism in the United States is population segregation. In Chapters 12 and 13, when discussing cities around the globe, we will also encounter the phenomenon of population segregation. But nowhere is the racial nature of this sociospatial effect as clear as in metropolitan areas across the United States.

The classic study of segregation is by the Taeubers (1965). They compiled statistics on American cities with regard to the relative locations of whites and blacks. To measure segregation, they constructed a very useful tool, an "index of segregation." If a city had a 30 percent African American population as a whole, they expected, in the absence of segregation, that the black population would be evenly distributed across space. The index of segregation refers to the percentage of African Americans who would have to move in order for all neighborhoods to reflect the 30 percent black composition of the entire city. If a neighborhood were 90 percent black, 67 percent of the black population would have to move, resulting in an index of .67.

On the basis of Taeuber and Taeuber's study, all U.S. cities were discovered to be highly segregated, that is, with indexes above .50 for African Americans. The Taeubers replicated their study in the 1970s and found little change in the degree of black population clustering. Some of the most segregated cities during the 1970s were Detroit, Michigan; Chicago, Illinois; Buffalo, New York; Cleveland, Ohio; and Birmingham, Alabama.

Some have argued that not all of the segregation observed in American cities is the consequence of involuntary segregation; the spatial cluster of population groups can also be voluntary. In the case of African Americans, however, we know that the urban ghettos were created by a form of racism and violence designed to prevent blacks from moving into "white" settlement spaces, federal housing policies that concentrated public housing in the inner city while subsidizing "white flight" to the suburbs through construction of the interstate highway system and home mortgage loans, and other factors. Bullard and Feagin (1991), for example, discuss various techniques used by housing-related institutions to prevent blacks from locating where they prefer, thereby fostering involuntary segregation. This is an example of institutional racism.

Douglas Massey and Nancy Denton (1993:74–77) identify five distinct dimensions that may characterize the spatial arrangement of ethnic communities across a metropolitan region:

1. Unevenness: African Americans may be distributed so that they are overrepresented in some areas and underrepresented in other areas.
2. Isolation: African Americans may be distributed so that they have little interaction with other groups.
3. Clustered: Black neighborhoods may be tightly clustered to form one contiguous enclave, or they may be scattered about in checkerboard fashion.
4. Concentrated: Black neighborhoods may be concentrated within a very small area, or they may be settled sparsely throughout the urban environment.
5. Centralized: Black neighborhoods may be spatially centralized around the urban core, or they may be spread out along the periphery.

These five dimensions together define geographic traits that social scientists think of when they consider segregation. A high score on any single dimension is serious because it removes blacks from full participation in urban society and limits their access to benefits. As segregation accumulates across multiple dimensions, the effects intensify. The indices of unevenness and isolation do not capture this multidimensional layering of segregation and therefore understate its real severity in American society. Not only are blacks more segregated than other groups on each dimension of segregation, but they are also more segregated on all dimensions simultaneously. In many metropolitan areas, they are highly segregated on at least four of the five dimensions at once, a pattern that Massey and Denton call hypersegregation.

One-third of all African Americans in the United States live under conditions of intense racial segregation. They are the nation's most spatially isolated and geographically secluded people, suffering extreme segregation across multiple dimensions simultaneously. They are unlikely to come into contact with whites within the particular neighborhood where they live; even if they traveled to the adjacent neighborhood they would still be unlikely to see a white face; and if they went to the next neighborhood, no whites would be there either. Massey and Denton note:

> No other group in the contemporary United States comes close to this level of isolation within urban society. U.S. Hispanics, for example, are never highly segregated on more than three dimensions simultaneously, and in 45 of the 60 metropolitan areas examined, they were highly segregated on only one dimension. Moreover, the large Hispanic community in Miami (the third largest in the country) is not highly segregated on any dimension at all. Despite their immigrant origins, Spanish language, and high poverty rates, Hispanics are considerably more integrated in American society than are blacks. (Massey and Denton, 1993: 74–77)

Rental and real estate agents may use a variety of methods to prevent blacks from locating in white-owned areas. One mechanism is called steering. When an African American couple comes to a rental or real estate agent, the agent will steer the couple to areas of the city populated by blacks. Agents will also simply refuse to divulge the existence of housing opportunities in white areas. Despite gains in family income earnings by a growing number of middle-class blacks, racial segregation remains a fact of life for the majority of African Americans.

Harris and Weinburg (1992) used nineteen different indexes of residential segregation for four groups (African Americans, Asians, Hispanics, and Native Americans) across all 254 metropolitan regions in the United States. This is one of the relatively few studies to incorporate a regional perspective, using the metropolitan area rather than the central city as the unit of analysis. They found that segregation levels had changed very little from 1980 to 1990, replicating the results of the Taeubers' studies for the 1960–1970 period. Although they found a very slight decrease in the segregation levels for blacks in some northern cities, segregation of Hispanics, Asian Americans, and Native Americans increased slightly in most metropolitan areas.

From the information presented in these and other studies, it is clear that the major determinant of racial segregation is not income, social class, or length of time in the United States, as suggested by Park's race relations cycle (see Chapter 8), but racial background. African Americans confront the highest levels of segregation, while Asian Americans have the lowest levels. Racial background is also important in determining segregation for various ethnic groups within these categories: Puerto Ricans are more segregated than Mexican Americans, for example. Cultural factors such as language and religion are associated with the level of segregation for particular ethnic groups. For example, Filipino immigrants are likely to speak English and are familiar with American schools and government, and are much less segregated than other Asian American populations.

Racial segregation is not restricted to urban settlement space but is regionwide. Taken as a whole, suburban settlement space may be even more segregated than central cities. Institutional racism, including government policies and the actions of developers and real estate companies, has effectively ensured that most suburbs remain racially distinct. As noted in Chapter 4, the first mass suburban community, Levittown, New York, took special precautions to exclude prospective home buyers who were African American. Many studies have shown that when African Americans do acquire suburban residence, they are most likely to find housing in older, industrial suburbs and in inner-ring suburbs adjacent to an expanding urban ghetto. This is referred to as spillover from the central city, and for many years it was argued that black suburbanization simply resulted in the formation of suburban ghettos. Since World War II, a significant number of African Americans have achieved middle-class status, and the rate of increase for blacks in the suburban ring has actually exceeded that of whites for many decades. Thus, this group is likely to live in a wide range of suburban communities, although these numbers are still small and disproportionate to their total population in the metropolitan community as a whole.

One effect on U.S. culture of these arrangements is that increasingly whites learn about blacks and blacks learn about whites only from the mass media, because they have little direct contact with each other. Styles of dress and language among teenagers, in particular, are highly influenced by the media and the mass marketing of youth-related fashions in clothing, cinema, and music. In the 1990s, an urban style of ghetto dress among black teenagers that is associated with rap music and inner-city dance styles was marketed nationwide. Many youths in suburbia copy the style that is marketed to them through television and films. At the same time, suburban fashions associated with active leisure wear, especially influenced by southern California, such as skateboarding and beachwear, are also marketed through the media nationwide. Teenage culture represents a battleground of these and other spatially generated lifestyles that are diffused across the country by the mass media (Chambers, 1986), and it is here, in popular culture, that urban African American culture has had its greatest impact on whites.

POVERTY

The issue of poverty is not confined to urban settlement space alone. People throughout the metropolitan region suffer from the effects of this problem. Poverty is caused by the uneven development of the economy. In the 1950s, despite growing affluence, large numbers of Americans were poor, with some living in appalling conditions (Harrington, 1962). At that time, it was recognized that there were poor people in rural areas as well as urban places. As a result of government programs such as the War on Poverty, the poverty rate declined to about 12.1 percent in the 1960s. In the 1970s and 1980s, however, the rate rose again and reached levels comparable to Depression-era statistics; roughly 20 percent of the total population was living at or below the poverty line in the 1980s (Wilson, 1987).

Although poverty rates were held constant over the 1990s, we must consider several aspects of the poverty problem in the United States. First is the meaning and measurement of poverty. In 2003, the poverty level was defined as $18,979 for a family of four. It is difficult to imagine a family making ends meet on just $1,500 per month, particularly for families living in urban areas with skyrocketing rents and high food costs. Second, despite the near record low unemployment of the 1990s under the Clinton administration, and the only slightly higher level under President Bush, the relative number of persons with incomes below the poverty line has remained at more than 12 percent—more than 35.9 million persons in 2003. A person working full-time at the minimum wage cannot earn enough to escape from poverty.

Poverty can be considered an urban problem because of concentrated poverty neighborhoods in large cities, as the sociospatial perspective suggests. The number of central city poor people climbed from 8 million in 1969 to 12.7 million in 1982, a 59 percent increase. Consequently, the city as a spatial form concentrates the poor in record numbers. As William J. Wilson has observed, "to say that poverty has become increasingly urbanized is to note a remarkable change in the concentration of poor people in the United States in only slightly more than a decade" (1987:172).

Furthermore, the demographic profile of the poor is a special cause for alarm. In 2003, more than 30 percent of young children were living in poverty; among all age groups, 24.4 percent of African Americans and 22.5 percent of Hispanics were living below the poverty line (U.S. Bureau of the Census, 2003). Because the minority population of the United States is overwhelmingly urban, these figures imply a concentration of poor minority group members in the large central cities. This presents a major problem for the entire society, not just for those living in central cities.

Economic Restructuring

Although poverty is a phenomenon of uneven development, the past two decades of deindustrialization and manufacturing decline have contributed greatly to the numbers of poor people. During the 1980s, many cities were transformed by the new realities of global location decisions (see Chapters 6 and 12). Manufacturing jobs declined drastically, and central city economies retooled into service centers. These changes created positions for highly trained professional workers, especially in information processing and banking, along with a limited number of low-skilled, poorly paid jobs in the service sectors of food, tourism, and delivery systems, among others. As job opportunities dried up during the recession-plagued years of the 1980s and early 1990s, unemployed workers among the less affluent and less educated found it increasingly difficult to make ends meet, and both poverty and crime increased.

The new conditions of poverty, however, are not just confined to the large cities. Deindustrialization and economic restructuring have also affected towns and suburbs that have relied on manufacturing. In Chapter 6 we discussed the case of Youngstown, Ohio, which was devastated by the closing of its pipe mill. There have been many other such cases since the 1980s.

The decline of manufacturing has resulted in the crushing of communities and a rise in poverty among working-class populations across the country. For example, Homestead, Pennsylvania, near Pittsburgh, was once a thriving town of 20,000 people. It was the site of a large steel mill that was typical of the kinds of businesses that failed due to deindustrialization. According to one account (Serrin, 1992), the community was simply abandoned by U.S. Steel Corporation in the 1980s. It is now an impoverished, bleak community of fewer than 4,000 people. The pattern that has been repeated in countless places such as Youngstown and Homestead is one of no planning and no transition phase for workers who suffer job loss due to plant closings. Many communities across the United States have been impoverished, and working-class whites have suffered the most because of this callous process of change.

Poverty and Race

Poverty in the inner city, and across the metropolitan region, is compounded by the consequences of racial discrimination. African Americans have always been spatially isolated in our society due to racism. Hence, the economic deprivation that they now suffer because of industrial restructuring has forced the quality of life in ghetto areas to decline drastically. Furthermore, the black unemployment rate, for example, is generally twice that of whites (except in 1975): from 9 percent for blacks and 5 percent for whites in 1954 to 10.5 percent and 4.7 percent, respectively, in 2004. The number of persons structurally unemployed (those who have ceased to look for work as well as those recently out of work) among black city residents is double that of the unemployed. Many of these inner-city residents are not just poor; they are ill equipped to participate in the economy because of the decline of manufacturing and the restructuring to services. They do not have the skills to obtain the jobs they need to rise above poverty.

The alarming increase in poverty among inner-city ghetto residents prompted several observers to suggest that there exists an urban "underclass" living in ghetto areas that is afflicted by isolation and deprivation (see Chapter 8). According to William J. Wilson, the underclass consists of a relatively permanent population that (1) is concentrated in poor areas of the city, (2) is chronically removed from the full-time labor force, (3) contains a large proportion of teenage and out-of-wedlock births, and (4) has a comparatively long history of welfare dependency (Wilson, 1987:172). The underclass is a problem because forces or institutions that give people economic and social opportunities, such as education, have ceased to function for a sizable proportion of the urban poor. As a result, there is no mechanism that might improve the condition of the underclass.

Since Wilson's important study, the term underclass has been adopted by those who blame the victims of poverty and racism rather than the structural causes and profit-seeking corporations that are responsible for the condition in the first place (Feagin, 1992). According to Herbert J. Gans, "while this word can be used as a graphic technical term for the growing number of persistently poor and jobless Americans, it is also a value-laden, increasingly pejorative term that seems to be becoming the newest buzzword for the undeserving poor" (Gans, 1990:271). As a consequence, Wilson and other prominent sociologists have recently called for an abandonment of its usage. We suggest the term ghettoized poor as closer to the original intent of the concept. Ghettoization is not just an effect of poverty and lack of skills but an outcome of overt discrimination against minorities.

The spatial effects of concentrating the poor in a few neighborhoods also contribute to urban problems. For example, ghetto areas are the sites of the most violent criminal and drug-related activities, so the urban poor are also the most likely to be crime victims and suffer the most from crime (Taylor, 1991). In addition, ghetto areas have much more limited access to medical care than other parts of the city. A study of infant mortality rates in New York found that the rate was almost twice as high in central Harlem and Bedford-Stuyvesant (23.4 and 21 per 1,000, respectively), both overwhelmingly black communities, as the city average of 13.3 per 1,000 (the national average was 10 in 1,000 in 1990).

As these studies suggest, the underlying structural problem of poverty in inner-city neighborhoods (and older industrial suburbs as well) is the consequence of the sociospatial effects of racism and economic changes due to the restructuring of the global economy and the decline of manufacturing. At present, potential solutions are unclear because even in times of prosperity, underclass areas lack the human resources to capitalize on opportunities; that is, urban poverty does not seem to decline when the economy as a whole improves, even when there has been a marked increase in the black middle class (as was the case in 1990s). As Wilson (1987) and others have maintained, special programs are needed to deal with the intractable problems of the poor. In the meantime, the effects of the pathology emanating from poverty-stricken ghetto areas will continue to drain society's resources for years to come.

The potential threat of a large, minority population that is racially and economically deprived has been graphically illustrated many times in the outbreak of violence and riots that have terrorized entire cities. Often ghetto violence of this nature occurs after the police, perceived to be a white racist institution, kill or injure an African American neighborhood resident. Such incidents have occurred countless times across the nation, most memorably during the days from April 30 to May 3, 1992. Following a verdict that acquitted four Los Angeles police officers in a case of excessive force against motorist Rodney King, rioting broke out on the streets of the south-central ghetto area. As reported in the daily press:

> Violence mushroomed as marauding gangs torched scores of structures and looted dozens of stores despite an all-night curfew and the deployment of the National Guard. Attacks spread to normally tranquil neighborhoods miles

away from the city's mean streets, and law enforcement officials dodged bullets. (Wilson, 1992:Al)

All told, at least 53 people were killed and 2,328 were injured in America's bloodiest urban riot. Damage estimates exceeded $1 billion, and an extensive area was devastated, including portions of Los Angeles adjacent to the south-central area.

CRIME AND DRUGS

Crime

News stories give the impression that crime is rampant in cities and that cities are unsafe as human environments. When people speak of crime, they usually mean violent crime, which includes murder, assault, rape, and robbery. However, a large amount of property crime—burglary, larceny, and auto theft—also occurs every year in cities and suburbs. White-collar criminals such as insider traders on Wall Street and the bankers involved in the savings and loan scandal are responsible for the theft of billions of dollars. The recent bankruptcy of ENRON and other corporations because of fraudulent accounting practices resulted in the loss of millions of dollars of retirement funds as well as personal investments of thousands of persons across the United States. But these white-collar crimes, as they are called, are not usually considered when people discuss criminal activity or describe dangerous criminals. White-collar criminals rarely appear in the photographs of the most wanted criminals in the post office or on the television screen in *America's Most Wanted*. For the most part, the crimes associated with metropolitan areas are of the violent variety or property crimes such as burglary and auto theft—the stuff of *Police Chase* and other television "reality shows" that continue to fascinate the American public. These crimes affect our view of public safety and the safety of our homes.

Table 10.1 shows the number of crimes reported in large cities across the United States in 2002. New York City, the nation's largest city, reported 63,839 violent crimes in 2002, including 587 homicides and 1,689 forcible rapes. Los Angeles, with less than half the population of New York, reported 51,695 violent crimes, including 654 murders and 1,415 forcible rapes. Detroit, a city that is less than one-ninth the size of New York, reported 19,940 violent crimes, including 402 murders, while Philadelphia, one-fifth the size of New York, reported 20,057 violent crimes and 1,035 forcible rapes—numbers that are proportionately greater than those reported in New York or Los Angeles. This comparison shows that the size of the city population is

TABLE 10.1   Crime Incidents for Largest Cities, 2002

City	Population	Crime incidents	Violent Crime	Property Crime	Violent Crime				Property Crime		
					Murder	Forcible Rape	Robbery	Aggravated Assault	Burglary	Larceny-Theft	Motor Vehicle Theft
New York	8,084,693	250,630	63,839	186,791	587	1,689	27,229	34,334	30,102	129,655	27,034
Los Angeles	3,830,561	190,992	51,695	139,297	654	1,415	17,197	32,429	25,374	79,813	34,110
Houston	2,040,583	149,247	24,958	124,289	256	892	11,212	12,598	26,905	73,445	23,939
Philadelphia	1,524,226	83,392	20,057	63,335	288	1,035	8,869	9,865	11,244	38,789	13,302
Phoenix	1,404,938	109,916	10,223	99,693	177	410	4,075	5,561	16,855	57,214	25,624
San Diego	1,268,346	50,124	7,193	42,931	47	330	1,627	5,189	7,639	24,577	10,715
Dallas	1,241,481	112,040	17,018	95,022	196	656	8,041	8,125	20,351	56,306	18,365
San Antonio	1,195,592	108,437	24,074	84,363	100	464	2,114	7,091	13,368	65,251	5,744
Detroit	961,987	85,035	19,940	65,095	402	708	6,288	12,542	14,399	26,839	23,857
San Jose	927,821	24,139	4,134	20,005	26	379	827	2,902	3,026	13,642	3,337
San Francisco	805,269	42,671	6,059	36,612	68	210	3,208	2,573	5,947	24,468	6,197
Jacksonville	769,253	51,021	7,043	43,978	90	277	2,016	4,660	9,173	29,391	5,414
Columbus	715,739	66,261	6,499	59,762	81	673	3,503	2,242	16,066	36,063	7,633
Austin	685,784	42,979	3,203	39,776	25	256	1,174	1,748	6,916	29,725	3,135
Baltimore	671,028	55,820	13,789	42,031	253	178	4,714	8,644	8,759	26,716	6,556
Boston	596,444	35,706	6,956	28,750	60	369	2,533	3,994	3,830	17,824	7,096
Washington, D.C.	570,898	44,349	9,111	35,238	264	262	3,731	4,854	5,167	20,903	9,168
Seattle	580,089	46,432	4,092	42,340	26	152	1,576	2,338	7,290	26,742	8,308
El Paso	588,750	26,998	3,892	23,106	14	221	575	3,082	2,221	18,887	1,998

SOURCE: U.S. FBI, *Crime in the United States*, annual. From *Statistical Abstract of the United States, 2004–2005* (Crime Index = number of crimes known to police per 100,000 population).

not directly associated with crime incidents or with the type of crime—and also that the number of crimes reported to the police must be standardized to make for useful comparisons across urban areas. For example, Houston reported nearly 25,000 violent crimes in 2002, but was it actually more violent than Baltimore, which reported only 13,700 violent crimes?

Table 10.2 reports on the crime rate for violent criminal offenses and property offenses. This information reinforces the general conclusion that city size has little effect on the rate of crime or type of crime. The city with the highest overall crime rate (9,257.7 per 100,000 residents) is Columbus, a medium-sized city (715,000 persons) and home to Ohio State University, which makes it an unlikely prospect for the highest crime rate! Three other cities stand out from the rest because of the high overall crime rate: Detroit (8,839.5), Baltimore (8,318.6), and Seattle (8,004.3). But these cities vary dramatically in the type of crime. Detroit and Baltimore report very high rates of violent crime (more than 2,000 per 100,000 persons) and murder (41.8 and 37.7 per 100,000 persons), while Columbus and Seattle reported relatively low rates of violent crime (908 and 705 per 100,000 persons, among the lowest rates of large cities) and murder (11.3 and 4.5 per 100,000 persons). The other information in Table 10.2 concerning property crime explains why Columbus and Seattle have overall crime rates similar to Detroit and Baltimore: Columbus reported 4610.0 larcenies per 100,000 persons (the third highest). These comparisons suggest that (a) much care must be taken when comparing crime rates across cities, and (b) the types of crimes associated with cities of different sizes and locations may be different from what we may expect.

Table 10.2 suggests that there is no simple relationship between city size and either violent or property crime. Detroit, Baltimore, and Washington, D.C. have the highest murder rates among large cities, figures twice as high as those of most other cities. One distinctive pattern does stand out in this table, however. The cities with the highest reported violent crime rate and homicide rates are Detroit (41.8), Baltimore (37.7), Washington, D.C. (45.9), Memphis (22.5), and Chicago (22.1). These represent several of the cities that perennially have been labeled the "murder capital" of the country. They also report high rates of rape (Detroit and Memphis rank highest on this measure) and burglary (Baltimore, Detroit, Washington, D.C., and Chicago rank highest on this measure). These cities share another important characteristic: they are all older cities that have lost population and employment over the last several decades; they have large numbers of households with incomes below the poverty line; and they contain large minority communities that are highly segregated. These results show the unfortunate cycle of violence within low-income neighborhoods in our large cities.

TABLE 10.2 Crime Index for Largest Cities, 2002

City	Total	Violent Crime	Property Crime	Violent Crime				Property Crime		
				Murder	Rape	Robbery	Assault	Burglary	Theft	Motor Vehicle Theft
New York City	3100.1	789.7	2310.6	7.3	20.9	336.8	424.7	372.3	1603.7	334.4
Los Angeles	4986.0	1349.8	1349.8	17.1	36.9	448.9	846.6	662.4	2083.6	890.5
Chicago	n/a	n/a	n/a	22.1	n/a	630.7	845.5	869.6	3280.1	859.2
Houston	7313.9	1223.1	6091.4	12.5	43.7	549.5	617.4	1318.5	3599.2	1173.1
Philadelphia	5471.1	1315.9	4155.4	18.9	67.9	581.9	647.2	737.7	2544.8	872.7
Phoenix	7823.5	727.7	7096.1	12.6	29.2	290	395.8	1199.7	4072.4	1823.9
San Diego	3951.9	567.1	3384.7	3.7	26.0	128.3	409.1	602.3	1937.7	844.8
Dallas	9024.7	1370.8	7654.0	15.8	52.8	647.7	654.5	1639.3	4535.4	1479.3
San Antonio	7873.3	2013.6	7056.1	8.4	38.8	176.8	593.1	1118.1	5457.6	480.4
Detroit	8839.5	2072.8	6767.2.	41.8	73.6	653.6	1303.8	1496.8	2790.0	2480.0
San Jose	2601.7	445.6	2156.1	2.8	40.8	89.1	312.8	326.1	1470.3	359.7
Indianapolis	6032.5	n/a	n/a	13.9	54.8	365.3	501.0	1201.7	3087.1	808.7
Jacksonville	6632.5	915.6	5409.3	11.7	36.0	262.1	605.8	1192.5	3820.7	703.8
San Francisco	5299.0	752.4	4546.5	8.4	26.1	398.4	319.5	738.5	3038.5	769.6
Columbus	9257.7	908.0	8349.9	11.3	94.0	489.4	313.2	2244.7	5038.6	1066.5
Austin	7267.1	467.1	5800.1	3.6	37.3	171.2	254.9	1008.5	4334.5	457.1
Baltimore	8318.6	2054.9	6263.9	37.7	26.5	702.5	1288.2	1305.3	3981.4	977.0
Memphis	9947.2	n/a	n/a	22.5	78.0	640.7	831.2	2469.7	4513.5	1391.7
Milwaukee	7647.8	n/a	n/a	18.3	53.8	527.9	354.7	1143.0	4363.3	1186.8
Fort Worth	8021.0	n/a	n/a	9.5	57.5	295.1	397.7	1743.3	4813.1	704.9
Charlotte	7512.7	n/a	n/a	10.4	44.7	447.2	670.0	1625.7	3997.7	717.0
El Paso	4585.6	661.1	3924.6	2.4	37.5	97.7	523.5	377.2	3208.0	339.4
Boston	5986.5	1166.2	4820.2	10.1	61.9	424.7	669.6	642.1	2988.4	1189.7
Seattle	8004.3	705.4	7299.0	4.5	26.2	271.7	403.0	1256.7	4610.0	1432.2
Washington	7767.9	1595.9	6172.3	45.9	45.9	653.5	850.2	905.1	3661.4	1605.9

SOURCE: U.S. FBI, *Crime in the United States*, annual. From *Statistical Abstract of the United States, 2004–2005* (Crime Index = number of crimes known to police per 100,000 population).

To understand the nature of urban crime it is necessary to view it as a spatial as well as a social phenomenon. The incidence of crimes varies within any given city by neighborhood. Typically, criminal incidents follow the lines of class and racial segregation; the most dangerous places are also the places where the poorest urban residents live. For example, "the typical New York City murder victim is a black man in his late teens or twenties, killed by an acquaintance of the same race with a hand gun during a dispute—most likely over drug-dealing" (Greenberg, 1990:26). In all cities, racially segregated ghettos are the places where violent crimes are committed the most. Furthermore, most incarcerated felons are either black or Hispanic, and virtually all are poor. They come from the ghetto areas of the city, and their crimes usually were committed in those areas. And as the urban environment is partitioned into areas of relative safety and terror, several extreme examples of violent crimes, such as shootings in public schools, indicate that the islands of safety are shrinking in size and availability.

Drugs

According to studies of arrestees, many robberies and burglaries are committed in association with drug trafficking. In fact, statistics show a disturbing relationship between violent crime and drug use. The National Institute of Justice surveyed arrestees in the twenty largest American cities and found that at least half tested positive for the use of illegal drugs. In New York City, as many as 83 percent of males tested positive at the time of arrest. The range for females was slightly lower, but not by much: a low of 44 percent testing positive in St. Louis and a high of 81 percent in Detroit (National Institute of Justice, 1990).

According to this report, the extent of drug use among arrestees varies from city to city, but the use of drugs by people who commit violent crimes is alarming. The most common drug for both male and female arrestees during the 1980s and 1990s was cocaine or crack.

The lack of safety in large cities results from a high crime rate that is compounded by illegal drug use. When city streets are not considered safe, it is difficult for urban areas to attract new residents and businesses. Consequently, the economic life of the city deteriorates further. In addition, when the enjoyment of public space becomes impossible due to crime and drugs, one of the primary enjoyments of urban culture is threatened with extinction.

The Costs of Crime

What effect does crime have on everyday urban life? Perhaps the greatest effect has occurred with regard to the use of city space. In less crime-ridden eras, public spaces such as parks, plazas, and streets were enjoyed by everyone. Parks in particular were used by diverse people at all hours of the day and evening; during intense summer heat waves families would sleep on the public beaches in Chicago and other cities. Today the use of public space is limited. People are afraid to venture into parks without friends nearby, and children must be supervised and kept away from strangers. The evening use of public spaces and facilities, such as streets and mass transit systems, has also been negatively affected. People leaving their offices late at night now take cabs or cars rather than public transportation. A few years ago, a young woman out for a jog in Central Park was brutally attacked by a group of teenagers. Beaten within an inch of her life and raped, she miraculously survived, but the story of this urban professional who was employed on Wall Street became a national news story and a symbol of the toll of crime on the enjoyment of urban space.

Crime increases the security budgets of private companies as well as public expenditures for security in schools and court buildings. Violent crime causes billions of dollars in unnecessary medical expenses. It can also devastate property values. In areas of the city with high crime rates, the value of property remains low and does not rise during times of prosperity (Taylor, 1991). Thus, innocent households suffer doubly in crime-infested sections because they are victims of crime and because the value of their housing declines. Poor areas remain in poverty because high crime levels chase away prospective investment.

Finally, crime makes the city an unattractive place to live, especially for families with small children. Crime chases families away from the city, which compounds the problem of population loss and the inability of the city to increase its tax base. This very real cost to communities can be demonstrated by a visit to the "Moving & Relocation Page" at the MSN House and Home Web site. In an article titled "Best and Worst Cities for Crime," the following blurb rests atop a listing of high- and low-crime cities:

> Feeling safe and secure is especially important to Americans these days. Recent events remind us that the safety of our loved ones and the security of our property can't be taken for granted. . . . So what are America's best and worst cities for crime? Are there certain cities with an especially high rate of violent crime? Where do car thieves thrive? [We] have mined the recently released FBI Uniform Crime Reports to identify those U.S. cities with the highest and lowest rates of crime during 2002.

White-collar crime also results in terrible costs to this society—criminologists maintain that the monetary cost of white-collar crime is many times that of other crime—but is not associated with the quality of urban life. Rather, it is violent crime that scares people away from the city. In addition to murder, which usually is committed among people who know one another, mugging is a particularly frightening crime, especially armed robbery. The frequency of this type of crime in the cities contributes greatly to the image of danger.

Recent Trends and the Changing Costs of Crimes

A recent report from the Justice Policy Institute (2005) summarized recent trends in national crime rates, urban crime, and gang activity in American cities in the following manner:

> *Serious adult crime has fallen.* The latest crime survey from the FBI's Uniform Crime reporting program examines the first six months of 2004. Compared to the first six months of 2003, violent crime fell 2 percent in 2004, and the number of homicides fell by 5.7 percent. The drop in violent crime and homicides over the one-year period was the biggest drop recorded since 2001, which came after the historic drop in crime of the 1990s. Violent crime, adult and juvenile, fell by 28 percent between 1993 and 2003, from 1,926,017 to 1,381259 respectively.
>
> *Serious crime has fallen in most cities.* Even in cities where law enforcement says there are "super-gangs," the latest federal surveys show crime on the decline. Compared to the first six months of 2003, the number of homicide arrests fell by 25 percent in Chicago in 2004, robbery arrests fell by 7 percent, and property crime fell by 4 percent.
>
> *Serious youth crime has fallen.* The latest crime survey from the FBI's Uniform Crime reporting program breaks down the ages of people arrested for serious offenses in 2003. The number of people under 18 arrested for homicide declined 30 percent. Between 1993 and 2003, youth homicide arrests declined by 75 percent. Youth violent crime fell by 46 percent from 1993 to 2000.

The changing discussion of crime and the costs of crime in the three editions of this textbook is instructive. In the first edition, written in the early 1990s, we spoke of crime as a growing problem for cities. This was in response to the increase in violence in American society and in urban areas in the 1960s and 1970s; by the late 1970s, violent crime had reached an all-time high. In the second edition, written in 1999, we spoke of the decline of criminal activity, in response to reports of a nearly two-decade decrease in crime rates for the country as a whole, and for most metropolitan areas as well. As we prepare the third edition, it is clear that the problem of crime in urban areas has taken on a new and different dimension. While violent crime is now

(2005) at the lowest level since 1974, the prison population in the United States has grown exponentially, now exceeding 2 million persons for the first time. Indeed, for many states and communities, the prison industry, as it is referred to, is one of the few growth sectors of the local economy. The United States now has more persons in prison than any other country in the world. The number of persons in the prison system in California alone is greater than that of all European countries combined.

The costs of maintaining and running this vast prison system are enormous. The figure currently is more than $32 billion a year. Each year that an inmate spends in prison costs the taxpayers approximately $22,000. An individual sentenced to five years for a $300 theft costs the public over $100,000. Over the past twenty years, the amount of money spent on prisons has increased by 570 percent while funding for elementary and secondary education was increased by only 33 percent. In several states—perhaps your own—more money is spent on prisons than is spent on public universities.

The cost of criminal activity and drugs, which so often go together, can be measured in other ways. In the 2000 presidential election, thousands of voters in Florida were purged from the list of eligible voters because they had been identified (incorrectly) as having a criminal record. One sidebar to this story is the fact that in the African American community, an entire generation has been disenfranchised because of their arrest for drug use and crimes associated with drug use. More than half of the prisoners in the American penal system are incarcerated for these crimes. Denial of the franchise—the right to vote—is a particularly sensitive issue for African Americans, and the events associated with the 2000 presidential election have resulted in a national movement to restore the voting rights of persons convicted of nonviolent crimes. The criminalization of drugs that are legal in many other countries has resulted in increased crime in metropolitan areas, the breakup of families, and the corruption of law enforcement agencies, and has drawn billions of dollars out of public budgets that could be used to rebuild urban infrastructure, fund public schools, and address many other important metropolitan issues.

The number of women incarcerated for drug offenses increased more than 800 percent from 1986 to 2005. More than 1,000,000 women are currently in prison, in jail, or on parole. In many cases, these women were not guilty of any crime but were caught in the expanding web of the drug war. The expansion of laws dealing with conspiracy, accomplice liability, constructive possession, and asset forfeiture unfairly punish women for the actions of boyfriends, husbands, and other family members involved in drug crimes. Not only are families disrupted when women are sent to prison, but they often lose custody of their children—resulting in the destruction of the family.

Caught in the Web: The Impact of Drug Policies on Families and Women, a report from the Brennan Center for Justice at the New York University School of Law (Levingston, 2005), documents the cases of 150 women found "guilty by association" because their husbands or boyfriends were involved in the drug trade. "This country can no longer ignore the devastation of families and communities when record numbers of women and mothers are locked up for drug offenses," said Kirsten Levingston, Director of the Criminal Justice Program at the Brennan Center for Justice. "It's time to promote drug policies that work, to stop wasting money and to use our social systems to help women, not hurt them." Others are aware of the problem. When Martha Stewart was released from the Alderson Federal Prison Camp in 2005, she posted a letter at her Web site that encouraged American citizens "to ask for reforms, both in sentencing guidelines, in length of incarceration for nonviolent first-time offenders, and for those involved in drug-taking."

Ultimately, the cost of crime is not borne simply by individuals, public budgets, and private security expenditures. The cost of crime is born by the larger society in ways that are often hidden from view, even though they threaten the well-being of our families and communities. Those costs are increasing with each decade.

STREET GANGS AND GANG ACTIVITY

One type of criminal activity with a strong sociospatial component involves street gangs. Although gangs are not a new phenomenon—Emory Bogardus studied Mexican gangs in Los Angeles in the 1930s—gang activity has grown significantly in many cities over the past several decades. Frederick Thrasher's classic work on street gangs in Chicago noted that gangs were likely to appear in the "interstitial areas" of urban neighborhoods, where there was a lack of institutional structures, and that children from recent immigrant families—Polish, Italian, and other groups from Eastern Europe—were more likely to become involved in street gangs (Thrasher, 1927). Street gang activity of the present day is often concentrated in the same neighborhoods, and children from recent immigrant groups are still more likely to be involved in street gangs. Many of the reasons for gang involvement are likely the same, including isolation from the dominant culture, peer group pressure, family stress, poverty, and the struggle for self-identity that all adolescents confront (Vigil, 1988). In other ways, however, street gangs of the present day are different: The children of immigrants are now Mexican and Asian, not Polish and Italian. Because of the loss of employment in the central city, there are fewer opportunities for gang members to "mature out" of the gangs (Hagedorn, 1988).

Gang members are more socially isolated from other adolescent groups than was the case in earlier generations (Moore, 1991). And the open availability of both legal and illegal handguns makes street gang activity more dangerous and unpredictable.

Street gangs develop among adolescent groups within the meaningful spaces of local neighborhoods; gangs are often named after the local neighborhood (Logan Heights in San Diego) or street coordinates (18th Street in Los Angeles), and they aim to defend their "turf" from encroachment by other gangs. It is common to refer to "black gangs" or "Latino gangs," but this characterization is very misleading. Street gangs are organized within specific settlement spaces, and because of the high levels of racial segregation, gang members from African American neighborhoods are likely to be black, while those from Latino neighborhoods are likely to be Hispanic. But there is no one-to-one correspondence; one may come across white members of the Black Gangster Disciples or black members of the Latin Kings. Because both gangs and schools are organized around urban spaces, gang activity may carry over into the public schools (Hutchison and Kyle, 1993).

In the past decade or so there has been a substantial increase in research on street gangs from sociologists and criminologists. This research has made a significant contribution to our understanding of street gangs in individual communities (in the case of field studies) and of gang activity more generally. We know that gang activity has spread from large cities and inner-city neighborhoods to suburban communities and small towns across the country. Some gang problems are associated with immigration from countries such as El Salvador and Guatemala. MS13, or Mara Salvatrucha, has developed into one of the largest and most violent gangs in Los Angeles, and there are said to be more than 100,000 members of the gang in El Salvador. Street gangs from the United States have also appeared in other countries, particularly Mexican gangs in Mexican cities and even Filipino gangs in Manila. But in many cases we have learned that the reality of gangs and gang activity is different from what one might expect from reports of gangs in the media and even from police reports of gang activity.

We know, for example, that street gangs are involved in criminal activity of many kinds, including drug dealing. But the actual level of gang involvement is much smaller than most persons would think. Joan Moore notes that when the Los Angeles Police Department began its program of massive sweeps to remove gang members from the streets and reduce drug trafficking, very little evidence of gang involvement in drug trafficking turned up. The first 2,300 arrests resulted in the confiscation of just 3 ounces of crack cocaine and some $10,000 (Moore, 1991). A review of criminal records revealed that fewer than

5 percent of the convictions for violent criminal offenses were connected with gang activity in Chicago—this study was done during a peak level of gang activity in the city (Bobrowski, 1998)—and a similar study in Las Vegas found that fewer than 3 percent of crimes were committed by known gang members (McCorkle and Miethe, 1998). The Justice Policy Institute (2005) concluded that "While many communities do experience unacceptable levels of serious crime, including gang crime, our measures of serious gang violence do not tell us that the problem is 'ravaging' all our communities. In 2002, gang homicides represented 7 percent of the known circumstances in which homicides occurred. Four times as many homicide victims were killed in relation to an 'argument' than in relation to a gang."

These results are not surprising to gang researchers. When Cheryl Maxson began research on black street gangs in Los Angeles, she was warned by police officers that all of the youth in the community were gang members and that the neighborhoods were not safe for her to work in. Looking back on the research, Maxson noted that she never encountered a neighborhood where even a majority of youth belonged to a gang or where street gangs controlled daily activity within the community (Maxson and Klein, 2002). We know that gangs have appeared in many smaller communities, but we also know that most often this is because the family has moved from another city, not because of "gang migration." Jody Miller's study of female gangs in St. Louis found that although the gangs styled themselves after Los Angeles gangs and identified themselves as Bloods and Crips, there was no one from Los Angeles in the gang (Miller, 2000). We know that gang members are involved in drug trafficking, but this most often is an individual activity, not the business of the gang. Gang members do commit acts of violence, but we also know that the daily life of gang members is pretty boring: hanging out, getting high, waiting for friends to show up, hanging out. Malcolm Klein, a senior researcher who has worked with several generations of gang members in Los Angeles, says that the only thing more boring than being a gang member is studying gang members (Klein, 1995).

A recent autobiography gives us a detailed description of three or four years in the Gaylords, a white gang that was involved in major gang conflicts on the northwest side of Chicago in the 1970s and 1980s (Scott, 2004). During this time, three members of the gang were killed (a fourth was shot and remains paralyzed). At the end of the book the author has a memorial page listing the twelve members of the gang killed in gang violence. But this list represents more than twenty years in the history of a gang that was involved in several "gang wars" and had hundreds of members. Any reasonable person would argue that the loss of just one young life is too many. But the pic-

FIGURE 10.1   Street Gang Graffiti in Chicago

ture of life in the street gang that emerges from this and other gang biographies is quite different from what we are likely to read and see in the popular media.

The graffiti produced by street gangs show their claims to particular neighborhoods and alliances with other gangs (Hutchison, 1993)—and here the semiotic analysis of the sociospatial approach is especially informative. The gang graffiti in Figure 10.1 shows the Latin Kings (of Kedzie Street) and Gaylords (of Palmer Street). An alliance between these groups is demonstrated by the Gaylord figure (a hooded figure) wearing the pointed crown of the Latin Kings. Symbols of opposing gangs are inverted, such as the Latin Disciple pitchfork and Imperial Gangster rounded crown. The networking of allegiances and opposition among Chicago street gangs represented by this photograph extends across the metropolitan region, into the public schools, and even within the prison system, where separate wings of the Stateville Federal Penitentiary are allocated to members of the Latin Disciple, Latin King, Vicelord, and Gangster Disciple "nations."

The alliances (and opposition) among street gangs represent a specific ordering of social space within the contemporary city. Street gangs may fight to defend their home neighborhoods and, in some instances, move into other neighborhoods to extend their power and reputation. A mapping of the 120 gang homicides committed in Chicago in 1980 and then again in 1990 clearly demonstrates the spatial nature of this gang activity: Maps such as these suggest how important street gangs and gang activity have become over the past three decades. Gang activity no longer is confined to urban barrios and ghettos but has spread across the metropolitan region, and it is not unusual to find "wannabes" and even bona fide gang members among middle-class youth in suburban settlement space.

SUBURBAN CRIME

Compared to crime in the large city, little research has been carried out on suburban crime (see Stahura, Huff, and Smith, 1980; Gottdiener, 1982). Most reports on suburban crimes identify the same factors that cause city crimes, that is, racism, poverty, and class conflict. As in the case of urban areas, the rate of suburban crime has increased dramatically since the 1980s (Barbanel, 1992). However, crimes in the suburbs differ in some ways from those in large cities. First, the property crimes of burglary, auto theft, fraud, and larceny dominate suburban crime, although rape is as serious a problem in suburbs as in cities. Thus, although violent crime is increasing in suburban areas, there is much less of it in suburbs than in large cities. In contrast, property crimes are most troublesome.

Second, there is a distinct spatial component to suburban crime that differs from the city. In the latter, high-crime areas are associated with urban ghettos. Although suburbs have ghettos, not all of these are high-crime areas. Instead, according to one study of a mature suburban region outside of Los Angeles (Gottdiener, 1982), police in Orange County, California, associate high crime rates with apartment buildings. These stand out because most residential dwellings in suburbia are single-family homes. In large cities, this distinction would not be effective since most residences are in apartment buildings. According to this study, police in suburbs pay particular attention to apartment dwellings and monitor the activities of their residents. Because of the lower density of suburban areas, surveillance of populations is an easier chore than in the large city (see Davis, 1990).

Aside from the above features, however, suburban crime seems very much like that found in large cities, although perhaps not at the same rate per capita. But given the diversity of suburban communities, ranging from declining industrial suburbs to communities with spillover from adjacent urban ghettos, it is likely that many suburban communities are less safe than many city neighborhoods. While overall crime rates in the United States decreased each year from 1993 to 1998, the public's perception of and fear of crime remained high. Violent crime, drugs, burglary, rape, and street gang activity have become a significant factor in daily life across the metropolitan region, affecting life in both urban and suburban settlement spaces.

THE FISCAL CRISIS AND PUBLIC SERVICE PROBLEMS

Urban problems are difficult to solve when insufficient money is available to local governments. A fiscal crisis starts when the revenues obtained by government fall short of the expenses of running a city. When this occurs, it is necessary to borrow money and incur debt. Long-term debt involves borrowing to improve resources and finance public works such as transportation infrastructure. This form of borrowing is usually considered healthy as long as the projects are well thought out. Long-term debt is considered an investment in the city's future; if it is successful, the city grows and its economy improves, resulting in an increase in revenues. In contrast, short-term debt involves borrowing to pay general operating expenses due to a shortfall in revenues and money transferred to the city from higher levels of government. Occasionally, cities must borrow simply to cover operating expenses, such as meeting a payroll, but this usually happens only in an emergency. However, as a regular practice it can ruin the health of a city by limiting the amount of money invested for future needs.

Fiscal Crisis

The fiscal crisis of the cities has two components. During the 1970s, many cities faced budgetary shortfalls because of rising costs coupled with decreasing revenues caused by the decline in manufacturing and the rapid deterioration of urban economies. These cities were forced to resort to short-term borrowing to cover their costs. Compounding the problem was the flight of middle-class families from the cities to the suburbs (traveling on highways built with federal money to homes subsidized by federal housing policies), taking with them potential tax revenue that the cities desperately needed. The lower-income and new immigrant communities in the cities required relatively higher levels of health care, education programs, and housing services. When New York and other cities appealed to higher levels of government for financial relief, they were rebuked, and this precipitated the urban fiscal crisis. Cities responded to this situation by cutting services and systematically laying off personnel. New York City, for example, almost went bankrupt during 1976 and was placed in the hands of a money management panel appointed by the state to bring expenditures back in line with revenues and limit the amount of borrowing. As a result of the changes caused by this fiscal crisis, New York was unable to offer a full range of services to its residents. The closing of firehouses, reductions in the numbers of police officers and the hours of policing, the shortening of library hours, and layoffs and firings at city agencies were some of the austerity measures enacted in response to the urban fiscal crisis.

In the 1980s many cities, such as Cleveland, which had defaulted in 1978, and New York, which was forced into austerity, regained their fiscal health. The banking community renewed its faith in the obligations incurred by municipal governments. Short-term borrowing was controlled, and many cities prospered. For a time, it appeared that the urban fiscal crisis was resolved (Gottdiener, 1986). However, the problem was simply transferred to higher levels of government. At present, many states face record deficits. In 2005 California was especially hard hit. Many states have had to cut back on budgets for social programs in education, health, and other areas, with perceptible effects on the quality of life. Because state governments can no longer aid cities, local jurisdictions must increase taxes or cut back services. Hence, the effects of the state fiscal crisis have been especially troubling for local communities, with no end in sight for the first decades of the twenty-first century.

The federal government has not been able to help, since it has acquired serious debt problems of its own for the first time in U.S. history. In 1980 the federal deficit was approximately $40 million, which was unprecedented but still manageable. During the 1980s, it rose to more than $150 billion a year. The interest payments on this massive debt made up 14 percent of gross national product (GNP), and the United States became the world's leading debtor nation. Although President Clinton made deficit reduction of the federal budget a priority, the resulting surplus completely disappeared under the leadership of the current President Bush. Little effort has been made to restore either programs or funding cut over the past two decades. In places such as New York and California, governments at all levels are suffering cutbacks of services and programs as a result of the fiscal crisis. The damaging effects of these cuts cannot be exaggerated. In Los Angeles, the police department and the district attorney's office blame California's Proposition 13, which froze property tax revenues, for cuts in social programs resulting in an increase in gang activity that has led to Los Angeles becoming known as the gang capital of the United States.

Social Service Cutbacks: Education and Infrastructure

Cutbacks in the services that municipal governments provide, such as firefighting and education, greatly affect the quality of life. Even before the fiscal crisis, however, questions were raised about the relative distribution of such services. Many scholars argued that poorer areas did not get the same level or quality of services that wealthier areas received. Thus, the distribution of city services had a spatial component, and the allocation pattern was inequitable. In Chapter 14 we will see how this sociospatial discrimination is reflected in environmental conditions that proportionately disadvantage the poor. The municipal cutbacks since the fiscal crisis of the 1970s have thus made an unfair situation much worse (Susser, 1982).

HOUSING PROBLEMS: AFFORDABILITY, ACCESS

In the United States, family well-being depends to a great extent on where one's home is located. Differences in wealth and the location of the family home determine the opportunities available to individuals. Where one lives determines the quality of the school one attends, as we have already discussed, but it also determines the safety of the local streets and how much one's property will increase in value. Over the years, the cost of well-situated housing, either owned or rented, has increased substantially as a percentage of income. Consequently, attractive neighborhoods are now out of reach for many people.

Since 1965, the cost of housing has risen more rapidly than has income. As a result, a growing number of people either cannot afford single-family home ownership or must devote more of their income to housing. In the mid-1950s, an average thirty-year-old worker could purchase a median-priced house for just 14 percent of his or her gross earnings. Thirty years later, it would take fully 44 percent of that person's income to purchase the same house (Levy, 1987). Shannon, Kleiniewski, and Cross (1991) illustrated the rapid increase in housing prices. In 1970, the median monthly rent in the United States was $108; by 1985, it was three times as high ($350). The median sales price of new homes went up four times, from $23,000 in 1970 to more than $92,000 in 1986. Now the boom in real estate values has accentuated the high cost of housing, which is approaching an average price of $200,000 nationally. Price rises have been most rapid on both the East and West Coasts, becoming almost prohibitively high in places such as Orange County, California, and Nassau County, New York. In the summer of 2005, the rapidly rising prices of real estate continued unabated, pricing an increasing number of people out of the market.

More than one-third of all households now pay an excessive amount for their housing (that is, more than 30 percent of their gross salary), and almost one-fourth of all renters are spending more than half their income for shelter.

Schwartz, Ferlauto, and Hoffman (1988:10) suggest that since 1975, the average family has not been able to afford an average-priced home, although most people continue to buy homes they cannot afford.

Suburban Inequities

Suburban areas of the metropolitan region present a clearer case than do central cities of differentials in the supply of housing. Each suburban municipality offers a bundle of services to prospective residents and, in many cases, a local property tax level that helps to finance the quality of life. Those wishing to live in suburbia choose the level of services and taxes that they can afford by purchasing a house in a particular community.

Fifty years of suburbanization in the United States have produced a pattern of clear differences among communities with regard to family income levels and race. There is extreme social segregation in suburbia (Muller, 1981); that is, classes as well as races are spatially separated. Due to the power of home rule, which grants local suburban governments autonomy over land use, several administrative mechanisms have been used to control the racial and economic makeup of prospective residents. Perhaps the most powerful tool is exclusionary zoning, which mandates large-lot zoning for residential homes. In general, the larger the lot, the more expensive the home. Moderate-income families are automatically priced out of areas with such zoning. After a period of development, many communities passed exclusionary zoning ordinances on remaining vacant land precisely to prevent rapid development of affordable dwellings. The result of such practices is income segregation, because the less affluent must search for suburban housing in the few communities that make it available.

The zoning ordinance was challenged by open-housing advocates. They were defeated, and the ordinance was upheld by the Supreme Court in a 1976 decision. The Court ruled that local areas indeed had the right to control their own zoning, despite the issues of social justice that had been raised. Since that time, it has been increasingly difficult to provide affordable housing in all suburban communities, and no less so because zoning has become a tool for the control of growth (see Gottdiener and Neiman, 1981).

Exclusionary zoning means that the quality of local services varies greatly in suburbia. Many states, such as New York, have tried to preserve minimum levels by enacting statewide standards for such things as educational levels. In practice, however, great variation still exists among suburban communities. A typical family moving into a suburban town will immediately be told precisely where the best schools are located, and in most places educational quality varies greatly from school to school. If the education of their children is utmost in importance, the family will try to purchase a home in the best district. Of course, this area will be among the most expensive in the town. In this way, segregation of family income by housing tract perpetuates inequalities of social services and remains an unfortunate characteristic of suburbia.

Homelessness

One of the first things visitors to the large city notice is individuals walking on the street carrying all their possessions. Both disconcerting and pathetic, the sight of homeless people makes us question the well-being of our society as a whole. A recent *New York Times* poll found that about 54 percent of Americans see homeless people in the community or on their way to work (Applebome, 1991).

We cannot say for sure how many homeless people there are at present. We do know, however, that the numbers have not been as great since the Great Depression of the 1930s (Blau, 1992). The homeless are not found in any single place; they are mobile. Their condition also varies. Some days or nights they may be inside charity shelters, and at other times they may have enough money for a room in a single-room-occupancy (SRO) hotel. In the mid-1980s one estimate was 350,000 homeless "on a given night" (Peroff, 1987), but later estimates have run much higher, to 3 million or more (Flanagan, 1990:320). In addition, the composition of the homeless population, including married couples with children, is more representative of the entire cross-section of U.S. society than during previous periods, such as the Depression.

In Manhattan, for example, the homeless seem to be everywhere, and the city has opened up public buildings such as armories to provide "temporary" shelter to those in need. The Fort Washington Armory in Manhattan, or "the Fort," is typical. It is a scary place where some men have lived for as long as five years. Roving bands of "jawbreakers" control the shelter, drug use is rampant, noise pierces the night and disturbs sleep, stealing is so endemic that residents must place their shoes under their bedposts at night, and security guards are scarce, unarmed, and poorly paid. It is a place, in short, very much like prison. However, the only alternative is to remain on the street at night, a fate that many homeless prefer to shelter life.

Recent reports indicate that both homelessness and squatting, phenomena once associated with Third World cities, have become increasingly common in European as well as American metropolitan areas (Adams, 1986). There are several reasons for homelessness (Flanagan, 1990; Leshner, 1992). Job loss since the 1970s has taken a terrible toll on families. Economic restructuring, as we saw earlier in this chapter, has caused job loss and community decline. In many cases, a loss of income results in an inability to afford housing;

for some families, even rental housing can be hard to obtain with limited financial means. But declines in welfare funding have been a principal cause of homelessness; fiscal austerity and cutbacks in the federal budget have limited the ability of local communities to support people in need.

But homelessness is not simply a question of social welfare; it is also a matter of land use issues connected with gentrification, displacement, and the cultural imaginings of what the city should be. Talmadge Wright notes that the "problem" of homelessness in American cities is especially challenging because the homeless, city officials, and other groups have very different visions of how urban space should be used. For low-income persons who cannot afford housing, vacant buildings may be seen as squatter properties. But for most people—including public officials and developers—urban space does not include a place for the homeless (Wright, 1998). This attitude has resulted in the "militarization" of urban space, including such things as concertina wire around dumpsters behind grocery stores and restaurants to prevent homeless persons from obtaining leftover food, park benches specifically designed to prevent people from sleeping, and sprinkler systems in public parks that are turned on during evening hours to prevent homeless persons from sleeping on the ground (Davis, 1990). In Chicago, San Jose, and other cities, homeless populations have mobilized to resist the displacement of their communities, including protests of urban redevelopment projects, squatting activities, and other forms of collective action (Wright, 1998).

Homelessness combines aspects of economic crisis, poverty, and the failures of U.S. health and housing policies. Remedies for this problem require integrated plans that address the root causes. It is clear that with the declining economy, poor people have fewer opportunities to improve their lot, and their relative standing in society is deteriorating.

Housing is a major problem in both urban and suburban areas because the stock of affordable units is on the decline. Due to the relationship between the location of a home and the quality of urban life, the lack of affordability will continue to be an important problem for new families and young couples just starting out in life.

SUMMARY

The effect of differences in the flow of resources to metropolitan communities due to racial and economic problems has created a landscape in which poverty and affluence exist almost side by side. While some individuals and families seem to be doing remarkably well, many are barely holding on to what they have been able to accumulate over years of hard work. Large numbers of Americans now find quality education and affordable housing slipping beyond their grasp or that of their children. In addition, a minority of people do not even have the advantages of this besieged majority. They are mired in an intractable syndrome of isolation and despair. Our central cities are becoming unlivable, with crime and social strife prevailing almost everywhere. In Chapter 14, we will take up other issues involved in social problems, particularly ones that involve the environment and planning. These issues will be related to the process of uneven development that informs the sociospatial approach. In Chapter 15, we will consider some possible solutions and the prospect for a positive urban future.

KEY CONCEPTS

social disorganization
compositional theory
subcultural theory
hypersegregation
institutional racism
economic restructuring
urban fiscal crisis
urban infrastructure
affordable housing
exclusionary zoning

IMPORTANT NAMES

Louis Wirth
Herbert Gans
Claude Fischer
William J. Wilson
Elijah Anderson

DISCUSSION QUESTIONS

1. What are the four theories for explaining social problems presented in this chapter? How does the sociospatial theory differ from the other theories?

2. How prevalent is residential segregation in metropolitan areas across the United States? Has residential segregation increased or decreased in the past several decades? What factors are responsible for the segregation patterns found in metropolitan areas? Which group (or groups) are the most highly segregated?

3. Urban problems are often associated with an "underclass" population. What is meant by this term, and why is it controversial? How does the spatial concentration of the urban poor relate to the underclass thesis?

4. What are the spatial implications of crime rates reported for urban and suburban settlement spaces? What differences (if any) are there between crime in cities and crime in suburbs? What are the social consequences of high crime rates in urban neighborhoods?

5. How does the sociospatial perspective help explain the nature of street gang activity in American cities?

6. Metropolitan regions in the United States will confront a number of important problems in the twenty-first century, including the infrastructure crisis, the fiscal crisis, housing problems, and the crisis in education. Select one of these problem areas and explain how changes in American society and developments within metropolitan regions in the era after World War II have affected the problem.

LOCAL POLITICS

City and Suburban Government

Until the 1950s, urban governments in the United States were quite powerful. This is somewhat remarkable because when the political structure of the country was carved out in the eighteenth century, no provision was made for the autonomy of local government. Power under our federal republic is shared between the states and the federal government. City governments exist only by permission of the state in which they are located.

In the 1800s, cities were granted specific powers that enabled them to prosper. It was considered beneficial for the entire society if local government could take care of environmental needs and provide services that supported the quality of daily life. As cities began to grow, they needed infrastructure, that is, paved streets, sewer lines, utilities, bridges, and harbors. Cities also needed to provide public services such as garbage collection, police protection, and education.

Through a mutual understanding among the different levels of government, the task of providing for infrastructure improvement fell to the locality. As a result, in the 1800s, states sanctioned the notion of the municipal corporation, which provided for city government and its services. In return, those same governments were given limited powers of taxation and, most significantly, control over the regulation of land. Hence, the responsibility for the quality of the local environment fell mainly on municipal shoulders.

From its earliest days, the powers of city government were viewed as a prize, even though their scope was limited. It was understood over one hundred years ago that in addition to control over capital and land, control of the bureaucracies and of the decision-making power of government was a separate means of acquiring wealth. The power to tax or regulate both land use and public services gave local government officials significant control over other people's money. Municipalities could, for example, tax the local economy and reap the benefits of growth in the value of land. In addition, city services expanded their domains through various departments or bureaucracies, thereby making the city a major employer. It was this power that made urban administrations central players in the generation and accumulation of wealth throughout the metropolitan period. But the ability of municipalities to influence factors that might affect the accumulation of wealth has largely disappeared with the increased mobility of capital in the era of global capitalism.

In previous chapters we have seen how capital investment operates to produce a built environment. Due to the uneven nature of development, growth brings with it problems of equity and social justice. The struggles involving these issues are carried out in the municipal arena. The government must also intervene to keep capitalists from destroying one another's opportunities in the mad rush for profits. As a result, local government becomes the forum within which issues of growth and change, of the local quality of life, of the demands of citizens for relief from inequities, and of the well-being of local neighborhoods are all addressed. Both conflict and accommodation mark the tenor of community public affairs.

Over the past century, the nature of local government changed dramatically. Unprincipled exploitation of municipal decision-making powers was opposed by a series of reform cycles, some of which were more equitable and enlightened than others. But always, individual city residents and interest groups sought over the years to make local government in the United States function better. Out of that struggle the ethos of self-rule has been fashioned, however imperfect the results may be. The following sections discuss the evolution of these changes and then deal with several important issues surrounding the exercise of municipal authority today—in particular, the decline of democracy in local decision making and the growing power of corporate and banking interests to define the local agenda.

MACHINE POLITICS

In the early days of municipal government, political groups that controlled city hall and utilized it to acquire wealth were called political machines. One of the most notorious machines was the New York–based Tweed Ring, run by Boss Tweed. His reign made city government synonymous with corruption. A more typical political machine, however, was the one founded by Boss Pendergast in Kansas City (Dorsett, 1968). Jim Pendergast came to that town in the 1880s and opened a popular saloon. It was located in West Bottoms, a typical poor section of the city—typical for any city at that time—with large numbers of low-income working people from a variety of backgrounds, including foreign countries. He entered politics by creating a local Democrats club and quickly extended his influence to adjoining wards within the city. Soon his organization was able to mobilize the majority of votes, and he took control of local government. Boss Pendergast's regime apparently was not corrupt and derived its income from the regulation of saloons, gambling, and prostitution. Its support came from the successful mobilization of the large working class and other lower-income groups in the city.

After 1910, Jim Pendergast died and his brother Tom took over. In the years that followed, Tom Pendergast remained in control of the city but increasingly followed the lead of corrupt bosses elsewhere by engaging in fraudulent voting practices and influence peddling; that is, when business needed some public decision for its own interests, the local political leaders would ask for money in return. Eventually, charges of corruption destroyed this machine as they did so many others.

The principal characteristic of the political machine was that it functioned as a mode of administration rather than one of social change or political ideology; that is, machines did not stand for anything in particular, although most of them ran on the Democratic Party line because that party represented new immigrant and working-class groups that had moved to the industrial cities. They worked as organizations that acquired and deployed citizen votes. As Lineberry and Sharkansky (1978:119) note, "Machines are almost never ideological. They are rather broad umbrellas that are large enough to cover every shade of opinion and interest." The members of machines aggressively sought the loyalty of voters, often by promising employment or other favors, a process that has become known as patronage. In return, those individuals behind the machine used their political influence to acquire wealth for themselves and their associates in the private sector.

Political machines often were organized efforts of corruption (Scott, 1972). Their power derived from their ability to mobilize large numbers of voters and thereby win elections. Once in power, they had control over the city resources. They helped redistribute wealth to those who really needed it—for example, by employing hundreds of thousands of recent immigrants in search of work. They institutionalized and enlarged city bureaucracies such as health departments. These became useful during times of crisis, such as when epidemics occurred, and they brought order to everyday city life.

PROGRESSIVE REFORM

The corruption of machine politics was attacked at a variety of levels at the turn of the twentieth century. Businesses that had been growing in strength and scope throughout the nineteenth century no longer sought to associate with corrupt regimes. Much of the city infrastructure was also in place across the country by 1900, and there was less for government to do aside from providing services. One remedy used to combat the machine was the movement to change the structure of local government known as progressivism. Progressivism attracted large numbers of voters, many of whom had recently attained middle-class status because of economic growth. Eventually the political machines whose base remained within working-class districts were thrown out of office. The control of urban governments was transferred to reformers, many of whom were from citizen and business associations known as "good government" coalitions. Some of the reforms that were enacted involved changing the way local leaders were elected and reorganizing city bureaucracies.

Changes in the Political Apparatus

Under the machines, most cities were carved up into local wards, with each sector able to vote for a councilperson who would sit in the government chamber. Most bosses, such as Pendergast in Kansas City and Tweed in New York, started by capturing a single ward. Machines could use their influence on the voters at the local levels to mobilize support for candidates. One characteristic reform of the progressives involved a switch from precinct to at-large elections in which candidates had to acquire an overall majority of votes across the city in order to win. It was felt that the open glare of publicity and the need to acquire support from all the citizens of the city would act to curb the insider trading and deal making that were characteristic of the ward system.

In short, this progressive reform changed the structure of the municipal government apparatus of citizen representation. To this day, the degree to which various individuals and parties influence city elections depends to a significant extent on the structure of local government. Specifically, it depends on how citizens are represented, in addition to other factors such as their desire for change. For example, at-large elections require consensus building that cuts across particular interests, whereas the ward system favors champions of local constituencies with their specific concerns. We will return to this point when we discuss power structure studies.

Reforming the City Bureaucracy

The reform discussed above refers to changes in the apparatus of representation. A second important progressive reform involved bringing apolitical, professional expertise into local government; that is, the progressives also changed the apparatus of administration. Because mayors often represented special interests, and because city bureaucracies were often staffed by cronies of the machine holding patronage positions, progressives sought to eliminate such abuse. They instituted "civil service" structures in bureaucracies, which then hired people according to their professional qualifications and ensured job security, especially immunity from being fired after a change in political leadership. Work in city agencies became a career as a result.

In place of an elected mayor, many cities turned to a *councilmanic* structure of government with elected officials serving on a council and the head of government appointed as a "city manager." This manager was chosen on the basis of professional background and experience, thereby bringing technical expertise into city government. To this day, the extent to which professional careerists and city managers are involved in local government or the apparatus of administration constitutes a second independent source of political effects in the running of the city in addition to the structure of representation discussed above; that is, the relationship between elected and appointed career officials represents an important source of variation in the relative success of local government.

For example, city managers are usually career civil servants and have considerable control over the day-to-day budget. When their level of expertise is low, they may be responsible for severe fiscal problems through the mismanagement of finances. Unsound fiscal management has contributed to many of the problems cities now face. Over the past two decades, professional managers have responded to the fiscal problems of cities by improving their ability to aid local government (Matzer, 1986). Several management techniques have been developed, including (1) trend monitoring systems, which enable financial forecasting and trend analysis; (2) fiscal impact analysis, which predicts how future changes will affect people; and (3) creative capital financing, such as floating capital improvement plans for public investment. In short, professional city managers can make a positive difference in the fight against fiscal distress and budget problems.

To summarize, whereas the machine embodied a vote-for-favor ethic, progressive reforms restructured the representative and administrative apparatuses of government so that influence operated according to general interests expressed in terms of overarching values that were often ideologies. We cannot say unequivocally whether one system was better than the other, although the serious excesses of machine politics were cleaned up by the progressives. The machine, while flawed, did champion the needs of the masses, whereas the progressives tended to represent the middle-class business community. What is clear is that explorations into the nature of political power and influence at the local level must consider the independent effects of structures of representation on the one hand and the role of city bureaucrats on the other, in addition to factors related to competition over votes.

The above discussion has demonstrated the importance of structure for understanding the role of local government. Much of politics, however, is high drama and involves constant interactions among various individuals and groups over the satisfaction of respective needs. Politics involves the way these actors utilize power to get what they want. In the following section, we examine a number of theories of politics that address this important issue of the nature of power.

THEORIES OF LOCAL POLITICS

Whether we consider city or suburban governments, the central feature of the local state—its ability to acquire wealth and channel social resources—has meant that organized interests must compete with one another for control. This struggle for control over urban and suburban settlement space provides the drama of local politics. Urban sociologists have made use of three competing theories to explain how the political process in metropolitan regions operates: elite theory, pluralist theory, and state managerialism.

Elite Theory

The elite theory of urban politics asserts that there is always a select group of influentials, or a "community power structure," that possesses the controlling interest in a town. The elite structure of power was discovered by Floyd Hunter (1953) in his study of Atlanta. The power structure in a community can be identified by using a reputational analysis approach to identify the most influential people in a town and those with whom they associate. While not actively involved in all government deliberations, this "elite" group monitors them and intervenes through personal influence when it appears that an impending decision or project may interfere with their interests. Hunter's conclusion that Atlanta was run by a group of powerful individuals, most of whom were not part of elected government, was confirmed some thirty years later by Clarence Stone (1989).

Community power structure case studies are very convincing because they capture the way government and the private sector combine to push development toward specific directions, often in spite of community opposition, in ways that usually avoid public scrutiny. One characteristic of elites is that they get together relatively often to establish and reaffirm their common interests.

Houston has been touted for years as a "free enterprise city." Joe R. Feagin (1988) discovered that despite the label, there was a select group in control that used the local state to improve its private interests. Members were called the "Suite 8F crowd" because they met regularly at a room in a local hotel. The Houston group was very effective in persuading government to enhance its own business interests by pushing for development projects that it preferred. In fact, this group had so much influence that it even got the federal government to fund the dredging of Houston harbor, turning it into a port that made many local elites wealthy.

Pluralist Theory

Pluralism represents the dominant theoretical paradigm within contemporary political science. According to the pluralist theory, political influence is exercised by interest groups that are widely dispersed across the political spectrum. These interest groups all compete more or less equally within the political system to influence political decisions. While large corporations might influence decisions by contributing to political candidates, for example, labor unions also contribute to their candidates, and over the long run these interest groups share equally in the decisions made by elected officials. Control of government by any one interest over the long term is not possible.

Robert Dahl (1961) used a decision analysis approach to study how the mayor and city council of New Haven, Connecticut, made decisions on important political issues, including public education and urban renewal. He found that specific groups of leaders emerged to argue for (or against) particular issues, based largely on their specialized knowledge of each issue. There was little overlap among these groups from one issue to the next. Following the classic pluralist model, Dahl concluded that all groups of people in the community were represented by the local leadership and that no single group had special power or influence in local decision making.

Several other case studies of community decision making have been carried out by other scholars subscribing to this theoretical model. But their results have likely been influenced by their methodology, which focuses only on those decisions decided by elected officials in the public arena. Much of what influences government policy takes place behind the scenes and is never brought up for public deliberation (Bachrach and Baratz, 1962). As we will see later in this chapter, many cities have created redevelopment authorities that have the power to condemn land and use public funds without any public oversight.

State Managerialism

Whenever the day-to-day workings of city hall are examined, it is sometimes difficult to discern whether pluralist or elitist powers are in operation. On the one hand, it often appears that many groups are seeking to be heard and that the mayor must spend a great deal of time with constituents. On the other hand, when big decisions are made, the private sector seems to prevail. Recently a third perspective on local government has been proposed that fills in the gaps, so to speak, of these two theories: the state autonomy or state managerialism thesis.

According to this view, local government itself possesses some autonomy from both community and business interests. The local state also has interests of its own. For example, since government agencies represent a principal sector of employment, the local state seeks to enlarge its power over the private sector just to generate jobs and justify expanding budgets. Leaders of local government are also aware that they must satisfy the majority of the population to remain in power. Hence, they find highly visible ways of catering to the populace that may on occasion offend individually powerful groups, such as demanding that developers make small but significant concessions to community interests before project plans can be approved.

Several studies (Lipsky, 1976; Hero and Durand, 1985) have confirmed the presence of "relative" government autonomy. In particular, it was found that bureaucrats in city agencies have considerable leeway in responding to the needs of clients. Public satisfaction with government varies greatly depending on personal experiences. Pluralist theory asserts that elected officials function by integrating conflicting demands. While that may be one response, bureaucrats may also choose to lead according to what they perceive is their own expert opinion. As studies of local government have noted, it is very difficult to hold public officials strictly accountable for their actions. We often discover their abuses of power only when scandalous incidents of corruption are brought to light. But the ability of city bureaucrats to act on their own has positive advantages as well. We already discussed in a previous section how greater expertise by city managers in handling fiscal problems has made local governments more efficient and sound. The relative autonomy thesis suggests that public bureaucrats' ability to pursue their independent interests is always present.

WHICH VIEW IS CORRECT?

Years of community power studies have given us a relatively clear picture of the functions of local government. We might say that the state and its officials act in a variety of ways depending on how they are viewed by researchers and on the methodology used to study the government decision-making process. However, it is clear that most cities are dominated by an elite, even if they are not "controlled" by this select group. What we are suggesting is that there are enough degrees of freedom in the activities of local government for observers to note both pluralist and state managerialist outcomes of local decision making. However, such results generally involve decisions that are not *critical* to the development of the area. When truly important decisions have to be made, generally involving large sums of money and local political subsidies to the private sector, elites usually have their way. Often, such decisions are made with limited public input, while lesser issues are given substantial coverage by town meetings and the like. In short, local government, like state and national government, subsidizes the private sector through the use of public resources.

As Gregory Squires noted, the public-private partnerships that developed in the 1980s and 1990s to link civic and economic interests have had negative impacts on American cities and metropolitan regions:

> Contemporary partnerships take many forms. Coalitions of business leaders have been organized, sometimes including prominent public officials, to generate local economic growth. Redevelopment authorities have been created to give selected private developers rights and responsibilities traditionally vested in the public sector, such as land clearance, administration of government grants, and approval of public subsidies. In the name of public-private partnership, public officials have provided an array of subsidies in efforts to stimulate private business development . . .
>
> What has frequently been overlooked, however, is the inherently unequal nature of most partnerships. Frequently they exclude altogether the neighborhood residents most affected by development decisions. Public goals often go unmet, and democratic processes are undermined. Public support for public goals can dissipate if it is perceived (incorrectly) that the private sector is picking up the slack. The principal beneficiaries are often large corporations, developers, and institutions because the tax burden and other costs are shifted to consumers. And perhaps the important public benefits—jobs—either are temporary and low paying, or in the case of good jobs, go to suburbanites or other out-of-towners recruited by local businesses. (Squires, 1989:3)

THE DRAMA OF LOCAL POLITICS

Empowerment: Ethnic and Racial Changes

The succession of economic elites is just one way to look at changes in local government, although it is perhaps the most important way. Politics is also a dramatic enterprise. It involves struggle, conciliation, coalition building, and conflict. For many years, our cities have been ruled by broadly based coalitions representing local neighborhoods as well as economic interests. The backgrounds of local politicians reflected immigrant origins in the early waves that arrived in this country. The late 1700s and 1800s witnessed the domination of WASPs such as Boss Tweed in New York. Later on, the Irish became adept at political control, as we have seen in the case of Boss Pendergast. For much of the twentieth century, cities were run by coalitions of Irish, Eastern Europeans, Italians, and Jews.

In recent decades, the populations of metropolitan regions have changed greatly (see Chapter 6). In some cities and suburbs, minority groups have become numerical majorities. More than three hundred American cities have elected minority mayors, including many communities where a coalition of ethnic and racial groups have joined together to defeat the incumbent. Many are African American, but others are Hispanic and Asian. In 2005, Los Angeles City Councilman Antonio Villaraigosa defeated Mayor James Hahn to become the city's first Hispanic mayor since 1872 (when the city had some 5,000 residents). The changeover from the ruling coalitions of Irish, Italians, Jews, and Eastern Europeans beginning with the industrial period to minority leadership reflects today's multicultural city, but the change has not gone necessarily smoothly. Logan and Mollenkopf's (2003) study of the transition of political power in American cities found that there is about a twenty-year lag in the time from population majority to the election of a minority candidate, and suggested that mayoral elections are visible reminders of ethnic and racial cleavages in American society—including new divisions among ethnic populations and new immigrant communities.

Asians, for example, have been considered a "model minority" because many of the third-wave immigrants have done well economically (see Chapter 8). Yet many Asian Americans have incomes below the poverty line and have needs that are being neglected by the existing power structure in local areas. In one such case, the Cambodians of Long Beach, California, decided to organize for empowerment rather than continue to be represented by other ethnic groups. Cambodians represent 10 percent of the Long Beach population. Previous ethnic groups relied on churches, ward machines, and even local taverns as the places where voting blocs could be organized. The

Cambodians had no such power bases. Under continual pressure to become active in politics because their needs were being neglected, they began to organize themselves through the only institutional channel at their disposal, the Cambodian refugee agencies. According to Riposa (1992:16), these organizations blended social services for immigrants and cultural support in the transition to U.S. society. As a result of the struggle for empowerment, they were assigned a third task of political advocacy as the voice of the Cambodian community. Today these refugee organizations are one of many organized interests in Long Beach competing within the political arena. Another such organization is TWO–The Woodlawn Organization, described in Box 11.1.

Urban Social Movements

The previous section depicts one aspect of the drama of local politics, namely, the quest for power and control by organized ruling coalitions. There is another aspect, however, based on the concerns of citizens regarding their everyday life. Individuals and community associations often organize to influence local government. Despite the old saying "You can't fight city hall," many people do just that. When there are large enough numbers and defined demands, mobilized constituencies may even aggregate to the level of an urban social movement, that is, an organized mass of citizens making demands on local government for structural change (Castells, 1983). The concept of *local social movement* is an important one in urban research. However, it must be noted at the outset that the concerns behind so-called urban social movements differ substantially from those in the suburbs. All areas of the multicentered metropolitan region possess their own, unique agendas when local social movements arise.

In many cases, local social movements are ad hoc and relate to a specific issue. There may be some persisting irritant that afflicts a community, such as inadequate police protection or garbage removal. Residents belonging to a city-based social movement mobilize their local community to appeal for more resources and the mayor's attention to their needs. Often these protests are resolved when the mayor's office negotiates with local citizens. These incidents constitute the very backbone of democratic freedom, even if the system itself cannot respond adequately to every demand. As might be expected, neighborhoods that are wealthier or better organized in the city may receive more immediate attention. There is, therefore, an incentive for communities to keep a standing association that represents an organized voice for their needs. Many localities in both cities and suburbs have such neighborhood associations, and there is even a national network of block associations representing the voice of local communities (Boyte, 1980; Logan and Rabrenovic,

BOX 11.1   The Woodlawn Organization and Community Redevelopment

Between 1960 and 1970, the Woodlawn community on Chicago's South Side lost half of its population to white flight to the suburbs. Economic institutions were the next to leave; in 1971, the last bank in the community closed its doors. By the end of the 1970s, the once-thriving business district along 63rd Street had been replaced by boarded-up storefronts, and residential areas had become vacant lots. The City of Chicago shut down the elevated train that ran above 63rd Street for repairs and later announced plans to dismantle the line.

A coalition of more than one hundred neighborhood organizations, led by religious and block club leaders and with the assistance of Saul Alinsky, the famous community organizer, formed the Temporary Woodlawn Organization (TWO), later to be known as The Woodlawn Organization. TWO organized community residents to picket and threaten boycotts against merchants, landlords, and city bureaucrats responsible for the decline of the community, including demonstrations in front of the suburban homes of absentee landlords. When the University of Chicago sought to use urban renewal funds to clear the land between 60th and 63rd Streets and construct a park and upper-income housing to establish a buffer zone against the low-income neighborhood, TWO used the community participation requirement of the urban renewal program to prevent the displacement of low-income families.

In the 1970s, TWO began a wide range of social service programs, including prenatal and infant health care, Head Start programs for early child development, and programs for substance abuse, teenage pregnancy, and mental health care. By 1997, the organization was operating a social service network with a total budget of $4.2 million serving more than 7,000 people each day. Recognizing that middle- and upper-class black families were following whites out into the suburbs, the Woodlawn Community Development Commission was created to attract middle-class black families back to the neighborhood and create a viable mixed-income community. Since 1968, TWO has rehabilitated or constructed more than 1,500 apartments and homes for low- and moderate-income families, senior citizens, and others.

TWO was the first organization in the country to sponsor a mixed-income homeownership project in which moderate- and low-income families would live next to one another. A small-business support program for local businesses gave way to large-scale commercial real estate development, including a shopping plaza to focus economic growth and create jobs within the community. Along 63rd Street and Stony Island Boulevard, vacant lots and abandoned hotels have been transformed into garden apartments for middle- and working-class families. In cities around the country, neighborhood organizations such as TWO have demonstrated that development strategies planned at the community level often produce results far superior to those of federal officials and city planners.

1990). Previously, we have made the distinction between a neighborhood and a community on the basis of the existence of standing, area-wide associations. These are characteristic of communities and are most often found in cities.

According to Castells (1983), typically, *urban* social movements are directed against city hall. They make demands for better services and may call for structural changes in local government, such as the representation of neighborhoods or districts. Other concerns involve the community quality of life that is dependent on public services, such as police protection, public school quality, sanitation, park management, traffic conditions, street repair, air pollution, and environmental quality. What characterizes these activities as urban social movements is not so much their content as their target—local government and bureaucrats. However, as mentioned above, the content of city-based concerns can differ considerably from suburban counterparts. This difference in content of local social movements constitutes an interesting research area.

Suburban Social Movements

Cities are not the only places where social movements occur. Suburbs also have their share. As with the city, organized efforts at influencing local government in suburbia can range from specific and temporary incidents to full-fledged movements that unite several communities. However, one common example of a typical *suburban* social movement that differs from urban social movements is neighborhood organization for greater traffic controls on streets, while others involve movements to control residential development or the tax revolts of home owners. In general, suburban social movements involve issues emerging from the developing character of suburbs. This is in contrast to city life, which takes place in an environment that was developed decades ago.

Growth Control Movements.   Another social movement that is typically suburban is the call for growth controls among home owners who have already moved into an area in order to limit the kind of housing of future inhabitants. To a great extent, suburban politics is home-owner politics, because most of the issues that mobilize citizens concern their interest as owners of single-family homes in regions that are becoming densely populated and, at times, sited with new housing that is cheaper than that previously built. The issue that represents the variety of concerns dealing with the desire to limit future private-sector construction is called "growth control." In such cases, we can say that organized efforts to control growth qualify as a suburban social movement. Simply put, when suburban areas grow, the increase in residents brings problems that have an impact on the quality of life for those people who settled there earlier. Increased traffic, pollution, taxes, crowding in schools, and overburdening of public facilities, such as recreational areas, are but some of the problems that result when a region experiences sustained development. Often original inhabitants of a suburb will try to prevent future growth by passing a growth control measure or amendment to the town's zoning code.

For example, in the medium-size city of Riverside, a rapidly growing suburban area in southern California, a movement arose to limit the development of hillsides and wild arroyos in the town. A growth control initiative was placed on the ballot for the 1980 election. Opposition to the measure was expressed by real estate interests and retailers who wanted to maintain the pace of growth. The initiative to block growth was passed by a majority of voters coming from a variety of backgrounds. In a statistical study of the election, class differences among voters were not found to be a significant factor (Gottdiener and Neiman, 1981). Rather, all social groups in the community expressed a concern for maintaining the quality of life, and this interest dominated local suburban politics. A principal function of local government is preserving or enhancing the quality of life, and support for this effort comes from all segments of the community. The non-class-based nature of suburban social movements has commonalities with those of the central city in the United States and other countries that are also concerned with government's role in maintaining the quality of life.

Growth control measures often result in "up-zoning," that is, the restructuring of land use by local planning departments to allow only larger plots for homes. Such measures prevent the construction of high-density development, thereby reducing growth pressures. But they also push the value of new homes sky-high. For this reason, many communities that are in the path of development often opt for local growth controls. This strategy places them at odds with state legislatures concerned about *equal access* to housing and developers who seek to build as many houses as they can, and often with landowners who want to sell their land to developers. The result is a potent brew for local political conflict. Consequently, growth control is a contentious issue that is often perceived as violating the civil rights of new home buyers in pursuit of affordable housing, on the one hand, and of violating the private property rights of landowners and home developers, on the other.

Tax Revolts and the Crisis of Suburban Social Services.   Another issue that is typically suburban concerns the way local residents perceive the need to support local government services with home-owner property taxes. Despite the fact that in almost all areas of the country, property taxes go to support public education, policing, and the like, area residents may oppose the costs for such services. When a sufficient number of home owners object to local tax rates, they may form a social movement, typically suburban, called a "tax revolt." In several states, the demand of home owners for tax relief not only cut across local suburban jurisdictions but struck a responsive chord in the majority of residents who were not newcomers. California voters, for example, passed the Jarvis-Gann initiative—Proposition 13—in 1979. This measure restricted the property tax that could be charged to existing owners while allowing tax increases when property was bought by those just moving into the region. In effect, Proposition 13 made new buyers of property the bearers of increased taxes while providing considerable relief to residents who had lived in the state for some time. Despite the obvious civil rights issue this proposition posed, in June 1992, the United States Supreme Court upheld its constitutionality. The initiative was so successful that it sparked tax revolts in other states, such as Massachusetts. Proposition 13 affects all the residents of California because it places limits on the ability of local government to raise tax revenue, necessitating cuts in social spending. At the same time, it has benefited longtime residents because it has kept their property taxes from rising, although it has greatly exacerbated social problems in the larger cities (see Chapter 10). Among other things, the quality of elementary school education plummeted after the passage of the measure. Moreover, chronic fiscal crises and deteriorating public services have continued to plague California since that time.

THE CONTRADICTORY NATURE OF LOCAL GOVERNMENT

Local politics in both cities and suburbs is directed at concerns regarding the quality of life, whether that quality is measured in services or in tax relief. City government is expected to provide services, maintain law and order, and promote economic development while not adding to the tax burdens of local residents. This highlights the great contradiction of local politics in the United States: On the one hand, people want government to improve their quality of life; on the other, they are not willing to pay for it in taxes even though taxes in the United States are by far the lowest of any developed nation.

Social movements that seek reforms and change are motivated by the same concerns that form the basis of local politics, namely, the role of local government in promoting the quality of life and in limiting taxation. One important outcome of research on urban and suburban social movements is that they are usually not class based; that is, their constituencies often cut across class lines. Hence, they constitute a second source of politics in society alongside worker-led

industrial conflict. In addition, these social movements expose the contradictory nature of local government in our society. People expect the public sector to do much, but they are unwilling to pay for it. This contradiction leads
everywhere and at every level of government to fiscal crisis. The fact that our
society has been burdened by problems associated with deficit spending since
the Great Depression is not an accident. Capitalism exploits workers, but, as
residents, these same workers demand a minimum quality of life from their
local government. When the private sector exploits tax relief rather than pay-
ing its fair share, the result is fiscal crisis and attendant cuts in public services,
which in turn lead to a decline in the community quality of life.

The cross-class basis of local social movements is most apparent in the suburban case of home-owner politics. As we have seen, in suburbia, concerns
over rising property taxes and the rate of growth and development are shared
by a variety of social groups. Threats to the quality of life cut across class lines
in the city as well. This is clearest in urban areas when diverse communities
unite to block proposed projects that would overdevelop local areas or when
traffic, crime, and other urban ills threaten neighborhood tranquillity. Urban
and suburban social movements are a form of politics that differs from traditional economic conflict. Whereas the latter involves workers clashing with
capitalists over wages and benefits, the former unites people of diverse backgrounds and confronts the state over concerns about taxation or the quality of
life. Americans perceive the function of local government to be the maintenance of a reasonably high quality of life. People pressure their local governments to gain concessions from business interests, such as real estate
developers or corporations, so that development benefits the public good.
Whenever this occurs and the negative effects of uneven development can be
avoided or mitigated, democratic politics functions as it was intended. For the
most part, however, corporations and other business interests are given considerable latitude and often win tax breaks. The fiscal burden of sustaining the
quality of life then falls on the shoulders of local residents, who cannot bear
the full weight of supporting society's needs.

THE DECLINING POWER OF LOCAL POLITICS

The strength of local government in our society is not only severely limited
by the paradoxical attitudes of the urban and suburban citizenry, it is also
considerably weakened by the decline in our political culture in general. This
is manifested in the incredible power of private business interests in our society that seem to go unchecked by the public sector. Control of city and suburban government brings certain benefits from control over public-sector

decisions. The quality of life can be either enhanced or frustrated by the acts of those holding public office. This offers an incentive for citizens to become involved in local politics, even when the apparatus of government discourages direct participation. Involvement in politics may also be a means of acquiring wealth. Lawyers and politicians, along with their friends in real estate, construction, public services such as medicine, and banking and commercial interests, may benefit greatly from influence in or control of city government. There is an incentive to fight for the right to manage city hall. In recent decades, local governments have clearly been dominated by powerful economic interests to the detriment of citizen control. This is not simply a matter of such interests actively being involved in local decision making. Rather it is a phenomenon of the general decline in the power of local government to do anything, given the new realities of a globally connected, information economy. Increasingly, states have also been sidestepped in their political abilities to control the private sector. Now, it is mainly the federal government that is the last line of public interest in this evolution of a world capitalist system.

The power of local government declined after World War II. Both city and suburban governments were hemmed in by powerful economic constraints, making local politics weak. And over the past several decades, the drama of politics has been replaced by fighting over dwindling public resources, which often heightens racial and ethnic divisions. There are three major reasons for this decline of city politics.

First, participation in local elections is limited. Voter turnout is consistently less than half of all those eligible to participate. Community life once was characterized by high levels of citizen involvement, but if we consider voting, participation in the community has declined drastically. Although some analysts do not consider this phenomenon as cause for alarm, it does suggest that a significant number of people have become alienated from the institution of politics and have limited faith in political leaders.

A *second* limitation of local politics is that, if we consider metropolitan regions as a whole, we discover they are excessively fragmented by multiple municipal jurisdictions and overlapped with special service districts. The Chicago region possesses a chaotic array of more than 1,000 separate public service districts. This makes metropolitan coordination of service delivery very difficult and regional planning almost impossible. In addition, central city governments are being overshadowed by their outlying suburban counties, which have matured and developed a strong array of services that rival those of the large city. In 1966, the city of Atlanta outspent its suburban counties by two to one in services. By 1987, however, Atlanta accounted for only

10 percent of spending on services among all places located within the metropolitan area. A single suburban county, Fulton, spent almost as much ($409.5 million) as the city of Atlanta itself ($586.7 million) (Fleischmann, 1991). Such differences in public-sector spending abilities are a direct consequence of the growth of multicentered metropolitan regions.

The *third* limitation of local politics is the ideology of privatism. According to Gregory Squires (1991:197), "the central tenet of privatism is the belief in the supremacy of the private sector and market forces in nurturing development, with the public sector as a junior partner whose principal obligation is to facilitate private capital accumulation."

Little connection is made between the need to promote the general quality of life and the desire of businesses to locate in areas that are attractive places to live as well as work. The ideology of privatism, therefore, is a very limited way of conceptualizing the guiding vision of local politics (see Chapter 15 for a more detailed discussion of privatism and public policy). It implies not simply the domination of business interests but a political leadership that has only a limited vision in addressing the social issues of growth.

Public subsidies to business have had only limited success in revitalizing cities. Redevelopment usually is centered on the downtown area and the construction of hotels, luxury housing, sports stadiums, and tourist attractions such as convention centers. These areas seem to function effectively by day but are devoid of life during other times. They provide only limited employment, usually in service industries and at minimum wage. They are places besieged by crime, the homeless, and deteriorating public facilities. Elsewhere in the city, neighborhoods and infrastructure deteriorate, and education declines for lack of funds. In short, downtown business may have been improved by the policy of privatism, but the rest of the city has deteriorated.

Even more important with respect to our democratic institutions, privatism removes the goals and operations of government from both the political process and public accountability. Government decisions become merely a technical matter of choosing which economic policy to pursue. Public-private partnerships ensure that an increasing number of decisions previously open for public discussion are decided instead in political backrooms or, more likely, corporate corridors.

Redevelopment has created nonelective super-agencies such as the Boston Redevelopment Authority and the Port Authority of New York and New Jersey, which carry out massive projects, such as the construction of the "Big Dig" tunnels under Boston, with only minimal public input. Consequently, the quality of local politics has declined, and residents' participation in urban policy making is diminished. In short, at present there is a crisis of political process and leadership at the local level and an alarming deterioration in the community quality of life for most residents of cities and suburbs.

SUMMARY

Since the 1950s, the power of city government has progressively declined. At the same time, the demands made on it to ensure the quality of life have increased. As suburbanization drained the tax-paying middle class away from the city, first the federal government and then state governments cut aid to the cities. Now urban governments are being asked to do more and more with less and less to help the neediest groups in our society: the poor, minorities, and the aged.

Suburban governments have not fared much better. Although residents tend to be more affluent than those in the city, political jurisdictions are relatively small and their economic base is weak. Competition among suburban areas for new investment is always keen and usually results in a zero-sum game. As a consequence, suburban government also possesses a limited scope. Only the wealthiest communities are able to provide the kind of extensive services that rival those of the central city.

Some people assert that limited government is a good thing and that only liberals seek an extended political sphere, which usually does no more than tax excessively and fritter away public money. However, the kind of decline highlighted in this chapter is not about the limitations of government intervention but about the diminished quality of local democracy. At the local level, the declining power of government has meant constraints on the political process and on the democratic participation of all citizens in making effective decisions about the future of their own communities.

The history of municipal politics in the United States involves a struggle over the form that the representative and administrative apparatuses of local government within urban and suburban settlement spaces will take. Each of these is important for an understanding of the daily operation of government. But local politics also encapsulates dramatic struggles and themes. Because of the power of political decision making, both the business and the local residential communities strive to make their respective needs known. Municipal government can be the forum within which the desires of ordinary citizens are expressed and the injustices of uneven economic development are remedied. That is a democratic ideal. However, local politics is often controlled by business interests and poor political leadership. Too often municipal policy merely helps subsidize capital accumulation for the wealthiest groups in our society. This crisis of democracy may be measured not only by the extent to which business dominates local decisions but also by the failure of citizen participation and political leadership.

Local politics within urban and suburban settlement spaces has some important commonalities but also differences. In both, local governments must provide for education and other public services such as libraries and police and fire protection. In many large cities, government has reflected the popular interests of immigrant groups. In some communities, leadership and power have shifted into the hands of minorities that have become empowered after a long political struggle. But corporate, banking, and real estate interests are likely to set the agenda for urban and suburban governments. And the increased participation of minorities in city government has not resulted in a stronger commitment to alleviate social problems affecting these groups.

In the suburbs, concerns about the community quality of life dominate. Metropolitan growth itself has been perceived as a threat to the quality of life, and suburban politics has shifted to ways of managing growth. Political concerns in the suburbs also hold in common with the large city the need to overcome the injustices of uneven development. In both cases, these concerns are based not on class alone but on a cross-section of community interests.

In the 1800s, municipal boundaries enclosed the significant economic resources of manufacturing and banking activities, so that local government and its bureaucrats had the capacity to enrich themselves as the economy prospered. This is not so today. At present, capital investing and manufacturing are dispersed not only across the metropolitan region but across world space. Attachment of capital to place is quite limited, although some businesses, such as public utilities, newspapers, and banks, have a permanent stake in neighborhood prosperity and growth. Consequently, local government lacks the same ability to raise revenue from the private sector that it once had.

Other factors add to the limitations of local politics. These include the continuing fiscal crisis at the state and local levels, the growing power of quasi-public agencies that push for economic development without community involvement; and the ideology of privatism, which restricts the redistributive role of local government and identifies private-sector interests as public subsidization of development.

The limitations on local government discussed in this chapter require reforms that address the nature of the local political process. Programs to address the social problems discussed in Chapter 10 will be effective only if we understand how government might work better in the future, rather than by endorsing wholesale spending programs such as the urban renewal of the 1960s. Our discussion of urban problems and politics over the past several chapters requires an examination of the nature of metropolitan policy. But first, let us survey the patterns of metropolitan growth in other countries of the world to obtain a comparative perspective on the issues raised in the preceding chapters.

KEY CONCEPTS

municipal corporation
political machine
city manager
elite theory
pluralist theory
growth control movements
privatism
unequal partnerships

DISCUSSION QUESTIONS

1. How do the elite theory, the pluralist theory, and the state managerialist theory of urban political structure differ from one another? Which is most accurate in explaining the political structure in your city?

2. What is the role of the city manager? Why did many urban governments adopt the city manager position?

3. What is meant by the ideology of privatism? How do you see this ideology working within local political structures in the United States?

4. What is meant by unequal partnerships? What are some of the recent redevelopment projects in your community? What type of partnerships were used for these projects?

5. How do the concerns of suburban politics differ from the political concerns of the large city? In what ways are the political concerns of both urban and suburban residents similar to one another?

URBANIZATION IN
THE DEVELOPED NATIONS

Western and Eastern Europe and Japan

rban development in the United States at the beginning of the twenty-first century is defined by a spatial pattern of multicentered regions resulting from the deconcentration of commercial, retail, and government services in the city center and reconcentration of these land uses in regional minicenters that are functionally specialized. This spatial pattern is the product of the political economy of American late capitalism, as we show in Chapter 6. Other societies around the world exhibit their own patterns of urban and regional development according to their political economy, although many share a similar fate of increasing regional sprawl characteristic of the United States. Although large cities remain important centers of commerce and culture, many have reached slow or stable population growth. Redevelopment and gentrification occurs within the central city, but most new development occurs in suburban settlement space. Land use is mixed and shared among densely populated cities, minicenters of various kinds, and expanding suburban regions of residential housing. Metropolitan regions confront problems that are intensified by locational inequities. Income and racial segregation are pervasive and have led to serious inequalities in employment, housing, education, medical care, and other aspects of everyday life.

For many years, the study of urbanization in Europe was a relatively predictable affair. This is the oldest part of the globe having fully urbanized societies. In recent years, however, profound transformations have been taking place in Western and Eastern Europe. Shifts in industry to high technology,

TABLE 12.1   Urbanization in Selected European Countries, 1980 and 2000

	Urban Population				Population in Urban Regions of 1,000,000 or More		Population in Largest City	
	millions		% of total population		% of total population		% of total population	
Country	1980	2000	1980	2000	1980	2000	1980	2000
Western Europe								
Belgium	9.4	10.0	95	97	12	11	13	11
France	39.5	44.5	73	76	21	21	23	22
Germany	64.7	71.9	83	88	39	41	9	9
Greece	5.6	6.3	58	60	31	30	49	49
Italy	37.6	38.7	67	67	24	11	14	11
Spain	27.2	30.6	73	78	20	13	16	13
Sweden	6.9	7.4	83	83	17	21	20	21
United Kingdom	50.0	53.5	89	90	25	14	15	14
Eastern Europe								
Belarus	5.4	7.0	57	70	14	18	24	25
Bulgaria	5.4	5.7	61	70	12	15	20	21
Czech Republic	7.6	7.7	75	75	12	12	15	16
Hungary	6.1	6.2	57	64	19	18	34	28
Poland	20.7	25.4	58	66	14	16	33	25
Romania	10.9	12.6	49	56	9	9	18	26
Russian Federation	97.0	106.4	70	73	18	19	8	9
Ukraine	30.9	33.7	62	68	14	15	7	8

SOURCE: Adapted from Table 3.10, *World Development Indicators 2002* (New York: World Bank, 2002).

declines in manufacturing, and growth in the service sector are common to both the United States and Europe. There are other similarities: the growing inequality among groups living within the city that results from the division between highly paid professionals and low-paid service workers; the growth of immigrant communities from former colonies, and the intractable problems of the poor resulting from the combination of job loss in manufacturing, segregation and social exclusion, and more recently, cutbacks in social welfare.

Table 12.1 shows four measures of urbanization for selected countries in Western and Eastern Europe: the number of persons living in urban areas, percentage of population living in urban areas, percentage living in regions with a population of 1 million or more, and the percentage of the population living in the largest city. Although Europe was part of the first great urban empire under imperial Rome and is one of the most urbanized areas in the world, the figures indicate differences in the level of urbanization within the region. Three countries in Western Europe (Belgium, Germany, and the United Kingdom) have about 90 percent or more of their population in urban regions, whereas none of the Eastern European countries has more than 75 percent in urban regions.

Two countries in Western Europe (Greece and Italy) have much lower levels of urbanization, comparable to many countries in Eastern Europe. There are more than 500 cities with populations of 150,000 or more, and relatively few persons live in urban areas with a population of more than 1 million persons (in most countries, the figure is less than 20 percent); Germany has the largest number—just more than 41 percent of the population lives in large cities. Moscow has emerged as the largest metropolitan region in Europe with a population of nearly 8.3 million persons, moving ahead of London (7.0 million) and Paris (4.7 million). Of the twenty largest cities in Europe, ten are located in Eastern European countries, including Kiev (2.6 million), Bucharest (2.0 million), Budapest (1.8 million), and Minsk (1.7 million).

The extent of urbanization in Europe is evident in the satellite photograph reproduced in Figure 12.1. Large urban agglomerations can be seen in the industrial areas of United Kingdom and in the Ruhr River valley in northern Germany. Also noticeable are the city lights of urban centers along the North Sea in northern Europe as well as individual cities in southern Europe. These urban agglomerations are similar to those shown in Figure 1.1 when we were looking at the large manufacturing regions along the Great Lakes and urban agglomerations along the east and west coasts of North America. As noted above, fully half of the largest urban centers in Europe are located in the former Soviet bloc, but here a different pattern of urban development is evident. The large capital cities (Bucharest; Budapest; Minsk, Ukraine) can clearly be seen, but they are distinct from one another and not connected to other large urban agglomerations.

We begin with an overview of urbanization in Western Europe, whose recent history offers many parallels to the U.S. experience. In subsequent sections we discuss Eastern Europe, or the former Soviet bloc countries, to examine urban conditions there. The final section deals with the case of Japan, which exhibits certain similarities to, but also differences from, the restructuring of settlement space that has characterized metropolitan development in the United States.

WESTERN EUROPE

The countries of Western Europe have been urbanized for centuries. There is a well-developed urban hierarchy within the region, and within individual countries as well. The United Nations estimated that 74.6 percent of the European population was urbanized at the beginning of the millennium. That number is expected to increase to around 82 percent by 2030 and then stabilize. As we saw in Table 12.1, not all of the urban population lives in large cities; about one-half lives in small towns of 1,000–50,000 persons; one-quarter

FIGURE 12.1   The City Lights of Europe
Source: NASA.

lives in medium-sized cities of 50,000–250,000 persons, and one-quarter lives in cities of more than 250,000 persons (UNCHS 2001a).

In recent decades, Western Europe has experienced a restructuring of population and economic activities similar to those occurring in the United States. The urban population increased at a steady pace during the 1960s and 1970s. Since the 1970s there has been significant sprawl due to limited housing in the urban core, changes in household size, higher household incomes, and increased infrastructure such as public transportation and interurban railroads (the last factor very different from the United States). Many central cities are declining, and there is a marked increase in the development of suburban settlement space. Many new towns are experiencing rapid growth, producing metropolitan regions similar to those found in the United States.

The pattern of urban change is not consistent. Some countries, such as the United Kingdom, Germany, and to a lesser extent, Italy, have experienced decentralization of the population away from the large urban centers. Others, such as Belgium, Luxembourg, and to some extent, France, continue to experience robust central city growth. Between 1970 and 1980, for example, Liverpool, Manchester, Birmingham, Belfast, and other cities in the United

Kingdom all lost population. In Germany, Berlin, Essen, Dortmund, and other central cities also declined even while the larger metropolitan regions grew (Hall, 1988).

As is the case in the United States, long-term changes in these metropolitan regions can be attributed to the restructuring of settlement space as a consequence of global economic shifts. Manufacturing has declined in many European countries, especially in the United Kingdom. Cities have reduced their labor forces and converted to service economies, but with smaller employment bases than in the past. High-technology corridors, the European equivalent of Silicon Valley, and other "new spaces" of production have emerged. These have become new sources of employment and growth based on a professional, skilled labor force along with low-wage services. Industrial restructuring has resulted in declining urban cores with considerable unemployment of the working class, while the periphery has grown and developed into an affluent, middle-class population base. Welfare state programs have been cut back, leading to continuing problems with poverty and related issues, just as in the United States. A look at individual countries shows the impact of the restructuring of settlement space in greater detail.

United Kingdom

The population of the United Kingdom's largest cities and their metropolitan regions is shown in Table 12.2. The prominent role of London in this urban system is quite apparent; with a population of more than 12 million persons, London is some five times larger than the second group of urban agglomerations (Birmingham, Leeds, and Manchester), the older industrial cities of the west and north. There are three other urban agglomerations of 1 million or more, but all include small central cities of less than 500,000 persons.

Deindustrialization, which followed World War II and has accelerated in the past quarter of the century, has had a drastic impact on the United Kingdom. All the older industrial centers have experienced sharp employment declines due to factory shutdowns and wholesale job loss. Between 1978 and 1985 alone, manufacturing in Great Britain declined by 24 percent (Sassen, 1991:131). This followed a decade of comparable job loss. During this same period, employment in business services increased by 44 percent. Like the United States, Britain has undergone a shift from manufacturing to service industries.

Statistics for London are most revealing. Between 1960 and 1990, London lost more than 800,000 jobs in manufacturing (Sassen, 1991:205). After 1980 it reaped a harvest of new jobs in the expanding service sector. It was not until 1985, and for the first time in twenty-five years, that net gains in employment

TABLE 12.2   Largest Metropolitan Areas in the United Kingdom, 2000

	City	Metropolitan Area
London	7,074,265	11,950,000
Birmingham	1,020,589	2,600,000
Leeds	726,939	2,150,000
Glasgow	616,430	1,550,000
Sheffield	530,375	1,275,000
Bradford	483,422	
Liverpool	467,995	1,350,000
Edinburgh	448,850	
Manchester	430,818	2,500,000
Bristol	399,633	
Kirklees	388,807	
Fife	349,300	
Wirral	329,179	
North Lanarkshire	325,940	
Wakefield	317,342	

SOURCE: Adapted from *City Mayors* (www.citymayors.com), 2000.

finally outstripped net losses. The shift from a manufacturing economy to a service economy is graphically represented by the following figures: "In 1971 27% of all London jobs were in manufacturing and 68.6% were in services. By 1986 the shares were 15% and 80% respectively" (Sassen, 1991:205). Almost all of the new service employment in London is a result of the city's continued historical role as a global center of financial activities. London, New York City, and Tokyo today form three global centers for finance capital whose companies command and coordinate the increasingly dispersed world economy of manufacturing and marketing (Sassen, 1991).

New manufacturing centers tied to high-tech development have also emerged as part of this global restructuring. The M-4 highway corridor between London and Reading represents a center for electronics development that is similar to the I-128 peripheral corridor outside of Boston, Massachusetts. In Cambridge, the government linked up with private venture capital and with the university to build a "science park." It contains thirty new enterprises on 55 hectares and is similar to the "research triangle" located near Duke University and the college town of Chapel Hill in North Carolina.

New employment bases have been unable to compensate for job loss due to deindustrialization. England is currently undergoing a change that requires retraining of the labor force along with a smaller industrial sector. The need for drastic changes provided support for the Conservative Party in the 1980s. The Conservatives dismantled the British welfare state by increasing privatism and reducing publicly supported benefits (King, 1990). Although a complete transfer from public financing to market-based services has not occurred in Great Britain, many welfare state programs have been partially converted to a pay-for-service basis or simply eliminated (Forrest, 1991). This record is comparable to the downsizing of domestic programs during the Reagan, Bush, and Clinton administrations in the United States. The selling off of formerly nationalized companies enabled the Conservative regime in the United Kingdom to avoid massive debt financing of the economy in the 1980s, unlike the case of the United States. Presently the Labour Party is in control of government, with Tony Blair as prime minister. Yet economic policies are little changed. Welfare, for example, remains under attack.

Privatization has brought increasing misery to the majority of the British working class. The appearance of uneven development on a national scale has also brought social changes to the entire country. According to one observer, shifts in national attitudes involve the replacement of a moral ethos that supported the welfare state and its reliance on redistributive policies to overcome uneven development with a new ethos based on social Darwinism, limited public programs, and a full reliance on the market economy (Mellor, 1989).

The outcome of restructuring over the past decade in the United Kingdom is that the police have had to expand their role as controllers of the population while crime and civil unrest have increased. As Mellor (1989:591) notes, "U.K. towns were, in international terms, safe places. Now burglary, often minimal in material effect, violates personal space and enforces discipline in the use of house and effects; assaults and/or harassment limit the freedom of movement of the elderly, children, black people, women and, increasingly, white men." In the 1980s, Edinburgh, Scotland, had the highest rates of heroin use and, as a result, AIDS infection, of any European city. The consequences of the global restructuring of economic opportunity are graphically shown in the film *Trainspotting*.

There is also evidence that after years of successful redistributive policies under the welfare state, *social exclusion*, a term similar to our conception of the underclass, has greatly increased. A survey of households revealed that families whose major breadwinner has lost a job have had only limited success in placing any member in gainful employment. At present, England is facing the "spectre of an increasing number of households where *no*-one works, while there are also households with multiple wage earners" (Dale and Banford, 1989:482). In short, when a family can consistently count on the resources of a single wage earner, it has the resources to support the employment of others, even if their positions are not in high-earning capacities. However, those families suffering from job loss and periodic unemployment are falling behind and floundering in a sea of chronic poverty. One consequence of economic restructuring has been the rise of anti-immigrant

TABLE 12.3   Largest Metropolitan Areas in France, 2000

	City	Metropolitan Area
Paris	2,152,000	10,562,000
Lyon	422,000	1,598,000
Marseille-Aix	808,000	1,398,000
Lille	178,000	1,108,000
Toulouse	366,000	917,000
Bordeaux	213,000	882,000
Nantes	252,000	674,000
Nice	346,000	557,000
Strasbourg	256,000	557,000
Grenoble	154,000	505,000
Rennes	204,000	484,000
Toulon	170,000	478,000
Rouen	102,000	470,000
Montpellier	211,000	446,000
Nancy	105,000	396,000

SOURCE: Adapted from *City Mayors* (www.citymayors.com), 2000.

and racist groups, particularly among urban youth. Opposition to these neo-fascist groups is brilliantly portrayed in *Rude Boy* (1980), the documentary film by The Clash.

France

The urban population in France and most other European countries has been growing steadily. In the two decades from 1980 to 2000, the urban population of France grew from 39.5 to 44.5 million persons, and the percentage of the population that is urbanized increased from 73 to 76 percent. The growth that has occurred has not been in large cities: In 1980 just 21 percent lived in urban areas with populations greater than 1 million, and this figure was unchanged in 2000. This is the third-lowest total for all Western and Eastern European countries (see Table 12.1).

The population of the fifteen largest cities in France is shown in Table 12.3. Most notable about this urban system is the large number of cities with populations of 300,000–500,000 and the dominant position of the capital city. With a population of approximately 10.6 million persons, the Paris metropolitan area has seven times the population of Lyon (1.6 million), the second largest city. Paris is by far the largest city in this urban system and is an example of how the presence of a primate city can influence the development of other urban centers (see Chapter 13 for a full discussion of the impact of primate cities on urban development). As a result of Paris's power, France has long had one of the more centralized systems of urban planning in Europe.

As in the United Kingdom, the restructuring of metropolitan regions in France has been the result of industrial decline. Coal mining, steel production, and textiles, located in the north and west, have been particularly hard hit by plant closings and layoffs. In one year alone (1982–1983), more than 185,000 industrial jobs were lost (Body-Gendrot, 1987:244). Cities such as Metz, Dunkirk, Nancy, Lille, and Roubaix have taken on the feel of declining Rust Belt cities in the United States. The French government intervened and propped up failing industries to retain jobs and the community quality of life. When these policies were not successful, however, supports were abandoned in favor of a competitive unburdening of unproductive businesses.

Industrial decline has resulted in a social crisis for many working-class families. According to one observer, "austerity brought about a deterioration of the social fabric: . . . racism, demonstrations of workers against arbitrary decisions benefitting other workers, and petty delinquency. At the workplace, competition rose between the working classes: . . . young vs. old, white vs. non-white, men vs. women, all fighting as the size of the pie was shrinking" (Body-Gendrot, 1987:244). The rise of right-wing racists can be attributed in part to this upheaval. Today racism is a major problem in France, and hate crimes target immigrants from North Africa, Jews, and Arabs.

Some French industries responded with modernization schemes, especially the French automakers Renault and Citroën. Post-Fordist changes, such as flexible production, just-in-time supplying, and computer-assisted manufacturing in the manner of the Japanese industries, have also been adopted (see Leborgne and Lipietz, 1988). The French government has been very aggressive in supporting electronics-related industries, software companies, and biotechnology. In conjunction with universities and business venture capital, new technopoles have sprung up in the Grenoble, Montpellier, and Toulouse regions, among others. These resemble the Oxbridge complex in Great Britain (that is, the region of development around Oxford and Cambridge) and the larger university/high-tech industry regions of Silicon Valley and the Research Triangle in the United States.

The push to high-technology industries has affected higher education in the country. As elsewhere, more emphasis is now placed on technologically sophisticated degrees in engineering and science. To date, the changeover to a modernized, flexible, and high-tech economy has met with some success; for example, the French military industries are world leaders. But the older industrialized cities and their problems of decline, unemployment, and renewed racism remain.

TABLE 12.4   Largest Metropolitan Areas in Germany, 2000

		Population	
City	*Region*	*City*	*Metropolitan Area*
Berlin	Berlin	3,275,000	4,200,000
Hamburg	Hamburg	1,686,100	2,550,000
München	Bavaria	1,185,400	1,950,000
Köln	Northrhine-Westfalia	965,300	1,850,000
Frankfurt	Hessen	648,000	1,925,000
Ruhr-Rhine			5,800,000
Essen	Northrhine-Westfalia	588,800	
Dortmund	Northrhine-Westfalia	587,600	
Duisburg	Northrhine-Westfalia	513,400	
Stuttgart	Baden-Württemberg	581,100	2,600,000
Düsseldorf	Northrhine-Westfalia	568,900	1,325,000
Bremen	Bremen	527,900	900,000
Hannover	Lower Saxony	516,300	1,025,000
Nürnberg	Bavaria	486,700	1,050,000
Leipzig	Saxony	486,100	n/a
Dresden	Saxony	473,300	n/a
Mannheim	Baden-Württemberg	320,000	1,600,000

SOURCE: Adapted from *City Mayors* (www.citymayors.com), 2000.

Germany

Table 12.4 shows the population for the fifteen largest metropolitan areas in Germany; also shown is the region where each is located. The capital city, Berlin, is the largest urban center with a population of some 3.2 million persons—twice that of Hamburg, the second largest city and former center of the Hanseatic League on the North Sea. München, the largest city in the southern half of the country, is the third largest metropolitan area with a population of more than 1.9 million. Beyond the large cities, the most important information about the urban system in Germany concerns the five cities in the Northrhine-Westfalia region (Köln, Essen, Dortmund, Düsseldorf, and Duisburg). These are the industrial cities of the Ruhr River valley, forming the Rhine-Ruhr urban agglomeration of more than 12 million persons. Fully half of the corporate headquarters for Germany's top one hundred companies are located in Düsseldorf itself. This is the large urban agglomeration that is visible in the northern part of Germany in the satellite photograph in Figure 12.1.

Economic restructuring and uneven development has had a pronounced effect on this region. Called the *sud-nord-gefülle* or the south-north cleavage in Germany, the older, northern industrial cities such as Bremen and Hamburg have been hardest hit by restructuring, while southern towns such as München and Frankfurt have become affluent. This pattern appears to be similar to the way economic changes have affected the United States, where the industrial manufacturing base of the Midwestern and northeastern Rust Belt (or Snowbelt) cities such as Buffalo, Detroit, and Pittsburgh has declined, and the "new" Sunbelt cities such as Phoenix, San Diego, and Los Angeles have prospered.

According to Haussermann and Siebel, the north-south split is a consequence of Germany's shift to an export-oriented economy, similar to the case in Italy. In Germany, the southern region contains the automobile industry and also high-technology-based manufacturing—two economic sectors that have done well in the global economy. Steel production and the shipping industry, which are concentrated in the north, have been unable to compete effectively in the world system; consequently, cities based on these sectors have declined. From 1980 to 1988, the northern region containing the cities of Bremen, Hamburg, and Bonn experienced a 6.4 percent decline in employment, while the southern region containing the cities of München, Baden, Frankfurt, and Stuttgart enjoyed an increase in employment (Haussermann and Siebel, 1990:377).

It is not clear how the reunification of West and East Germany will affect urban areas. West Germany has committed more than $2 billion toward rebuilding East Germany, but that region still lags behind West Germany and is blamed for the increasing budget deficits and the lagging growth of what a decade ago was the strongest of the European economies. A poll conducted in 2005 reported that 24 percent of West Germans responded positively when asked, "Would it be better if the wall between east and west still stood?" The same newspaper account noted that stereotypes and resentments persist in both regions of the country, with some West Germans regarding East Germans as backward, while some East Germans regard West Germans as bossy know-it-alls (Associated Press, 2005).

It is expected that population will shift to centers of increasing employment wherever they are located in the nation. There is continuing difficulty in absorbing the labor force of former East Germany. Unemployment is on the rise, as is racism. Fascist skinheads perpetrating violence and hate crimes against immigrants and Jews threatened to destabilize the government in 1992. In May of 2005 the celebration of the sixty-year anniversary of the end of World War II brought more than 3,000 neo-Nazis to Berlin's central plaza to protest against German guilt for the war and the opening of a new memorial to Jews killed in the Holocaust. They were opposed by an even larger group of 6,000 protesters, and some 10,000 police were used to keep the two groups separated (*Washington Post*, 2005). As in Italy and France, the renewal of racism in Germany has complex causes, although economic uncertainties following reunification are a contributing factor. Most Germans believe their economy can absorb the population of former East Germany; nevertheless, the long-term effects of reunification remain unpredictable. Urbanization and conditions of life in the former Soviet bloc countries is examined in greater detail below.

Italy

As we saw in Chapter 2, the historical development of urban life in Europe after 1000 led to the formation of a number of very important cities in Italy. By the 1500s, three of the five largest cities in Europe were located in Italy (Naples, Milan, and Venice). After this period, economic development would focus on Northern Europe, and the great Italian cities of the Renaissance have remained relatively small through recent times. As we saw in Table 12.1, while about two-thirds (67 percent) of the Italian population lives in urban areas, only about 10 percent live in large cities of 1 million or more persons. Table 12.5 shows the largest cities in Italy and Spain. Rome is the largest city in Italy with a population of 2.6 million, and there are two other cities with populations of about 1 million or more (Milan and Naples). Other great cities of the Renaissance—Florence and Venice—have populations of less than 400,000.

For decades Italy remained one of the underdeveloped areas of Western Europe. The north was highly industrialized with an urbanized labor force centering on Milan and Turin. The south, in contrast, remained rural and dependent on agriculture (Martinelli, 1985). Population in the south was unstable, as native sons often left home to migrate to cities in the north or immigrated to other countries (including Australia, Argentina, Canada, and the United States) in search of employment.

Since the 1960s, the same force of economic restructuring that has operated in the rest of the industrialized West has changed the sociospatial pattern of development in Italy as well. The middle and southern regions, known as the *mezzogiorno,* have developed a vibrant industrial employment base concentrated in the small-craft tradition of the region. This includes apparel, textiles, footwear, wood products such as furniture, metal working, and clay and glass products. Firms in this region have been very successful by adopting custom design and flexible industrial methods. They engage in small-batch production, which can be changed and customized for new orders relatively easily. Some observers believe that these firms are a model for the new type of "flexible" manufacturing that will prosper in the global economy (Scott, 1988; Piore and Sabel, 1984), called post-Fordism.

Due to foreign competition, especially in the automobile industry, the northern region has been threatened with decline. By the 1990s, the cities of

TABLE 12.5 Largest Cities in Italy and Spain, 2000

City	Population
Italy	
Roma (Rome)	2,648,843
Milano (Milan)	1,305,591
Napoli (Naples)	1,046,987
Torino (Turin)	921,485
Palermo	689,349
Genova (Genoa)	655,704
Bologna	385,813
Firenze (Florence)	381,762
Catania	341,685
Bari	335,647
Venezia (Venice)	297,743
Messina	262,524
Verona	254,146
Trieste	222,589
Padova (Padua)	213,072
Spain	
Madrid	2,824,000
Barcelona	1,454,000
Valencia	736,000
Sevilla	695,000
Zaragoza	601,000
Málaga	542,000
Las Palmas de Gran Canaria	354,000
Bilbao	351,000
Murcia	350,000
Valladolid	317,000
Córdoba	307,000
Palma de Mallorca	302,000
Vigo	287,000
Alicante	272,000
Gijón	264,000

SOURCE: Adapted from *City Mayors* (www.citymayors.com), 2000.

Turin and Milan no longer were the employment meccas they had been in the past. Changes were made in the industrial base to regain the competitive edge of such companies as Fiat Automobiles and Pirelli Tires. In Turin, existing plants were modernized according to the Japanese style that has also been copied by American automakers. Automation was introduced, and aspects of the assembly line were turned over to robotics. Wholesale use of electronic or computer-assisted manufacturing was also incorporated into production. Finally, the "just-in-time" system (discussed in Chapter 4) was adopted by assembly plants to reduce operating costs by eliminating inventory problems.

Under this system, assembly plants do away with holding large inventories of items they require in production. Instead, they work with suppliers outside the plant but within the region to provide what they need at the time they require it in the assembly process. Coordination of supplies is accomplished with the use of computers that monitor all aspects of the distribution and production schedules.

The successful adaptation of Italian industries to changes in the global marketplace has stabilized the migration patterns within the country. Transformations as a consequence of restructuring have been celebrated by some observers as a new model of growth that other advanced nations undergoing change should copy (Piore and Sabel, 1984). The fate of cities depends progressively more on their ability to attract and retain mobile capital investment. Capital, in turn, must restructure and acquire greater flexibility in responding to the increasing demands for small-batch, customized production. Caught by the decline in manufacturing employment and the threat of plant closings or layoffs, workers must settle for less job security and a growing need to work closely with business for the sake of their mutual survival.

Much of Italian industry is oriented toward exports. In the 1990s, the slowdown in the global economy hit Italy hard, especially in the *mezzogiorno* region. Once again the specter of layoffs and recession has destabilized politics as the standard of living for both working-class and middle-class households is threatened by economic restructuring. Fascist skinheads emerged in the 1980s, and anti-Semitism is on the rise despite the very small Jewish population. Not all of this activity is directly related to the current recession, and other, as yet undocumented factors may be playing a role as Italy enters a new period of social transformation.

Spain

We saw in Chapter 2 that during the early Middle Ages, the cities of Spain were the largest in all of Europe; Córdoba, the capital of the Moorish empire, was for several centuries the largest city in the world. In the 1500s, Catholic Spain rose to world dominance, and millions of dollars of wealth poured into the country from colonies in the Americas and Asia. But the wealth generated by this mercantilist empire did not produce a well-developed urban system, nor did it lead to industrialization in the 1700s and 1800s. The Spanish Civil War of the 1930s, which resulted in the triumph of the fascist state that survived until the 1960s, created further divisions that made development more difficult. As a consequence, and unlike most other European countries, Spain is not highly industrialized, and agricultural production remains important for a significant proportion of the population. Most of the manufacturing has been centered over the years in the Madrid region, and the urbanization pattern in this country is not as balanced as in the other European nations we have so far considered.

As we saw in Table 12.1, the proportion of population living in urban areas increased from 73 percent in 1980 to 78 percent in 2000, while the number of persons living in large cities of 1 million or more declined from 20 percent in 1980 to just 13 percent in 2000. The populations of the largest cities in Spain are shown in the bottom half of Table 12.5. The two largest cities are Madrid (the capital, with a population of 2.8 million) and Barcelona (1.4 million). There are four other cities with populations more than 500,000 and a large number of regional centers with populations ranging from 250,000 to 350,000 persons. This urban system is very different from what we have seen in other areas of Europe, in large measure because the level of industrialization did not lead to the concentration of population in large industrial cities. But in recent years, Spain too has been affected by the worldwide restructuring of the global economy.

Older industrial districts, such as Villaverde, have declined and are plagued by job loss and poverty. Small manufacturers, much like the businesses of Italy's *mezzogiorno,* have remained successful, especially those involved in metal working, crafts, and printing. In addition, a new, high-tech corridor running from Madrid past the airport and toward Barcelona has appeared recently that is expanding in employment. And the city of Madrid itself has been changing from a manufacturing economy to a service economy. A building boom of office towers along La Castellana boulevard caused by the growing importance of finance-related business services has produced an increase in service-related employment.

Spain is an interesting case because of the success of its industries during the 1980s under the direction of a socialist government. The 1992 summer Olympics served to showcase Spain's other large metropolis, Barcelona, as well as stimulate the nation's economy. The global recession of the 1990s, however, hit this country hard, as it did all other export-oriented economies. Consequently, there was a slowdown in the sociospatial restructuring of metropolitan areas in Spain.

EASTERN EUROPE

The countries in Eastern Europe were occupied by the Soviet Union at the end of World War II and lived under communist domination for seventy years. They now have joined the capitalist West, but there are many questions about how this heavily urbanized area will develop in the future. The United Nations summarized these concerns in the following manner:

The countries of Eastern Europe and the former Soviet Union are undergoing an economic, political, and administrative transition which is reflected in shrinking gross domestic products, high unemployment and declining fertility and life expectancy. While some countries have shown signs of economic stabilization (e.g., reduced rates of inflation and economic contraction), it will take time to establish new institutions and redefine the role of the public and private sectors. . . . Wasteful consumption and productive patterns, long-term neglect and misdirected policies have led to serious environmental degradation. Toxic industrial pollutants affect health and agriculture. The transition to market economies calls for new regulatory regimes to accommodate greater participation by non-governmental organizations and the private sector. (UNFPA, 1996)

The complicated history of Eastern European cities, and the important social and political issues surrounding their reintegration into European urban history more generally, is described in Box 12.1, which presents the statement of a 2005 conference titled "Cities After the Fall: European Integration and Urban History Conference."

By 2000, some 68 percent of the population in Eastern Europe lived in urban areas—one of the highest levels of urbanization in the world. But as we saw in Table 12.1, the level of urbanization varies substantially from country to country.

This included some seven cities with populations of more than 2 million persons, as shown in Table 12.6. Many Eastern European countries exhibit a pattern of primate city development, where one large urban center dominates the country. Only Russia seems to have been able to develop a balanced urban hierarchy.

Table 12.6 shows the population for the largest metropolitan centers in Eastern Europe. There are several distinctive features about this regional urban system. It is dominated by Moscow, the capital of the former Soviet Union, with a metropolitan region population estimated at 15.2 million in 2003 (citymayors.com, 2005). The second largest metropolitan area, St. Petersburg, with a population of 6.3 million, is the former capital built in the 1700s as Russia sought to become a world power alongside the European monarchies. These are followed by a group of cities with populations of 1.5 to 3.0 million that for the most part represent the capital cities of older nations in Eastern Europe (Warsaw in Poland, Budapest in Hungary) or the newly independent countries of the former USSR (Minsk in Belarus, Kiev in Ukraine).

In 1970 only six Russian cities had more than 1 million persons. By 2000 there were more than a dozen cities with a population of at least 1 million.

BOX 12.1 Cities After the Fall

In his book *Images of the American City,* when Anselm Strauss posed a simple question, "What time is this city?" he was asking about the character of urban temporal orientation and about how it had a formative effect on the character of a city. One could pose the same question in contemporary East Berlin, Riga, Lviv, Vilnius, Minsk or Wrocław, in Gdansk, Kaliningrad, Novgorod, Szczecin, Tallinn, or Odessa; in each case, either storied pasts or supposed European futures would probably insinuate themselves into the contemporary answer. The post-communist projections of the past and the future engender Janus-faced imageries of era and geography in these cities, which, in turn, are strongly influencing their representation and (planned) reconfiguration. A process of cultural reorientation and European integration that began circa 1990 continues.

The reorientations are geopolitical as attempts are made to integrate into a "Western" and "European" context after the fall of the Soviet Union. The transformation of these cities is helping redefine the regions and the modern borders of Europe. One could claim that a "New Europe" takes place and form in these cities, which gravitate to Habsburg, Baltic, Imperial Russian, or Germanic past and propose their own futures in ethnic-national, European, Western, and global contexts. The tourist industry as well as political parties, private heritage societies and government organizations, and other political and economic interests are all involved in this historical and geographical repositioning. Concretely the shift in urban time and place expresses itself in the grand and subtle changes to the urban fabric, which is beginning to accommodate the new order and orientation. The primary object of this conference would be to describe and analyze the significant and concrete changes in the fabric, architecture, commemorative practices, and plan of these cities in relation to their reorientation and repositioning—i.e., in regard to projected ethnic, national, regional, and European frameworks. In most cases, there is a strained discourse between the versions of an urban past and the variously envisioned future(s); meanwhile the opposing arguments are being set in stone or in steel and glass.

SOURCE: "CITIES AFTER THE FALL: EUROPEAN INTEGRATION AND URBAN HISTORY CONFERENCE," MINDA DE GUNZBURG CENTER FOR EUROPEAN STUDIES, HARVARD UNIVERSITY, SPRING 2005.

HTTP://WWW.FAS.HARVARD.EDU/~CES-LIB/WROCLAW.HTML

The two largest cities—Moscow and St. Petersburg—are most similar to cities in the United States and Europe in having a regional formation. The relative size of these two cities is a consequence of the long history of Russia as a centralized state. Moscow is not only the largest city in Eastern Europe, but it also is larger than any other European city. It accounts for half of all banking activity in Russia, along with one-third of its retail sales and one-third

TABLE 12.6   Largest Cities in Eastern Europe, 1975 and 2003

City	Country	Population (1,000,000s) 1975	Population (1,000,000s) 2003	% of Urban Population 1975	% of Urban Population 2003
Moscow	Russian Federation	7.6	10.5	7.3	10.0
Saint Petersburg	Russian Federation	4.3	5.3	3.7	5.0
Katowice	Poland	3.0	3.0	7.7	12.4
Kiev	Ukraine	1.9	2.6	5.4	8.0
Warsaw	Poland	1.9	2.2	5.7	9.2
Bucharest	Romania	1.8	1.9	8.3	15.2
Budapest	Hungary	2.0	1.7	17.3	26.6
Minsk	Belarus	1.1	1.7	17.2	24.3
Kharkov	Ukraine	1.4	1.5	3.0	4.5
Novosibirsk	Russian Federation	1.3	1.4	1.0	1.4
Nizhni Novgorod	Russian Federation	1.3	1.3	0.9	1.2
Ekaterinburg	Russian Federation	1.1	1.3	0.9	1.2
Prague	Czech Republic	1.1	1.2	11.4	15.4
Samara	Russian Federation	1.1	1.2	0.8	1.1
Omsk	Russian Federation	0.9	1.1	0.8	1.1
Kazan	Russian Federation	0.9	1.1	0.8	1.1
Chelyabinsk	Russian Federation	1.0	1.1	0.8	1.0
Sofia	Bulgaria	1.0	1.1	13.6	19.5
Rostov-on-Don	Russian Federation	0.9	1.1	0.8	1.0
Tbilisi	Georgia	1.0	1.1	20.8	40.0
Dnepropetrovsk	Ukraine	1.0	1.1	2.2	3.2
Ufa	Russian Federation	0.9	1.0	0.7	1.0
Odessa	Ukraine	1.0	1.0	2.1	3.1
Volgograd	Russian Federation	0.9	1.0	0.7	1.0
Donetsk	Ukraine	1.0	1.0	2.1	3.1

SOURCE: Adapted from United Nations, Department of Economic and Social Affairs, Population Division, *Urban Agglomerations 2003* (http://www.un.org/esa/population/publications/wup2003).

of national wholesale trade. Although there are more than a dozen Russian cities with populations of 1 million or more, the concentration of economic power and political control under the Soviet state meant that none of these cities developed as metropolitan centers for a larger urban region. This role was reserved for the two cities with former federal status, that is, Moscow and St. Petersburg.

In the past, discussion about Eastern European cities among urbanists focused on whether there is a specific difference in patterns of growth that can be attributed to communism—was there a particular urban form that might be identified as the Socialist City? But according to Friedrichs, "except for a short period in the early 1920s, there are no specific socialist types of land use, distribution of new housing, internal organization of residential blocks, or location of companies" (1988:128). There was some effort to develop urban structures more friendly to the working population in the years following World War I, when much of Europe was governed by a succession of socialist and left-wing political movements, before the solidification of rightist regimes under Fascism. Consequently, communist societies have built environments similar to those in capitalist countries. Yet there are fundamental differences between communism and capitalism, especially with regard to the absence in the former of separate factions of capital and separate markets. There are some peculiarities of land use and population distribution among such cities that differ from patterns in the West. These involve the nature of the central city due to an absence of the finance capital sector, the pattern of population distribution and the housing shortage, and most important, an absence of a capitalist real estate market.

Central City Decline

All Eastern European countries have large capital cities. Some, such as Hungary and Poland, approach the condition of primate status due to the dominance of their main centers—Budapest and Warsaw, respectively. Others, such as the Czech Republic and Russia, have a more balanced system of cities. In every case, the central sections of the major cities are quite old, dating back several hundred years to their founding. Under the communist governments, original buildings in the city center were not torn down. They remain standing and are, in most cases, in terrible shape. The lack of ambitious office building schemes, characteristic of the communist city, stands in contrast to the capitalist city, where finance capital and its associated business services, such as accounting and legal consulting, have taken over the downtown. In most communist countries, the state directed investment; thus, their downtowns do not contain an active real estate market of office buildings that services the needs of corporate and finance capital. As a result, the shift to the service-oriented economy is occurring more slowly in these countries than elsewhere in Europe.

The Demographic Pattern of Land Use

Family income differences in Eastern European cities are not as segregated as in the rest of Europe or the United States (Ladanyi, 1989). In the United States, both the wealthy and the poorest classes are highly segregated. In Eastern European cities, such as Budapest, the upper classes are highly segregated, but the poorest people are only somewhat segregated, and the rest of the population is evenly spread out in the city despite some differences in family income.

The reason for this contrast seems to be the operation of government subsidies for housing, which has prevented the poorest people from being concentrated within urban spaces. Thus, a major difference between formerly communist societies and capitalist ones such as the United States is the active role of government in providing affordable housing for the poor (although, as we will see below, the total volume of housing provided is inadequate). Paradoxically, however, under the communist governments, the more affluent people have also enjoyed considerable state housing subsidies (Ladanyi, 1989). Consequently, it is not the market that has created uneven development in formerly communist countries, as it does under capitalism, but state intervention itself. This kind of uneven development and privilege produced by state favors for the elite has been a common complaint about communist practice for decades; however, it is comparable to the economic advantages of the capitalist class in the United States.

With the fall of communism, housing subsidies are declining, and as the market takes over, segregation is also increasing. More privately produced housing represents efforts to alleviate the chronic shortage of housing in these societies. However, a shift to an active capitalist real estate market is also producing the first significant signs of capitalist-style uneven development within urban settlement spaces, such as a growing number of homeless people and a sharp rise in the cost of rental housing, which hits elderly pensioners particularly hard.

The Emergence of Free Markets

Eastern Europe is now the scene of immense social changes as the changeover is made from communism to a market economy. Potentially the most significant change is the growth of the real estate market and a new, second circuit of capital for formerly communist countries. It remains to be seen how this restructuring will affect settlement space; however, we can use the U.S. case as a guide for future projections. Some indications already suggest that within the large cities, segregation will increase, deconcentration of population will accelerate as suburbanization occurs, and the service economy will replace manufacturing as the principal sector. It remains to be seen how slowly or quickly land use in the centers of cities such as Budapest, Warsaw, Prague, and Moscow will also change. Old buildings remain, and to date there is little new office construction, but this situation most likely cannot last as the capitalist urban land market takes over and the pressures to switch to a service-based economy prevail there as they have in the capitalist West. We can even expect drastic renovation or renewal programs, led by private

BOX 12.2   Social Problems in Eastern Europe

The contraction of state-sector employment without commensurate growth of private-sector employment has led to a decline in real wages, pensions, and social transfers within a general context of high inflation. The breakup of the former Soviet Union generated severe disruptions in the old trading and monetary regimes, which resulted in catastrophic declines in GDP of about 45 percent during the 1990–1996 period.

The region saw subsequent rising income inequalities. Open poverty and unemployment also increased significantly. It has been observed that the failure of rapid privatization in Russia, for instance, "was not an accident, but a predictable consequence" of the absence of competition policies and the institutional and legal infrastructure needed to support successful reform efforts. The region's poor housing conditions are reflected in recent slum estimates, which reveal that in transition economies about one-tenth of the urban population live in slum conditions, without adequate access to basic services, or in crowded housing units. In 2002, about 46 percent of residents of the former Soviet Union and Eastern European countries lived on less than US$4 per day, compared to 10 percent in Western Europe. Fifty-three percent of the Russian population, 23 percent in Romania, 28 percent in Latvia, 62 percent in Kazakhstan, and 88 percent in Kyrgyzstan have to survive on even less.

Trafficking and smuggling of human beings operated by organized crime networks in countries whose economies are in transition has become of particular concern to national governments and the international community. Although Asian countries have been the primary suppliers of women to the sex trade for decades, the collapse of the Soviet Union has made former Soviet republics such as Ukraine, Belarus, Latvia, and Russia major source countries of women into prostitution. Trafficked women from this region are delivered into prostitution throughout the world, and there are estimated to be a half million women from Central and Eastern Europe working in prostitution in the European Union alone.

Today the dream for a better life seems to have vanished in the face of the millions of new poor exposed to living conditions that can be similar to those living in the least developed nations. Across Eastern Europe and Central Asia, household poverty has increased fivefold during the last twelve years and its social by-products are discernible everywhere: sharp increases in alcoholism—especially among men—suicide, and mortality, as well as a decline in marriage and a rise in divorce rates.

SOURCE: ADAPTED FROM "POVERTY, CRIME AND MIGRATION ARE ACUTE ISSUES AS EASTERN EUROPEAN CITIES CONTINUE TO GROW," *CITIES IN EASTERN EUROPE*, CITY MAYORS SOCIETY, WWW.CITYMAYORS.COM/SOCIETY/EASTEUROPE_CITIES.HTML.

investment, for the construction of high-rise office towers in the Eastern European cities of the future.

JAPAN

One of the world's greatest economic powers, Japan has contained large cities for hundreds of years (Bestor, 1985). Tokyo, for example, had over 1 million people as early as the 1700s when it served as the capital (called Edo at the time) of the shogun empire. The modernization of Tokyo following the Meiji Restoration has resulted in a continuous migration from rural areas to the expanding metropolitan region surrounding the capital city. Since World War II, Japanese cities have developed as large regional agglomerations or multicentered metropolitan regions. The greater Tokyo metropolitan area is estimated to contain 34 million people, a quarter of the entire population of Japan, while the city of Tokyo alone had more than 8 million persons in 2000. This large urban agglomeration is comparable to that of New York and Los Angeles combined. The overall level of urbanization of the Japanese population, some 80 percent of the total, is comparable to that of Western countries such as the United States and Britain.

The population of the largest metropolitan areas in Japan is shown in Table 12.7. Two urban centers dominate this urban system. The Tokyo metropolitan area includes the cities of Tokyo (8.1 million), Yokohama (3.4 million), and Kawasaki (1.2 million) and another 20 million persons living in other cities and urbanized areas linked to these cities. The greater Osaka metropolitan area (16.8 million persons) includes the cities of Osaka (2.6 million), Kobe (1.5 million), and Kyoto (1.5 million), and another 11 million persons in the urbanized areas linked to these cities. There is one other great metropolitan area (Nagoya, with a population of 8 million), and two metropolitan areas of more than 2.5 million (Sapporo and Fukuoka). Table 12.7 includes eight other metropolitan areas with populations of more than 1 million, and there is some variation in the structure of these regions: In Hiroshima and Kitakyushu the city population accounts for more than half of the metropolitan area, while the populations of the cities of Naha and Himeji account for less than a third of their metropolitan regions.

Japanese cities developed trading and commercial centers during the sixteenth and seventeenth centuries. When industrialization was occurring in the nineteenth century, it was embraced by Japanese business along with the aid of the monarchy. By the beginning of the twentieth century, Japan was already a major industrial power. After the massive loss of labor and industrial production as a consequence of World War II, Japan initiated ambitious in-

TABLE 12.7 Largest Metropolitan Areas in Japan, 2000

City	City Population	Metropolitan Area
Tokyo	8,130,000	34,000,000
Yokohama	3,426,000	
Kawasaki	1,249,000	
Osaka	2,598,000	16,750,000
Kobe	1,493,000	
Kyoto	1,467,000	
Nagoya	2,171,000	8,000,000
Sapporo	1,822,000	2,500,000
Fukuoka	1,341,000	2,250,000
Hiroshima	1,126,000	1,725,000
Kitakyushu	1,011,000	1,600,000
Okayama	627,000	1,375,000
Naha	301,000	1,125,000
Himeji	471,000	1,125,000
Kumamoto	662,123	1,100,000
Hamamatsu	582,000	1,100,000
Shizuoka	470,000	1,000,000

SOURCE: Adapted from Thomas Brinkerhoff, *Principal Agglomerations and Cities of the World* (http://www.citypopulation.de, 5.0.05).

dustrialization schemes focusing on exports, which were remarkably successful in establishing Japan as a global economic power (Lee, 1982; Berry, 1989).

Japanese cities have not experienced the same forms of deconcentration that we observe in U.S. cities, nor have they undergone a shift to services on the same scale as cities in the United States and older industrialized countries. Today manufacturing remains important to the Japanese economy. Work is highly centralized within city boundaries even though the suburban population is growing. Each day several million commuters ride into the central city by public transportation, often traveling as much as two hours each way. Japan is unlike the United States in other respects as well. Due to a free market in real estate, a general shortage of land in the country, and the centralization of employment within large cities, housing and rental prices are astronomically high. It has become increasingly difficult to own one's own home there, and most housing space, in terms of square feet, is extremely small by U.S. standards.

The success of Japan's export-oriented industries in the global economy has resulted in important changes in settlement space patterns for the entire Pacific Rim. Japanese industries innovated a number of techniques, such as "just-in-time" methods, that increased their competitiveness. They also embarked on regional schemes of manufacturing in search of cheap labor (much like U.S. companies), which had an impact on other Asian countries, in particular South Korea and Taiwan. But the real impact occurred because of Japan's success in foreign trade earnings. Within a few decades, it became a major repository of the world's finance capital.

Several notable trends characterize Japanese industrial and urban development. Most significant is the profits squeeze from the increasing costs of Japanese labor. This has resulted in the kind of response adopted by U.S. firms, namely, the shift of some production to other countries with cheaper and more compliant sources of labor. While marketing and control remain located in Japan, the past two decades have witnessed an increase in the amount of component part production farmed out to Taiwan, South Korea, and Singapore (Douglas, 1988; Berry, 1989:203).

Japan is experiencing another trend common to the United States and Europe. Japan has always restricted its immigration, which is why its labor force and urban populations have remained more stable than those in countries such as the United States. Lately, however, illegal immigration is becoming noticeable as the global flow of investment and people integrates the Pacific Rim countries. Typically, such immigration occurs because the low-wage, menial jobs that are necessary in a developed economy are no longer being filled by the domestic population because of increases in the quality of life and training levels. This has been the experience of the United States and, increasingly, of Japan. Sassen (1991:308) notes that since the late 1980s, there has been a rapid increase in the number of illegal aliens working in Japan; typically, they enter the country with tourist visas and overstay their officially permitted time. It is estimated that in the 1990s there were 200,000 illegal male workers in Japan in manual work, from construction to restaurant kitchens. Almost all of these were from Asia. The largest groups were from Taiwan, South Korea, Bangladesh, the Philippines, and Pakistan.

Japanese cities are not characterized by the kind of social segregation found in the West, although the wealthy are isolated from the rest of the masses. However, they exhibit uneven development with regard to the lack of services and facilities. Extreme housing and space shortages still affect the city's inhabitants. There are few parks, medical facilities, and community centers in Tokyo. The city does contain an extensive mass transit network, as do other Japanese cities, but all Japanese cities suffer from pollution, smog, noise, and overcrowding (Nakamura and White, 1988). Other areas of the country are plagued by extensive pollution resulting from industrial development that the government has not controlled.

Population demographics will have an impact on Japanese cities and metropolitan areas in the coming decades, but in a way very different from other

Asian countries (see Chapter 13). The fertility rate is very low and is expected to decrease rapidly, as we have already seen in some Western European countries. It is estimated that Japan's population in 2050 may be only 100 million—a decrease of 17 percent (Fujii, 2005). Changing demographics will have an impact on the metropolitan region. Japan generally has not seen the decline of urban centers similar to that of Detroit (Chapter 6) or Liverpool (earlier in this chapter). Fujii suggests that Osaka may be the most appropriate urban comparison. Osaka reached its peak population of 3.0 million in 1985 but has decreased since then (to 2.6 million in 1995). Some observers suggest that cities in Japan may be shrinking for a number of reasons: port cities such as Nagasaki and Kobe have declined relative to other cities; manufacturing centers such as Kitakyushu are "company towns" vulnerable to the relative success of just one company or economic sector; and in some instances companies have moved out of older industrial cities to locate in the capital. As a consequence, the Tokyo metropolitan region prospers while other cities may decline.

Much recent development in Japan involves the construction of new spaces that bypass traditional urban agglomerations. This is especially the case for the new technopoles that have been energetically constructed with massive government support, a feature that differs from the United States, which has yet to undertake such federally sponsored development. Most projects are joint ventures by the state, universities, and private capital, such as the giant Tsukuba "science city" centered on Skuba university outside of Tokyo. More recently, technopoles have been developed in the peripheral regions of Japan—those areas previously bypassed by development—such as Hokkaido, Tohoku, Kyushu, and the area along the Sea of Japan. One of the most ambitious of these projects is the "silicon island" developed on Kyushu, centered in Kumamoto City. This region has become a leading producer of microchips and contains a population of over 1.1 million persons (Fujita, 1988).

Japan exhibits some of the characteristics of Western industrialized countries. Its traditional urban centers continue to grow. At the same time, new spaces have been created to house the "knowledge industries." These are similar to technopoles found elsewhere, but Japan's government is energetic in its support of such new development. Japan's urban system shows symptoms of overurbanization and is dominated by Tokyo and other large agglomerations, such as Osaka and Nagoya. Due to the high cost of land and the very high price of housing, there is little suburbanization or residential construction. As a result, many Japanese must contend with long commutes from regional towns to work in crowded facilities and cramped living quarters at home.

SUMMARY

Cities and metropolitan regions in the developed nations have undergone significant economic restructuring to service-based economies, with a reduced scale of government aid similar to that in the United States. New techniques of post-Fordist manufacturing have been introduced in the successful industries, including automation and Japanese-style flexible methods of production. High-technology corridors, similar to Silicon Valley in the United States, have also appeared, such as the M-4 corridor in England. Finally, there is an increasing integration of large corporations and transnational firms that, like their American counterparts, conduct business around the globe.

Economic restructuring has also brought an increasing array of urban problems. Crime, poverty, and the declining quality of life, almost unheard of as European concerns, are now becoming serious problems. Hate crimes, anti-immigrant sentiments, and racism are on the rise. Poverty and unemployment are growing because of related economic changes that have hit the working class especially hard.

Cutbacks in the traditional European welfare state have made the problem of poverty more severe. Since the level of funding for public assistance varies greatly among the countries of Western Europe, despite recent EU programs, fears have been expressed about the possibility of "social dumping." This phenomenon arises when one geographical area has appreciably better social programs than another during a time of economic hardship. Poor populations migrate to the area with better benefits.

A different form of social dumping has already been experienced by European countries and, to an extent, the United States. Since the 1970s, large numbers of workers from the Third World have entered developed societies in the hope of obtaining work. Several million Turks, Kurds, and Greeks, for example, live in Germany. Millions of North Africans have migrated to France, and even the Danes, who have always lived in a homogeneous society, are now concerned about the high Muslim birth rate in their country. It is now quite common to have African, Middle Eastern, or Asian cab drivers in Paris, London, and Berlin (not just Los Angeles and New York). Domestic servants, undocumented workers, and low-skilled, labor-intensive factories or sweat shops composed of Third World workers are increasingly common in all these cities. Even Japan, which restricts immigration, has a growing number of illegal aliens from Asia who come there in search of work.

Global economic restructuring therefore brings an increasingly mobile flow not only of capital investment and goods but also of people. Immigration from Third World countries to Europe has affected the social order of these once relatively homogeneous societies in notable ways. The growing presence of foreigners is reflected in the increasing mix of ethnic restaurants that have sprung up in city centers. This drawing together of the First and Third Worlds in a common urban experience is increasingly characteristic of contemporary Western cities.

All of these elements have combined to produce changes in the social order of once homogeneous European societies. Uneven development in wage levels creates a growing disparity between well-off professionals and low-wage service workers. Migration and ethnic cultural influences have met with increasing numbers of hate crimes, racism, and most ironically, anti-Semitism in a post-Holocaust Europe.

Asian urban development is led by the modern economy of Japan and, more recently, of China (see Chapter 13). It too suffers from uneven development. Japanese housing and real estate issues are worrisome, and the shortage of affordable units will provoke a crisis of business location as fewer and fewer workers find places to live within commuting distances of jobs. But many negative effects are outweighed by the success of Japanese economic growth. Industrial expansion brings the growth of multicentered metropolitan regions outside of Japan's traditional manufacturing centers—Tokyo, Osaka, and Nagoya. Financial investment flowing from Japan fuels the economies of the Asian tigers and thereby restructures the entire Pacific Rim (as well as the United States, Canada, and Australia, in addition to the less developed countries of Asia and Latin America) for a new round of growth.

Common problems abound in Europe, Japan, and the United States, including the growing lack of affordable housing, challenges from the flow of immigrants who are often illegal aliens, declines in manufacturing employment, and the uneven development of economic opportunities for city populations due to the restructuring of the economy and the emphasis on high-tech skills. With few exceptions, however, no industrialized country has experienced the kind of inner-city collapse and decline in the conditions of everyday life comparable to the U.S. experience. In this respect the United States presents a unique case to the world—although parallels may be found in Third World cities such as Calcutta and Nairobi, as we will see in the next chapter.

KEY CONCEPTS

Fordist means of production
global restructuring
welfare state

deindustrialization
social dumping
social exclusion

DISCUSSION QUESTIONS

1. How is the pattern of urbanization in other industrialized countries similar to that found in the United States? In what ways does it differ from that in the United States? What factors are responsible for these differences?

2. Many of the changes in urban systems and metropolitan areas in other industrialized countries are similar to those in the United States. How have changes in the global economy affected metropolitan areas in Western Europe? Have these changes made these cities more similar to or more different from those in the United States?

3. What are the effects of deindustrialization and other changes in the global economy on cities in Western Europe? What are some of the important differences in the ways in which national governments responded to these changes?

4. How are the patterns of urbanization in Eastern Europe different from those in Western Europe? Explain the effects of the housing shortage and central city decline.

5. How are the history and pattern of urbanization in Japan different from those of other industrialized countries? How have changes in the global economy affected new urban developments in Japan?

GLOBALIZATION AND
THIRD WORLD URBANIZATION

In 2005, the world's urban population is estimated to be more than 3 billion persons. That is approximately ten times the total population of the United States. The number is expected to increase to some 5 billion persons by 2030, representing an annual growth rate of about 1.8 percent (nearly double the increase of the world population as a whole). At this rate of growth, the number of persons living in urban areas will double in thirty-eight years. These figures are overwhelming, and not simply because it is difficult to think of 1 million people at anything more than a conceptual level, much less 1 billion persons. The figures are overwhelming because almost all of the growth in the world's urban population in the future is expected to take place in the cities and metropolitan regions of the less developed nations.

Table 13.1 reflects the dramatic changes that have taken place in world urban population over the past fifty years. In 1950 there were just two metropolitan areas with a population of 8 million or more persons—New York and London, reflecting the concentration effects of urban growth under industrial capitalism in the developed nations. By 1970, there were nine metropolitan areas in this category, four in the developed nations (New York, London, Tokyo, and Los Angeles) and five in the developing nations (Shanghai, Buenos Aires, Mexico City, Beijing, and São Paulo). In 2000 two new metropolitan areas in the developed nations were added to this list, but an astonishing eighteen new metropolitan areas in the developing nations crossed the threshold. Of the twenty-two metropolitan areas with populations of 8 million or more persons in less developed regions, four are located in South America, one is in

FIGURE 13.1   City Lights of Asia
Source: NASA.

sub-Saharan Africa, and three are in the Middle East. Fifteen of the metropolitan areas are located in Asia, including six on the Indian subcontinent. Population estimates for 2030 show further growth—overwhelming growth—in metropolitan regions across the developing nations, particularly in Asia.

One way to think of the significance of the increase of large urban agglomerations in the developing world is that most of us would recognize the names of the cities shown in 1970—Mexico City, Buenos Aires (capital of Argentina), São Paulo (capital of Brazil). And many would recognize the cities in 1990—Manila (capital of the Philippines), Seoul (capital of South Korea). But few of us would recognize the cities that by 2030 will take their place alongside these more familiar names.

In Chapter 12 we studied metropolitan regions in Europe and Japan. In many ways the growth of cities in the more developed nations is similar to the postwar development of cities in the United States: There has been extensive

TABLE 13.1 Urban Agglomerations with Populations Exceeding 8 million, 1950–2030

1950	1970	1990	2000	2030
More Developed Regions				
New York	New York	Tokyo	Tokyo	Tokyo
London	London	New York	New York	New York
	Tokyo	Los Angeles	Los Angeles	Los Angeles
	Los Angeles	Moscow	Moscow	Osaka-Kobe
		Osaka-Kobe	Osaka-Kobe	Moscow
		Paris	Paris	Paris
				Chicago
Less Developed Regions				
	Shanghai	Mexico City	Mexico City	Bombay
	Mexico City	São Paulo	São Paulo	Delhi
	Buenos Aires	Shanghai	Shanghai	Mexico City
	Beijing	Calcutta	Calcutta	São Paulo
	São Paulo	Buenos Aires	Buenos Aires	Dhaka
		Bombay	Bombay	Jakarta
		Seoul	Beijing	Lagos
		Beijing	Jakarta	Calcutta
		Rio de Janeiro	Delhi	Karachi
		Tianjin	Buenos Aires	Buenos Aires
		Jakarta	Lagos	Cairo
		Cairo	Tianjin	Shanghai
		Delhi	Seoul	Manila
		Manila	Rio de Janeiro	Rio de Janeiro
			Dhaka	Istanbul
			Cairo	Beijing
			Manila	Tianjin
			Karachi	Lima
			Bangkok	Seoul
			Istanbul	Sante fe de Bogata
			Tehran	Lahore
			Bangalore	Kinshasa
			Lima	Tehran
				Bangalore
				Chennai (Madras)
				Wuhan

SOURCE: Adapted from United Nations, *World Urbanization Prospects: The 2003 Revision*; and United Nations, Department of Economic and Social Affairs, Population Division, *World Agglomerations 2003*.

growth in the suburban areas, resulting in urban sprawl. Infrastructure development has kept pace with the expansion of the metropolitan area. While there are troubling social inequalities that often are compounded by spatial segregation, most people have adequate housing, with access to basic utilities including electricity, clean water, and sanitary facilities. In the past this pattern of development was sometimes described as urbanization with industrialization, emphasizing the importance of economic development to provide for the needs of a growing urban population.

Despite problems of uneven development and economic transition, most people living in cities in the developed nations are well housed and well fed. The majority can find work and pursue careers that offer opportunities for advancement as their communities respond to changes in the new global economy. But in many other parts of the world, cities have a different relationship to society, and people's individual fortunes are plagued by dangers and disparities unheard of in more affluent societies. In this chapter, we examine the urban condition in Asia, Africa, and Latin America. These regions contain three-fourths of the world's population and most of its landmass. The societies range from democracies to totalitarian dictatorships. What they have in common is an inability to sustain economic development and, with some notable exceptions, a declining quality of life for most of their urban residents. In the past, this pattern of development was described as urbanization without industrialization, emphasizing the problems in providing basic needs for an ever-increasing population in cities in the developing world.

CHANGING PERSPECTIVES ON THIRD WORLD URBANIZATION

In approaching the issue of urbanization in developing countries, a number of misconceptions must be dispelled. First, persons living in the developed nations, and especially persons in the United States, commonly think of these regions as being primitively developed compared to the United States. In fact, however, countries such as China, Mexico, and Korea are highly industrialized, with factory workers numbering in the millions. Some of the largest cities in the world, such as Shanghai, São Paulo, and Bangkok, not only are located in developing countries but also are dynamic urban centers (see the next section). But many Third World countries share a pattern of uneven development that is even more extreme than that found in the older, developed nations. The prospects for persons living in these cities are very different from those of urban residents in New York, London, or Tokyo.

Second, the ecological theory that continues to dominate mainstream urban sociology argues that developing countries are much like the developed societies, only at an earlier stage of development, and that they will "modernize" in time (Kasarda and Crenshaw, 1991). The sociospatial perspective conflicts with this view in that it considers factors such as the roles of the state, socioeconomic class, global capital investment, and economic changes in the First World—all of which are neglected by the ecological approach—as critical for an understanding of urbanization in developing countries. Thus, the sociospatial perspective suggests that countries having different economic structures will develop in different ways. Close observers of growth patterns in areas such as Latin America (Roberts, 1978) and Asia (Berry, 1989) seem to agree that the explanatory variables stressed by the sociospatial approach are most important, while not necessarily subscribing to the perspective itself. Contrary to what the human ecology and modernization theory would predict, the process of urbanization in the developing nations is *different* from what we have observed in the more developed nations. The key differences involve factors such as elite power, state policies, integration into the global economy, and the effects of class structure (Smith and Timberlake, 1993).

A third change in perspective concerns the increasing relevance of the global economy. Prior to the 1970s, there seemed to be a sharp distinction between First and Third World economies. Countries such as the United States were still operating under "Fordist" arrangements of production during this time, meaning that most manufacturing was carried out domestically, and foreign countries were viewed principally as a source of raw materials and as markets for U.S. goods. Less developed countries were sources for agricultural goods such as coffee or winter fruits but were otherwise thought to be disconnected from our own society, except perhaps as places for tourists to visit and strategic locations for military bases. Developmental theories of the time proposed the concept of "peripheral urbanization," which emphasized the marginal nature of the Third World (Harvey, 1973; Castells, 1977; Walton, 1982). In other words, countries were seen to be either part of the core of the world system (the developed nations), or they were relegated to the periphery (the developing world).

Since the 1970s, however, vast changes have occurred in the developed nations as Fordist arrangements of production have been replaced by post-Fordist production and the country underwent deindustrialization. During the 1970s and 1980s, much U.S. manufacturing employment was shipped overseas, and countries such as Mexico, Malaysia, Singapore, Brazil, and the Dominican Republic were used as effective sites for labor. By the 1990s, it had become commonplace for consumers in the United States to find that the products they purchased, whether articles of clothing, sports equipment, or cars, were assembled in foreign places. Thus, a pattern of manufacturing for world markets was established in many areas of the Third World, and people's lives in the United States were connected by multinational corporations to formerly peripheral societies (Peet, 1987).

Recent studies of Third World urbanization now reject previous approaches that emphasized world system marginality or dependency (Datta, 1990). Instead, it is argued that these countries are increasingly linked to the global economy. The cycle of investment, manufacturing, consumption, and

BOX 13.1   The Impact of Globalization on Third World Cities

Globalization at the national level leads to the economic restructuring and global linking of particular regions within the nation, particular cities in these regions, and particular geographical segments within these cities. Thus, various levels of change permeate society. Unfortunately, the globalized population and geographical regions sponge on the population and regions lacking global links. In developing countries, government policies play an integral role in bridging inequalities. But in their eagerness to push rapid global economic integration, governments strengthen the processes of exclusion through fragmentation of employment, housing, and social services.

As nations compete, cities too begin to compete with each other under the neoliberal agenda. These cities differ from those of an earlier era in terms of the way urban space is utilized, governed, contested, and represented. Capital mobility, leading to competition for investment, has forced city governments to adopt innovative and entrepreneurial approaches to local growth. Local governments take up selective projects to improve the urban environment, which end up either displacing or excluding segments of population or, through privatization, lead to fragmentation of housing, infrastructure, and services as well as institutional structures. City plans give priority to business, and scarce city resources are diverted to cater to the needs of business. Many local economies providing employment to the poor are de-legitimized and face eviction from productive locations sought after by elite groups.

An increase in inequality in cities leads to issues of internal security. This pushes the rich to live in enclaves that are well protected. The city gets segmented between the rich and the poor. Segregation may not be total, but some segments of the city would have a concentration of the rich and others of the poor, as observed in the case of Mumbai. In Buenos Aires, one finds rich enclaves cropping up. In Mumbai, the privatization of basic services could exclude poorer areas from receiving an adequate level of services. In Buenos Aires, the rich have avoided contributing to the costs of services at the city level. In the wake of the outbreak of suspected plague in Surat city in 1995, some city planners came up with the idea of bifurcating the Surat Municipal Corporation into two—a corporation consisting of residential areas where the rich and middle classes live, and another where the poor and industrial workers live and where the plague originated. Thus, the social and spatial segmentation of the mega-city into "citadels" and "ghettos" takes place, and the city's geography changes.

Infrastructure projects based on the principle of public-private partnership or privatization, including those for water supply and sanitation, increase the cost of living for the poor and may altogether exclude the poorest. Land development becomes an intensely contested area. The new environmental agenda, under the concept of

(continues)

Sustainable Cities, also ends up expelling the poor from the city space and economy. Low-skilled workers in industries or industrial zones, services, and the informal sector congregate at the fringes where systems are inadequately developed, or in areas of the mega-city that are environmentally stressed or hazardous. The development processes that unwind are exclusionary. Large sections are first expelled from the economic space and then excluded from various city-level social systems. Women in poor communities suffer the most.

The influence of multilateral international development agencies, such as the World Bank and Asian Development Bank, and of some bilateral development agencies is increasingly felt in development policy making. Most of these agencies promote privatization in urban areas. The conditions for urban development lending often include clauses such as allowing transnational or multinational utilities to enter the city. Such policies lead to exclusion in the city through the process of privatization and also increase debt liability, thereby reducing the city's ability to address the issue of sustainable poverty reduction.

ADAPTED FROM D. MAHADEVIA, "INCLUSIVE MEGA-CITIES IN GLOBALISING ASIA," INFO CHANGE URBAN INDIA, HTTP://INFOCHANGEINDIA.ORG/URBAN_INDIA_10.JSP.

profit making that leads to greater investment integrates consumers and producers in the developed nations with manufacturing, banking, and consumption activities in other countries, including the Third World. This effect is often called the "internationalization of capital." The once meaningful "comparative" study of urbanization in Third World countries and urbanization in the United States and other developed nations has been replaced by the study of globalization—of the growing interconnections and interdependence between the core and periphery because of government policy, international trade agreements, and other recent developments.

The sociospatial perspective acknowledges the influence of the global system of capital on locality. The case of the Philippines is of some interest in this regard. As one of the capital cities in the Spanish colonial empire, Manila has been part of the capitalist world system from the 1500s on. Its position as a regional city within the global system of capital was increased when it became an American colony following the Spanish American War and again in the post–World War II years. Over the past two decades, however, Manila's importance and influence in the Southeast Asian economy has declined. Capital flows and investments in the new system of global capitalism have bypassed Manila in favor of Hong Kong and Singapore and, more recently, Shanghai. While many countries in Southeast Asia have prospered during the past decade, the economy of the Philippines has registered a negative growth rate, and urban development in Manila lags behind that of other cities that have emerged as more important in the global system of capital.

But it is important to recognize that urbanization processes in both developed and developing nations often involve combinations of global, national, and local factors that may operate independently of the global economy. The form of government at the national level has played a key role in the success—or failure—of development schemes in many Third World countries. China, South Korea and Singapore, for example, have aggressive national policies in pursuit of growth and governments that actively aid capital investment (Barone, 1983). Other countries, such as many Latin American societies, are plagued by "crony capitalism" and government corruption and dictatorships that squander national wealth.

At the most local level, there are also independent effects that are related to but not determined by the global level. Third World cities are moving rapidly from the stage of developing economies to postindustrial relations, that is, skipping many of the features of industrialization that inform the experience of Western, developed nations (Roberts, 1991). Large cities in the Third World, like their First World counterparts, are experiencing shifts to a service-oriented employment base due to their increasing role as command and control centers of capital investment. As a result of new employment opportunities created for professional workers, there is a growing wage differential between well-paid and working-poor residents. How this increasingly diverse class structure manifests itself politically varies from country to country and involves new patterns of local political activity that are independent of, and in some cases oppositional to, global system needs (see the section on social movements).

The sociospatial perspective on Third World urbanization emphasizes global linkages, differences in class structure, the effects of national state arrangements, and differences in local politics as key factors for an understanding of current trends. Third World urbanization processes also have many features in common that contrast with First World experiences. These can be identified by considering the nature of population growth and change, or demography, which we discuss next.

DEMOGRAPHY AND THIRD WORLD URBANIZATION

When dealing with rapid population changes such as those that affected the United States in the 1800s and affect developing countries today, the science of demography can offer important insights. Demographers track the dynamics of population growth, concentrating on rates of change, such as the frequency of births and deaths and the average number of children per mother. Demographers are also interested in rates of migration, especially changes in the rural and urban populations. For any given population, the rate of increase that depends on the number of births minus deaths is known as the *natural increase*. Population changes within any given settlement space can arise from natural increase or from migration.

For most of human history, the high birth rate was offset by an equally high death rate, and populations grew very slowly. Following World War II, the introduction of modern medical techniques and preventive measures to the Third World resulted in a population explosion that is called the *demographic transition*. When new techniques of medical intervention lowered the death rates in these countries, the societies experienced a permanent rise in the rate of natural increase because they maintained a high birth rate. In the developed world, the demographic transition was eventually adjusted by means of a declining birth rate, as the rising standard of living associated with industrialization led to smaller family size. Many European countries now have low or even negative growth rates. That stage has yet to occur in the Third World, although some countries, such as Brazil, have drastically lowered their growth rates in recent years. But for most of the Third World, birth rates still outstrip death rates, and overpopulation is a serious social and environmental problem.

The demographic problems of the Third World are compounded by the limited success of economic development. Faced with a population explosion, rural areas have been hard-pressed to grow enough food for domestic consumption. Despite the best efforts of developmental economists, the standard of living in rural areas has declined drastically since the 1950s in most Third World countries. There are simply too many mouths to feed. The dilemma facing families was poignantly depicted in a Mexican film by Luis Buñuel, *Los Olvidados*. A farmer comes to the city with his young son. They move toward a crowd in the center of the city. When the father is satisfied that his son is distracted, he seizes his chance and runs away. Many Third World cities are teeming with such abandoned children, many of whom are exploited by a growing sex industry catering to foreign tourists. As might be expected, they have a short life span.

The failure of rural agricultural efforts to mass produce enough to sustain the quality of life has led excess population to migrate to the cities. Despite the hardships of life found there, the move holds out the promise of improvement, and this encourages others to come. As a result, Third World cities suffer from a *double* population explosion: a high rate of natural increase *and* a high rate of in-migration. In the city, there is little room for poor people's housing. In many cities, urban migrants find space on the outskirts and put up makeshift shelters that lack the basic necessities of homes, such as running water, sanitation facilities, and even adequate ventilation for heating. These shantytowns, or squatter settlements, have many names all over the world—*favellas* (Brazil), *bustees* (India), *barriadas* (Mexico), *poblaciones* (Chile), *villas miserias* (Argentina), *bidonvilles* (Africa), and *Kampongs* (Southeast Asia). But they have many features in common, including frequent public health crises, crime, crushing poverty, and no future for the next generation since few countries provide them with schools. We will discuss shantytowns in more detail later.

A third effect of demographic changes in Third World countries involves their common experience of social, economic, and political exploitation under European and American colonialism. Western powers took control of underdeveloped countries in Africa, Asia, and South America beginning in the sixteenth century. In 1898 the United States gained control of the former Spanish colonies: the Philippines, Hawaii, Cuba, and Puerto Rico. The principal goal was to acquire natural resources such as gold, spices, and later, cheaply produced manufactured goods. Because colonialism or imperialism depended on trade with the conquering country, effective links to the global world system were established early. A result of colonialism was the construction of large cities that were usually located near the coast, such as Hong Kong, Manila, Lagos, Singapore, Bombay, and Bangkok. Over the years these cities grew immensely, but few other cities were founded because the colonial powers did not deem them necessary.

Over the years, many Third World countries have been able to launch development programs that have overcome the legacy of colonial control. However, the success of these programs has been limited due to changes in geopolitics and in the world economy, as well as to national issues such as crony capitalism and civil conflict. These factors hinder the balanced growth of cities in these countries. As a result, many Third World countries today possess a single, gigantic *primate city* that is *overurbanized*, or excessively populated, and remains the center for most investment and economic growth, while retaining a relatively *underurbanized* interior with no large cities. Primate cities are characteristic of an unbalanced pattern of urbanization that remains quite different from that found in the developed countries of the world. Let us examine this unique feature in more detail, as well as other characteristics of Third World urbanization, including shantytown development, household coping strategies and the informal economy, and new urban social movements.

PRIMATE CITY DEVELOPMENT PATTERNS

In developed countries such as the United States, there is an even distribution in the number of cities according to size (see Chapter 4). Some, such as New York City with more than 8 million people, are quite large; others fill in the ranks with smaller populations of between 500,000 and 1 million, such as San Francisco, and between 100,000 and 500,000, such as Minneapolis, and so on down the hierarchy. Such a profile constitutes "balanced" urbanization, and it provides a range of urban environments and locational options for both businesses and people.

Primate cities dominate and distort development within their countries. *Overurbanization,* or the presence of primate cities, is measured by comparing the size of the largest city with other large cities within a given country. In the developing world, the disparities among urban centers may be very great. In Thailand, for example, the population of the capital city of Bangkok was 6,685,000 in 2000, more than thirty times larger than that of the next largest city (the population figure applies to the total urbanized area of the capital city). Countries with primate cities lack locational flexibility: If one is looking for investment opportunities within the country, there typically is only one area that has the population and infrastructure to support development. If one is looking for employment, there is only one area where new jobs are being created. As a consequence, countries that have primate cities are locked in a migratory cycle. Like a magnet, primate cities pull mobile populations from the countryside at the expense of other locations.

The pattern of primate city development not only is inconsistent with models of urban growth based upon location theory but also calls into question the legitimacy of ecological theory. You may recall from Chapter 3 that urban ecologists sought to apply the model of factorial ecology to cities in developing nations with the belief that a single model could explain urbanization in all countries around the world. Another part of this perspective holds that developed nations should be the model for poorer countries, asserting that Third World countries should industrialize and urbanize as rapidly as possible. Ecological theory suggests that when they do, those living in industrialized cities will increase their incomes and acquire a better quality of life. By encouraging urban growth, the entire society benefits.

The sociospatial perspective disagrees with this view. Third World countries may grow through industrial development and as part of the new postindustrial economy, but economic growth is likely only when it occurs in conjunction with world system priorities and investment flows. Consequently, rapid urbanization may have negative effects because its principal cause is the needs of global capital and not the quality of life for local populations (Smith, 1985). As a result, Third World countries can suffer from extremely uneven development despite impressive modernization efforts, and primate cities are often the consequence. While the *average* income of primate city residents may be greater than that of rural counterparts, the inequality of income and of quality of life is so severe in primate cities that the standard of living is lower than in rural areas (Bradshaw and Fraser, 1989). Thus, the growth of primate city economies does not help the majority of citizens who are victims of uneven and inequitable development.

SHANTYTOWN DEVELOPMENT

Each month more than 20,000 people come to Mexico City from impoverished rural states looking for employment. The sheer number of urban migrants is too great for either the private or public sector to provide adequate housing or shelter, and thus many families end up in *barriadas*, or squatter settlements. The common conception is that life in these places is totally peripheral to the urban economy of the city. But many shantytowns support robust economies in themselves—including areas of real estate investment—and many have developed into large residential districts where the working class often lives. Perlman (1976) argued that the marginality of shantytown inhabitants in Rio de Janeiro is largely a myth.

The status of shantytowns varies from city to city and country to country. In many places, they are simply illegal settlements built on the outskirts of cities, and they exist under the threat of annihilation by state authorities. In other places, however, shantytowns have acquired legitimate status through political activism, and they constitute working-class suburbs that have many services, including electrical power, running water, and schools. Shantytowns differ not only in location, building materials, and physical appearance but also in the types of groups that live in them. Some settlements suffer from social disorganization and crime, while others have been characterized as "slums of hope." In older shantytowns, many families may rent their building from other squatters. Charles Abrams (1977) discovered five different types of squatters during his research in South American cities:

1. *Owner squatters.* This group conforms to our common idea of the urban squatter: the individual or household owns its own building but not the land on which it was built.

2. *Squatter tenants.* This group is composed of new in-migrants to urban centers who do not live in their own buildings but rent this space from other squatters. Because the "landlord" does not pay taxes or upkeep of the structure, substantial profit may be realized from this business enterprise.
3. *Speculator squatters.* Like regular landowners, this group understands that occupying land and gaining property rights is a way to make a profit. Squatting is viewed as a business venture in the hope of obtaining title to the land.
4. *Store or business squatters.* This group consists of individuals who operate businesses and often live within the squatter settlement. Because they pay no rent or taxes, they may be able to make substantial profits.
5. *Semisquatters.* Individuals or households in this group construct a building on private land but later come to terms with the owner on the rental or even purchase price for the space. The boundary between the legal tenant and the semisquatter may be blurred, particularly within Third World economies.

Some shantytowns possess a robust social order (Aina, 1990; Cooper, 1987). They often are the location for small-business enterprises started by urban migrants. Shantytowns may also be the location for small and medium-size factories employing residents from the surrounding area. The more recent penetration of multinational corporations into metropolitan areas in the developing nations as part of the restructuring of the global economy has created new manufacturing jobs and support for local entrepreneurs. In these and other ways, shantytowns may be integrated into the world economy.

In many developing nations, shantytowns may be the only places where the working class can find affordable housing. According to one estimate, a majority of shantytown dwellers actually live in rental housing (Datta, 1990). Individuals who construct housing in these settlements become real estate entrepreneurs, and form an important real estate submarket within the larger metropolitan economy. Real estate investment brings in much needed income for individuals and households living within the shantytown. However, as in the First World, there may be problems with this privatized housing market. The increased cost of construction materials has meant that shantytown housing around Mexico City has become excessively expensive, and new pressures have been placed on the Mexican government to address the issue of affordable housing (Schteingart, 1990).

It has been suggested that shantytowns should be viewed as workers' suburbs that require greater attention and services from local government, not as slum areas. But the recent projections of population growth in urban areas of the developing nations raise new concerns and may eclipse the earlier discussions of working-class suburbs. The United Nations reports that more than a third of all urban residents now live in slums, most of them in cities in the Third World. By 2030 that figure is expected to increase to more than half—or some 2.5 billion persons living in urban slums (UN-Habitat 2005). This is likely to be accompanied by increased poverty in urban areas. Of the 14.5 million people living in metropolitan Manila in 2000, for example, it is estimated that 60 percent had incomes below the poverty line and that 40 percent lived in slums and shantytowns in areas outside of the urban core.

THE INFORMAL ECONOMY AND COPING STRATEGIES

In previous chapters we noted that many urban sociologists follow the ecological approach. They focus on individual behavior and the aggregation of separate interests in the public and private sectors. The sociospatial perspective, in contrast, recognizes that while society is composed of individuals, a focus on groups, such as classes and networks, is a preferred way of understanding metropolitan dynamics. In Chapter 11 we saw that urban politics has a class component but cannot always be explained by class conflict alone. Homeowner politics and the struggle to control territory and its quality of life are also important political considerations. When studying the Third World, the nature of class structure and especially the control by select elites through the government and military are important factors. Urban researchers also assert that Third World urban dynamics is not exclusively a class phenomenon. They suggest that the appropriate unit of analysis for the study of urban populations in developing nations is the household (Datta, 1990).

Roberts (1991) argues that the household and its coping strategies are basic to an understanding of urban life everywhere, that is, in the First as well as the Third World. Households are collective units that share housing and food, trade clothing and other consumer durables, and are composed of individuals who pool monetary resources. According to Mingione (1988), not all the members of a given household are immediate family. Households may contain distant relatives and even friends. The collective pooling of resources does not preclude differences among household members, such as conflicts between men and women. What counts most with this emphasis is that it conforms better to the reality of urban life in many countries than does the focus of mainstream sociology on individual decision making or of Marxists on class alone.

The study of household survival strategies shows that the poor do not accept their adversity in a passive manner. They innovate and find ways to support themselves and others. This dynamism makes shantytown life quite complex and leads to both positive and negative outcomes such as the reproduction of generations despite poverty and the existence of criminal activity. Households cope with adversity by making collective decisions rather than allowing the burden of poverty to fall on each individual's shoulders alone. To reduce expenses they may engage in *self-provisioning*, which "includes domestic processing or production of food, making clothes, undertaking repairs, self-construction of housing" (Roberts, 1991:142). Other household coping strategies include reducing the number of members (often children, as in the earlier example of the Buñuel film) and connecting with the *informal economy*.

The issue of the informal economy is an important focus of Third World urbanization research and is increasingly an equally relevant topic for the First World (Safa, 1987). In this sector, whose activities are considered "off the books" or illegal, people sell everything from drugs, cigarettes, and convenience store items (such as sodas) to produce (such as fruits and vegetables)—and even their own bodies for sex. As global restructuring expands in Third World cities, bringing with it highly paid professional services, poor people find informal or casual employment as shoe shiners, messengers, delivery persons, and domestic helpers, in addition to the burgeoning demand for restaurant and other commercial laborers. Many laborers, especially domestic servants and babysitters, are hired off the record.

The informal sector is dominated by a market economy, although this is not the same as capitalism because barter or trade as well as monetary exchange prevails, and no formal structures dominate pricing (Korff, 1990). Work is precarious and does not bring the kinds of benefits that people in the First World identify with full-time employment, such as health insurance or social security. Researchers of this phenomenon note that the numbers of people and activities in the informal sector are growing in all countries (Datta, 1990), a fact we have noted in connection with the illegal drug industry's role in poor ghetto areas of the United States.

The study of household coping strategies and the informal economy paints a multidimensional picture of shantytown life and illustrates how individuals may take advantage of opportunities in cities that are not usually noted when attention is given only to formal economies and our own limited, culture-bound conceptions of everyday life.

URBAN SOCIAL MOVEMENTS AND POLITICS

Another important topic that is often neglected in discussing urbanization in the Third World is the significance of political struggles within the city (see Castells, 1983; Walton, 1987; Cooper, 1987). According to one observer, Third

World urban movements are characterized by a gradual transition during the past decade from essentially comprising local movements with limited sociopolitical goals to being more conscious movements making much greater demands on the state and with social and political effects no longer limited to the local arena (Datta, 1990:44).

An example of this change concerns the broadening movement for affordable housing (Castells, 1983; Ramirez, 1990) and the drive to make squatter and shantytown settlements legal. Organized efforts of poor people have pitted them against the government with demands for better health, education, and neighborhood services—a phenomenon that is also characteristic of First World communities and that transcends class distinctions. Another recent development is the growing number of class-based union activities that take place in cities. Deindustrialization has meant the decline of manufacturing jobs in the First World and with it the drastic decline in the power of unions. But as manufacturing jobs have been shunted to the Third World, an associated rise in union activity and class struggle has resulted. Countries such as Brazil and India, for example, have formidable industrial labor forces, and with them have come active trade union movements and class-based political action.

Special attention must be given to the role of women in Third World politics. When women migrate to the city in traditional Third World countries, they acquire new opportunities for marriage and male-female relations, "even if social conservatism may also be exacerbated by the novelty and difficulties of urban life" (Coquery-Vidrovitch, 1990:77). African and Latin American studies show that women take advantage both of the informal economy and of shantytown dwellings to earn a living, although some fall victim to male domination and criminal exploitation such as prostitution (Schlyter, 1990). One important measure of the freer status of city women is their important role in urban social movements. Coquery-Vidrovitch suggests that this important representation may be the result of the active involvement of women in voluntary associations connected with urban shantytown life.

Uneven development and the proliferation of shantytowns may lead to political instability. The national government is not viewed as an avenue for the solving of ordinary people's problems. This makes struggles at the most local level increasingly important as a vehicle for change. According to one African study (Mabogunje, 1990:361), the government of Nigeria is seen as no more than the instrument of the dominant class, committed to perpetuating an unbalanced distribution of income and wealth and preserving the dominance of capitalist ideology and political power. Reports of the performance in government of different groups, whether military or civilian, reveal a cynical use of state apparatus to enrich individuals at the expense of the commonwealth.

From time to time, leaders arise claiming to address the immense disparities of wealth. Often this occurs at the local level, and urban social movements help organize residents to fight for political influence. Beneditas Das Silvas, a black from the major *favella* in Rio de Janeiro, Brazil, ran for the office of mayor in December 1992 on the Socialist Party (PT) ticket. Beneditas, as her supporters call her, symbolizes the forces of change that challenge the inequities of uneven development. Her presence in a local election shows how relevant this issue is for growing urban areas.

Urban social movements are connected to the global economy. Workers in Third World countries constitute a complex social order with many different class statuses (Portes and Walton, 1981). Changes in the activities linked to global investment have differential effects on the Third World working class. These differences are reflected in different political positions and complex ideological issues among trade union parties, some of whom are active socialist or communist organizations, although there are conservative and reactionary political elements as well. In other words, Third World national and urban politics involves a variety of organized political positions despite the greater presence in many countries of worker-oriented or left-wing movements than in the developed nations.

The global economy also affects urban social movements directly through its agents of international control. In the 1970s, for example, the International Monetary Fund (IMF), which controls most of the Third World debt and national financing, called for austerity measures and reductions in state expenditures among all its client countries in the Third World. In turn, national governments responded by eliminating subsidies on food and other consumer goods. This placed a severe burden on households. In response to the threat of hunger or increased misery, residents of cities began rioting in protest of food subsidy cutbacks. The "IMF" riots (Walton, 1987; Cleaver, 1989), as they came to be called, were powerful political events that affected the stability of state regimes in diverse places around the globe, including Africa, Latin America, and Asia. As summarized by Datta (1990:45), "food riots caused the fall of the Tolbert regime in Liberia in 1979 and threatened the imminent collapse of the regimes in Tunisia and Morocco in 1981, in the Dominican Republic in 1984 and 1985, in Brazil in 1983, in Chile in 1983 and 1985." As a result of organized opposition to global restructuring agents such as the IMF or to multinational corporations and industrial development, urban social movements have broadened their perspectives to deal with issues that affect all levels of society, including the local, the national, and the global.

Urban social movements are important in the Third World and take many forms. In Chile, for example, between 1968 and 1972, 400,000 people converged on the city of Santiago and established free squatter settlements, or *campamentos* (Schneier, 1990:349). Similar self-governing squatter communities can be found in Mexico, where they are a powerful political force in urban areas (Castells, 1983). In Nigeria, shantytowns have been organized into neighborhoods that have demanded greater political representation. According to one African study, "the mobilization of people at such a level within a city should at least encourage improved information flows and increase the prospect of greater participation by all in the governance (as distinct from the government) of the city" (Mabogunje, 1990:364). Thus, as we saw in Chapter 10, urban social movements are common among city dwellers in both the developed and undeveloped countries of the world.

We have been discussing phenomena that Third World countries have in common. These include the presence of primate cities, the complex social order of shantytowns, household coping strategies and the informal economy, and the changing complexion of urban social movements and politics. Much of the research on these topics has been published only since the 1970s, when they were brought into sharper focus for those in developed, Westernized countries.

Above all, studies show that the "comparative" perspective on global urbanization that conceptualized a break between the First and Third Worlds must give way to the sociospatial perspective, which acknowledges the growing commonalities and links between metropolitan restructuring patterns in both the First and Third Worlds. Along with increasing acknowledgment of global links is the recognition of certain differences that exist among countries. Not everything is determined by global processes alone. National and local differences also add to the complexity of Third World urbanization. In the final section of this chapter, we survey briefly these local sources of variation in a region-by-region analysis.

PATTERNS OF THIRD WORLD URBANIZATION

Latin America

Latin America contains one of the world's largest cities, Mexico City, with a population of some 18.5 million persons in 2000, and several of the world's most rapidly growing metropolises: Rio de Janeiro and São Paulo in Brazil, Buenos Aires in Argentina, Caracas in Venezuela, and Bogotá in Colombia. The continent of South America, along with Central America and Mexico, was urbanized hundreds of years ago as a result of the Aztec, Mayan, and Inca civilizations, which founded great cities during the European Middle Ages. In the seventeenth and eighteenth centuries, the Spanish and Portuguese con-

TABLE 13.2 Urbanization in Selected Latin American Countries, 1980–2000

	Urban population				*Population in Urban Regions of 1,000,000 or more (% of total population)*		*Population in Largest City (% of total population)*	
	millions		*% of total population*					
	1980	*2000*	*1980*	*2000*	*1980*	*2000*	*1980*	*2000*
Argentina	23.3	33.1	83	89	43	41	43	38
Bolivia	2.4	5.4	46	65	14	18	30	27
Brazil	80.5	138.5	66	81	32	34	16	13
Chile	9.0	12.9	81	85	33	36	41	43
Colombia	18.2	31.7	64	75	26	32	20	20
Cuba	6.6	8.4	68	75	20	20	29	27
El Salvador	1.9	2.9	42	47	16	22	39	48
Guatemala	2.6	4.6	37	40	11	28	29	79
Mexico	44.8	72.9	66	74	28	28	31	25
Peru	11.2	18.7	65	73	25	29	39	40
Uruguay	2.5	3.0	85	91	42	37	49	41
Venezuela	12.0	21.3	79	87	28	29	21	15

SOURCE: Adapted from Table 3.10, *World Development Indicators 2002* (New York: World Bank, 2002).

quests founded new towns and administration centers. Uneven spatial development engendered by colonialism created primate cities in most countries. Many of the cities were located on the coast because of the dominance of trade with the colonial power, although Mexico City, the capital of the ancient Aztec empire, remains an inland magnet for migration.

Recent urbanization patterns in South America are shown in Table 13.2. Although Latin America is one the most urbanized areas in the world, there is substantial variation within the region. Countries such as Argentina, Brazil, Chile, Uruguay, and Venezuela have between 80 and 90 percent of their populations living in urban areas, whereas the figures for El Salvador and Guatemala are less than 50 percent. South America includes several countries with urban populations concentrated in large cities: 40 percent of the population of Argentina lives in cities with populations of 1 million or more, and more than a third of the populations of both Brazil and Chile lives in these larger metropolitan areas. Table 13.2 also shows the strong presence of primate cities in this urban system. In Guatemala, nearly 80 percent of the population lives in the capital city, and in Chile, El Salvador, Peru, and Uruguay more than 40 percent of the population lives in the capital city (38 percent of the population of Argentina lives in Buenos Aires).

Countries such as Brazil, Argentina, and Mexico have benefited from the global search for cheap labor. Mexico, for example, is host to the successful *maquilladoras* program, which locates primary manufacturing in a band of space along the U.S. border for shipment back to the United States as finished products to be sold in this country. Maquilladoras systems, such as enterprise zones, are becoming increasingly popular with Third World countries as First World deindustrialization continues. They allow First World multinationals to retain control of production and marketing while still benefiting from the exploitation of cheap labor in foreign countries with the active support of their governments. The maquilladoras program relies heavily on the use of female labor, which has been made compliant by the culture of paternalism (Fernandez-Kelly, 1991), and enjoys active subsidies from both the Mexican and U.S. governments.

Some Latin American countries, such as Argentina and Brazil, have industrialized. However, in order to be successful and compete with foreign competition, they must use the most sophisticated techniques to make products that will sell on the global market. Most often this means using capital-intensive methods, such as automation, that require little labor. Consequently, even in countries that have achieved some industrialization, factories are run without significant labor forces. New employment opportunities are not created at a pace that could absorb the excess rural population. The result is the perpetuation of shantytown growth despite industrial development.

Brazil is a prime example of the dilemma presented by world system competition. Brazil has a rather successful indigenous steel industry. It can compete on the world market principally because it is capital intensive and uses the latest techniques of production. But this also means that it employs comparatively few people. Hence, it is not a major source of employment, something Brazil also desperately needs. As Cochrane (1982:16) explains, in the 1870s England was the world's leader in steel production, reaching the million-ton mark. At that time, England's steel industry employed 400,000 workers. Brazil today routinely produces four times that amount of steel but does so using only around 28,000 workers. Modern technology and production techniques make a difference that is surely a mixed blessing to developing countries, and the need to compete in the world system constrains the types of development policies those countries can pursue.

Latin America is the scene of the most explosive growth in the world. For example, São Paulo, Brazil, had a population of less than 3 million in 1950, but its population is approaching 24 million today. Estimates assert that the total Brazilian population, which was 136 million in 1985, will almost double to 246 million by the year 2025 (United Nations, 1985). Of this population, it is estimated that over 90 percent will reside in urban areas. In the next thirty years, Brazil will become a country of giant cities. To feed these people, Brazil can exploit its arable landmass—but many of these new lands are part of the rain forest. A potential ecological disaster of global magnitude is in the making.

Unlike Brazil, Mexico is semiarid and lacks appreciable agricultural resources. It has already cultivated virtually all of the available land. Population pressures will force people into the cities or to "El Norte," the United States. As observers note:

> The urban population is expected to increase from 55 million in 1985 to 131 million in 2025, the equivalent of 13 cities of ten million each. Is there a limit to Mexico City's growth, this bowl constrained by a circle of pollutant-trapping mountains? Guadalajara and Veracruz might become enormous metropolises. How many new cities of over a million will spring up in the Mexican "desert"? How many Mexicans will head for California, either legally or clandestinely? (Dogan and Kasarda, 1988:24–25)

In addition to immense population pressures, Latin American countries share a history of political instability. They have been controlled for over a century by the dictates of U.S. foreign policy and by the demands of its corporations. Over the years, developmental strategies have been hemmed in by such global constraints. There is a great need to nurture domestic industrial development. Yet political problems and periodic military coups seem to hamstring such efforts. Instability is also fostered by inequalities in the class system, which is one of the most skewed in the world. The factors of class structure, government control, and global power figure prominently in understanding development in Latin America.

Asia

The global region of Asia represents great diversity and contains at least half of the world's population. The two largest countries, China and India, share a similar pattern of settlement. In the case of India more so than China, they are "overurbanized" because of the presence of primate cities.

Table 13.3 provides further information about urbanization in selected Asian countries. Most of these countries do not show the same high levels of urbanization that we saw in the previous table for Latin America. In 2000, Korea, Malaysia, and the Philippines each had more than 50 percent of their population living in urban areas, but the level of urbanization in other countries, including India, Thailand, and Vietnam, was less than 30 percent. A relatively small proportion of the population lived in large cities of 1 million

TABLE 13.3 Urbanization in Selected Asian Countries, 1980–2000

	Urban population (millions)		Urban population (% of total population)		Population in Urban Regions of 1,000,000 or more (% of total population)		Population in Largest City (% of total population)	
	1980	2000	1980	2000	1980	2000	1980	2000
China	192.3	405.2	20	32	12	14	6	3
India	158.8	288.5	23	28	8	10	18	13
Indonesia	32.9	86.1	22	41	8	10	18	13
Korea	9.8	13.4	57	60	11	14	19	24
Malaysia	5.8	13.4	42	57	7	6	16	10
Myanmar	8.1	13.2	2	28	7	9	27	32
Philippines	18.0	44.3	38	59	14	16	33	25
Thailand	7.9	13.1	17	22	10	12	59	56
Vietnam	10.3	18.8	19	24	14	13	34	24

SOURCE: Adapted from Table 3.10, *World Development Indicators* 2002 (New York: World Bank, 2002).

persons—only the Philippines had more than 15 percent of its population in large cities. Interesting facts not apparent in the table include the following: In 2000, 56 percent of the population of Thailand lived in the capital city (Bangkok), and in three other countries (Korea, the Philippines, and Vietnam) one-quarter or more of the population lived in the largest city.

India and China display differences in their patterns of urbanization because of different national policies; as in Latin America, the factors of state control and local class structure explain a great deal about development. For example, up until the 1980s, China's communist government restricted the size of China's largest cities. China's largest city, Shanghai, had a population of under 7 million, Beijing had 5,550,000 people, and Tianjin had 5,130,000 in 1982 (Chen, 1988:233), although their surrounding areas also had large populations. In contrast, India's largest city, Bombay, contained 16.4 million people in 2000, while Calcutta had 13.2 million and Delhi had 12.8 million. The populations for the largest cities and metropolitan areas in India and China are shown in Tables 13.4 and 13.5.

Of all the rapidly growing population areas of the globe, only China seems to have controlled the rate of urbanization to match its development potential. China's government pursues a balanced growth process of rural and urban development. Under the *hukou* system, the rural population is prevented by law from moving to cities (Kim, 1988). This outlaws the kind of inmigration to the cities from rural areas that is common in the rest of the developing world.

TABLE 13.4 Largest Cities and Metropolitan Areas in India, 2000

	City Population	Metropolitan Population
Mumbai (Bombay)	16,368,000	19,400,000
Kolkata (Calcutta)	13,217,000	15,350,000
Delhi	12,791,000	19,400,000
Chennai	6,425,000	7,450,000
Bangalore	5,687,000	6,900,000
Hyderabad	5,534,000	6,550,000
Ahmadabad	4,519,000	5,450,000
Pune	3,756,000	4,350,000
Surat	2,811,000	3,550,000
Kanpur	2,690,000	3,150,000
Jaipur	2,324,000	2,850,000
Lucknow	2,267,000	2,700,000
Nagpur	2,123,000	2,450,000
Patna	1,707,000	2,100,000

SOURCE: Adapted from City Mayors, *The World's Largest Cities,* and Thomas Brinkhoff, *The Principal Agglomerations and Cities of the World,* 2003.

Such balanced growth has had positive effects, and living in one of China's large cities may actually improve the quality of life (Bradshaw and Fraser, 1989). Over the past fifteen years, however, China has launched an extensive drive to integrate into the world economy, particularly by manufacturing consumer items. The government adopted rapid modernization policies that canceled China's measured urban growth. It remains to be seen whether or not they will also develop the characteristic pattern of uneven development that plagues other societies.

China and India can also be contrasted with regard to the quality of life in their cities. Just the mention of India's cities (Calcutta, Bombay, Delhi) conjures up images of extreme poverty. To an extent, these images are accurate. The first two cities have large homeless populations, and all possess a declining quality of life. India's cities are surrounded by shantytowns, called *bustees,* that grow each day. Their presence has not prevented the city center from experiencing terrible overcrowding. The population density of Calcutta, for example, has been estimated at 45,000 residents per square kilometer, with the overwhelming majority living below the poverty line. Misery, disease, squalor, and malnutrition afflict the hordes of urban street people. The urban implosion of India is the consequence of rural push factors as well as urban pull. The "green revolution" that modernized India's agriculture has been relatively successful, and has led to a decline in the number of people needed to grow food in rural areas. As a result, in recent years more Indians are looking toward the cities for livelihood.

TABLE 13.5   Largest Cities and Metropolitan Areas in China, 2000

	City Population	Metropolitan Population
Shanghai	8,214,000	12,800,000
Beijing	7,362,000	10.800,000
Tianjun	5,855,000	9,300,000
Hong Kong	6,843,000	6,800,000
Wuhan	4.040,000	5,700,000
Shengyang	4,669,000	4,900,000
Chongging	3,127,000	4,800,000
Guangzhou	3,935,000	3,900,000
Chengdu	2,954,000	3,400,000
Xian	2,872,000	3,200,000
Changchun	2,192,000	3,000,000
Haerbin	2,990,000	2,900,000
Nanjing	2,678,000	2,800,000
Zibo	2,484,000	2,700,000
Dalian	2,483,000	2,700,000
Jinan	2,403,000	2,600,000
Taipei	2,640,000	2,500,000
Taiyuan	2,051,000	2.500,000
Gingdao	2,101,000	2,400,000
Guiyang	1,741,000	2,400,000
Zhengzhou	1,796,000	2,200,000
Zaozhung	1,793,000	2,100,000

SOURCE: Adapted from City Mayors, *The World's Largest Cities*; and United Nations, Department of Economic and Social Affairs, Population Division, *Urban Agglomerations 2003*.

The uncontrolled influx of people to India's cities is making a bad situation worse. As one observer notes:

> The most serious problems are related directly or indirectly to the extreme shortage of housing, and to inadequacy of physical and social infrastructures to meet the needs of the urban low- and middle-income groups. . . . The shortages are the principal cause of the progressive deterioration of the urban environment during the past 20–25 years. Proliferation of slums is the most visible symptom of the environmental deterioration. The other major symptom is the rapid increase in the levels of air and water pollution in or near the cities, far above the internationally accepted levels for maintaining human health and safety. (Nath, 1989:264)

Some of India's cities, such as Delhi, have large areas that are middle class and quite prosperous. Bombay was planned by the British as a colonial center and retains its planned streets and residential districts that

BOX 13.2   Urban Poor Made Homeless in India's Drive for More "Beautiful" Cities

Large areas of habitation of India's urban poor have been forcefully taken over by city government—regardless of political make-up. The groups of people affected are often the ones who have been employed in informal sectors or are self-employed in the tertiary services sector. Their displacement has as much to do with the space they live in as with the work they perform.

The areas that they occupied are being transferred into larger private corporate entities such as commercial complexes and residential developments. These units are also often coupled with labor-replacing devices ranging from automatic tellers and computer-aided machines to vacuum cleaners and home delivery services, thus eliminating the work earlier done by the lower rungs of the urban population. While the driving force behind these changes is manifestly the new globalized economy, it is offered on an environmental platter of "cleanliness" and "beautification."

In Chennai City 40 percent of the population lives in slums—there are 69,000 families who have been identified to be living on government land, and they are to be relocated to areas far removed from the city. The areas vacated will be taken over by railway tracks, hotel resorts, commercial and residential complexes, and modern businesses. Much of the "clearance" is being undertaken in the name of "beautification" and tourism.

In Kolkata (Calcutta) the Left Front government also is working on "environmental improvement" projects. Operation Sunshine was launched in 1996 to evict over 50,000 hawkers from the city's main streets. Currently over 7,000 hutments are being forcibly demolished along the sides of storm water drains and the metro and circular rail tracks. At the same time, lavish commercial and residential complexes are coming up unhindered along the metropolitan bypass, where the real estate prices rival those in the elite areas of South Calcutta.

Delhi, where sub-standard settlements house as much as 70 percent of the city's population, leads the way in environmental activism. Not only have vendors, cycle-rickshaws, beggars, shanties, polluting and non-conforming industries, and diesel buses already been "evicted," a recent addition to the hit list are the 75,000 families who live on the banks of the Yamuna River. They are being held responsible for the river's pollution. The resettlement colonies and industrial areas, that were once supposed to be at the fringe of the city, have been drawn into its ambit. The ring towns are now contiguous urban sprawls and the arterial roads and national highways are the most congested in the region. Increasing numbers of poor inhabitants continue to live in shantytowns without services. Rapidly shrinking employment opportunities and crusading environmental activism have made the situation significantly

(continues)

worse for them. While the city gets the Clean City Award from far-off California, its own citizens grimly face critical inadequacies of work, shelter, civic amenities, and governance.

In vicious combination these three trends are changing the urban landscape from "homes" to "estate ownerships" in the name of liberalization, privatization, and globalization. The replacement of housing of poor urban dwellers with commercial and upmarket developments raises several questions about the nature of "planning" itself. Who makes these plans? Who are they made for?

ADAPTED FROM DUNU ROY, "URBAN POOR INCREASINGLY MADE HOMELESS IN INDIA'S DRIVE FOR MORE 'BEAUTI-FUL' CITIES," CITY MAYORS DEVELOPMENT, HTTP://WWW.CITYMAYORS.COM/DEVELOPMENT/INDIA_URBAN1.HTML.

allow services to be delivered with some efficiency. It is a major center of industrial and service employment. In short, despite the declining quality of life, India's cities are not all mired in extreme poverty and deprivation (Misra, 1978).

Chinese cities fared comparatively better under communist rule. One of the first acts of the Maoist regime in the 1950s was to eradicate the poverty and prostitution endemic to the streets of Shanghai, the focal point of global colonial interests. City services throughout China are regulated by the state and function to maintain the quality of life. The Chinese government has also pushed strict measures of birth control. In fact, most families are not permitted to have more than one child. This state policy of restricting population growth in a country of more than 1 billion people has had some success in the cities but is less successful in the countryside.

There is a visible contrast between cities in India and cities in China, as noted by Whyte and Parish (1984:2–3):

Slums and squatter settlements seemed absent, conspicuous consumption and foreign oriented life styles were not visible, a high degree of economic equality and security seemed to prevail, unemployment seemed absent, close-knit neighborhoods and families seemed to persist, and crime, drug addiction, prostitution, and other forms of deviance seemed minor or nonexistent.

The urban system in China dates back many centuries, and the current clustering of large cities follows from a pattern that was evident during the imperial period. Recent economic reforms and industrial development have generally reinforced the earlier clustering of towns and cities (Xeh and Xu, 1984). There are four main urban agglomerations:

Liaodong Peninsula (Shenyang-Dalian): Shenyang in the north and Dalian in the south are the dominant cities in this region; Shenyang is the major industrial town and Dalian is the major port. Other cities include Anshan, Fushun, Benxi, and Liaoyang.

Beijing-Tianjin: Beijing (the capital city) and Tianjin are the dominant cities of this cluster located in the Yellow River valley. Other important cities of the region include Tanggu and Tangshan.

Yangtze River Delta (Nanjing-Shanghai-Hangzhou): Shanghai (the largest city in China) is the dominant city of this cluster, which also includes the industrial centers of Nanjing and Hangzhou.

Pearl River Delta: The former British colony of Hong Kong and the older Chinese city of Guangzhou are the dominant cities in this region.

Cities located within these clusters are connected by railway, expressway, and canals and are dominated by heavy industry. The Beijing-Tianjin and Liaodong Peninsula regions contain China's metal, machinery, petrochemical, and industrial centers. Newer cities have emerged within these clusters, including Dongguan, Shenzhen, and Zhuhai in the Pearl River Delta, and Changzhou in the Yangtze River Delta. Two other urban agglomerations have emerged in the past few decades:

Shandong Peninsula: Jinan and Qingdao are the dominant cities in this region, with Yantai as the major port of the region.

Fuzhou-Xiamen (Minnan): Fuzhou and Xiamen are the important cities in this region, although they are not as dominant as the major cities in other clusters. Development in this area will depend to some degree on relations with Taiwan (Yeh and Xu, 1984).

In all the countries of Asia, primate cities—Tokyo-Yokohama, Pyongyang, Seoul, Taipei, Jakarta, Kuala Lumpur, Manila, and Bangkok—represent the centers of economic growth and development (Yeung, 1988:162). For example, in the 1980s Tokyo accounted for 60 percent of Japan's elite business leaders and 60 percent of the total capital invested, along with a third of all department store sales; Seoul contained 78 percent of South Korean business headquarters and 90 percent of all large enterprises, while accounting for 27.9 percent of South Korea's GNP; and Bangkok housed one-third of Thailand's manufacturing and almost 80 percent of its banking, and contributes 26.8 percent toward the country's GNP (Yeung, 1988:162).

In all of these countries, urban development programs are often given a high profile. Among the issues that must be confronted is the lack of an adequate infrastructure to meet the demands of the growing urban population. The case of urban redevelopment in Manila is instructive. The Philippines suffered from the crony capitalism of the Marcos dictatorship for two decades before electing Cory Aquino (wife of the political opposition leader assassinated by Marcos's security forces) president of the country in 1986. Millions of dollars from the World Bank and other international agencies lined the pockets of the military leaders, while underdevelopment continued to plague the country; more than 80 percent of its export crops are owned by the Dole pineapple conglomerate, and many Filipinos in rural areas work in a plantation system characterized by Ligaya McGovern (1996) as a "militarized zone." With perhaps the highest birth rate in all of Asia, overpopulation has led many Filipinos to leave rural communities for the capital city of Manila. The result has been uneven development within the metropolitan Manila region, where neighborhoods not much different from those in any modern city exist alongside squatter settlements.

In recent years several Asian nations, such as Korea, Taiwan, and Singapore, have exploded the myth of Third World dependency and the notion of "peripheral" development by growing rapidly as industrialized countries. They have been helped along by the influx of capital investment from Japan and the search for cheap labor by multinational corporations from across the globe. Many of the enterprises are joint domestic and foreign operations. Analysts today refer to the four "Asian tigers"—Hong Kong, Taiwan, South Korea, and Singapore—as especially successful areas of industrial development. In the 1980s, the Asian tigers led the world in percentage growth of gross domestic product at 7 percent a year (Berry, 1989:176), helped by the continuing demand for consumer goods—especially electronics, textiles, and clothing. This pattern of "export-led" development has also been tried successfully in Spain and Italy (see Chapter 12) among other countries.

An important characteristic of the Asian tiger development is the large role played by the national government in promoting growth. This intervention is not restricted to subsidization of capital investment and development but also includes strong control of unions and, often, harsh methods of regulating the working-class population; unions are not allowed, and child labor, low wages, and sweatshop conditions are common (Lee, 1982; Palen, 1990).

The presence of the Asian tigers changes the dynamics of global capital investment. In the future, China may prove to be as competitive in manufacturing as established First World economies, or more so. This Asian *Pacific Rim,* which is linked to Japan (see Chapter 12) as well as the United States, contains economic forces that are emerging as a major sphere of power and development in the new century (Berry, 1989).

Africa and the Arab Countries

Of all the continents, Africa presents the clearest case of the overurbanization-underurbanization dilemma. For the most part, this reflects a legacy of years of colonial rule (Simon, 1989). South of the Sahara, the primate cities were all founded as trading centers and located near the coasts or with easy access by water to the coast. Some countries, such as Nigeria, have a moderately developed urban hierarchy containing several cities: Lagos, Ibadan, Kano, and Oshogbo. However, most, such as Kenya, are classic cases of primate city development. Kenya's capital, Nairobi, contains over half (57 percent) of the country's population. Here, as in most of Africa, the intermediate level of the urban hierarchy (that is, cities with populations greater than 100,000 but less than 1,000,000) is notably absent.

Africa contains fifty-four separate countries, and it is sometimes difficult to generalize about the scale of development or urbanization. The north, which contains Arab countries, is highly urbanized. In 2000, 88 percent of the Libyan population and 56 percent of Morocco's population were living in cities. Egypt contains one of the world's most populated cities, Cairo, with more than 8 million people. Most African countries have rates of urbanization of between 40 and 50 percent, although countries in eastern and central Africa generally have lower levels of urbanization. Table 13.6 provides information on urbanization for selected African countries.

Most African countries have a primate city land-use pattern similar to that of other Third World countries. The center consists of wide boulevards loaded with traffic and passing in between high skyscrapers built in the common "international style" of the developed West. Affluent natives and the foreign community make their home there. Beyond the glitter domes of development, the core is surrounded by mile upon mile of shantytowns—the most depressing agglomeration of ersatz housing imaginable—where entire families follow a precarious existence and play the "life lottery," hoping to acquire some meager portion of the wealth circulating through the center.

According to O'Connor (1978:86), around the central city "is an extensive peripheral zone of crudely built shacks sometimes disparagingly termed a 'septic fringe.' In several cities such areas . . . now house over half the urban population and informal sector housebuilding constitutes a major economic activity."

Years of dominance by colonial powers, coupled with political conflict and poor local leadership, have left Africa in an undeveloped state. Countries continue to rely on natural resources and tourism for economic growth. With the discovery and exploitation of oil, Nigeria has acquired considerable capital, as

TABLE 13.6   Urbanization in Selected African Countries, 1980–2000

	Urban population				Population in Urban Regions of 1,000,000 or more (% of total population)		Population in Largest City (% of total population)	
	millions		% of total population					
	1980	2000	1980	2000	1980	2000	1980	2000
Angola	1.5	4.5	21	34	13	20	63	60
Cameroon	2.7	7.3	31	49	11	21	19	23
Congo	7.7	15.4	29	30	8	10	28	33
Egypt	17.9	28.9	44	45	23	23	38	36
Ethiopia	4.0	11.3	11	18	3	4	30	23
Libya	2.3	4.6	69	88	26	34	38	39
Morocco	8.0	16.1	41	56	15	18	26	22
Nigeria	19.1	55.8	27	44	8	12	23	24
Senegal	2.0	4.5	36	47	17	22	48	46
South Africa	13.3	23.5	48	55	27	32	12	13
Sudan	3.9	11.2	20	36	6	9	30	24
Zambia	2.3	4.5	40	45	9	16	23	37
Zimbabwe	1.8	4.5	22	36	9	14	39	39

SOURCE: Adapted from Table 3.10, *World Development Indicators 2002* (New York: World Bank, 2002).

is the case with Libya. However, most countries remain locked in the grip of poverty, with limited industrial schemes and weak rural economies. Without extensive agricultural development, migration to the cities is an inevitable result. Extensive squatter settlements, or *bidonvilles,* are characteristic of urban development (Aina, 1990; Schlyter, 1990).

The Arab cities are also scenes of uneven development. Cairo is known for its cosmopolitan population but also for its squatter settlements, such as the inhabitants of the immense cemetery, the City of the Dead, or the people known as the *zebaleen,* who live off of other people's garbage at the massive city dump (Abu-Lughod, 1969). Most Arab countries have medium-size cities and have not experienced a large rural exodus because their hinterlands have always been sparsely settled. The oil kingdoms of the Middle East have utilized their great wealth to create cities with modern architecture, such as Riyadh in Saudi Arabia. These cities have remained showcases that are dependent on the oil industry monoculture.

SUMMARY

Many Third World countries are mired in the vicious cycle of overurbanization-underurbanization. The failure of agriculture means future populations face starvation or migration. The limited success of urban economic growth means that Third World cities will continue to play a marginal role in the global economy. Without balanced policies of development, these countries will face a bleak future. The issue is not simply growth and industrial development financed by the wealthy First World. Rather, there is a need for linked policies that improve agricultural production on the one hand and urban economies on the other. Especially in places such as Asia and Africa, it is essential that rural populations be stabilized so that the migration pressures on cities can be relieved. Yet development that is simply led by global capital investment will not head countries in that much-needed direction.

For example, more than twenty years ago the World Bank and the International Monetary Fund encouraged developing countries to build enterprise zones of manufacturing that would capture global investment. However, this development has come with a price. Much of the labor force consists of young women between sixteen and twenty-five years old. The movement of young women from their home villages to employment in the city disrupts traditional family structures, and often this cheap supply of labor simply expands the patriarchal dominance over females in Third World countries. These women once constituted the backbone of traditional agriculture. With the young female population working in factories, rural agriculture in many countries is on the verge of collapse (Fuentes and Ehrenreich, 1987:203). Decline of rural economies pushes more and more people into the cities to seek a livelihood. As we have seen, this cycle of growth has disastrous results.

Shantytowns are growing rapidly in response to continued population expansion. São Paulo, Brazil, and Calcutta, India, respectively, have more than 1 million and 2 million residents in their *favellas* and *bustees,* while Mexico City's *barriadas* contain more than 4 million. The pattern of shantytown/central core uneven development is the exact opposite of that in the United States. As we have seen, the latter possesses maturing and relatively affluent suburbs surrounding a declining urban core. Third World cities exhibit the reverse of this pattern. But more important, the gap between the wealthy and the majority of the population is quite enormous.

For the most part, Third World governments have failed to achieve a better quality of life for their citizens. The domination of the economy and the government by the ruling class leads to harsh measures of social control, hyperaggressive police, death squads, and repressive political dictatorship rather than enlightened policies of social reform. The passion of the Third World peoples manifests itself as a political clash between the fortunate few backed up by the government and the afflicted and disadvantaged. As the urban population in these countries grows to some 5 billion persons in the next twenty years, with a majority having incomes below the poverty line and living in massive urban slums, the demands for social reform are likely to increase. It is unlikely that the expansion of global capitalism will be able to meet the needs of these persons. The response of people and governments in the developed world is equally uncertain.

KEY CONCEPTS

uneven development
colonialism
internationalization of capital
demographic transition
primate city
balanced urbanization
shantytown
informal economy
crony capitalism
overurbanization / underurbanization

DISCUSSION QUESTIONS

1. The global economic system is increasingly important to the Third World. Discuss the relationship between the two. In what ways has modernization theory changed because of the influence of the global system?

2. Discuss the importance of demographic change in studying Third World urbanization. How is urbanization in the Third World different from that in the industrialized nations?

3. Urbanization in Third World countries often is characterized by the dominance of a primate city, overurbanization, shantytown development, and the important role of the informal economy. Define and discuss these concepts and give an example of each.

4. Discuss how urban social movements in Third World countries have addressed poverty, uneven development, women's rights, and other social issues.

5. What are some of the important differences in urban development in Latin America, Asia, and Africa? What factors might account for these differences? Which theoretical model (dependency theory, modernization theory, world systems theory, or the sociospatial model) might best explain these differences?

ENVIRONMENTAL ISSUES AND
METROPOLITAN PLANNING

O n October 1, 1980, the Love Canal section of the small town of Niagara, New York, located near the Canadian border, was declared an environmental disaster by President Carter. He ordered the permanent evacuation of all families from their homes. This action followed after two previous evacuations beginning in 1978 (Gibbs, 1981:5). Between 1920 and 1953 the area, an uncompleted canal, was used as a dump site for toxic chemicals from both the private sector and the federal government, particularly the U.S. Army. Homes had been built on top of landfill after the site was no longer used for dumping. Residents who lived along the canal had been exposed for many years to carcinogens from the toxic wastes that leaked into groundwater and oozed to the surface. In the 1970s, some of the 1,000 families that lived near the canal site began to complain about the high incidence of cancer, birth defects, miscarriages, and central nervous system diseases (Gibbs, 1981:3). Once the full extent of the poisoning became known, evacuations proceeded, but this action came too late to save many people from contracting cancer and other environmentally caused health problems from the area.

On April 26, 1986, a nuclear power plant located in Chernobyl, near the Ukrainian capital city of Kiev, exploded. The blast ignited the graphite moderating core of the reactor and resulted in the unleashing of intense radiation across a wide area of the former Soviet Union and Western Europe. Fallout from the disaster was measured as far away as the United States and showed up in the dairy production of countries such as Norway, but the most severe effects were to hundreds of thousands of people living in the small towns of the area (Marples, 1988). Had the winds been blowing northward at the time, the Ukrainian people's historic city of Kiev (population 2.4 million) would have been destroyed along with countless lives.

Official figures from the Soviet Union listed 31 people killed by the accident, but other estimates are as high as 500 (Marples, 1988:42). It was also estimated that as many as 50,000 people may have been directly exposed to excessive radiation, with nearly 500,000 premature deaths predicted over the next few decades. The disaster forced permanent evacuation of persons and homes from a 30-kilometer zone, but over 100,000 children outside this area were also taken from their families to avoid exposure. Thousands of people were treated for radiation sickness. To this day, the region contains "hot spots" that are a threat to life.

Unfortunately, the above examples are not isolated cases. The United States, for instance, had its own potential nuclear catastrophe when the Three Mile Island reactor near Middletown, Pennsylvania, began emitting radioactive steam on March 28, 1979. That emergency was controlled without immediate loss of life or property. Many countries around the world have toxic pollution sites and unsafe radioactive facilities within their borders that affect the health of citizens every day.

In this chapter, we will use the sociospatial perspective to study environmental issues that result from, and create problems for, the expansion of urban and suburban settlement space. Because the living and working arrangements in modern societies impact the health and well-being of all residents, questions raised about environmental quality have as much to do with spatial issues as they do with economic development.

The environmental question and its relation to sociospatial development raise a variety of issues. One set deals with the nature of constructed space, or "second nature," as Henri Lefebvre (1991) calls it. These issues involve the activity of planning, which seeks to obtain the best living and working arrangements in developing cities. The built environment, any built environment, such as a city or a mall, possesses attributes that may enhance or hinder the functioning of its use. Elements of the environmental fabric such as streets, pedestrian pathways, automobile corridors, and housing complexes can be placed in harmony with one another to facilitate the movement of people and vehicular traffic throughout the constructed space. Planning and architectural design address these kinds of issues, and we will consider them in the second section of this chapter. In addition, urban and metropolitan governments have sought to incorporate sound environmental principles into future plans. This type of planning is called "sustainable growth," and it has emerged as a very important perspective today.

A separate set of questions involves the inherent quality of the environment. What are the outcomes and by-products of social activities? What effects do the different types of activities, such as manufacturing, have on population groups within their vicinity? Who pays the environmental costs for development? What is the environmental impact of growth on the health and well-being of citizens? These and other questions frame the discussion of urban and suburban settlement spaces as a built environment. Let us explore this topic first and relate it to metropolitan considerations.

ENVIRONMENTAL QUALITY

All societies seek to improve their quality of life through industrial development. Some countries, such as the United States, already possess a heritage of over one hundred years of industrialization. Although all human activities produce waste products that may adversely affect others, such as the effluent problem in an ancient city like Beijing, the scale and intensity of the environmental costs of industrialization are unprecedented. Manufacturing results in by-products that are toxic to animal and plant life; energy generation affects the temperature and quality of water and air with consequent effects on living things; and the extraction of natural resources, such as gold, results in environmental damage, such as the releasing of toxic metals into forest streams.

Societies around the globe have always put developmental desires above environmental concerns. In places such as China, Brazil, and sections of Europe, the health-related impacts of industrialization weren't even publicly recognized until quite recently, as we saw in the Chapter 13 discussion of Shanghai's waste water pollution. For many centuries, all societies have held an unwavering belief in the idea of progress. Technology, science, and industrial growth, it is commonly understood, hold the promise of making our lives better and better. At present this assumption, which is at the core developmental ideology (discussed shortly), has been called into question by some environmentally conscious individuals. According to Murray Bookchin (1990:20), the certainty that technology and science would improve the human condition is mocked by the proliferation of nuclear weapons, by massive hunger in the Third World, and by poverty in the First World.

Most Americans appreciate the quality of life made available to them by the accomplishments of industrialization, but environmental activists suggest that this comfort for the relative few, globally speaking, has been acquired at a phenomenal cost to the many around the world. Furthermore, the unprecedented scale of human development today has resulted in global effects such as the widening hole in the ozone layer, global warming, acid rain, the eradication of plant and animal species, and the increasing threats to fresh drinking water. In response, environmentalists have called for a new ordering of global priorities that would seek out environmentally enhancing methods of industrial production and safe technologies (Naess, 1989; Gore, 1992). This means redefining the relationship between humans and settlement space on this planet.

As the level of awareness about these environmental issues increases across the globe, perhaps the issues of growth and development will be reexamined. New, environmentally sound methods of production and safe technologies such as rechargeable electric cars may usher in a transformed relation between people and the earth that preserves the well-being of both. Environmental concerns translate into new jobs and industries so that ecologically conscious development can be compatible with saving the planet (Kazis and Grossman, 1982).

The above concerns have been part of the environmental movement in the United States for some time. In the classical phase of activism, which began in the 1800s, Americans sought to protect large areas of the country from development and endangered species from destruction. Naturalists such as John Muir (1838–1914), who won protection for places like Yosemite and led the fight to establish the national parks system, and organizations such as the Audubon Society, which has been at the forefront of the fight to save native birds and other wildlife, are examples of the classical phase of environmentalism (Bullard, 1990).

In the twentieth century, the mature phase of activism attacked the unbridled nature of industrialization in the United States. Concerned citizens fought for regulatory agencies, the passage of environmental statutes, and the establishment of industrial standards for control of pollutants. Over the years, regulations and legally binding statutes have been passed by both the federal and state levels of government. In 1970 the mature phase efforts culminated in the establishment of a separate federal agency under the executive branch, the Environmental Protection Agency (EPA), which serves as the public's advocate and coordinates research on environmental issues. In the 1970s the EPA was granted powers to regulate mileage standards for automobiles, thereby leading to the production of fuel-efficient engines. Although there is still much work to be done and an imminent need for residents of the United States to rethink their relationship with the settlement space of advanced industrial society, the classical and mature phases of environmental activism have accomplished a great deal. This is especially the case when we consider the sensitivity many Americans have acquired in the past several decades to the need for fuel economy, recycling of waste products, and the search for safe technologies.

A third type of activism is grassroots or community efforts. Advocates of grassroots mobilization point out that while social concern about environmental quality is quite high in the United States, there is little appreciation for the social equity and social justice aspects of environmental impacts (Gale, 1983). These impacts are distributed inequitably across settlement space, creating a particular sociospatial dimension to the differential impact of costs. As one observer puts it, "an abundance of documentation shows blacks, lower-income groups and working-class persons are subjected to a disproportionately large amount of pollution and other environmental stressors in their neighborhoods as well as in their workplaces" (Bullard, 1990:1).

The classical and mature phases of environmental activism have drawn in thousands of people, but the overwhelming majority of them and the concerns they express are those of the middle class. The environmental costs paid by poor and minority people have largely been ignored. This sociospatial pattern of environmental costs is most revealing. Love Canal in New York State was situated within a white, working-class community, and it was these people who paid the price of toxic pollution. In Alabama, the town of Triana was judged to be the unhealthiest town in America (Reynolds, 1980:38). The residents of Triana are black, and they have been poisoned by the pesticide DDT and the chemical PCB from a creek whose quality is the responsibility of the federal government. Time and again research shows that society continues to produce toxic pollution and that poor and minority communities are its victims (Bullard, 1990; Berry, 1977; Blum, 1978).

Many of the hazards that differentially affect minorities and the poor are the consequence of industrial location patterns. Factories, chemical plants, mills, and the like are located in areas isolated from middle-class residential space. Because housing costs are lower in settlement spaces constructed around manufacturing areas, this is where poor people are more likely to live. Chemical emissions, spillovers of toxic by-products, unpleasant smells, and loud noises are just some of the hazards that affect these relatively powerless communities. These areas are often selected for unwanted land uses (or LULUs) such as landfills, toxic waste dumps, and effluent treatment plants. Hence, even though regulations have increased for safeguarding environmental quality, they have also led to injustices in the disposal of environmental threats, especially because of the inequitable siting of toxic dumps and landfills. For example:

> Four landfills in minority zip code areas represented 63 percent of the South's total hazardous-waste disposal capacity. Moreover, the landfills located in the mostly black zip code areas of Emelle (Alabama), Alsen (Louisiana), and

Pinewood (South Carolina) in 1987 accounted for 58.6 percent of the region's hazardous-waste landfill capacity. (Bullard, 1990:40)

The differential locational impacts of environmental costs and the issues of social equity that they raise have yet to be addressed. Most communities seek to avoid becoming hosts to activities that represent social problems, such as outpatient mental clinics, halfway houses for criminals, and drug treatment centers. They advocate not in my backyard or NIMBY politics, which makes location a struggle that the least powerful community loses. The same is true for LULUs such as hazardous waste dumps or landfills. But allowing the stronger to make the weaker pay for all of society's costs violates principles of social justice.

In recent years, grassroots activists have organized poor and minority communities to fight for their rights. They are forcing the larger society to rethink environmental issues. If toxic dumps are unfair to any community, why not design production operations to minimize environmental damage? If landfills are becoming a problem, can't recycling and other, even more imaginative schemes be considered for the ever-increasing volume of garbage we all produce? How can we reorder our priorities to avoid having people pay unfairly for pollution? These and other questions frame the agenda for grassroots organizing and environmental activism in the years to come. This agenda has also become central to the "environmental sustainability" movement.

SUSTAINABLE GROWTH

Local governments deploying this concept frame future growth in terms that also relate to environmental goals. They pursue planning for development that, at the same time, asks the following question: How can we sustain and improve the environmental quality of life defined as a series of concrete planning targets? Another term for this approach is the "livable cities" movement.

Environmentalists define the impact of any activity as its "ecological footprint." Taken together, the way in which a metro region uses resources and the effects of its activities on the environment define its unique "footprint." The stated goal of sustainable growth is to reduce that footprint to as small an impact as possible. The use of recycling, mass transit, electric or hybrid vehicles (at the bare minimum, government owned), use of solar energy and other "renewable" energy resources, and citizen activities aimed at cleaning up vacant lots, streets, and highways are but a few of the tools applied in the pursuit of sustainable growth.

Sustainable growth has meant a renewed role for local government; in this case, it becomes the manager of environmentally aware development. Activist positions by administrators instigate change and mandate that environmental concerns be addressed. This approach also means that local communities and neighborhoods must be transformed into activist organizations that pursue improvements in environmental quality. In fact, the local community component of sustainable growth is quite critical to its success.

One problem emerging in recent years with this movement is that more cities and metropolitan areas claim to be pursuing sustainability than are actually doing so. Consequently, there is a danger that the term may just be used as an election slogan rather than a concrete goal of local administrations. A study by Portney (2003) found that, of twenty-five cities in the United States that have proclaimed a pursuit of sustainability, only eight had actually taken that goal seriously. Furthermore, Portney uncovered another problem. Cities and metropolitan regions vary considerably with regard to what they understand to be sustainable environmental issues. Some places emphasized environmental quality most directly. Others included adequate health care, proper schools, and an acceptable standard of living as goals. According to Portney's study, then, there is no guarantee that pursuit of sustainability necessarily means pursuit of environmental quality. When the term is found as part of a governing agenda, there is also no guarantee that measures deployed will be pursued actively until they are successful. Despite these drawbacks, the sustainable development movement is becoming increasingly popular in the United States as public awareness grows regarding serious environmental problems and the costs of growth.

Environmental concerns also raise issues relating to the way we design or "plan" settlement space and how we can improve our arrangements for living and working together through more enlightened techniques of urban planning. The remainder of this chapter looks at people's attempts to change their circumstances through the specific manipulation of space, design, and public policy. We consider the case of planning, the use of rational schemes of land use, home construction, and environmental design to make metropolitan life better in general and to improve the quality of life of specific groups of individuals. We will consider public policy, the active intervention of the government at various levels to bring about social changes through public means, in Chapter 15.

METROPOLITAN PLANNING

Pruitt-Igoe was a massive public housing project constructed in the early 1950s in St. Louis, Missouri. It was inspired by the work of the leading architect of the postwar generation, Le Corbusier of France, and executed in design by several famous architects, including Minoru Yamasaki. The project consisted of thirty-three eleven-story buildings with a total of 2,700 apartment units on a site that encompassed almost 60 acres (about one-tenth of a square mile). The project represented the zenith of government-sponsored high-rise/low-income housing construction. Yet residents experienced problems almost immediately after Pruitt-Igoe opened in 1954 (Montgomery, 1987). Elevators broke down and were not repaired. Children were injured playing in corridors or stairwells that could not be monitored adequately by adults. Crime began to terrorize residents due to the large scale of design that allowed muggers to remain hidden. People complained of isolation from friends and neighbors.

Within five short years after opening, occupancy rates were already on the decline despite the subsidized rent. By 1970, vacancy rates in the buildings had reached more than 50 percent. The St. Louis housing authority made the fateful decision that the problems with the project were insurmountable and ordered its complete demolition. By 1976, the entire project was torn down. Pruitt-Igoe was a combination of architecture design following modernist principles that pursued progress in human/spatial relations and, simultaneously, a type of government intervention that made apartments at subsidized rents available to poor people. Architectural critic Charles Jencks sets this date as the time when modernist ideas about the promise of architecture as promoting social progress gave way to the postmodern period with its abandonment of such lofty aspirations (Holston, 1989). With the failure of Pruitt-Igoe and other public housing projects, came the realization that modernist architecture and government intervention in public housing required reexamination. In Chicago, the Cabrini-Green housing projects are now being dismantled and replaced by single-family town houses (see Box 14.1).

Within the metropolitan region, we find separate agencies devoted to planning that employ significant workforces at each level of government, including each city, suburb, and township within the metropolitan area, plus a countywide and regional planning department! Yet our metropolitan environments seem to be characteristically unplanned. This "planning paradox" (see Gottdiener, 1977) exists because in the United States planners have very little direct power to enact their schemes and for the most part are confined instead to advisory roles. The civic culture of the United States has always resisted direct intervention in the market by government. Compounding this restriction is the problem of the urban planning profession in our society. Most schemes come from the private sector, but even when they emerge from public bureaucracies, like Pruitt-Igoe or Cabrini-Green, they most often reflect the ideas of architects who believe they can create successful living and working arrangements for people through principles of design and the control of the built environment alone. Recall that the former project

BOX 14.1 Redevelopment of Cabrini-Green

In 1929 Harvey Zorbaugh published his study *The Gold Coast and the Slum,* a description of Chicago's wealthy lakefront neighborhoods along Lake Michigan (the Gold Coast) and of the slum area of tenement housing just half a mile inland. In the 1950s, the slum area was cleared and replaced with some two dozen high-rise public housing units called Cabrini-Green. In the early years most of the occupants were white, but by the 1960s the area was almost entirely composed of poor black families. The film *Cooley High* (1966) was shot at the local high school of the same name. By the 1980s the projects, sometimes called the worst in America, had become symptomatic of all that was wrong with public housing in the United States: All of the residents had incomes below the poverty line; most units were single-parent households; and drugs, gangs, and crime were rampant. In 1996 Dantrell Davis, a seven-year-old boy, was shot and killed while walking to the elementary school across the street from the project, still holding his mother's hand.

For years the site remained not simply a black spot in the city's history but also a controversial area with respect to plans for urban redevelopment. Many floors of the buildings were boarded up and some of the buildings were vacant, while the remainder sported large graffiti showing which gangs controlled the buildings. The *Chicago Tribune* sponsored a design competition for the best redevelopment plan for the area. Neighborhood organizers charged that the city wanted to turn the land over to real estate developers for middle- and upper-class housing close to the downtown area, and city planners looked for ways to relocate low-income households that would be displaced by the removal of the buildings. Finally, in 1998 and 1999, eight of the high-rise buildings were demolished in a scene reminiscent of the earlier destruction of the Pruitt-Igoe projects in St. Louis.

In the area adjacent to the project, new town houses selling for $180,000 were built by a developer, and in 2003 a Starbucks opened in a strip mall across the street from the projects, seeming to confirm the fears of neighborhood activists. But along with the 65 new units in the Mohawk North condominium development are 16 units of public housing. From the outside, the public housing units are indistinguishable from the private development, and the floor plans of each unit are similar "railroad flats" common to both older and newer housing in this area of the city. By dispersing low-income households and creating, in effect, a mixed-income housing development, the city hopes to eliminate the problems of concentration and isolation of poor families described by Massey and Denton in *Urban Apartheid.* In the coming decade, the high-rise public housing developments will disappear, to be replaced by new row houses—perhaps the end of the slum described some seventy-five years earlier in *The Gold Coast and the Slum.*

appeared to be first-rate on paper and represented the highest ideals of the modernist school of architecture but turned out to be a total failure in practice. These limitations to urban planning invite a sociological analysis, which is presented in the next section.

THE SOCIOLOGY OF LAND-USE PLANNING

The Advisory Role of Planners

The most basic kind of planning involves zoning for land use. Based on the principles that like activities should be located near one another and that industrial activities and residential areas should be separated, zoning partitions metropolitan space into distinct areas for each activity. Space is partitioned into zones reserved for residential use, commercial activities, and industrial work, among other functions. Planners use detailed maps to draw up land-use guides that constitute the zoning master plan. In most cases, such a plan needs to be adopted by local residents or their elected representatives. Thus, the ability to plan is restricted by the advisory role of planners. In the end, the public and elected officials determine whether a plan will be accepted and, also, whether it will be accepted in total or with modifications. Changes and modifications are always a possibility with land-use schemes, and both planners and architects may not like the final result.

Planners also work with elected officials and representatives from the business community to develop new uses of land. They may set aside land or help design an industrial park for factories and businesses, an office tower or city skyscraper complex, a mall, or a large residential development. New developments require infrastructure planning as well as the construction of the buildings themselves.

Roads have to be put in along with sewer and utility lines and the like. The impact on the surrounding area also requires careful thought and planning. New developments, just like zoning schemes, must be approved by local political authorities. Sometimes citizens object to new growth, and developments can be blocked or changed according to local resident desires. Most of the time, however, local elected representatives approve growth, since that is the priority of city government. Local communities often feel they must compete against one another to develop new industrial parks, shopping malls, and office centers, adding to the pressures for growth across the metropolitan region.

Physical Determinism

Architects who like to plan for social effects, as well as many planners, believe that optimal living and working arrangements for people can be achieved through the use of construction, design, and landscaping technology. This approach assumes that people's behavior can be controlled or channeled into desirable forms through the manipulation of physical design. As Herbert Gans (1968:28–33) has argued, this commits the fallacy of assuming that physical design will determine personal behavior. As social scientists are aware, behavior is determined by a complex relation of various social processes interacting in and with spatial forms rather than through the influence of the physical environment alone. In practice, planners and architects seem to ignore the social basis of behavior and falsely believe that construction design by itself can bring about desired change, such as increasing the frequency of neighborly interaction. Physical determinism, which privileges the abstract space of the planning professional over social space, has been responsible for some spectacular failures of planning, including the Pruitt-Igoe and Cabrini-Green housing projects, where it was thought that new architectural designs would somehow alleviate the social problems brought about by social exclusion. Perhaps the newest and most important example of the fallacy of physical determinism is the ideology of the "New Urbanism."

THE NEW URBANISM

This contemporary movement of architects and planners includes among its members Andres Duany, Elizabeth Plater-Zyberk, Jaime Correa, Steven Peterson, Barbara Littenberg, and Daniel Solomon. More so than any other single factor, New Urbanists are opposed to the present-day pattern of metropolitan sprawl and see it as both an immense waste of resources and a blow to the well-being of central cities. Calthorpe and Fulton (2001), for example, critique the existing form of urban planning, which designs zoning areas that separate residential from commercial and industrial use. They see such restrictions as being old-fashioned and more relevant to a time when industry was messy and polluting. Now our economy is based on information processing, and most of its economic activities are environmentally clean. For this reason, Calthorpe and Fulton, as New Urbanists, advocate planning for cities that have a mix of residential, commercial, and manufacturing or global economic functions. According to them, plans respecting these new realities would, among other things, do away with regional sprawl.

A major criticism of their approach is that they take as given the activities of both planning agencies and local governments. Their argument centers around the belief that metropolitan regions would look better "if only" planning were better. This belief fails to respect the way private interests in pursuit of profit circumvent and even subvert plans. Real estate interests have a habit of taking what is best, from their point of view, about urban planning and disregarding the rest of the recommendations in order to make money. In short, it is not an outdated form of planning, as Calthorpe and Fulton contend, that is the culprit behind sprawl and inefficient land-use schemes but the relentless pursuit of profit through real estate. The latter is often followed by subverting government regulations and by having planning schemes modified or even discarded.

Another aspect of the New Urbanism is the belief that the behavior of people can be altered for the better through more enlightened architectural design alone. As the enemy of the present-day sprawl pattern of development, New Urbanists seek, through architectural design, to create residential communities with a high degree of both neighboring and street life. According to their charter, "We are committed to re-establishing the relationship between the art of building and the making of community, through citizen-based participatory planning and design" (Fichman and Fowler, 2003:18). New Urbanists seek to build up cities by first constructing neighborhoods and communities with active citizen participation that are then connected to larger districts and areas within the metropolitan region. At the most local level, architects like Duany and Plater-Zyberk believe that residential communities can be physically designed to promote neighboring, even though many metropolitan residents prefer networking and possess communities without locality. For this reason, their designs feature houses with porches and emphasize pedestrian pathways rather than streets for automobiles. An excellent example of their ideas put into practice is the new residential development Seaside, located 100 miles west of Tallahassee, Florida. It is a community of 300 homes and 200 apartments that lies on 80 acres. Its human scale is accentuated by residential housing that is consciously based on the forms of one hundred years ago. All houses have front porches, and most are located on pedestrian paths rather than roads. Lots are small and narrow to facilitate social interaction among neighbors. Communities such as Seaside also incorporate many construction features dictated by architects that play an uncertain role in promoting a new sense of community, such as the mandated use of tin roofs or tall, narrow house windows. The elitism of architectural choice may not appeal to everyone.

New Urbanists, like many architects, believe that social goals like encouraging neighboring and stemming sprawl can be achieved through the physical means of design and construction. This is a fallacy. Residents of communities do not behave in certain ways simply because well-known architects direct them to do so. Neighboring, in particular, may be facilitated by the presence of porches, but it is not the determining factor. Rather, people create neighborhoods by establishing primary relations with neighbors. They have to want to do so. Many do not because their local reference groups are spread out across the metropolitan region and elsewhere, and yet they can keep in constant communication with these significant others through cell phone and Internet technology. This pattern is known as "community without locality," as we have already discussed. Studies of Seaside and another New Urbanist Florida development, Celebration, confirm that, because the housing is quite expensive, the residents are almost exclusively affluent middle-class Americans. These people prefer their far-flung "communities without locality" to reliance on neighbors alone. Furthermore, communities cannot be created merely by facilitating pedestrian traffic. Many people are so dependent on their automobiles that they ignore the role of the sidewalk in their daily life. While commercial shopping facilities may be located in New Urbanist developments, residents are more likely to use their cars in order to shop where they please throughout the metropolitan region, as exemplified by the failure of a project, the "Uptown District" in San Diego, California.

Some of the most influential planned projects today have come not from contemporary architects and theorists of community development but from utopian thinkers who created coherent plans for growth involving theories of design that are still considered important today. The final section of this chapter addresses these ideas.

UTOPIAN SCHEMES:
HOWARD, LE CORBUSIER, AND WRIGHT

Idealistic thinkers in centuries past lamented the evils of civilization and created a genre of literature known as utopian writing. Plato's *Republic* might be the earliest example, but the consummate vision belongs to Thomas More's *Utopia*. These accounts of some fictional paradise provide us with a means of measuring the prospects of human endeavor by showing how we can perfect ourselves and our society even while exploring our all too frail shortcomings as a species. Over the centuries, utopian literature has provided important inspiration to socially concerned individuals, as has the equally fascinating genre of dystopian writing, especially science fiction's dystopian accounts of life in future cities (such as the film *Blade Runner*).

Utopia, from the Greek word meaning "no place," and dystopia, a more recently coined expression that means an imaginary place of dread, are examples of places that exist elsewhere in time and space. While the former usually signals the modernist theme of progress, the latter represents our fears about the myth of progress. This yearning for the perfection of settlement space and the realization that it may never be attained due to the limitations of our civilization constitute an important strain in Western literature and cinema. The philosopher Henri Lefebvre (1991) calls all such spaces that exist in our minds as imaginary places heterotopias. As mental conceptions, heterotopias have the ability to influence our behavior and to define prospective schemes for architects and planners.

In nineteenth-century Europe, when the evils of industrialization and urbanization became a major social concern, individuals exercised the utopian spirit by conceiving of alternative urban environments. Some of these modernist visions were highly influential in the planning and architectural professions, and indeed by the twentieth century, architects no longer confined themselves to the design of individual buildings but composed manifestos and schemes that addressed the living and working arrangements of the entire city space itself. Among the important conceptualizers of new urban environments are Ebenezer Howard, Le Corbusier, and Frank Lloyd Wright. The modernist vision of each was expressed, respectively, as the Garden City, the Radiant City, and Broadacre City.

The Garden City

Ebenezer Howard, who lived during the turn of the last century, was a social reformer in England. Like others of his time, including Friedrich Engels, he was appalled at the social costs of British industrialization. Some thinkers, such as Robert Owen, responded by founding a utopian movement that advocated the construction of communities (such as New Harmony, Indiana) that would counteract the evils of the industrial city but required a fundamental break with acceptable ways of family or social life. Howard's response was to propose an alternative way of living that everyone could follow, even those uninterested in the utopian movement's social change.

To Howard, the city represented the future of economic growth, but it was, to express it directly, a lousy place to live. In contrast, the rural areas remained in organic harmony with their surroundings, but they were afflicted with limited economic opportunity. Howard's vision combined the two. He proposed that all new industrial growth be channeled to new locations in outlying areas that would combine industrial employment with country living on a moderate, human scale. These "garden cities" would represent the very best of city and country living.

The concept of the garden city proved to be very powerful. Capitalist industrialization in the nineteenth century knew no bounds. The older cities were crowded and polluted, and large cities gobbled up their adjacent countrysides in a relentless process of accretion. Because planners understood that growth was inevitable, they were attracted to Howard's idea of breaking urban expansion off and aspiring to locate new industry and housing in moderate-size communities.

Howard's ideas influenced the "new town" movement in England, which was responsible for building hundreds of such places, as well as the measured establishment of medium-size cities in Russia, although the latter case does not embody the ideal of the "garden," or suburbanized urban environment. In the United States a group of architects, notably Clarence Stein, popularized Howard's approach. Working with local authorities and developers, they constructed several places across the country, including Garden City, New York, outside of Manhattan, and Baldwin Hills, California, located in Los Angeles. Ebenezer Howard lived to see the opening of the New York community in 1928.

In practice, most of the American garden cities lack their own industry and hence are little more than middle-class suburban housing developments with some interesting features, such as shared public spaces. These ideas, all derivative of Ebenezer Howard's vision, are still put in practice by developers of large suburban residential projects such as planned unit developments, or PUDs.

The Radiant City

Le Corbusier was the professional name of the Swiss-born French architect Charles-Edouard Jeanneret (1887–1965). Along with several German architects, such as Walter Gropius and Ludwig Mies van der Rohe, Le Corbusier is considered the founder of the international style of design and one of the leaders of the modernist movement in architecture. The type of building associated with this movement is familiar to anyone who has seen the skyline of a large city, because the design concepts took over the world of architecture following World War II. International-style buildings are clean, straightforward, rectangular shapes with flat roofs. They are framed in steel and feature large glass windows that are sealed shut. Not until the postmodern architectural revolt of the 1980s were downtown office buildings liberated from the dictates of this concept.

Le Corbusier was influential because he propagated certain ideas about city living instead of confining his practice to building design. He believed in the triumph of technology over social conditions of industrialization. Buildings themselves were to be "machines for living," that is, the most efficient designs for the sustenance of everyday activities. The urban environment would itself have to be changed to conform to the dictates of more enlightened architectural design. Because Le Corbusier lamented the terrible social costs of industrialization, he proclaimed the modernist rallying cry, "Architecture or Revolution," sincerely believing that capitalist countries had little choice but to follow his ideas or confront the revolt of the urban masses.

Le Corbusier's ideas and those of his contemporaries constituted the ideology of modernism, which legitimated the notion of progress and the improvement of human conditions year after year through the intervention of technology. Modernist ideology asserted that the lot of individuals could be improved by the acquisition and application of knowledge—scientific, technological, architectural, social, and psychological. Part of modernist culture was the celebration of architecture and "modern" ideas about city planning.

Le Corbusier's plan for an entire metropolis, the "radiant city," reordered social space across a large, industrial aggregation. Instead of the relatively low density of housing and chaotic land use that was characteristic of the cities at that time, Le Corbusier proposed that buildings should be high-rises. By condensing the living space using building height, open spaces would be liberated, and Le Corbusier envisioned these spaces as parks that would surround residential clusters, thereby transforming the congested, sprawling industrial city into an open, airy, and efficient place of mobility and light.

A second important feature of the new design followed from Le Corbusier's and the modernist belief in the virtues of technology. Le Corbusier believed that the widespread use of public transportation and auto modes of transport would vastly improve the efficiency of urban scale. He proclaimed the "death of the street," that is, the pedestrian thoroughfare characteristic of all cities in the past. He envisioned instead rapid movement facilitated by autos, trains, highways, and feeder roads of people and commodities between the various nodes of urban space, residences, factories, shops, and government buildings.

The lesson of Pruitt-Igoe and Cabrini-Green (see discussion above) illustrates the deeply ingrained physicalist fallacy of Le Corbusier. Construction design, which disregards social process, cannot alone change everyday life. Unfortunately, the modernist ideas of the international style, and especially the concepts of Le Corbusier, were highly influential in urban planning through the 1960s. Along with Pruitt-Igoe, another major tragedy of planning in this vein is exemplified by the case of Brasilia, the capital city of Brazil, which was constructed following Le Corbusier's idea of the radiant city. Designed by the architects Lucio Costa and Oscar Niemeyer in 1960 and located in the interior 600 miles from the Rio de Janeiro coast, Brasilia looks like a giant bird from an aerial view. But on the ground, its limitations have become legendary. The "death of the street" produced an austere, alienating environment in which urban life is shrouded in anonymity. Neighboring and community interaction have all but disappeared because of the inability to overcome the automobile-based lifestyle and the imposing superhuman social scale, which has led to feelings of isolation and anonymity among residents (Holston, 1989).

The city was built to be the country's new capital, and so government administrators and their support staffs find employment there. However, Brasilia has failed to attract the diverse kinds of industry and everyday life that would convert it to a major city. Brasilia, among other austere creations of modernist city planning, reminds us of the perils of physical determinism and the need for architects to work in conjunction with social science to bring about an improvement of urban conditions.

Broadacre City

Frank Lloyd Wright (1869–1959) was the premiere American architect for most of the past century. His ideas, unlike Le Corbusier's, are still appreciated today, even if some of his designs have become outdated. Wright was no modernist. In fact, he was much influenced by the crafts movement in the United States and by Oriental architecture, particularly the Japanese use of interior space. Wright believed that structures should be organic extensions of natural environments. Houses, for example, should emerge from the crown of the hill rather than being built at the top, since the latter should be reserved for nature. They should embody a fluid connection with the world outside, and their construction should celebrate natural materials and settings, as exemplified by the Kaufmann home, Falling Water House (built in 1936), outside Pittsburgh, Pennsylvania. This summer home is made of concrete that is stacked like pancakes on three levels (called cantilevering) so that it sits on a rock above a forest stream. The water flows under the lower level and out over a falls. Sitting in the living room, one can watch the water flow and hear the stream as it runs over the rock below.

Frank Lloyd Wright was not enamored with the American city that he saw developing after World War II and wrote that with each new skyscraper he saw only the death of the city. Wright's vision of the new city possessed some similarities with that of Ebenezer Howard, especially the desire to merge the city and the country, except Wright thought in modular terms. Instead of a single, human-scale community, Wright envisioned an immense metropolis whose internal structure reduces space to a human scale through modular design. Each family would be assigned a single-family home on an acre of land! The space would enable families to grow their own food and to modify their surroundings according to their own personal tastes. Houses would be arrayed on an expansive grid. Wright also liked the possibilities of the auto, and his Broadacre City assumed that the car would be the basic means of transportation. Each place would be accessible by interconnected roads and highways feeding into and out of grids. Commercial shopping would take place in regularly spaced shopping centers, and industry would be isolated in specifically designed factory areas that were zoned exclusively for business.

Wright's scheme seems almost like the massive suburban environments of today—and indeed Wright saw little need for the city. He was one of the earliest architects to envision the concept of the shopping center, and his factory-zoned area is recognizable as the industrial park of the present, a common feature of metropolitan environments. The key element of Wright's vision, however, seems elusive, namely, the one-acre allotment of land that resolved the city/country dilemma at the smallest scale of each individual family. While suburban residences often have ample backyards, these are reserved for leisure activities, including, perhaps, a swimming pool. But Wright's vision of every family providing for its sustenance through backyard farming seems far removed from the realities of metropolitan life.

Our review of architectural visionaries provides us with some alternative ways to think about massive metropolitan environments and reminds us that urbanized landscapes do not necessarily have to assume the form they now possess. The present-day approach to metropolitan development seems oblivious to other ways of building except unending sprawl. But alternatives are possible; only the continuing belief in physical determinism, which wrongly suggests that architecture and urban planning can alter social processes, needs to be abandoned. Developers combining proper design with environmentally aware social science that uses the legacy of utopian ideas have had some successes, such as the new towns of Columbia, Maryland, and Garden City, New York.

PLANNING CRITICS: JACOBS AND KRIER

Ideas about planning have benefited from the work of critics who have taken both architects and the planning profession to task for neglecting the human values embodied within social space (Mayo, 1988). Two of the most influential critics are Jane Jacobs and Leon Krier.

Jane Jacobs

Jane Jacobs (1961) is concerned that we preserve the city as a viable place to live. She believes that the best cities have a vital and active street life. Her critique of urban planning claims that too many projects have ignored the role of human interaction as providing the lifeblood of city culture when most city inhabitants live in apartments with restricted space. For Jacobs, active urban life can never be planned because people invent uses for space. They accommodate the pursuit of their needs to the streets, parks, and playgrounds that they find around them. City planning that discourages this social interaction through the limiting of public or social space results in the destruction of the city itself.

For example, adolescents in the city spend a good deal of time out on the streets where they live. Over the years, an incredible variety of street games has arisen using this space, and many of these have been handed down through the generations, such as "Ring-a-Levio," "Johnny on the Pony," "Hop-Scotch," rope-jumping games, and stick ball. Skateboarders and others make use of urban spaces in ways never envisioned by architects and planners (Bordan, 1999). Projects planned only in terms of efficient automobile traffic (such as Le Corbusier's radiant city or Brasilia) arrange for wide thoroughfares that are heavily traveled. But such efficiency in the name of transportation destroys the ability of children to use the streets for play. Can you imagine active street games in the immense auto corridors of Los Angeles or on the well-traveled two-way streets in your own community? In contrast, Jacobs celebrates the streets and advocates blocking them off on a periodic and temporary basis to allow for neighborhood interaction. This is just what many cities now do when they sponsor neighborhood festivals during the summer months.

According to Jacobs, human-scale public spaces in the city, such as sidewalks, parks, and playgrounds, provide people with a number of resources: (1) They constitute learning environments for children, (2) they allow for parents' surveillance of the neighborhood and their children's activities, and (3) they facilitate intimate, primary relations among neighbors, thereby providing a strong sense of community (see the case studies of street corner societies in Chapter 7).

Jane Jacobs's ideas have had a strong impact on the way urbanists and planners think about city life. Local governments encourage park use, street festivals, temporary blocking of community roads, and toleration of sidewalk vendors. But not all of Jacobs's ideas have been accepted. Some of her followers advocated the elimination of elevators in apartment buildings to facilitate neighborly interaction, but with disastrous results for the residents of these buildings. Planners who emphasize revitalizing streets and city parks must take the high crime rate into account; in many cities, downtown revitalization efforts using Jacobs's ideas have failed due to the fear of urban crime on the part of suburban residents.

Jacobs's ideas about community may also be passé. Many city residents socialize with networks of friends and relatives who do not live nearby, as we saw in Chapter 9. Teenagers may prefer to travel to their own friendship networks rather than socialize on the street. On the whole, however, Jane Jacobs's ideas have influenced urbanists because she has captured the heart and soul of urban culture. Her importance lies in convincing us that urban culture depends on the relationship between personal interaction and public space. The fact that this culture is in danger of dying today is certainly not the fault of her conception. As we direct our attention to metropolitan regions, it is important to ask whether her ideas are equally relevant for suburban settlement spaces.

Leon Krier

Although a contemporary architect practicing in Germany, Leon Krier's ideas have been highly influential in the United States in recent years. Like Jacobs, his main concern is revitalizing urban culture. He views this as principally a problem of scale: The contemporary city has grown too large to shelter a livable environment, and it is necessary to return urban building to a human scale. Krier's model of the city is the pre-industrial town, and he advocates a return to the type of building characteristic of societies hundreds of years ago. In this sense, Krier is a critic of modernist ideology and one of the inspirations for postmodern architecture.

According to Krier, settlement space should be divided into districts with no more than 15,000 people in each subdivision. Ample use is made of squares, monuments, and public spaces, which should have the proportions of the classical pre-industrial towns. These changes, inspired by "retro" thinking, would return urban space to a human scale.

Krier also has his critics (see Dutton, 1989). More so than Jacobs, he commits the fallacy of physical determinism. He ignores social process and the larger societal forces that make up the modern city, and the kind of transition in scale that he envisions would be difficult for all but the most affluent residents. Krier's proposal, like those of most architects, also commits the elitist/populist fallacy. He never asks what people want; he only dictates design prescriptions through abstract space.

Despite these drawbacks, Leon Krier's work has had an enormous influence on architects designing new communities in the United States who seek to overcome modernist ideology, especially the New Urbanist movement (see above). Among the most significant disciples is the team of Andres Duany and Elizabeth Plater-Zyberk. Krier's ideas have been influential because there is a growing sense that typical suburban communities have isolated people unnecessarily. At the same time, these ideas seem destined to be realized by the most affluent but to be unavailable to the average family interested in a suburban home.

OTHER TRENDS IN PLANNING TODAY

In contrast to the New Urbanism and its projects, which dictate a design of human scale, other recent developments in both urban and suburban settlement spaces have embraced projects that are notably large in scale. Projects such as the building of the garden city Columbia, Maryland, and the construction of Battery Park City at the tip of Manhattan are large in scope and encompass many acres. Large tracts of land have been converted from agricultural use in the suburbs or cleared of slums in the city core. These megaprojects usually incorporate mixed-use developments of housing and commercial shops. Due to the influence of planning critics, however, many of these designs incorporate human scaling despite their large size.

Among the most successful developers of large but human-scale projects is James Rouse, whose corporation built the Baltimore Inner Harbor, Faneuil Hall in Boston, the New York South Street Seaport in Manhattan, and the Santa Monica Mall. The Baltimore, Boston, and New York projects in particular were constructed on deteriorating, unused land that was revitalized. Rouse's success involved a blending of open spaces, reasonably priced eating places of great variety, and upscale shops. Such redevelopment transformed spaces of bleak prospect into vital urban centers with an active public life. The Baltimore Harbor project, for example, consists of a large horseshoe of open space that surrounds the shore of the harbor inlet. Concrete steps lead to benches and play areas. One section is devoted to an array of alternative and moderately priced eateries. Two attractions, the Baltimore Aquarium and the Revolutionary War battleship Constellation, also draw visitors.

Rouse also successfully developed Columbia, Maryland, a new town that mixes apartment and single-family home construction with accessible and usable open space and shopping areas. The entire project has been planned to conform to human scale and includes pathways totally dedicated to pedestrian use that link the various sections of the town. As one observer notes:

> In Columbia the size of residential areas was determined primarily by the number of households needed to support an elementary school. The Rouse Co., as developer, insisted that within a block of the school there be a swimming pool, a community building, and a convenience store, and that people be able to walk or bike to these facilities without crossing any major streets. Three to five neighborhoods made up a village, which offered more facilities, including a supermarket, a bank branch, and other businesses, also accessible by the community's forty-seven miles of walking and biking paths, as well as by car. (Langdon, 1988:52)

The success of the Rouse Corporation has influenced the way other megaprojects have been designed. In New York City, for example, a 92-acre section of the dilapidated downtown with few residential units was demolished to

BOX 14.2 Enclaves of Fear?

The phenomenon of walled cities and gated communities is a dramatic manifestation of a new fortress mentality growing in America. Gates, fences, and private security guards, like exclusionary land-use policies, development regulations, and an assortment of other planning tools, are means of control, used to restrict or limit access to residential, commercial, and public spaces.

Gated communities are residential areas with restricted access in which normally public spaces are privatized. They are security developments with designated perimeters, usually walls or fences, and controlled entrances that are intended to prevent penetration by non-residents. They include new developments and older areas retrofitted with gates and fences, and they are found from the inner cities to the exurbs and from the richest neighborhoods to the poorest. Some communities with round-the-clock security require all cars to pass the guard, issuing identification stickers for residents' cars. Others use video cameras to record the license plate numbers and sometimes the faces of all who pass through. Entrances without guards may have intercom systems, some with video monitors, that residents may use to screen visitors.

These developments in part reflect the notion of community as an island, a social bulwark against the general degradation of the urban social order; they also reflect the increasing attempt to substitute private controls for public organization, for the joint responsibilities of democratic citizenship all of us share. Gates and walls are not necessary or natural consequences of these social trends or causes of them; they are, rather, a dramatic manifestation of them.

Gates and fences around our neighborhoods represent more than simple physical barriers. Gated communities manifest a number of tensions: between exclusionary aspirations rooted in fear and protection of privilege and the values of civic responsibility; between the trend toward privatization of social public services and the ideals of the public good and general welfare; and between the need for personal and community control of the environment and the dangers of making outsiders of fellow citizens.

The gated communities phenomenon has enormous policy consequences. It allows some citizens to secede from public contact, excluding others from sharing in their economic and social privilege. This result raises an ideological question that prompts polarized viewpoints. Are gated communities a metaphor of the exclusionary fortress, creating walls between citizens, or are they refuges from the forces that threaten family, economic security, and quality of life?

The real issue is not about the actual gates and walls but about why so many feel that they need them. What is the measure of nationhood when the divisions between neighborhoods require guards and fences to keep out other citizens? When public services and even local governments are privatized, when the community of responsibility stops at the subdivision gates, what happens to the function and the very idea of a social and political democracy? (Blakely and Snyder, 1997).

build Battery Park City. The project consists of high-rise apartments, offices, and shopping facilities. Located at the tip of Manhattan, the new development makes ample use of its view of the Hudson River. Residential blocks are integrated with an esplanade that includes spaces to sit and socialize with neighbors. Many other projects across the country, such as Riverplace along the Willamette River in Portland, Oregon, have adopted the successful approach of human-scale residential blocks, mixed commercial and housing land use, and pedestrian amenities to provide a more attractive environment for residents.

While the above cases provide examples of developers' attempts to encourage the formation of community, other trends are symptomatic of the many problems cities and suburbs face. For example, it is also popular to construct gated developments where security and surveillance are given prime importance. These barricaded communities do not seek integration into their urban surroundings nor an active street life but instead isolate themselves from the city fabric (see Box 14.2). Fences surround the perimeter. Guards supervise the coming and going of both residents and their guests. The uninvited are simply not allowed in. One such project, Studio Colony, is located in the Studio City section of Los Angeles and consists of 450 upper-middle-class apartments. The residences are sealed off in high-rise buildings with parking garages located underneath the guarded structures. Studio Colony provides security from the high crime rate of Los Angeles, but as one observer notes, "what Studio Colony does not do is shape the outdoor areas into coherent, genuinely inviting spaces; it is hard to imagine that anyone would want to walk from one end of Studio Colony to the other even once" (Langdon, 1988:59).

In sum, principally due to the increase in the social problems of metropolitan living, architectural schemes for communities have changed in recent years. The shift is from the utopian-influenced plans of the nineteenth century to the current mix of postmodern design that seeks a return to human scale, as exemplified by the New Urbanism, on the one hand, and the barricaded, guarded environments that seek isolation from the dystopia of the city, on the other. Both types of building, however, are associated more with creating housing for the affluent middle class than with providing affordable housing within metropolitan areas.

SUMMARY

People in the United States regard planning with suspicion. They prefer to defend individual property rights and the home rule prerogative of local government control over land use. Although every jurisdiction, no matter how small, seems to have its own planning department, professional experts are relegated to an advisory position. Planners must maneuver within this politically constrained milieu by exercising their influence on developers, speculators, homeowners, renters, local community activists, and public officials (Weiss, 1987). It is not an easy task. In the main, the professional planners employed by business and government devote their time to working out the ordinary details of mandated land use and construction requirements. They pursue the unglamorous job of drafting site usage plans for developers, reviewing and updating zoning maps for local governments, and assessing traffic studies. They also collect and review demographic information on the present and future growth patterns of individual towns. But this bureaucratic domain of activity remains removed from the active task of fashioning environments in which other people will live.

As we have seen, the limitations placed on professional planners have not prevented individuals from dreaming their dreams of the perfect city. Visionaries and utopian thinkers have tried their best to lead citizens of modern society toward some Eden that actualizes the promise of industrial progress. Some ideas, such as Howard's garden city, have been influential enough to affect future generations. Colossal failures, such as the superhuman building blocks of Le Corbusier's radiant city (actualized in every high-rise public housing project, not to mention the ashes of Pruitt-Igoe), have also been helpful because they have shown what we cannot or should not do. Happily, visionary plans are tried sometimes, and, even more happily, most of the time on a small enough scale so that the human cost of failure is not dear. We learn from mistakes and successes as our knowledge of planning human environments accumulates.

One important lesson that has recently been learned concerns the yearning for human-scale places in the face of unending metropolitan sprawl and the experience of immense, impersonal city space. Developments today feature an informed use of space. Macro-environments, such as the Santa Monica enclosed mall, are composed of many mini-environments that nurture sociability. The huge Battery Park City project opens itself out to the surrounding urban fabric and natural setting, providing for social interaction through human-scale public spaces and the extended esplanade on the Hudson River. Finally, as we have seen, new towns developed in their entirety (such as Columbia, Maryland) succeed by devoting space to pedestrians and thereby providing alternatives to automobile transportation to perform everyday tasks such as shopping, leisure activities, and commuting to work and school.

A return to human scale alone, however, even through the best efforts of planners, will not save the declining quality of life in either our central cities or our massive, sprawling suburbs. As discussed in Chapter 10, the high level of crime has taken an immense toll on the free use of urban space, not to mention its cost in lives. We can rightly wonder what will happen to the Hudson River esplanade and its pedestrian traffic if it becomes a haven for muggers. How enjoyable would the miles of pedestrian paths of Columbia, Maryland, be if the community were not isolated from the realities of homelessness and destitution characteristic of inner-city districts? The growing problems of land use, congestion, traffic jams, housing blight, environmental pollution, and suburban sprawl spur the public to search for planned solutions to urban growth. These and other problems may yet encourage local citizens to give up their traditional and narrow concern with protecting their own property rights in favor of a more coordinated approach to development. Yet the problems of the metropolitan region have societal roots that are not easily addressed by technical recommendations without massive social change.

These contradictions are clearest when we study the impact of environmental pollutants on communities. As we have discussed, the burden of costs for society's progress seems to fall on poor and minority neighborhoods. Government at all levels participates in producing this pattern of discrimination. In many communities, air pollution affects and endangers the lives of everyone, rich and poor. Environmental problems are found in all metropolitan regions and require economic, political, and social responses in addition to better-quality spatial design.

As sociologists have noted, professional planners, government officials, and architects would probably remain limited by their own outlook even if they were provided with more power. They preach the fallacy of physical determinism, which holds a blind faith in the power of construction technology and design to alter social relationships. Rarely do they profess what Frank Lloyd Wright saw as the organic, holistic needs of families and households. They are more comfortable with limited prescriptions that conform to the dictates of their professions' focus: building design and construction for architects, landscaping or land-use schemes for planners, or political expediency for politicians. Much more is needed to control the forces of development in the United States, but little public debate seems to be devoted to the issue of planning or the search for alternatives to our deteriorating environment.

Increased public involvement in the planning process is needed to refocus attention on those issues that affect our daily lives rather than on the profits to be reaped from development and the increased tax revenues that accompany urban growth. It is up to the leaders of our society and citizens to become more involved in a protracted dialogue regarding the kind of environments they would prefer to live in.

One last source of reform remains unexamined so far: the activities surrounding the drafting and execution of public policy and state intervention. We will consider this topic in the next chapter.

KEY CONCEPTS

planning paradox
physical determinism
New Urbanism
gated communities
sustainable development

IMPORTANT NAMES

Ebenezer Howard
Frank Lloyd Wright
Jane Jacobs
Leon Krier
Andres Duany

DISCUSSION QUESTIONS

1. Environmental problems must be considered as a sociospatial issue. What are some examples of sociospatial inequalities and environmental problems that you are aware of in your community?

2. The textbook suggests that physical determinism and the elitist-populist dilemma are major shortcomings with urban planning. What do these terms mean? What can be done to overcome these limitations?

3. We have discussed three utopian planners—Howard, Le Corbusier, and Wright. How did these planners differ in their ideas for improving urban life? Which has had the most influence on urban development in the United States?

4. What is meant by New Urbanism? Why are some observers critical of this movement? Do you think that New Urbanism can solve the social problems confronting metropolitan regions discussed in Chapter 10?

5. Are there gated communities in the area where you grew up? Do these communities match the description given by Blakely and Snyder? If not, in what ways are they different?

METROPOLITAN
SOCIAL POLICY

In the previous chapter, we considered one form of intervention: planning. We have examined both its prospects and its limitations. Attempts by society to fashion a living environment that is beneficial to all citizens do not end by exhausting planning options. A separate approach, one that is often initiated in conjunction with planning, involves government intervention guided by policy. The state has the authority to allocate money from tax revenues for social programs and to authorize deficit spending to address social needs. Government actions not only can direct behavior by prohibition, that is, by passing laws that prohibit certain acts, but also can provide incentives and opportunities to channel resources in specific ways. This push-versus-pull feature of policy is an important one to keep in mind when examining the issue of political intervention. Although this chapter is devoted to the role of government in improving metropolitan life, it is worthwhile noting that intervention, such as the publicly directed dumping of toxic waste in poor communities, can also create problems. Just "how much" intervention is needed and in "what forms" remain critical issues for any discussion of government policy.

THE TRAGEDY OF THE COMMONS
AND UNEVEN DEVELOPMENT

The United States possesses a civic culture that is averse to government intervention in the market. We have identified this perspective as *privatism*, the belief that government should restrict its role to supporting the business community and should seek market solutions to social problems. However, this reliance on the market can lead to problems. In the previous chapter, we saw that the desire to plan the development of metropolitan regions arose because the private market is not capable of providing the infrastructure required in our modern metropolis. There are other problems with the market as a mechanism for allocating resources. These include the difficulty of maintaining the quality of life when public resources are involved and the problem of uneven development in a capitalist society.

The Tragedy of the Commons

There is an old fable in academic circles that economists use to show why individual choice can lead to socially undesirable effects. The fable has many variations. Here is ours: Consider a village of farmers, each with a herd of cows and an open field adjacent to the village that is held in common. Each farmer seeks to use the public resource of the field to private advantage. Therefore, they all attempt to graze their cows as often and as long as possible on the common green. Pretty soon the grass is all eaten, and the common field is reduced to a muddy, barren plot of land.

If the farmers are interested in improving their situation, they have few alternatives. They could each buy a farm that would be owned privately with sufficient grazing land—an expensive move. Or they could band together and create a community scheduling agreement that would recognize the need of each farmer and the need of the field to regenerate itself. Because the users of this public resource might have disputes, the individuals involved would also have to arrange for arbitration in the event of disagreements or abuse. In short, this tragedy of the commons points to the need for the social institution of public authority or local government, which safeguards the benefits to the many from the abuses of the few.

Settlement spaces in modern society contain many public resources such as air, water, and recreational areas. Safeguarding these common environmental resources becomes increasingly difficult as the population and frequency of use rise (see Chapter 14). As a consequence, government must develop active public policies to deal with the many problems arising from large populations living in the same settlement space. Often these policies involve laws or regulations that restrict individual rights but are considered necessary to preserve public resources.

Consider one brief example: In New York City, partly as a consequence of a rising crime rate, apartment dwellers purchased dogs in great numbers. By the 1970s, piles of dog excrement made walking the city streets a hazardous affair. The city was compelled to pass a "pooper scooper" rule mandating that owners clean up after their dogs in public. This regulation made it a crime not to comply. To this day, any tourist can observe dog owners from all social backgrounds scooping up after their animals to keep the streets clean. The rule is an infringement on individual rights, but it is sanctioned by our society because it leads to a greater good: public enjoyment of a common resource, public space. Most environmental policy is of this type, and support for such measures requires a public culture that is committed to protecting environmental resources.

In the United States, many laws limit the free market for the public good. Some of the most restrictive are the southern California anti-air-pollution statutes, which are regulated by an independent state agency and affect everything from automobile exhaust systems to emissions from industrial activity, to the burning of trash and the use of outdoor barbecue grills. The air-quality control board has the authority to limit daily activities when air pollution reaches hazardous levels in the Los Angeles metropolitan region. Over the years, southern California has lost many businesses because they preferred to relocate rather than pay the extra cost of compliance. But that has not diminished public support for air-quality regulation. Rather, in such an environment, where pollution is an ever present danger, intervention is the only solution until the causes of air pollution are eliminated by other means. Hence, although we dislike government intervention, we find it useful. Sustaining the quality of life in metropolitan regions is an especially difficult task without the aid of government policy and regulation because the free market is incapable of doing so on its own.

Uneven Development and Policy: Redistributive Programs

In capitalist society, resources tend to flow to those who are most powerful. There are many reasons for this, and not all of them imply wrongdoing on anyone's part. Under pure market conditions, when individuals compete in business with one another, one's prosperity is supposed to spur the others to copy success. Thus, the market serves to discipline businesspeople to adopt the best and most efficient means of pursuing a profit. What holds for business, however, does not necessarily apply to individual people. Issues of inequality plague our society (as we saw in Chapter 10) and those of other countries (see Chapters 12 and 13). They also undermine the social order and lead to conflict.

Although our nation embraces the political philosophy of privatism, we also have a right, guaranteed by the Constitution, to equality of opportunity. This presents a dilemma for Americans, however, because powerful special interests lead to patterns of uneven development and hence inequalities. For example, all children have a right to a quality education. What do we do when we find that schools in more affluent neighborhoods have more resources than schools in poorer ones? Can we all afford to move to the best districts? Should we do so, even if we could? Should only the affluent have access to a quality education, including college, when education is supported by everyone's taxes?

Consider another example: Doctors in the United States are capitalists; they charge what the market will bear. Those people who have the most money can get the best medical care. But what happens to people who are too poor to pay? Why do some people have adequate insurance while others do not? Shouldn't all Americans, as a right of citizenship, have equal access to adequate health care? Or should quality of care depend on ability to pay?

Finally, the housing industry in our society is also a capitalist enterprise. Those individuals who can afford a private home can get one. The more you can afford to spend, the better your home will be. But what about those individuals who cannot afford the price? What happens to the truly poor who cannot even afford rent? Should we sanction poverty, homelessness, premature death, or the ruination of elderly persons who must pay for health and housing expenses they cannot afford?

Over the years, all capitalist societies have had to face the social costs of uneven development. In the United States, government has enacted legislation at all levels supporting social programs that address social ills. Social welfare programs are designed to pool resources so that all persons may have access to them (as is the case with Medicare programs for the elderly) or to redistribute them (in the case of rent vouchers for low-income households). Using certain criteria of inclusion, government officials decide what is needed and who should be eligible to receive assistance. These programs are supported by taxing the more affluent or by special government borrowing; hence, they redistribute the wealth from the relatively well-off to the poor, although, as we will discuss shortly, such schemes are not without their abuses or critics (Jencks, 1992).

In its most basic form, then, the issue of uneven development and public policy involves a question of money, because sustaining the quality of life has private and social costs. Government programs may address the issue of inequitable wealth, but as Christopher Jencks (1992) has argued, only income redistribution can directly address the problem of poverty. Hence, many social programs are destined to fail because they do not consider the fundamental cause of the problems they seek to address.

Public policy is created by government representatives in conjunction with research staffs and various academic aides. Some policies find the government directly intervening in the production of new resources such as the building of dams, highways, housing, and nuclear energy facilities. These directly aid private-sector business interests as well as the general welfare. In other cases, incentives are created to channel individual behavior in certain directions, such as the tax subsidy provided to people who purchase single-family homes. The enactment of programs often requires new staff and administrators. Government at all levels is a major employer in the United States, accounting for more than 25 percent of the entire workforce. Social programs run by government also support immense bureaucracies, such as the welfare departments in each state. Hence, not only the less affluent but also state workers benefit from public intervention.

There are many ways that government policy redistributes wealth and channels resources toward the public good. The welfare program and Medicaid are meant to protect the quality of life among those individuals who are less affluent or whose incomes are restricted because they are single parents or elderly. State boards of education try to equalize school resources among different public districts, regardless of neighborhood family incomes. Public health crises such as the AIDS epidemic are also addressed by government policy. Finally, housing programs exist in a variety of forms; there are even public programs to deal with homelessness.

In addition, government policies aid the business community directly and subsidize its activities, as the discussion of privatism suggests (see below). Public programs aimed at aiding individuals in need may be co-opted by private-sector involvement toward the pursuit of profit by business. This co-optation of government intervention is a serious limitation of public policy in the United States, and it alone causes programs to fail, as the experience with low-income housing programs run by HUD shows. Other limitations include the failure of individual programs themselves because they cannot attain desired goals as in the case of welfare aid or because intervention actually makes problems worse (Jencks, 1992).

Most of the examples discussed so far concern the general problems of inequity in our society rather than issues specifically relevant to metropolitan areas, although issues of inequity certainly have major impacts on the quality of life of urban spaces. Let us look more closely at some of the programs aimed particularly at the needs of both cities and suburbs, and the various political, economic, and social ramifications of government policy in metropolitan areas. In the previous chapter, we discussed how the desire for planning is associated with the modernist belief that increased rationality of land use and architectural design can improve our lives and lead to progress for all. Some countries, such as the welfare capitalist societies of Scandinavia, hold a modernist belief in government policy as also aiding progress through rational state intervention. The United States is characterized by a different public ideology called privatism, which requires government to aid business interests through the market. While our approach has had some success, it also leaves public programs vulnerable to co-optation by powerful interests. As we will see next, due to the characteristics of public policy, the pursuit of social justice often fails even when government intervenes with the best intentions.

URBAN AND METROPOLITAN POLICY

There is no escaping the fact that public policy is shaped by fundamental philosophical positions and ideologically held beliefs regarding government intervention. As we have seen, the dominant belief in the United States is that government should always play a limited role in the economy and that market solutions are usually best; however, it is not inappropriate for the government to subsidize private business. This attitude contrasts with those of industrialized countries in Western Europe, for example, which have more active public policy and more publicly supported benefits such as national health care schemes (although, as we discussed in Chapter 12, some of these countries, including the United Kingdom, have lately limited their public welfare programs).

The United States, therefore, is ambivalent regarding government intervention. Different political positions support various points of view in regard to state programs. On the one hand, many liberals lament the takeover of public programs by powerful business interests. On the other, many conservatives point to the inefficient and deleterious effects of government intervention. In addition to the philosophy of privatism, a second obstacle to intervention is that under the federalist arrangements between the national government and the states, the condition of cities is the responsibility of the states, despite the fact that many urban problems, such as crime and inadequate health care, are national in scope. Over the years, the respective roles of the federal government and the state government have become an issue of political debate (see the concluding section).

The urban renewal program of the 1950s, 1960s, and 1970s provides an illustrative case of the relationship between business and government as well as the limitations of policy. Urban renewal grew out of the Roosevelt administration's commitment to rescue the housing and banking industry from the Great Depression, a serious economic crisis indeed. The Housing Act of 1934, for example, established the Federal Housing Authority, which guaranteed home loans. The 1937 Housing Act mandated the government to provide funds for the support of low-income house construction and slum clearance. These powers were amplified in the Housing Act of 1949 under Title I assistance and in subsequent acts passed in 1954, 1961, 1968, and 1970. The Department of Housing and Urban Development (HUD) grew into a massive bureaucracy that oversaw the many programs associated with urban renewal.

It is important to note that housing intervention was aimed primarily at aiding the real estate industry, one of the three largest industries in the U.S. economy, rather than a showcase of modernist ideas mixing planning with policy, as in the Scandinavian countries. Providing homes for people and caring for their community needs was only a secondary goal of the U.S. program. As a result of this contradiction, metropolitan housing policy has had only mixed results. It proved to be a great boon to business but was less effective in attaining its social goals.

During the period from 1950 to 1990, government intervention aimed at aiding cities went through three separate phases, each of which reflected the dominant role of business in defining the interventionist agenda. Initially, funds targeted slum removal and construction of affordable housing. Then social goals were dropped, and the focus turned to the support of economic development for local business. Finally, government funds were used to subsidize economic development for global competition. In all three phases, local government operated less as a vehicle for social justice than as an aid to businesses experiencing declining profits.

Support for Slum Removal

Beginning with the late 1950s, the amount of federal money allocated for central city slum clearance and renewal increased greatly each year. Combined expenditures were $706 million in 1960, $1.8 billion in 1966, and $3.8 billion by 1970, or an increase of over 500 percent in 10 years (Mollenkopf, 1975).

There were many reasons for HUD's spending spree. By the 1950s, central cities were being devastated by the immense outflow of people to the suburbs. This shift, as we already discussed, was made possible by government highway and housing programs. As a result, downtown retailers and their department stores were in danger of being shut down because of the success of suburban shopping malls, while entire residential sections of the city gave way to blight and decline as middle-class people moved out. City politicians appealed to the federal government for help in rescuing downtown areas. A second cause involved the national response to the ghetto riots of the 1960s, which also highlighted the deterioration of inner-city areas. Funding for HUD projects more than doubled after 1966, the year of the worst rioting.

During the 1950s, urban renewal was aimed at revitalizing the downtown areas of cities and clearing away slums or blighted dwellings. Programs were supposed to replace cleared land with affordable housing and income-earning civic projects. According to some estimates, over 5 million low- to moderate-income housing units in U.S. cities were candidates for destruction and replacement (Flanagan, 1990:292). By the end of 1961, renewal programs had eliminated over 126,000 substandard housing units, but only 28,000 new dwellings were built (Robertson and Judd, 1989:307). The net result was a decline in the number of dwelling units for low-income households and an increase in housing costs in poor neighborhoods.

At that time, observers noted that the policy seemed to be more effective in the removal of black and/or poor residents than at replacing slums with affordable housing. In fact, during the 1960s, urban renewal was dubbed "Negro removal." Over 75 percent of all people displaced by renewal projects were black (Robertson and Judd, 1989:307).

While some low-income residents were helped by the ambitious redevelopment schemes subsidized by the federal government, much of urban renewal involved the clearing away of slums to allow private real estate interests to use downtown land for profit making, including the building of middle- and upper-middle-income housing projects and the regeneration of central city commerce through the construction of plazas, civic centers, and pedestrian malls.

Paradoxically, at the same time HUD programs were intervening in renewal, another federal housing policy in the form of tax subsidies to homeowners was destroying city neighborhoods by promoting suburbanization. These subsidies, which amounted to billions of dollars each year, were responsible for the massive shift to the suburbs, or white flight. By the 1970s, it was already clear that the United States had become segregated by race and class, with middle-class whites dominating the suburbs while the inner cities were increasingly populated by minorities and those whites who either could not afford to move to suburbia or preferred to live in the city in newly built or renovated upper-middle-income housing. Thus, government intervention not only was less interested in social justice than in subsidizing business but was also not rational, and it worked against itself in the fight to save the city.

Support for Economic Development

By the late 1960s, the goals of urban policy had changed as a result of political pressures. Commitment to the revitalization of slums was abandoned in favor of using government programs to bolster private business interests in the city. It was now apparent that urban economies, which had been dependent on manufacturing, were in decline. Deindustrialization had taken over the country, and cities needed to retool themselves to compete with other communities within their metropolitan region for new employment. Downtown business interests, along with local politicians, regrouped and worked together to use federal funds for revitalization projects. The focus of renewal shifted from slum clearance to support for economic development, such as the construction of sports stadiums, hotel and tourist complexes, and high-rise service centers. For example, in the 1960s the city of Los Angeles used urban renewal funds to bulldoze the blighted section of Bunker Hill near the downtown. But instead of replacing the structures with affordable housing and preserving the community, the city and its partners in the business sector constructed a music center, high-rise banking offices, and expensive high-rise apartment complexes. Slightly east of this redevelopment, the city eradicated another blighted residential neighborhood and replaced it with a sports facility, Dodger Stadium, instead of low-income housing (Davis, 1990).

Such projects, backed by powerful political and business interests, were responsible for the eradication of inner-city neighborhoods and small businesses, while the signs of progress greeted all residents with visible advertising for the joint government/business ventures. In many cases, city neighborhoods that did not represent high-yield profit making for business were bulldozed despite the objections of local residents. Gregory Squires (1989) illustrates this trend by presenting a dozen cases studies drawn from cities around the country in *Unequal Partnerships: The Political Economy of Urban Redevelopment in Postwar America,* and other researchers have studied unequal partnerships in individual cities (Robertson and Judd, 1989; Stone, 1989; Davis, 1990).

In the 1960s and 1970s, economic development as an urban policy meant that privatism had taken over not just through co-optation as it had in previous periods but overtly as part of city revival schemes. As the argument went, business concerns come first in a period of recession because when business prospers, the tax coffers of the city are also enriched. Housing programs and community redevelopment had to take a back seat, as did the fight against the problems of uneven development and for social justice. As in other periods, while some federal programs directly aided business, others also helped the middle class. City government could not stem the tide of middle-class white flight during this period because the pull of subsidized suburbanization was too powerful (see Chapter 6). Government could try to make the city a better place to do business, but it could not make it a better place to live.

Support for Global Competition

The shift to a financial and service economy for the downtown had now turned into global competition. Each place was in competition for limited investment that was attuned to worldwide opportunities within the market-place of global capitalism. National programs that supported private enter-prise would bypass local bureaucracies and downsize the role of government planning. Issues of social justice were ignored. This restructuring of the fed-eral/city government relationship reached its zenith during the eight years of the Reagan administration and resulted in the cutback of urban policy until there was little left of renewal funding.

Several reasons have been advanced for the federal abandonment of HUD city renewal programs, most of which are political. The Republican adminis-tration in the 1980s ran on a platform that de-emphasized the needs of cities. The plurality of active voters lived in the suburbs, and they were attracted by President Reagan's call to get government "off the backs" of people. This meant that under the Reagan and Bush administrations, there were severe cuts in public welfare programs but not in military spending. The new regime followed a conservative philosophy that favored market solutions to social problems. It also reaffirmed the political principle of federalism (mentioned at the beginning of this chapter), which made the condition of cities a responsi-bility of the states. This principle suggests that local and state governments were better able to deal with local problems and that urban revitalization should be market driven rather than pulled along by federally financed and planned projects. Such sentiments were supported by a majority of voters, who backed President Reagan's conservative agenda and later elected George Bush. The cuts to federal programs were unprecedented. Robertson and Judd (1989:314) made these observations about national aid to cities:

> Overall spending dropped from $6.1 billion in fiscal year 1981 to $5.2 billion in fiscal year 1984. The $5.2 billion spent for the fiscal year 1984–1985 amounted to a decline of almost 20 percent when corrected for inflation. By the 1989 budget year, money for urban programs was cut $4.4 billion, a fur-ther reduction of about 40 percent when the effects of inflation are consid-ered. Nearly all subsidies for the construction of public housing were ended. Urban mass transit grants were reduced 28 percent from 1981–1983 and were cut another 20 percent by 1986. CETA [Comprehensive Employment and Training Act] funds were eliminated after 1983.

The Clinton administration in the 1990s brought little in the way of new ideas or new aid to urban areas. Cities and states have had to fend for them-selves in supporting metropolitan programs. As discussed in Chapter 10, the fiscal crisis that set in during the 1970s severely restricted the ability of local areas to finance policy aimed at social goals, even when good ideas had public support. As the fiscal crisis spread to the states in the 1980s and 1990s, both cities and states had to scrap many social projects and have since concentrated on economic development.

The situation for cities, counties, towns, and metropolitan areas is now much worse under the Bush administration. Although the Clinton administration managed to achieve a budget surplus by the end of the second term, which might have been used to shore up local governments in the throes of fiscal crisis, no such outcome is remotely possible now under President Bush. His administration has turned a sizable surplus into a deficit of historical proportions. Much of the spending has gone to support the U.S. military presence in Iraq, although highly respected reports claim that billions of dollars of this effort remain unaccounted for and are probably lost forever. A deficit of such magnitude may not bother ordinary citizens, but they forget that such a situation has its most deleterious effects on local government. When cities and towns are in fiscal crisis and cannot support services or the community quality of life or repair needed infrastructure, they will not be able to turn to the federal government for relief. This might have been possible when the federal government had a surplus, that is, in the latter years of the Clinton presidency. However, all hope for such relief now is gone. This means that the immense and quite incomprehensible level of federal deficit spending has a very damaging, critically injuring effect on local government. Furthermore, current projections state that our foreign entanglements will lead to astronomical deficit spending for many years to come. To be sure, this is terrible news for cities, towns, counties, and even state governments in the United States.

Local politicians now work directly with business to revive ailing urban economies as their only way out of fiscal distress. Such a strategy only works when the business community has the resources to help. Public/private partnerships in the face of fiscal crisis also represent an extreme example of privatism, because the reduction or elimination of policies aimed at improving social well-being has occurred at every government level since the 1980s. This trend continued through the 1990s as the Clinton administration issued waivers to states that sought to eliminate welfare programs and replace them with a variety of "work incentive" programs. The result has been a substantial reduction in the number of welfare recipients, but this does not mean that former welfare recipients now participate in the paid labor force. Fewer than half of the persons removed from welfare rolls over the last decade have found permanent employment, and the number of families seeking assistance from food pantries and other private-sector charities has increased substantially.

Abandonment of public policy in support of the quality of life continues today under President Bush, who has offered no support for local government, despite touting "enlightened" social programs, such as those associated with education. The rhetoric is there, but the money isn't. It is one thing for the federal government to claim that the local quality of life is a matter for local jurisdictions, but it is quite another matter when no level of government addresses this need due to fiscal crisis and the subsidization by taxpayers of wasteful, irresponsible federal government spending in support of foreign adventures that have not been defended with sound, irrefutable arguments.

According to Desmond King (1990), local policy has been reduced completely to the subsidization of the private sector through either supply- or demand-side incentives to business. The former consists of packaging incentives such as tax breaks, rent-free land, and local bond financing designed to attract capital to the area. The latter consists of city development activities that attempt to create new industries with the aid of the private sector by underwriting development costs, such as in the creation of high-tech industrial parks. In both cases, the policies of the 1990s stand in stark contrast to those of thirty years ago, because the emphasis is on economic recovery without the rhetoric that once obscured the emphasis on privatism by, at least, acknowledging issues of social equity and injustice.

PRIVATISM AND ISSUES OF SOCIAL JUSTICE

Has the support of private enterprise and abandonment of active intervention in cities been successful? Our analysis of metropolitan problems (Chapter 10) shows just the opposite. What are the limitations of the ideology of privatism and the present constraints on pursuing social justice? The limitations of privatism and government subsidy for economic development include the failure to realize benefits from development, especially by low-income residents; the proliferation of beggar-thy-neighbor competition among different cities, which does not benefit local areas; the subsidization of capital investment that is not reinvested locally; and the destruction of public resources without benefit from the public subsidization of private-sector growth (Barnekov and Rich, 1989).

Lack of Community Benefits from Public Investment

Oakland, California, obtained a package of loans and tax subsidies to support the private development of airport improvements and an industrial park. The rationale for the public subsidy of the project was that it would help provide steady work for the city's hard-core unemployed. But only an estimated sixty-five jobs out of many hundreds that were created went to hard-core unemployed workers (Pressman and Wildavsky, 1973). Other studies indicate that publicly supported growth does not bring the kind of benefits purported by boosters of public/private partnerships. In Houston, which claims to be a city based on private enterprise, business has used government funds in many ways to develop infrastructure, subsidize industry, and grease the wheels of profit making. During the city's growth, the costs of development were passed along to residents. By maintaining a low tax rate on business, the city failed to plan adequately for highways, sewage systems, garbage collection, water quality, and road maintenance. Houston's traffic jams are legendary. And future residents will be saddled with the immense public bill to finance the missing infrastructure and the costs of growth (Feagin, 1988). The experience of Houston has been duplicated in other U.S. cities, which now face immense infrastructure problems of their own while continuing to spend millions in taxpayer money on "development" projects such as sports stadiums, convention centers, and luxury housing. The alleged "crisis" of the infrastructure and of public support for the quality of life is not, as some political leaders maintain, a crisis of funding alone, but represents some skewed priorities when all available money is spent on civic development projects of dubious value.

Other case studies reveal that privatism twists the intent of public/private partnerships to the full benefit of business. As Barnekov and Rich observe, "local economic development programs designed to use public funds to leverage private investment frequently result in reverse leverage; that is, private enterprise often leverages public funds to accomplish its own development objectives and, in the process, may hold local governments hostage if they do not come forth with generous subsidies" (1989:216).

Case studies have shown how the competition for investment dollars simply forces local jurisdictions to make excessive sacrifices. This is especially the case as capital has become increasingly mobile in the global economy. In the past decade, we have seen cities and states offering incredible tax breaks and other incentives to attract new or relocating industrial plants, another use of public funds to support private business. Some observers have called this ruthless competition among places for investment the "new arms race." In the chase after global dollars, social equity programs are cut or abandoned. As a result, cities have a diminished capacity to support socially beneficial programs and to sustain the community quality of life (Kanter, 1987:510–511). The problems of uneven development within and between metropolitan regions are of deep concern (see Chapter 6).

The Decline of Democracy in Local Politics

The new public/private partnerships in pursuit of economic development usually work outside the democratic process of government decision making.

Non-elective super-agencies such as the Port Authority of New York and New Jersey and similar ad hoc development agencies are not monitored by the voters. This means that public investment and oversight through the democratic process is itself diminished in the pursuit of policies of continued growth (see Chapter 11).

Government policy involves an often unproductive struggle between the dominant priority to support business and the lesser goal, often passionately pursued by social movements, of social justice. Spatial competition among places for limited public and private investment also affects the success of policy, because the United States has no overarching national program for metropolitan revitalization. In the 1950s, competition was between central cities and their suburbs; in the 1960s, it was between regions of the country, especially between areas that were not experiencing a decline in manufacturing (such as the Sunbelt) and those that were (for example, the Snowbelt). By the 1980s and 1990s, however, all places were involved in a universal global competition for scarce resources. These policies pitted place against place to the advantage of capital and at the expense of local taxpayers. Only recently have government policy experts been willing to reexamine this one-sided relation between people and increasingly mobile capital, because in many areas the benefits of business decisions to locate have been stripped away by the costs of incentive packages.

As homelessness, housing deterioration, and other urban problems intensify, renewed pressure is being placed on the federal government to intervene once more to stem the decline in the quality of community life. If such a turnaround does occur, it will come only with a renewed debate on the philosophy of intervention. This is unlikely to occur under the Bush administration.

URBAN POLICY: THE POLITICAL DEBATE

Over the past two decades, debate has raged regarding whether traditional liberal or conservative solutions to the urban crisis should be applied. Most analysts of urban problems discuss solutions in terms of precisely this clash of ideologies. In this section, we discuss policy recommendations along ideological lines. In a later section, we will point to a course of action that offers the possibility of rising above this clash of perspectives by addressing the limitations of present public policy arrangements.

Liberal Positions on Urban Problems

Liberals tend to focus on the limitations of existing social institutions and to seek remedies that equalize the ability of all citizens to overcome those limitations. They support government intervention and spending as a means of combating social ills. Most urban problems are caused, in this view, by the inequities of the resource distribution system in our society. Poverty and associated problems of uneven development are the inevitable consequence of the fact that economic rewards and social opportunities are not equally available to all citizens.

The liberal agenda uses government intervention as a tool to overcome uneven development. It supports active involvement of policy to identify, address, and help resolve serious urban problems of the less affluent. Economic deprivation and persistent racial segregation are contributing factors in the rise of crime and drug use rates. Programs could be designed, as they were in the 1960s, for job training, long-term unemployment assistance, and even government-subsidized corporate internships that might provide job possibilities for the most disadvantaged city residents. In addition, government-subsidized medical care, family assistance, and aid for the homeless, such as TANF, or Temporary Assistance for Needy Families, could provide a social safety net below which U.S. citizens would not fall. This would improve the life chances of the less affluent and remove from the city streets some of the worst cases of need that threaten the quality of life for everyone.

Conservative Approaches to Urban Problems

Conservatives, in contrast, believe in limited government intervention and severely restricted government spending. They accuse liberals of squandering society's wealth through excessive public spending. Consequently, they are opposed to the kinds of programs sponsored by liberals precisely because they cost money and must be supported by taxes on private income or corporate profits. Conservatives also address the issue of uneven development. In their view, less advantaged people and places must make themselves more competitive so that they will be in the contest for capital investment. It's up to people and places themselves to become more attractive.

Conservatives believe that many of the problems of the poor reside in their own personalities and family traits. Many suggest that poor people are not motivated to find legitimate jobs and that they prefer welfare programs because they have been encouraged to do so by liberals seeking to exercise their agenda and support the growth of government bureaucracy (see Banfield, 1974; Jencks, 1992). James Murray's influential book, *Losing Ground* (1984), argued that welfare and other government programs actually increased poverty and caused the increase in the number of unwed mothers. This book was referred to (by conservatives) as the Bible of the Reagan administration and continues to influence government policy in the Bush administration.

Recently a variant of the conservative position has been taken up by black critics of liberalism such as Shelby Steele (1990). They argue that urban liberals and their programs, such as affirmative action, have ruined the moral character of blacks while the latter have languished in the ghettos of northern cities. Blacks have been made dependent and are losing the ability to cultivate their own inner resources due to city bureaucracies and their liberal programs of aid. Consequently, the immense problems of the ghettoized poor (formerly called the "underclass") are really the outcome of decades of liberal policies that forced blacks to become wards of the state.

It must be pointed out that even if people favor government intervention for the pursuit of social justice, our study of the record of government metropolitan policy over the past fifty years shows that expensive public programs have continually been co-opted by the business community. Hence, there is considerable evidence against returning to the blind faith of liberals and active public spending to combat social ills, even if we could do so.

Overcoming the Liberal–Conservative Impasse

What hope exists for the urban future? The lessons of history teach us that either/or choices are unfair. We must look beyond the clash of liberal and conservative ideology and beyond all ideological means of understanding urban problems. What possible solutions might overcome the liberal–conservative ideological impasse?

An important but neglected dimension to the debate on urban problems involves recognizing the fact that local governments have only limited ability to plan adequately for social change. The ideological debate between liberals and conservatives misses an important dimension, namely, the limitations of local government as administrative structures. It also fails to address the particular relationships among the federal, state, and local levels that have always worked against adequate planning and public policy in the United States.

Within metropolitan areas, there are so many levels of government, each with its own limited administration, that power is both highly fragmented and weakly applied. Social programs initiated by cities are ineffective because they must tackle problems that are regional in scope. So cities simply control too small a piece of the regional pie to fight the immense problems of uneven development, such as the need for affordable housing. In fact, it can be argued that the city is not the place to initiate programs aimed at social problems of broad scope or at alleviating the inequities of uneven development. Suburbs and cities share similar problems, and the growth patterns of one are linked to those of the other. Hence, a metropolitan perspective on improving the quality of life becomes imperative for adequate public policy. Problems that are national in scope, such as crime or the crisis of health care, must be returned to the responsibility of the national and state levels of government, where they belong. By understanding the relationship between spatial and social levels in the study of policy, we can sort out what should and should not be the responsibility of local government. And by adopting a metropolitan, regional perspective, we can design better ways of attacking the problems of social justice and uneven development.

There is strong evidence that the political fragmentation of metropolitan regions in the United States contributes to and may be responsible for uneven sociospatial development. For example, Detroit and Toronto are industrial cities located just some 230 miles apart. Detroit, like many other American cities, has long been in the throes of economic crisis. While the metropolitan region contains more than 4.5 million people (and many wealthy suburbs), the city of Detroit itself lost half of its population between 1950 and 1990. The murder rate increased ten times during this same period, from 6 per 100,000 persons in 1950 to 60 per 100,000 in 1989. From 1990 to 2000 population for the Detroit metropolitan region remained at 4.5 million, while the city population declined by some 75,000 persons—from 1,028,000 to 951,000 persons—the first time that the population of Detroit has been below 1,000,000 persons since before World War II.

Most of us are familiar with the Detroit of popular culture—from the vibrant Motown sound of the 1960s to troubled rap music of Eminem and the film *Eight Mile* of the 2000s. The comparison is of some interest. Detroit of the 1960s was still a booming industrial city. Now entire city blocks are vacant, the housing long since abandoned due to white flight to the suburbs and destroyed by arson. Some of these neighborhoods have actually been reclaimed by "urban forests," and deer have returned to the city. Today the city is overwhelmingly black and poor, with apparently few opportunities for economic revival due to the restructuring of the auto industry that brought the city to greatness in the 1950s.

In contrast, Toronto has doubled its population since 1950, going from slightly more than 1 million to 2.5 million persons in 2000. The metropolitan region has also grown rapidly, from 3.9 million in 1990 to 4.7 million persons in 2000. Compared to Detroit, Toronto is relatively crime free, with a murder rate of less than 5 per 100,000 people, lower than any U.S. city of 1 million or more population. Yet Toronto has a diversity of people with a mix of racial, ethnic, and class groups that is comparable to any major American city. According to one report:

One thing does much to explain Toronto's success: the enactment in 1953 of a federal form of government for the 13 previously independent municipalities in the area. The original 13 have consolidated into six. They are responsible for local affairs, while the Metro council handles area affairs, including Metro-wide planning. (*The Economist,* May 1990:17)

The Metro-wide government consolidates resources in the entire region and coordinates the growth of both the central city and its suburbs. As a result, many of the problems brought about by uneven sociospatial development that have plagued Detroit have been avoided by the Toronto region. For example:

Metro-wide co-ordination of the education system has given Toronto civilized schools. Detroit has some civilized and well financed schools too, but they are in the suburbs; the city schools are mainly deprived, like their pupils. (*The Economist,* May 1990:18)

Regional government has worked in Toronto. In contrast, Detroit cannot possibly find the resources to address its problems because it is cut off from the affluent suburbs. Should this society tolerate the extreme forms of deprivation and affluence that can be readily seen in this region, even if all metropolitan Detroit residents suffer from the continued downsizing and outsourcing of the auto industry?

Due to the autonomous home rule of local communities that discourages regional forms of government, suburban settlement spaces have effectively insulated themselves from the need to address the problems of uneven sociospatial development. But the contrast is not only one of spatial organization. Canada has a system of health care that is run by the national government; the United States does not. The two federal governments differ regarding what they have chosen to bear as national responsibilities, and this also affects the quality of life for metropolitan residents. The issue of national concern for social justice cannot be separated from that of local policy.

In sum, we may not know all the answers to the present case of urban decline, but one very good try at finding a solution that avoids ideological debates focuses on the structural limitations of city government and the excessive fragmentation of local jurisdictions. Along with these sociospatial concerns are jurisdictional dilemmas among local, state, and national levels that must be faced to determine who shares the burden of responsibility for the quality of life in the United States—the individual alone (as conservative policy dictates), the city, the state, or the federal government.

Without metropolitan coordination, and lacking support from higher levels of government, cities simply do not possess the resources they need to address commanding problems of everyday life. At some point in the future, national leaders must provide the vision necessary to share the responsibility for social concerns at the federal and state levels, where it belongs. Until then, the quality of life not only in central cities but across metropolitan regions as a whole will be dependent on the well-being of local business concerns within an increasingly competitive global economy.

KEY CONCEPTS

tragedy of the commons
uneven development
redistributive policies
urban renewal
public housing
public subsidy
liberal / conservative approaches to urban problems
metropolitan government

DISCUSSION QUESTIONS

1. Why is the market system unable to adequately determine the allocation of resources across the metropolitan region? What is the rationale for public intervention in urban planning and metropolitan development?

2. The United States has a federal system of government. What does federalism mean, and what are the consequences of federalism for urban planning and government programs in metropolitan areas in the United States?

3. What is the ideology of privatism? Where did it originate, and what effect does it have on urban policy? What are two of the limitations of privatism? What are some of the consequences of these limitations?

4. What are some of the important differences between liberal and conservative positions as to the causes of urban social problems? How can we overcome the liberal/conservative impasse? What are some of the changes that have occurred recently in federal urban policy as a consequence of the Reagan, Clinton, and Bush presidencies?

THE FUTURE OF URBAN SOCIOLOGY

The beginning of the twenty-first century marks a new era in human history. The world's urban population is some 3 billion persons. For the first time, more than half of the world's population lives in urban areas. As we have noted earlier, in the next twenty-five years the number of persons living in urban areas will increase by some 2 billion persons—an amazing 60 percent increase—to some 5 billion persons. In 2030, it is expected that some 70 percent of the total world population will live in urban areas (United Nations, 2003).

We know that these urban areas are linked in exciting and new ways that would have been unimaginable just a short time ago. We are connected by a global economy where the life opportunities of persons in one country may be dependent upon capital flows of new investments from a nation on the other side of the world. The mass media brings us world music from Africa and the Middle East. We use the Internet to keep in touch with old friends who move to other countries, and to make new friends in places we have never even heard of. It is a global world, to be sure, but more than that, it is, for the very first time, an *urban world*.

The people living in this new urban world, the urban world of the twenty-first century, will confront many new and important issues. We know that more than a third of the world's urban population now lives in shantytowns, many with inadequate drinking water or sanitation, substandard housing, and few economic opportunities. The number of persons living in urban slums will increase to more than half of the world's urban population by 2030—some 2.5 billion persons. Problems of pollution will increase as the less developed nations industrialize and create new urban infrastructures that require the same resources for development that we find in the developed nations. This is already happening in China and India. A changing global climate may lead to major changes in crop production and weather patterns around the world, creating new scarcities of food and water that we have barely begun to consider.

Global society is urban society. And no field of study is more important for understanding these changes than Urban Sociology. Will urban sociology step up to this challenge?

UNDERSTANDING THE NEW URBAN WORLD

Urban studies is a comparatively new field of study. Perhaps because of the exciting changes—and important challenges—that the new urban world of the twenty-first century presents, urban studies and its related disciplines— urban sociology, urban geography, architecture—have emerged as something of a growth industry in academic publishing for the past decade or more. This work is built around both new and old perspectives in the field and offers some insight as to where urban research will lead in the future. In this final chapter, we explore several topics that are important to our understanding of the new urban world. These topics include globalization, world cities, theming of the urban environment, racialization of urban space, and cyberspace and the end of the city.

Globalization

First, there is an extensive literature on globalization and world cities. We have discussed some of the important characteristics of globalization and the impact of globalization on urban development in the industrialized countries (Chapter 12) and in the developing world (Chapter 13). It is important to remember that globalization is not a new phenomenon, nor is it a new area of study in sociology. Although globalization is sometimes presented as having begun with the European discovery of the Americas and the development of European colonial empires, there are earlier precedents. The great Chinese empires of an even earlier period linked trading centers across Southeast Asia with the great Chinese urban centers, then the largest cities in the world. Even earlier, Rome, the first truly urban civilization, depended upon wheat grown in Egypt to sustain its growing urban population, and Roman cities across Europe and the Middle East were linked with an extensive road system.

The European colonial system connected cities across the world in a new and more systematic fashion. During this period of mercantile capitalism, raw materials (silver from the Americas, spices from the Far East) were brought back to the European trading cities. The neocolonial empires of the twentieth century reestablished and intensified this system of economic dominance (as we saw in Chapter 13, the majority of export crops produced in the Philippines is under the control of just one American corporation). This system of globalization and colonial dependence is described by the world systems theory of the 1970s and 1980s, in which the industrialized countries and the former European colonial powers are seen as part of the core, and countries in the developing world are seen as part of the periphery (Wallerstein, 1976). The current literature on globalization builds upon these earlier models to describe an increasingly complex system of economic competition and urban growth.

Many of the significant issues of economic and social justice associated with globalization have been contested on college campuses across the United States and in protests against the International Monetary Fund and the World Bank in cities across the world. We know something about the costs of globalization in terms of job loss and economic restructuring in metropolitan regions across the United States (Chapter 6) and in other industrialized countries. Perhaps less well understood is the impact of globalization on urbanization and urban systems in the developing nations. The growth of urban centers in China—the number of metropolitan areas with populations of more than 2.5 million persons will increase from a dozen in 2000 to eighteen or more by 2030—is largely a consequence of the concentration of industrial production in the urban clusters identified in Chapter 13. In many other countries in the developing world, the growth of urban centers is a consequence of continuing migration from rural areas as individuals and households are unable to support themselves from simple agricultural work and come to the cities looking for work. Most of the growth of urban populations in the developing nations in the coming decades will be of this type (United Nations, 2003). These urban centers will not be part of the world urban system in the ways currently described in the literature; instead, they are likely to become part of what has been called the Fourth World—areas that are left behind in the globalization process (Giddens, 2000).

Globalization remains a topic that is studied closely among urbanists in all countries. One key area of globalization research involves the study of how it affects local labor markets. Changes in the demand for high- and low-tech labor, retail workers, or financial service workers, for example, can directly affect the economic well-being of cities. Commercial growth and housing development are all tied to the ebb and flow of local jobs, including the quality of wages.

American metropolitan regions have been adversely affected by the flight of industry and people from the urban core. Industrial decline has been attributed to the power of multinational corporations and their acquisition of local businesses. Some transnational corporations have purchased American companies just to shut them down or downsize them in order to increase corporate profits and strengthen market position. These actions have contributed to urban decline. Other places have benefited by new investment, much of it also involving multinationals. Sustained growth in places like Los Angeles, San Diego, and New York owes a considerable amount to the continuing viability of those cities as sites of global investment. Future research on globalization needs to examine the many contradictory impacts of this international business activity and determine how they affect different parts of the metropolitan region.

World Cities

Peter Hall's work on *The World City* highlighted seven world cities (London, Paris, Moscow, New York, Tokyo, Rhine-Ruhr, and Randstadt-Holland) and brought attention to cities as places of political and economic power (Hall, 1966). But the study of global cities emerged more directly from world systems theory and political economy models of urban growth (Chapter 4). Friedman and Wolff (1982) introduced the concept of a global network of cities where urbanization was linked to the internationalization of capital, and a later article by Friedman (1986) suggested that the way in which cities are connected to the world economy is the key to their growth and development. Cities connected to the world economy in similar ways would be alike regardless of differences in history, national policies, and cultural influences. The global city is the site of the concentration and accumulation of world capital and has a characteristic division of labor, with a large number of professionals in specialized control functions such as lawyers, computer programmers, and accountants.

Saskia Sassen's study of global cities argues that the presence of global cities has important consequences for the nation and for the global economy (1994; 1999; 2001). Sassen's work is different from the earlier world system theory in that Sassen asserts that the leading global cities, not the nations themselves, have emerged as the key structures in the world economy. The global city is characterized by specific forms of urban development, including the redevelopment of the urban core and displacement of the poor, construction of high-rise office towers, and an increasing social and spatial polarization. The transformation of cities into high-tech international business centers privileges global corporations at the expense of other groups in the city, particularly minorities, immigrants, and women. Sassen presents the corporate office building as a metaphor for the polarization that characterizes the global city: During the day, the building is occupied by highly educated, well-paid executives making global transactions; at night it is cleaned by female immigrant workers paid minimum wage. The influence of global firms on urban development raises important moral claims: Whose city is it? (Sassen, 2001).

While this literature has focused on major world cities, more recent work has emphasized that many cities compete to become global cities. The decline of manufacturing means that cities must find new ways to link to the global economy; they compete with one another to attract corporate headquarters, sports facilities, and new businesses in response to globalization and to achieve world-city status (Short, 2004). Abrahamson (2004) suggests that almost all cities are likely to have some features that make them global and that the focus on a small group of cities—such as Sassen's work on New York, London, and Tokyo—underestimates how widely the global city construct may be generalized. Chicago and Frankfurt, for example, are significant global cities when concentration of economic activity is used as a measure, but not cultural activity; Los Angeles figures prominently in cultural activity but is less important in economic activity.

In his study of global cities, Abrahamson ranks thirty cities on a composite economic index (including the number of stock exchanges, banks and financial institutions, multinational corporations and services) and cultural industries index (recorded music, movies, and television). The resulting global economic hierarchy puts New York at the top of both indexes, with London, Paris, and Tokyo grouped in a second tier with similar economic and cultural profiles. Abrahamson (2004:164) notes that "everyone else lags substantially far behind them." He finds evidence of regional economic centers—Chicago and Frankfurt—as well as regional cultural centers—Mumbai, Rio de Janeiro, Manila—cities that could move to world-city position by increasing their cultural activities (something that both Chicago and Frankfurt have sought to do) or by increasing their economic potential. These sorts of development activities are the focus of Short's (2005) work on global cities. He notes that the discourse on globalization leads cities to seek development that will better connect them to the new world economy: the construction of international airports, the establishment of international business centers, the building of world-class sports facilities, and the successful competition for events such as the World's Fair, the Olympics, and the World Cup.

Although current research gives considerable attention to world cities, from our perspective, the concept is misguided. At times these urban spaces act as cities, because some of their global functions are concentrated in their cores. At other times, however, these spaces function as multicentered regions, not cities, and it is necessary to study them in this larger configuration in order to understand them. When speaking of stock and bond trading, for example, the spaces corresponding with these activities would be lower Manhattan, the City of London, and downtown Tokyo, respectively. Market trading is generally a centralized city phenomenon, although stock markets like NASDAQ have no physical space at all and are, instead inscribed in telephone and computerized telecommunication links worldwide. To be sure, such activities are considered "command and control functions," but they are not the only kind. Multinational corporate headquarters are the other major component of the global economy, and these are increasingly located outside the cores of large cities in separate centers. When urbanists like Sassen speak of "world cities" as if this regional array did not exist, they overlook the very significant fact that the "world city" is embedded in a larger metropolitan region.

Employment in financial services within the City of London, for example, has significantly declined in recent years (Buck and Gordon, 2003). Increasingly, nationally tied business services have moved into the area. Furthermore, since the late 1960s a large number of corporate headquarters have left Manhattan for areas in the multicentered region of New York, New Jersey, and Connecticut, or for places in other parts of the country. And if we return to Sassen's metaphor of office buildings in the global city, it should be clear that the maintenance staff and service workers who make these buildings work on a day-to-day basis live their daily lives in a very different area of the metropolitan region than the office staff and executives who occupy the buildings during the 9–5 workday. The deconcentration and reconcentration of "command and control" centers across regions, the increasing divide—both spatially and socioeconomically among those who occupy these centers, and similar sociospatial factors make it imperative for future research to take the multicentered metropolitan region as the focal urban form.

Theming of the Urban Environment

Most of us have visited theme parks (Disneyland, Disney World, Busch Gardens), eaten at themed restaurants (Hard Rock Café, Rain Forest Café) and even visited themed nightclubs (House of Blues). Research on the role of theming in American culture and, more exactly, the way theming is used to sell products and places that, on their own, may not be markedly different, is a relatively undeveloped area (for an exception, see Gottdiener, 1995; 2001). In Las Vegas, for example, every casino sells the identical product, gambling, although they might vary slightly according to their house odds. However, on the outside, every casino is different, and each offers a thematic fantasy as an attraction. According to Gottdiener (2001), many of the themes can be bunched together: the Wild West, the romanticized desert, famous cities of the world, and exotic tropical locales. These motifs work because they have already been well established as familiar symbolic forms by Hollywood cinema and by television.

The success of places like Las Vegas over the decades as a gambling mecca, in contrast to the decline of American cities with industrial/manufacturing traditions, pinpoints both the prospects and problems facing places as they attempt to attract new investment and residents, because not every location can depend on casino gambling for economic stability (Gottdiener, 1994). Tourism, on the other hand, which is a more abstract way of looking at the success of Las Vegas, can be successfully promoted in most places. What we can all learn from Las Vegas is precisely the way architectural *theming* can be used to attract people to locations. In Las Vegas, theming is the major weapon in the competition of casinos for customers. In fact, they go to previously unheard of lengths in the creation of spectacular environments that provide fantasy stimulation and entertainment. When theming is used by other American metropolitan regions in order to attract tourists, however, popular Las Vegas motifs may not work. Consequently, the promotion of local tourism as a new growth industry requires places to research precisely what themes make sense within the local context. Future research should pay attention to these efforts and their variation among urban places.

Racialization of Urban Space

The racialization of urban space refers to the process by which social space becomes associated with various population groups. The racialization of space affects the activities of groups and individuals both within and beyond particular urban spaces: For persons living within racialized spaces, there is a stigma attached to the address they include on applications for employment; for persons living outside the racialized space, the neighborhood (and its residents) are to be avoided. The racialization of space is a clear example of how the sociospatial perspective takes us beyond human ecology to analyze the meanings that are given to urban spaces. As we saw in Chapter 1, urban spaces are meaningful spaces—they have specific meanings (sometimes contradictory) to persons within and outside of the local community. They often are contested spaces, and groups within the community may struggle to define these spaces in particular ways.

The concept of racialized space is also important for understanding particular patterns of development in cities. American cities by and large are not designed with public space, particularly in the city center. In the United States, housing projects have become associated with minority populations and with violent crime. Gotham (2004) describes how racialization was a fundamental part of the debate over urban renewal and the future development of black and white space in Kansas City. When the downtown areas of cities become racialized space, there is a decline in business of all kinds. The redevelopment of the Chicago Loop required the elimination of downtown movie theaters that featured black films and the removal of other institutions that served this population. This was followed by the development of a new arts district that brings in a very different clientele, such as new Borders and Barnes and Noble bookstores. The project has been viewed as a success as the area has become deracialized.

Although the racialization of space most directly brings to mind the image of inner-city neighborhoods, the concept has been used by scholars in Europe to study ethnic populations in the multicultural city and by scholars in the United States to study ethnic neighborhoods and populations. One of the most visible and long-lasting of these neighborhoods is the ubiquitous China-town; other areas such as Italian or Irish neighborhoods are also prominent features of the American urban environment. In many cases, these neighbor-hoods were defensive—the Chinese, Italian, and Irish immigrants experi-enced prejudice and discrimination when they first arrived in the United States, and the ethnic neighborhood provided a safe haven and opportunity for members of the ethnic group (Chapter 9).

Although much of the research on the racialization of space focuses on negative labels that are given to these communities by members of the dom-inant group living outside of these spaces, it should be recognized that there are forces that create racialized spaces from within the neighborhood or group, and there also are racialized spaces that have positive images as well. Street gang graffiti advertises the presence of groups competing for control of urban space and creates racialized spaces that may appear dangerous and mysterious to the outsider (Chapter 10). In many ethnic neighborhoods one finds murals that have been painted to create a racialized space that becomes a source of pride and identity for the group. Tourist bureaus in major cities supply maps that show the location of ethnic neighborhoods, such as China-town in New York and San Francisco, along with lists of ethnic restaurants and stores. The example of Chinatown is very interesting in this respect; it is an example of how a racialized space that long held negative meanings (opium dens and prostitution) in the popular imagination has been given a positive meaning (an important tourist destination) that has now become part of the city's advertising campaign (Hutchison, 2005).

Cyberspace and the End of the City

Finally, there is a literature that emphasizes the growth of new technologies and the new information society, resulting in a declining importance of geography and space and, ultimately, of the physical structures of the metropolis. This dis-cussion is connected in some interesting ways to the decline of the public realm (Chapter 9): the more time that persons spend on-line, whether talking with friends, shopping in cyber malls, or trolling Web sites, the less time they spend participating with fellow citizens in their local community. Manuel Castells (1998) describes contemporary society as an informational global economy, where the global structure of the world system is based upon a logic of flow, connectivity, networks, and nodes. The core activities of the global economy are linked in real time, and the daily work schedule is now on a planetary scale. While your credit card company may have service lines open from 8 AM to 8 PM, this means that the call operators in India on the other end of the line are working from 8 PM to 8 AM. Capital flows in the emerging markets—the urban clusters in Japan and China discussed in Chapters 12 and 13—bypass the corporate headquarters of the West. Global cities are no longer defined by the presence of the corporate headquarters, but by a space of flows.

Castells's view is unsettling. If the new global economy is in fact a system of flows as he describes, there is no longer a geography of spatial location, and urban sociology will have no grounding in the study of cities, suburbs, and metropolitan regions. What of the people left behind by the new global economy—those persons in inner-city neighborhoods, in older industrial towns, in the growing megacities of the developing world, no longer connected to the world system and now bypassed by the new information technologies? A new term has been used to describe the spaces left behind in the new global economy: the *Fourth World,* but this is clearly no compensation to the millions of people ignored by the "information economy."

Interestingly, it was Karl Marx who wrote that capitalism would destroy space and time. This brings us back to work of Henri Lefebvre, the social production of space, the emergence of metropolitan regions, and the origins of the new urban sociology discussed in Chapter 4. It seems clear that Marx was correct: Modern capitalism has created new technologies that have collapsed time and space; our very casual references to the powerful idea of cyberspace indicate how quickly and pervasively this transformation has taken place. Yet the core of the global economy remains manufacturing, as Marx also asserted. The important question for urban sociology, of course, is whether the information economy makes the city and the metropolitan region irrelevant.

There is already a growing body of literature arguing that these physical spaces are still important—that even if we order goods produced in a country in a different part of the world on-line through Internet stores, the places where the goods are manufactured are grounded in time and space, as are the locations where the goods are stored and shipped. This suggests that we need to base our understanding of the spaces of flows within those areas where productive activity and social reproduction occur; in other words, we are still interested in specific spatial locations and in the everyday lives of persons who live in multinucleated metropolitan regions of developed as well as developing nations. But it also seems clear that the city, as a physical entity, is less and less relevant as the metropolitan region expands and the new information technologies link nodes of activity across these metropolitan spaces. Louis Wirth would likely struggle to reconceptualize how size, density, and heterogeneity would inform our analysis of the urban world of the twenty-first century.

URBAN STRUCTURE AND URBAN CULTURE

In *Urban Sociology: Images and Structure,* William Flanagan (2001) divides the field of urban sociology into what he labels the culturalist approach and the structuralist approach. In general terms, what Flanagan means by the culturalist approach is the human ecology of the Chicago School and the later development of urban ecology by Amos Hawley, John Kasarda, and others. We have referred to this as the mainstream urban sociology of the present. Under the structuralist approach, Flanagan includes urban political economy, world systems theory, and the related areas of study that began with the revolt against mainstream urban sociology in the 1970s. These theoretical models are structural because they emphasize the importance of social structure (and in some cases, the role of the state) in determining urban development and social interaction within the urban environment. As we have presented these ideas in earlier chapters, the structuralist approach would view urbanization as a result of factors outside of the metropolitan region, whereas the culturalist approach would study urbanization by focusing on factors within the metropolitan region.

As we saw in Chapter 3, the Chicago School of urban sociology was very diverse in subject matter and research methodology, and we drew a sharp distinction between the work of Robert Park and his students (which reflected the ideas of human ecology) and the later work of Amos Hawley and others (which we refer to as urban ecology). Flanagan also includes the tradition of community studies, including the work of the Lynds (*Middletown* and *Middletown in Transition*), Herbert Gans (*The Urban Villagers* and *The Levittowners*), and others under the culturalist approach.

In Chapter 4, we described the emergence of a new urban sociology, in the work of Henri Lefebvre and others in the 1960s. This also is a diverse area of study, including the Marxist urban sociology of David Harvey and others, the urban growth model of Logan and Molotch, and the like. This work has now merged in what we refer to as the sociospatial model of urban development.

In the final chapter of *Urban Sociology: Images and Structure,* Flanagan suggests that the field is developing a unified perspective for urban sociology. The competing models of the past may not have merged into a single model, according to this view, but it seems clear that neither the culturalist approach nor the structuralist approach can adequately explain recent developments in the urban world. The culturalist perspective focuses on events within neighborhoods (community studies) or the city (urban ecology), but it does not place the everyday lives of individuals within the new global society. The research methodology and theoretical models that are used by urban sociologists following the culturalist approach do not make the necessary link between daily life in the metropolis and the larger urban structures that connect persons around the world in the twenty-first century.

The structuralist approach, on the other hand, focuses attention on the global system of capitalism and on the political economy of urban life at the national and sometimes metropolitan level. This approach is necessary for understanding the development of the world urban system, and it helps to explain patterns of economic development and urban change within and across nation states. The importance of this perspective is obvious if we want to understand how environmental policies in the developed nations have led to the movement of industrial jobs to developing nations, or how the new global economy has created the "dual city" pattern of high technology coupled with a growing service sector in cities in the developed nations. What the structuralist approach does not do, according to Flanagan, is help us understand the impact of these changes on the daily lives of persons in cities and metropolitan regions across the world.

Flanagan suggests that a unified perspective for urban sociology will result in a better understanding of both the structural forces that have created our new urban world and the impact of these changes on the lives of individuals living in the growing urban agglomerations that now account for more than half of the world's population. The structuralist approach is essential for understanding the powerful forces of global capitalism that have swept across the globe, creating a new urban world in its image. In this new world of growing social inequality and troubling exploitation of the world's diminishing resources, future generations will most likely live in larger and larger urban agglomerations, in a built environment that is far removed from the urban-rural world that our grandparents knew. To understand the new modalities of urban life—whether it be in older metropolises of Europe with urban histories stretching back hundreds of years or the newer and larger megacities of the developing world—we will need the ethnographic accounts and community studies of the culturalist approach.

Flanagan's argument concerning the need of a unified perspective for urban sociology is reasonable, and it follows from recent trends in a field that has become increasingly eclectic. Recent work in what is known as cultural studies offers us glimpses into the lives of persons around the world and emphasizes the ways in which global urban cultures have developed as our world shrinks and our lives become more dependent on other groups and other cultures. At the same time, we know that although there are differences from one area of the world to another and that there are distinctive urban cultures because of historical traditions, religion, and the like, the emerging urban metropolis of the twenty-first century shares some important characteristics regardless of country or region. It is not simply that they are linked with one another in the ever-expanding system of global capitalism. Most importantly, these urban agglomerations increasingly look like the multicentered urban region studied by the sociospatial perspective.

THE FUTURE OF THE URBAN INQUIRY

For many urbanists, analyzing metropolitan phenomena involves a choice between the competing paradigms of human ecology and political economy. While human ecology has been useful because it appreciates the role location plays in social interaction, it under-theorizes this role and adopts one-dimensional, technologically deterministic explanations for sociospatial processes. In contrast, the political economy approach deals with a host of important concepts and issues that ecology neglects, such as the role of capital and class in the urban drama. It, too, is limited, however, because it neglects aspects of culture and politics that cannot be reduced to class phenomena. Unfortunately, it also ignores the important features of spatial relations by considering location merely as a container for economic processes.

By adopting the sociospatial perspective, we pass beyond the limitations of political economy to explain how the built environment changes and develops. Political economy's focus on the restructuring of global capitalism cannot alone explain the changes experienced by metropolitan development. The missing element is supplied by a focus on real estate interests as the leading edge of change that channels growth in specific directions. Once spatial patterns are altered in one region of the metropolis, this alteration affects all other parts. Hence, social space operates as both a product and a producer of changes in the metropolitan environment.

Both ecological and political economy perspectives assume that the state has only a weak role as an agent of change. Ecology simply ignores government intervention. Political economy often treats the state as simply the direct agent of capitalist interests. But the involvement of the state in sociospatial development is both critical and complex. First, government policies help provide the "pull" factors of growth. Second, they are the focus of urban and suburban social movements that aim for a redistribution of both wealth and social costs. Third, government officials are relatively autonomous agents who do not simply follow the needs of capital alone but pursue interests of their own to bring about social change. Finally, national policies of taxation and spending can transfer wealth from one region of the country to another; hence, programs such as military spending are critical causes of regional growth or decline, in addition to private-sector investment patterns. As we have seen demonstrated in a variety of contexts, private- and public-sector efforts often work hand in hand.

The sociospatial perspective utilizes a semiotic approach to understand how culture and ideology define sociospatial processes, such as the appeals to progress and modernism in urban renewal or the use of religious belief to structure the ancient cities of the past. The sociospatial approach considers all built environments as meaningful social spaces. Behavior occurs within these social spaces, but our own behaviors may change the actual meaning and use of that space. The sociospatial approach further captures the special articulation between territory and culture that produces lifestyle networks and variation in daily community life within the metropolis. Ethnic, gender-oriented, or racially defined lifestyles enact themselves within the built environment. The street corner, the mall, the game arcade, the local bar, the school cafeteria, and the commuter train, car, or bus are all special venues where social networks interact.

Finally, the sociospatial perspective takes an integrated view of the multicentered metropolitan region. We have considered both urban and suburban settlement space. The traditional field of urban sociology possessed too narrow a focus on the central city. Urban texts invariably treat suburbs only in a special chapter devoted to that purpose, while the remainder of the text specializes in the study of the large, central city, even though a majority of population, employment, and business activity is located within expanding metropolitan environments. Urban or suburban concerns are largely metropolitan concerns, and any governmental efforts should begin from a regional rather than a local perspective.

The future of the metropolitan inquiry will require important conceptual changes. In place of the traditional urban sociology, we should have a field called the "sociology of settlement space" that would deal with all forms of human settlement—towns, cities, suburbs, metropolises, the multicentered region, and megalopolises, so that we no longer privilege the city as the sole urban form of space. In place of a contentious and often confusing clash of different paradigms (ecology for aggregate data analysis, political economy for economic issues, and the culturalist approach for ethnography), we can look forward to integrated discussions at all levels (micro, macro, and meso) following the synthesis of the sociospatial approach. Finally, by critically evaluating the planning efforts of the present and requiring them to recognize the importance of space, we have a means by which we can construct and live in more humane and enjoyable environments that confront, rather than hide from, the seemingly intractable issues of environmental, representational, and social justice.

KEY CONCEPTS

cyberspace
globalization
world system theory
world city
racialization of urban space
theming
information society
space of flows
multicentered metropolitan region

IMPORTANT NAMES

Manuel Castells
Saskia Sassen
Immanuel Wallerstein

DISCUSSION QUESTIONS

1. What is the relationship between world systems theory, neocolonialization, and globalization? How did these concepts develop? Have you encountered them in other courses or books that you have read? How is the use of these terms in urban sociology different from their presentation in other courses?

2. What is the relationship between world cities and global cities? What are some of the factors that might be used to determine whether a city might be included in a list of global cities? Why do the authors critique the recent emphasis on the global city in urban sociology?

3. What is meant by the racialization of space? How is this concept linked to some of the basic propositions of the sociospatial perspective presented in Chapter 1? Can you think of examples of the racialization of space in the community where you grew up?

4. What is meant by "theming" of the urban environment? What examples are given in the chapter? Can you think of other examples of theming in commercial development in your community? In new residential development or in the redevelopment of older neighborhoods of your community?

5. Manuel Castells's work on the new information society and the space of flows might lead some to suggest that cities are no longer important. What do you think of this argument? How would you critique Castells's argument using the concept of the multinuclear metropolitan region and sociospatial theory more generally?

BIBLIOGRAPHY

Abrahamson, M. 2004. *Global Cities.* New York: Oxford University Press.

Abrahamson, P. 1988. *Welfare States in Crisis: The Crumbling of the Scandinavian Model.* Copenhagen: Forlaget Sociologi.

Abrams, C. 1965. *The City Is the Frontier.* New York: Harper & Row.

———. 1977. "Squatting and Squatters." In J. Abu-Lughod and R. Hay, Jr., eds., *Third World Urbanization.* Chicago: Maaroufa Press.

Abu-Lughod, J. 1969. "Testing the Theory of Social Area Analysis: The Ecology of Cairo, Egypt." *American Sociological Review* 34 (April):313–343.

Adams, C. 1986. "Homelessness in the Postindustrial City." *Urban Affairs Quarterly* 21:527–549.

Aina, T. 1990. "Shanty Town Economy: The Case of Metropolitan Lagos, Nigeria." Pp.113–148 in S. Datta, ed., *Third World Urbanization: Reappraisals and New Perspectives.* Stockholm: HSFR.

Alicea, M. 1990. "Dual Home Bases: A Reconceptualization of Puerto Rican Migration." *Latino Studies Journal* 1 (3):78–98.

Alihan, M. 1938. *Social Ecology: A Critical Analysis: Ideological and Interest Group Barriers to Reform.* New York: Columbia University Press.

Allen, O. 1990. *New York, New York: A History of the World's Most Exhilarating and Challenging City.* New York: Atheneum.

Anderson, E. 1978. *A Place on the Corner.* Chicago: University of Chicago Press.

———. 1990. *Streetwise: Race, Class, and Change in an Urban Community.* Chicago: University of Chicago Press.

———. 1999. *Code of the Street: Decency, Violence, and the Moral Life of the Inner City.* New York: W. W. Norton.

Applebome, P. 1991. "Although Urban Blight Worsens, Most People Don't Feel Its Impact." *New York Times,* January 28, p. A20.

Arax, M. 1987. "Monterey Park: Nation's First Suburban Chinatown." *Los Angeles Times,* April 6.

Armstrong, R. 1972. *The Office Industry: Patterns of Growth and Location.* Cambridge, MA: MIT Press.

———. 1979. "National Trends in Office Construction, Employment and Headquarters Location in the United States Metropolitan Areas." In P. Daniels, ed., *Spatial Patterns of Office Growth and Location.* New York: John Wiley.

Auletta, K. 1983. *The Underclass.* New York: Random House.

Bachrach, P., and M. Baratz. 1962. "Two Faces of Power." *American Political Science Review* 56:947–952.

Bacon, E.N. 1967. *Design of Cities.* New York: Viking Press.

Banfield, E. 1974. *The Unheavenly City Revisited.* Boston: Little, Brown.

Baran, P., and P. Sweezy. 1966. *Monopoly Capital.* New York: Monthly Review Press.

Barbanel, J. 1992. "Robberies on the Rise on Long Island." *New York Times,* February 18, p. A15.

Barnekov, T., and D. Rich. 1989. "Privatism and the Limits of Local Economic Development Policy." *Urban Affairs Quarterly* 25:212–238.

Barnes, J.A. 1954. "Class and Committees in a Norwegian Island Parish." *Human Relations* 7:39–58.

———. 1972. *Social Networks.* Addison Wesley Modular Publications, Number 26.

Barone, C. 1983. "Dependency, Marxist Theory, and Salvaging the Idea of Capitalism in South Korea." *Review of Radical Political Economy* 16:1.

Barthes, R. 1973, *L'Empire des Signes.* Geneva: Albert Skira.

———. 1986. "Semiology and the Urban." Pp.87–98 in M. Gottdiener and A. Lagopoulos, *The City and the Sign.* New York: Columbia University Press.

Baumgartner, M. 1988. *The Moral Order of a Suburb.* Oxford: Oxford University Press.

Bean, F., and M. Tienda. 1987. *The Hispanic Population of the US.* New York: Russell Sage.

Benard, D., and E. Schlaffer. 1993. "'The Man in the Street': Why He Harasses." Pp.338–391 in L. Richardson and V. Taylor, *Feminist Frontiers III.* New York: McGraw-Hill.

Berger, B.M. 1960. *Working Class Suburb.* Berkeley: University of California Press.

Berman, M. 1981. *All That Is Solid Melts into Air: The Experience of Modernity.* New York: Simon & Schuster.

Bernard, R., and B. Rice. 1983. *Sunbelt Cities: Politics and Growth Since World War II.* Austin: University of Texas Press.

Berry, B. (ed.). 1977. *The Social Burden of Environmental Pollution.* Cambridge, MA: Ballinger.

Berry, B., and J. Kasarda. 1977. *Contemporary Urban Ecology.* New York: Macmillan.

Berry, B.J.L., and P. Rees. 1969. "The Factorial Ecology of Calcutta." *American Journal of Sociology* 74:445–491.

Berry, M. 1989. "Industrialization, De-industrialization and Uneven Development: The Case of the Pacific Rim." Pp.171–216 in M. Gottdiener and N. Komninos, eds., *Capitalist Development and Crisis Theory.* New York and London: Macmillan.

Bestor, T. 1985. *Japanese Urban Life.* Palo Alto: Stanford University Press.

Blake, W. 1977. "London." P.150 in *Songs of Innocence and of Experience.* New York: Oxford.

Blakely, E.J., and M.G. Snyder. 1997. *Fortress America: Gated Communities in the United States.* Washington, DC: Brookings Institution.

Blau, J. 1992. *The Visible Poor: Homelessness in the United States.* New York: Oxford University Press.

Bluestone, B., and B. Harrison. 1982. *The Deindustrialization of America: Plant Closings, Community Abandonment, and the Dismantling of Basic Industry.* New York: Basic Books.

Blum, B. 1978. *Cities: An Environmental Wilderness.* Washington, DC: Environmental Protection Agency.

Blumer, M. 1984. *The Chicago School of Sociology: Institutionalization, Diversity, and the Rise of Sociological Research.* Chicago: University of Chicago Press.

Bobrowski, L.S. 1998. *Collecting, Organizing, and Reporting Street Gang Crime.* Chicago: Chicago Police Department, Special Functions Group.

Body-Gendrot, S. 1987. "Plant Closures in Socialist France." Pp.237–251 in M. Smith and J. Feagin, eds., *The Capitalist City.* Oxford: Blackwell.

Boer, L. 1990. "(In)formalization: The Forces Beyond." *International Journal of Urban and Regional Research* 14:404–422.

Bollens, J., and H. Schmandt. 1965. *The Metropolis: Its People, Politics, and Economic Life.* New York: Harper & Row.

Bookchin, M. 1974. *The Limits of the City.* New York: Harper & Row.

_____. 1990. *The Philosophy of Social Ecology: Essays on Dialectical Naturalism.* Montreal: Black Rose Books.

Borchert, J. 1967. "American Metropolitan Evolution." *Geographical Review* 57:301–332.

Bordan, I. 1999. "Skateboarders, Urban Space, and Urban Planning." In R. Hutchison, ed., *Research in Urban Sociology,* Vol. 5. Greenwich, CT: JAI Press.

Bositis, D.A. 2003. *Black Elected Officials: A Statistical Summary 2001.* Washington, D.C.: Joint Center for Political and Economic Studies.

Bott, E. 1971 [1957]. *Family and Social Network.* New York: Free Press [London: Tavistock].

Boudon, P. 1986. "Rewriting of a City: The Medina of Tunis." Pp.303–322 in M. Gottdiener and A. Lagopoulos, eds., *The City and the Sign.* New York: Columbia University Press.

Bourne, L., and J. Simmons (eds.). 1978. *Systems of Cities: Readings on Structure, Growth, and Policy.* New York: Oxford University Press.

Boyte, H. 1980. *The Backyard Revolution: Understanding the New Citizens Movement.* Philadelphia: Temple University Press.

Bradshaw, Y., and E. Fraser. 1989. "City Size, Economic Development, and Quality of Life in China: New Empirical Evidence." *American Sociological Review* 54:986–1003.

Braudel, F. 1973. *Capitalism and Material Life: 1400–1800.* New York: Harper & Row.

Brinkerhoff, T. 2005. *Principal Agglomerations and Cities of the World* (http:/www.citypopulation.de, 5.0.05).

Buck, N. and Gordon I. 2003. *Working Capital.* Oxford: Blackwell.

Bullard, R. 1990. *Dumping in Dixie: Race, Class, and Environmental Quality.* Boulder, CO: Westview Press.

Bullard, R., and J. Feagin. 1991. "Racism and the City." Pp.55–76 in M. Gottdiener and C.G. Pickvance, eds., *Urban Life in Transition.* Newbury Park, CA: Sage.

Burgess, E. 1925. "The Growth of the City: An Introduction to a Research Project." In R. Park, E. Burgess, and R. McKenzie, eds., *The City.* Chicago: University of Chicago Press.

Calthorpe, P., and W. Fulton. 2001. *The Regional City: Planning for the End of Sprawl.* Washington, DC: Island Press.

Castells, M. 1977. *The Urban Question.* Cambridge, MA: MIT Press.

_____. 1983. *The City and the Grass Roots.* Berkeley and Los Angeles: University of California Press.

_____. 1989. *The Informational City.* Oxford: Blackwell.

_____. 1998. *The Rise of the Network Society.* New York: Blackwell.

Cavan, R.S. 1928. *Suicide.* Chicago: University of Chicago Press.

Chambers, I. 1986. *Popular Culture: The Metropolitan Experience.* London: Methuen.

Chase-Dunn, C. 1985. "The System of World Cities, A.D. 800–1975." Pp.269–292 in M. Timberlake, ed., *Urbanization in the World Economy.* Orlando, FL: Academic Press.

Chen, X. 1988. "Giant Cities and the Urban Hierarchy in China." Pp.225–251 in M. Dogan and J. Kasarda, eds., *The Metropolis Era,* Vol. 1. Newbury Park, CA: Sage.

Childe, V.G. 1950. "The Urban Revolution." *Town Planning Review* 21:4–17.

_____. 1954. *What Happened in History.* New York: Penguin Books.

City Mayors. 2005. www.citymayors.com.

Clavel, P. 1985. *The Progressive City: Planning and Participation, 1969–1984.* New Brunswick, NJ: Rutgers University Press.

Cleaver, H. 1989. "Close the IMF, Abolish Debt, and End Development: A Class Analysis of the International Debt Crisis." *Capital and Class* 39:17–50.

Cochrane, A. 1982. *Patterns of Urban Development.* Unit 29, Block 7. Milton Keynes: Open University Press.

Cooper, F. 1987. *On the African Waterfront: Urban Disorders and the Transformation of Work in Colonial Mombasa.* New Haven, CT: Yale.

Coquery-Vidrovitch, C. 1990. "A History of African Urbanization: Labor, Women, and the Informal Sector: A Survey of Recent Studies." Pp.75–89 in S. Datta, ed., *Third World Urbanization: Reappraisals and New Perspectives.* Stockholm: HSFR.

Coughlin, R. 1979. "Agricultural Land Conversion in the Urban Fringe." In M. Schept, ed., *Farmlands, Food, and the Future.* Ankers, IA: Soil Conservation Society of America.

Crary, D. 2005. "Private Prisons Experience Business Surge." *Associated Press,* July 30.

Cressey, P. 1932. *The Taxi-Dance Hall: A Sociological Study in Commercialized Recreation and City Life.* Chicago: University of Chicago Press.

_____. 1956. "The Ecological Organization of Rangoon, Burma." *Sociology and Social Research* 40:166–169.

Crump, S. 1962. *Ride the Big Red Cars: How Trolleys Helped Build Southern California.* Los Angeles: Crest Publications.

Dahl, R. 1961. *Who Governs? Democracy and Power in an American City.* New Haven, CT: Yale University Press.

Dale, A., and C. Banford. 1989. "Social Polarization in Britain: 1973–1982, Evidence from the General Household Survey." *International Journal of Urban and Regional Research* 13:482–494.

Darley, J., and B. Latane. 1970. *The Unresponsive Bystander: Why Doesn't He Help?* New York: Appleton-Century-Crofts.

Datta, S. 1990. *Third World Urbanization: Reappraisals and New Perspectives.* Stockholm: HSFR.

Davis, M. 1986. *Prisoners of the American Dream: Politics and Economy in the History of the U.S. Working Class.* London: Verso.

———. 1987. "Chinatown, Part Two? The Internationalization of Downtown Los Angeles." *New Left Review* 164:65–84.

———. 1990. *City of Quartz: Excavating the Future in Los Angeles.* New York: Verso.

Defoe, D. 1966 [1722]. *A Journal of the Plague Year.* New York: Penguin.

Dogan, M., and J. Kasarda. 1988. *The Metropolis Era,* Vols. 1 and 2. Newbury Park, CA: Sage.

Dorsett, L. 1968. *The Pendergast Machine.* New York: Oxford University Press.

Douglas, M. 1988. "Transnational Capital and Urbanization on the Pacific Rim: An Introduction." *International Journal of Urban and Regional Research* 12:343–355.

Drake, St. Clair, and H. Cayton. 1945. *Black Metropolis: A Study of Negro Life in a Northern City.* New York: Harcourt Brace.

DuBois, W.E.B. 1899. *The Philadelphia Negro.* Philadelphia: University of Pennsylvania Press.

Duranton, G. and D. Puga. 2005. "From Sectoral to Functional Urban Specialization." *Journal of Urban Economics* 57:343–370.

Durkheim, E. 1933 [1893]. *The Division of Labor in Society.* Translated by George Simpson. Glencoe, IL: Free Press.

Dutton, T. 1989. "Cities, Cultures, and Resistance: Beyond Leon Krier and the Postmodern Condition." *JAE* 42:3–9.

The Economist. 1990. "Toronto and Detroit: Canadians Do It Better," May 19, pp.17–20.

Egan, T. 2005. "Vibrant Cities Find One Thing Missing: Children." *New York Times,* March 24.

Ehrenreich, B. 1990. *Fear of Falling: The Inner Life of the Middle Class.* New York: HarperCollins.

Eisenstadt, S., and A. Shachar. 1987. *Society, Culture, and Urbanization.* Beverly Hills, CA: Sage.

Engels, F. 1973. *The Condition of the Working Class in England: From Personal Observations and Authentic Sources.* Moscow: Progress Publishers.

Espiritu, Y., and I. Light. 1991. "The Changing Ethnic Shape of Contemporary Urban America." Pp.35–54 in M. Gottdiener and C.G. Pickvance, eds., *Urban Life in Transition*. Newbury Park, CA: Sage.

Fagan, J. A. 1990. "Social Processes of Delinquency and Drug Use among Urban Gangs." In R. C. Huff, ed., *Gangs in America*. Newbury Park, CA: Sage.

Farley, R., and W. Allen. 1987. *The Color Line and the Quality of Life in America*. New York: Russell Sage.

Fava, S. 1980. "Women's Place in the New Suburbia." Pp.125–149 in G. Wekerle, R. Peterson, and D. Morley, eds., *New Space for Women*. Boulder, CO: Westview Press.

Feagin, J. 1983. *The Urban Real Estate Game: Playing Monopoly with Real Money*. Englewood Cliffs, NJ: Prentice-Hall.

_____. 1988. *Houston: The Free Enterprise City*. New Brunswick, NJ: Rutgers University Press.

_____. 1992. "Why Not Study the American 'Overclass'?" *Contemporary Sociology* 21(4):449–451.

Feagin, J., and M. Smith. 1987. "Cities and the New International Division of Labor: An Overview." Pp.3–36 in M. Smith and J. Feagin, *The Capitalist City*. Oxford: Blackwell.

Fernandez-Kelly, M. 1991. "Labor Force Recomposition and Industrial Restructuring in Electronics." Paper presented at symposium: "Crossing National Borders: Invasions or Involvement." December 6, Columbia University.

Fichman, M., and E. Fowler. 2003. "The Science and Politics of Sprawl." Unpublished paper. Toronto: York University.

Firey, W. 1945. "Sentiment and Symbolism as Ecological Variables." *American Sociological Review* 10:140–148.

Fischer, C. 1975. "Toward a Subcultural Theory of Urbanism." *American Journal of Sociology* 80:1319–1341.

_____. 1976. *The Urban Experience*. New York: Harcourt Brace.

_____. 1982. *To Dwell Among Friends: Personal Networks in Town and City*. Chicago: University of Chicago Press.

Fishman, R. 1987. *Bourgeois Utopias: The Rise and Fall of Suburbia*. New York: Basic Books.

Flanagan, W. 1990. *Urban Sociology: Images and Structures*. Boston: Allyn and Bacon.

_____. 2001. *Urban Sociology: Images and Structure*, 4th ed. New York: Allyn & Bacon.

Fong, T.P. 1991. *The First Suburban Chinatown: The Remaking of Monterey Park, California*. Philadelphia: Temple University Press.

Form, W. 1954. "The Place of Social Structure in the Determination of Land Use." *Social Forces* 32:317–323.

Forrest, R. 1991. "The Privatization of Collective Consumption." Pp.169–195 in M. Gottdiener and C. Pickvance, eds., *Urban Life in Transition*. Newbury Park, CA: Sage.

Frazier, E.F. 1932. *The Negro Family in Chicago*. Chicago: University of Chicago Press.

French, R., and F. Hamilton (eds.). 1979. *The Socialist City: Spatial Structure and Urban Policy*. New York: J. Wiley and Sons.

Frey, W. H. 1979. "Population Movement and City-Suburban Redistribution: An Analytic Framework." *Demography* 15:571–588.

_____. 2003. "Melting Pot Suburbs: A Study of Suburban Diversity." Pp. 155–179 in B. Katz and R.E. Long, eds., *Redefining Urban and Suburban America: Evidence from Census 2000*. Washington, DC: Brookings Institution.

Frey, W., and A. Speare. 1988. *Regional and Metropolitan Growth and Decline in the United States*. New York: Russell Sage.

Friedmann, J. 1986. "The World City Hypothesis." *Development and Change* 17:69–84.

Friedmann, J. and G. Wolff. 1982. "World City Formation: An Agenda for Research and Action." *International Journal of Urban and Regional Research* 3:309–344.

Friedrichs, J. 1988. "Large Cities in Eastern Europe." Pp.128–154 in M. Dogan and J. Kasarda, eds., *The Metropolis Era*, Vol. 1. Newbury Park, CA: Sage.

Fuentes, A., and B. Ehrenreich. 1987. "Women in the Global Factory." Pp.201–215 in R. Peet, ed., *International Capitalism and Industrial Restructuring*. Boston: Allen and Unwin.

Fujii, Y. 2005. "City Shrinkage Issues in Japan." Fuji Research Institute Corporation, Urban and Regional Issues. http://www.mizuho-ir.co.jp/english/knowledge/shrinkage 0405.html.

Fujita, K. 1988. "The Technopolis: High Technology and Regional Development in Japan." *International Journal of Urban and Regional Research* 12:573–581.

Fussell, P. 1983. *Class: A Guide Through the American Status System*. New York: Summit Books.

Gale, R. 1983. "The Environmental Movement and the Left: Antagonists or Allies?" *Sociological Inquiry* 53:179–199.

Gans, H. 1962. *The Urban Villagers: Group and Class in the Life of Italian-Americans*. New York: Free Press.

_____. 1968. "Urbanism and Suburbanism as a Way of Life: A Reevaluation of Definitions." Pp.34–52 in H. Gans, *People and Plans: Essays on Urban Problems and Solutions*. New York: Basic Books.

_____. 1990. "Deconstructing the Underclass: The Term's Dangers as a Planning Concept." *American Planning Association Journal* 56 (Summer):271–277.

Geruson, R., and D. McGrath. 1977. *Cities and Urbanization*. New York: Praeger.

Gibbs, L. 1981. *Love Canal: My Story*. Albany: SUNY Press.

Giddens, A. 2000. *Runaway World: How Globalism Is Reshaping Our Lives*. New York: Routledge.

Girouard, M. 1985. *Cities and People: A Social and Architectural History*. New Haven, CT: Yale University Press.

Glaab, C., and A.T. Brown. 1967. *A History of Urban America*. New York: Macmillan.

Glazer, N., and P. Moynihan. 1963. *Beyond the Melting Pot: The Negros, Puerto Ricans, Jews, Italians, and Irish of New York City.* Cambridge, MA: MIT Press.

Goffman, E. 1963. *Behavior in Public Places: Notes on the Social Organization of Places.* New York: Free Press.

_____. 1971. *Relations in Public: Microstudies of the Public Order.* New York: Basic Books.

Golledge, R., and G. Rushton (eds.). 1976. *Spatial Choice and Spatial Behavior.* Columbus: Ohio State University Press.

Goodman, P., and P. Goodman. 1974. *Communitas: Means of Livelihood and Ways of Life.* New York: Vintage.

Gordon, D. 1977. "Class Struggle and the Stages of Urban Development." In A. Watkins and R. Perry, eds., *The Rise of the Sunbelt Cities.* Beverly Hills, CA: Sage.

_____. 1984. "Capitalist Development and the History of American Cities." Pp.21–53 in W. Tabb and L. Sawers, eds., *Marxism and the Metropolis,* 2nd ed. New York: Oxford University Press.

Gordon, M. 1964. *Assimilation in American Life: The Role of Race, Religion, and National Origins.* New York: Oxford University Press.

Gore, A. 1992. *Earth in the Balance: Ecology and the Human Spirit.* Boston: Houghton Mifflin.

Gorrie, P. 1991. "Farewell to Chinatown: An Era of Isolation Ends with the Transition to Toronto's Suburbs." *Canadian Geographic,* August/September:17–28.

Gotham, K.F. 2002. *Race, Real Estate, and Uneven Development: The Kansas City Experience, 1900-2000.* Albany: State University of New York Press.

Gottdiener, M. 1977. *Planned Sprawl: Public and Private Interests in Suburbia.* Beverly Hills, CA: Sage.

_____. 1982. "Suburban Crime: Testing the Police Hypothesis." *Journal of Police Science and Administration* 10 (4):425–434.

_____. 1985. *The Social Production of Urban Space.* Austin: University of Texas Press.

_____. 1986. *The Decline of Urban Politics: Political Theory and the Crisis of the Local State.* Beverly Hills, CA: Sage.

_____. 1990. "Crisis Theory and State Financed Capital." *International Journal of Urban and Regional Research* 14:383–403.

_____. 1995. *Postmodern Semiotics: Material Culture and the Forms of Modern Life.* New York: Blackwell.

_____. 2001. *The Theming of America,* 2nd ed. Boulder: Westview Press.

Gottdiener, M., and J. Feagin. 1988. "The Paradigm Shift in Urban Sociology." *Urban Affairs Quarterly* 24:163–187.

Gottdiener, M., and G. Kephart. 1991. "The Multinucleated Metropolitan Region: A Comparative Analysis." Pp.31–54 in R. Kling, S.S. Olin, and M. Poster, eds., *Postsuburban California.* Berkeley and Los Angeles: University of California Press.

Gottdiener, M., and N. Komninos. 1989. *Capitalist Development and Crisis Theory.* New York: Macmillan.

Gottdiener, M., and A. Lagopoulos. 1986. *The City and the Sign: Introduction to Urban Semiotics.* New York: Columbia University Press.

Gottdiener, M., and N. Neiman. 1981. "Characteristics of Support for Local Growth Control." *Urban Affairs Quarterly* 17:55–73.

Gottdiener, M., and C.G. Pickvance (eds.). 1991. *Urban Life in Transition.* Newbury Park, CA: Sage.

Greenberg, J. 1990. "All about Crime." *New York Times,* September 3, pp. 20–32.

Grief, G. 1985. *Single Fathers.* Lexington, MA: Lexington Books.

Habermas, J. 1989. *The Structural Transformation of the Public Sphere: An Inquiry into a Category of Bourgeois Society.* Cambridge, MA: MIT Press.

Hacker, A. 1992. *Two Nations: Black and White, Separate, Hostile, Unequal.* New York: Scribner's.

Hagedorn, J. 1988. *People and Folks: Gangs, Crime, and the Underclass in a Rustbelt City.* Chicago: Lakeview Press.

Hall, P. 1966. *The World City.* London: Weidenfeld and Nicolson.

_____. 1988. "Urban Growth and Decline in Western Europe." Pp.111–127 in M. Dogan and J. Kasarda, eds., *The Metropolis Era,* Vol. 1. Newbury Park, CA: Sage.

Handlin, O. 1951. *The Uprooted.* Boston: Little, Brown.

Hannerz, U. 1969. *Soulside: Inquiries into Ghetto Culture and Community.* New York: Columbia University Press.

_____. 1980. *Exploring the City: Inquiries Toward Urban Anthropology.* New York: Columbia University Press.

Hareven, T. 1982. *Family Time and Industrial Time: The Relationship Between the Family and Work in a New England Industrial Economy.* New York: Cambridge University Press.

Harrington, M. 1962. *The Other America: Poverty in the United States.* New York: Macmillan.

Harris, C., and E. Ullman. 1945. "The Nature of Cities." *Annals of the Academy of Political and Social Science* 242:7–17.

Harrison, R., and D. Weinberg. 1992. "Changes in Racial and Ethnic Residential Segregation, 1980–1990." Paper prepared for the American Statistical Association Meetings in Boston, MA, August.

Harvey, D. 1973. *Social Justice and the City.* Baltimore: Johns Hopkins University Press.

_____. 1975. "Class-Monopoly Rent, Finance Capital, and the Urban Revolution." In S. Gale and E. Moore, eds., *The Manipulated City.* Chicago: Maaroufa Press.

_____. 1976. "Labor, Capital, and Class Struggle Around the Built Environment." *Politics and Society* 6:265–295.

_____. 1982. "The Urban Process Under Capitalism: A Framework for Analysis." Pp.91–122 in M. Dear and A. Scott, eds., *Urbanization and Urban Planning in Capitalist Society.* New York: Methuen.

_____. 1985. *The Urbanization of Capital: Studies in the History and Theory of Capitalist Urbanization.* Baltimore: Johns Hopkins University Press.

Haussermann, H., and W. Siebel. 1990. "The Polarization of Urban Development in the Federal Republic of Germany and the Question of a New Municipal Policy." *International Journal of Urban and Regional Research* 14:369–382.

Hawley, A. 1950. *Human Ecology: A Theory of Community Structure*. New York: Ronald Press.

———. 1956. *The Changing Shape of Metropolitan America: Deconcentration Since 1920*. Glencoe, IL: Free Press.

———. 1981. *Urban Society: An Ecological Approach*, 2nd ed. New York: J. Wiley and Sons.

Hayden, D. 1981. *The Grand Domestic Revolution: A History of Feminist Designs for American Homes, Neighborhoods, and Cities*. Cambridge, MA: MIT Press.

Hayner, N. 1936. *Hotel Life*. Chapel Hill: University of North Carolina Press.

Henslin, J. 1972. "What Makes for Trust?" In J. Henslin, ed., *Down to Earth Sociology*. New York: Free Press.

Hero, R., and R. Durand. 1985. "Explaining Citizen Evaluations of Urban Services." *Urban Affairs Quarterly: A Comparison of Some Alternative Models* 20:344–354.

Higham, J. 1977. *Strangers in the Land*. New York: Atheneum.

Hightower, J. 1975. *Eat Your Heart Out: Food Profiteering in America*. New York: Crown Publishers.

Hilkevitch, J., and P. Kendall. 1999. "Infrastructure Rust Never Sleeps: Aging Roads, Utilities, Sewers Are Reaching the Breaking Point." *Chicago Tribune*, February 8.

Hobbs, F., and N. Stoops. 2002. "Demographic Trends in the 20th Century." Census 2000 Special Reports, Series CENSR-4. Washington, D.C.: U.S. Census Bureau.

Holston, J. 1989. *The Modernist City: An Anthropological Critique of Brasília*. Chicago: University of Chicago Press.

Hoover, D. 1971. *A Teacher's Guide to American Urban History*. Chicago: Quadrangle.

Hoyt, H. 1933. *One Hundred Years of Land Values in Chicago*. Chicago: University of Chicago Press.

Hughes, E. 1928. "A Study of a Secular Institution: The Chicago Real Estate Board." Ph.D. dissertation, University of Chicago.

Hummon, D. 1986. "Urban Views: Popular Perspectives on City Life." *Urban Life* 15:3–36.

Hunter, F. 1953. *Community Power Structure: A Study of Decision Makers*. Chapel Hill: University of North Carolina Press.

———. 1963. *Community Power Structure: A Study of Decision Makers*, 2d edition. Chapel Hill: University of North Carolina Press.

———. 1980. *Community Power Succession: Atlanta's Policy Makers Revisited*. Chapel Hill: University of North Carolina Press.

Hutchison, R. 1988. "The Hispanic Population in Chicago: A Study in Population Growth and Acculturation." Pp.193–229 in C. Marrett and C. Leggon, eds., *Research in Race and Ethnic Relations*. Greenwich, CT: JAI Press.

———. 1993. "Blazon Nouveau: Gang Graffiti in the Barrios of Los Angeles and Chicago." Pp.137–172 in S. Cummings and D.J. Monti, eds., *Gangs: The Origins and Impact of Contemporary Youth Gangs in the United States.* Albany: State University of New York Press.

———. 2005. "The Racialization of Urban Space." In S.H.C. Lennard and H.L. Lennard, eds., *Proceedings of the 43rd International Making Cities Liveable Conference on True Urbanism and the European Town Square.* Venice, Italy, 2005.

Hutchison, R., and C. Kyle. 1993. "Hispanic Street Gangs in Chicago Public Schools." P.136 in S. Cummings and D.J. Monti, eds., *Gangs: The Origins and Impact of Contemporary Youth Gangs in the United States.* Albany: State University of New York Press.

Jackson, K. 1985. *Crabgrass Frontier: The Suburbanization of the United States.* New York: Oxford University Press.

Jacobs, J. 1961. *The Death and Life of Great American Cities.* New York: Random House.

———. 1970. *The Economy of Cities.* New York: Vintage Books.

———. 1984. *The Mall.* Prospect Heights, IL: Waveland Press.

Janowitz, M. 1956. *The Community Press in an Urban Setting.* Chicago: University of Chicago Press.

Jefferson, T. 1977. *Notes on the State of Virginia.* Edited by B. Wishey and W.G. Leuchtenberg. New York: Harper & Row.

Jencks, C. 1992. *Rethinking Social Policy: Race, Poverty, and the Underclass.* Cambridge, MA: Harvard University Press.

Jencks, C., and P. Peterson (eds.). 1991. *The Urban Underclass.* Washington, DC: Brookings Institution.

Jezierski, L. 1988. "Political Limits to Development in Two Declining Cities: Cleveland and Pittsburgh." Pp.173–189 in M. Wallace and J. Rothschild, eds., *Deindustrialization and the Restructuring of American Industry.* Greenwich, CT: JAI Press.

Judd, D. 1995. "The Rise of the New Walled City." Pp.146–166 in H. Ligget and D.C. Perry, eds., *Spatial Practices.* Newbury Park, CA: Sage.

Justice Policy Institute. 2005. "Fact Sheet: Ganging Up on Crime." Justice Policy Institute, April 11, http://www.justicepolicy.org/article.php?id=505

Kanter, P. 1987. *The Dependent City: The Changing Political Economy of Urban America.* Glenview, IL: Scott, Foresman.

Karp, D., G. Stone, and W. Yoels. 1977. *Being Urban: A Social Psychological View of City Life.* Lexington, MA: D. C. Heath.

Karp, D., and W. Yoels. 1986. *Sociology and Everyday Life.* Itasca, IL: Peacock Publishers.

Kasarda, J. 1988. "Economic Restructuring of America's Urban Dilemma." Pp.56–84 in M. Dogan and J. Kasarda, eds., *The Metropolis Era,* Vol. 1. Newbury Park, CA: Sage.

Kasarda, J., and E. Crenshaw. 1991. "Third World Urbanization: Dimensions, Theories, and Determinants." *Annual Review of Sociology* 17:467–501.

Kazis, R., and R. Grossman. 1982. *Fear at Work: Job Blackmail, Labor, and the Environment.* New York: Pilgrim Press.

Keller, S. 1968. *The Urban Neighborhood: A Sociological Perspective.* New York: Random House.

Kephart, G. 1991. "Economic Restructuring, Population Redistribution, and Migration in the United States." Pp.12–34 in M. Gottdiener and C.G. Pickvance, eds., *Urban Life in Transition.* Newbury Park, CA: Sage.

Kim, J. 1988. "China's Modernizations, Reforms, and Mobile Population." *International Journal of Urban and Regional Research* 12:595–608.

King, D. 1990. "Economic Activity and the Challenge to Local Government." Pp.265–287 in D. King and J. Pierre, eds., *Challenges to Local Government.* London: Sage.

Klein, M. L. 1995. *The American Street Gang.* New York: Oxford University Press.

Kling, R., S.S. Olin, and M. Poster. 1991. *Postsuburban California.* Berkeley and Los Angeles: University of California Press.

Korff, R. 1990. "Social Creativity, Power, and Trading Relations in Bangkok." Pp.168–185 in S. Datta, ed., *Third World Urbanization: Reappraisals and New Perspectives.* Stockholm: HSFR.

Ladanyi, J. 1989. "Changing Patterns of Residential Segregation in Budapest." *International Journal of Urban and Regional Research* 13:556–566.

Lagopoulos, A. 1986. "Semiotic Urban Models and Modes of Production: A Semiotic Approach." Pp.176–201 in M. Gottdiener and A. Lagopoulos, eds., *The City and the Sign.* New York: Columbia University Press.

LaGory, M., and J. Pipkin. 1981. *Urban Social Space.* Belmont, CA: Wadsworth.

Lamarche, F. 1976. "Property Development and the Economic Foundations of the Urban Question." Pp.85–119 in C. Pickvance, ed., *Urban Sociology: Critical Essays.* New York: St. Martin's Press.

Lamb, M. (ed.). 1986. *The Father's Role: Applied Perspectives.* New York: Wiley.

Langdon, P. 1988. "A Good Place to Live." *The Atlantic* 261 (3):39–60.

Lawson, C. 1991. "A Writer Reveals the 'Dark Underside of Suburbia': Car Pools," *New York Times,* September 12, p. C–1.

Leborgne, D., and A. Lipietz. 1988. "Two Social Strategies in the Production of New Economic Spaces." *CEPREMAP Working Papers* #8911. Paris: CEPREMAP.

Lee, E. 1982. *Export-Led Industrialization and Development.* Geneva: ILO.

Lefebvre, H. 1991. *The Production of Space.* Oxford: Blackwell.

Lemann, N. 1991a. "Four Generations in the Projects." *New York Times Magazine,* January 13, pp. 16–21, 36–38, 49.

_____. 1991b. *The Promised Land: The Great Black Migration and How It Changed America.* New York: Alfred A. Knopf.

Leshner, A. 1992. *Outcasts on Main Street: Report of the Federal Task Force on Homelessness and Severe Mental Illness.* Washington, DC: National Institute of Mental Health.

Levingston, K. 2005. *Caught in the Web: The Impact of Drug Policies on Families and Women.* New York: New York University School of Law, Brennan Center for Justice.

Levy, F. 1987. *Dollars and Dreams: The Changing American Distribution.* New York: Russell Sage.

Lewis Mumford Center for Comparative Urban and Regional Research. *Metropolitan Ethnic and Racial Change, Census 2000.* Albany: State University of New York at Albany, Lewis Mumford Center for Comparative Urban and Regional Research.

Lieberson, S. 1962. "Suburbs and Ethnic Residential Patterns." *American Journal of Sociology* 67:673–681.

_____. 1980. *A Piece of the Pie: Black and White Immigrants Since 1880.* Berkeley and Los Angeles: University of California Press.

Lieberson, S., and M.C. Walters. 1988. *From Many Strands: Ethnic and Racial Groups in Contemporary America.* New York: Russell Sage.

Lin, J. 1998. *Reconstructing Chinatown: Ethnic Enclave, Global Change.* Minneapolis: University of Minnesota Press.

Lindio-McGovern, L. 1997. *Filipino Peasant Women: Exploitation and Resistance.* Philadelphia: Pennsylvania State University.

Lineberry, R., 1977. *Equality and Urban Policy: The Distribution of Municipal Public Services.* Beverly Hills, CA: Sage.

Lineberry, R., and I. Sharkansky. 1978. *Urban Politics and Public Policy,* 3rd ed. New York: Harper & Row.

Lipsky, M. 1976. "Toward a Theory of Street-Level Bureaucracy." In W. Hawley et al., eds., *Theoretical Perspectives on Urban Politics.* Englewood Cliffs, NJ: Prentice-Hall.

Lobo, S. 2003. "Urban Clan Mothers: Key Households in Cities." *American Indian Quarterly* 27 (3):505-522.

_____. 2005. *Census Taking and the Invisibility of Urban American Indians.* Washington, D.C.: Population Reference Bureau.

Logan, J. 2002. *Metropolitan Ethnic and Racial Change, Census 2000.* Albany: State University of New York at Albany, Lewis Mumford Center for Comparative Urban and Regional Research.

Logan, J., and J. Mollenkopf. 2003. *People and Politics in America's Big Cities.* New York: Drum Major Institute.

Logan, J., and H. Molotch. 1987. *Urban Fortunes: The Political Economy of Place.* Berkeley and Los Angeles: University of California Press.

Logan, J., and G. Rabrenovic. 1990. "Neighborhood Associations: Their Issues, Their Allies, and Their Opponents." *Urban Affairs Quarterly* 26 (1):68–94.

Long, J. 1981. *Population Deconcentration in the United States.* Washington, DC: Bureau of the Census.

Lynch, K. 1964. *The Image of the City.* Cambridge: MIT Press.

Lynd, R.S., and H.M. Lynd. 1937. *Middletown in Transition: A Study in Cultural Conflicts.* New York: Harcourt Brace.

Mabogunje, A. 1990. "Organization of Urban Communities in Nigeria." *International Social Science Journal* 42:355–366.

MacDonald, M. 1984. *America's Cities: A Report on the Myth of Urban Renaissance.* New York: Simon and Schuster.

Mandel, E. 1975. *Late Capitalism.* London: Verso.

Marples, D. 1988. *The Social Impact of the Chernobyl Disaster.* New York: St. Martin's Press.

Marshall, D. 1990. "Continuing Significance of Race: The Transformation of American Politics." *American Political Science Review* 84:611–616.

Martinelli, F. 1985. "Public Policy and Industrial Development in Southern Italy." *International Journal of Urban and Regional Research* 9:48–56.

Marx, K. 1967. *Capital*. New York: International Publishers.

———. (n.d.). *The 18th Brumaire*. Moscow: Progress Publishers.

Massey, D.S., and N.A. Denton. 1993. *Urban Apartheid: Segregation and the Making of the Underclass*. Cambridge, MA: Harvard University Press.

Mathews, F.H. 1977. *Quest for an American Sociology: Robert E. Park and the Chicago School*. Montreal: McGill-Queen's University Press.

Matrix Collective. 1984. *Making Space: Women and the Man-Made Environment*. London: Pluto.

Matzer Jr., J.. 1986. "Local Control of Fiscal Stress." Pp.63–80 in M. Gottdiener, ed., *Cities in Stress*. Newbury Park, CA: Sage.

Maxson, C. L. 1995. *Street Gangs and Drug Sales in Two Suburban Cities*. Washingtion, D.C.: National Institute of Justice.

Maxson, C. L., and M. L. Klein. 2002. "Play Groups No Longer: Urban Street Gangs in the Los Angeles Region." In M. J. Dear, ed., *From Chicago to L.A.: Making Sense of Urban Theory*. Newbury Park, CA: Sage.

McCorkle, R. C., and T. D. Miethe. 1998. "The Political Organizational Response to Gangs: An Examination of a Moral Panic." *Justice Quarterly* 15:41–61.

McGovern, L. 1997. *Filipino Peasant Women: Exploitation and Resistance*. Philadelphia: University of Pennsylvania Press.

McKenzie, R. 1933. *The Metropolitan Community*. New York: McGraw-Hill.

———. 1944. *The Metropolitan Community*. Chicago: The University of Chicago Press.

McKeown, T. 1976. *The Modern Rise of Population*. London: Edward Arnold.

Mehta, S.K. 1969a. "Patterns of Residence in Poona (India) by Income, Education, and Occupation, 1937–1965." *American Journal of Sociology* 73:496–508.

———. 1969b. "Patterns of Residence in Poona (India) by Caste and Religion, 1822–1965." *Demography* 6:473–491.

Mellor, R. 1989. "Transitions in Urbanization: Twentieth-Century Britain." *International Journal of Urban and Regional Research* 13:579–592.

Melman, S. 1983. *Profits Without Production*. New York: Knopf.

Miller, J. 2000. *One of the Guys: Girls, Gangs, and Gender.* New York: Oxford University Press.

Mingione, E. 1988. "Urban Survival Strategies, Family Structure, and Informal Practices." Pp.297–322 in Michael Smith and Joe Feagin, eds., *The Capitalist City*. Oxford: Blackwell.

Minsky, H. 1989. "Financial Crises and the Evolution of Capitalism: The Crash of '87." Pp.391–403 in M. Gottdiener and N. Komninos, eds., *Capitalist Development and Crisis Theory*. New York: Macmillan.

Misra, R. (ed.). 1978. *Million Cities of India*. New Delhi: Vikas Publishing House.

Mollenkopf, J. 1975. "The Postwar Politics of Urban Development." *Politics and Society* 5:247–296.

Mollenkopf, J., and M. Castells. 1991. *The Dual City: Restructuring New York.* New York: Russell Sage.

Monkkonen, E. 1986. "The Sense of Crisis: A Historian's Point of View." Pp.20–38 in M. Gottdiener, ed., *Cities in Stress.* Newbury Park, CA: Sage.

_____. 1988. *America Becomes Urban.* Berkeley and Los Angeles: University of California Press.

Montgomery, R., and K. Bristol. 1987. *Pruitt-Igoe: An Annotated Bibliography.* Chicago, IL: Council of Planning Librarians.

Moore, J.W. 1976. *Mexican Americans,* 2nd ed. Englewood Cliffs, NJ: Prentice-Hall.

_____. 1978. *Homeboys: Gangs, Drugs, and Prison in the Barrios of L.A.* Philadelphia: Temple University Press.

_____. 1991. *Going Down to the Barrio: Homeboys and Homegirls in Change.* Philadelphia: Temple University Press.

Morawska, E. 1990. "The Sociology and Historiography of Immigration." Pp.187–238 in V. Yans-McLaughlin, ed., *Immigration Reconsidered: History, Sociology, and Politics.* New York: Oxford University Press.

Muller, P. 1981. *Contemporary Suburban America.* Englewood Cliffs, NJ: Prentice-Hall.

Mumford, L. 1961. *The City in History.* New York: Harcourt Brace Jovanovich.

Murray, J. 1984. *Losing Ground: American Social Policy, 1950–1980.* New York: Free Press.

Naess, A. 1989. *Ecology, Community, and Lifestyle: Outline of an Ecosophy.* New York: Cambridge University Press.

Nakamura, H., and J. White. 1988. "Tokyo." Pp.123–156 in M. Dogan and J. Kasarda, eds., *The Metropolis Era,* Vol. 2. Newbury Park, CA: Sage.

Nash, G. 1974. *Red, White, and Black: The People of Early America.* Englewood Cliffs, NJ: Prentice-Hall.

Nash, N. 1992, November 15. "Latin America's Shantytowns Grow as People Flock to Cities." *Press Enterprise,* p.A18.

Nath, V. 1989. "Urbanization and Urban Development in India." *International Journal of Urban and Regional Research* 13:258–269.

National Institute of Justice. 1990. *Drug Use Forecasting, Annual Report, 1988.* Washington, DC: U.S. Department of Justice.

National Council of Black Mayors (NCBM). 2005. (www.ncbm.org).

_____. 1991. "Wider Mosaic: Suburbs' Jobs Lure Immigrants to Greater Opportunity." December 7 (Metro Section), L–28.

Noyelle, T., and T.M. Stanback, Jr. 1984. *The Economic Transformation of American Cities.* Totowa, NJ: Rowman and Allanheld.

Oakes, J. 1985. *Keeping Track: How Schools Structure Inequality.* New Haven, CT: Yale University Press.

O'Connor, A. 1978. *The Geography of Tropical African Development,* 2nd ed. Oxford: Pergamon.

Ogunwole, S. U. 2002. *The American Indian and Alaska Native Population 2000: Census 2000 Brief.* Washington, DC: U.S. Department of Commerce, Economics and Statistics Association, Bureau of the Census.

Olin, S. 1991. "Intraclass Conflict and the Politics of a Fragmented Region." Pp.223–253 in R. Kling, S.S. Olin, and M. Poster, eds., *Postsuburban California*. Berkeley and Los Angeles: University of California Press.

Omi, P., and H. Winant. 1992. *Racial Formation in the United States: From the 1960s to the 1990s*. New York: Routledge.

Ong, P.M., H. Sung, and D. Houston. 2003. *The Status of American Indian Children in Los Angeles*. Los Angeles: University of California–Los Angeles, Ralph and Goldy Lewis Center for Regional Policy Studies, Policy Brief, Paper 3.

Ong, P.M., H. Sung, A.M. Uchida, and J. Heintz-Mackoff. 2004. *American Indian Adults in Los Angeles, California, and the U.S.* Los Angeles: University of California–Los Angeles, Ralph and Goldy Lewis Center for Regional Policy Studies, Policy Brief.

Orfield, M. 1997. *Metropolitics: A Regional Agenda for Community and Stability*, rev. ed. Washington, DC: Brookings Institution.

Palen, J. 1990. "Singapore." Pp.626–640 in W. Van Vliet, ed., *International Handbook of Housing Policies and Practices*. New York: Greenwood Press.

———. 1991. *The Urban World*. New York: McGraw-Hill.

Park, R.E. 1915. "The City: Suggestions for the Investigation of Human Behavior in an Urban Environment." *American Journal of Sociology* 20:577–612.

Peet, R. (ed.). 1987. *International Capitalism and Industrial Restructuring: A Critical Analysis*. Boston: Allen and Unwin.

Perlman, J. 1976. *The Myth of Marginality: Urban Poverty and Politics in Rio de Janeiro*. Berkeley: University of California Press.

Peroff, K. 1987. "Who Are the Homeless and How Many Are There?" Pp.33–45 in R. Bingham, R. Green, and S. White, eds., *The Homeless in Contemporary Society*. Beverly Hills, CA: Sage.

Perry, M.J., and P.J. Macun. 2001. *Population Change and Distribution, 1990–2000: Census 2000 Brief*. Washington, D.C.: U.S. Department of Commerce, Economics and Statistics Admininstration, U.S. Census Bureau.

Philips, K. 1990. *The Politics of Rich and Poor: Wealth and the American Electorate in the Reagan Aftermath*. New York: Random House.

Pickvance, C. (ed.). 1976. *Urban Sociology: Critical Essays*. New York: St. Martin's Press.

Piore, M., and C. Sabel. 1984. *The Second Industrial Divide: Possibilities for Prosperity*. New York: Basic Books.

Polsby, N. 1980. *Community Power and Political Theory*. New Haven, CT: Yale University Press.

Popenoe, D. 1977. *The Suburban Environment: Sweden and the United States*. Chicago: University of Chicago Press.

———. 1980. "Women in the Suburban Environment: A U.S.–Sweden Comparison." In G. Wekerle, R. Peterson, and D. Morley, eds., *New Space for Women*. Boulder, CO: Westview Press.

Population Reference Bureau. 1990. *1990 World Population Sheet*. Washington, DC.

Portes, A., and R. Rumbaut. 1990. *Immigrant America: A Portrait*. Berkeley: University of California Press.

Portes, A., and J. Walton. 1981. *Labor, Class, and the International System.* New York: Academic Press.

Portney, K. 2003. *Taking Sustainable Cities Seriously.* Cambridge, MA: MIT Press.

Pred, A. 1973. *Urban Growth and the Circulation of Information: The United States System of Cities, 1790–1840.* Cambridge, MA: Harvard University Press.

Press Enterprise. 1992a. "School Integration into Revenge." January 19, pp.A1, A7.

_____. 1992b. "Our Altered Planet." May 17, p.AA1.

Pressman, J., and A. Wildavsky. 1973. *Implementation.* Berkeley: University of California Press.

Pye, R. 1977. "Office Location and the Cost of Maintaining Contact." *Environment and Planning* 9:149–168.

Quante, W. 1976. *The Exodus of Corporate Headquarters from New York.* New York: Praeger.

Ramirez, R. 1990. "Urbanization, Housing, and the (Withdrawing) State: The Production-Reproduction Nexus." Pp.204–234 in S. Datta, *Third World Urbanization: Reappraisals and New Perspective.* Stockholm: HSFR.

Reckless, W. 1933. *Vice in Chicago.* Chicago: University of Chicago Press.

Reynolds. 1980. "Triana, Alabama: The Unhealthiest Town in America." *National Wildlife*, August 18.

Rhodes, R.F. 1995. *Architecture and Meaning on the Athenian Acropolis.* Cambridge, UK: Cambridge University Press.

Riposa, G. 1992. "Urban Empowerment: The Cambodian Struggle for Political Incorporation in California." Working Paper. Department of Political Science, Long Beach State College.

Roberts, B. 1978. *Cities of Peasants: The Political Economy of Urbanization in the Third World.* Beverly Hills, CA: Sage.

_____. 1991. "Household Coping Strategies and Urban Poverty in a Comparative Perspective." Pp.135–168 in M. Gottdiener and C. Pickvance, eds., *Urban Life in Transition.* Newbury Park, CA: Sage.

Roberts, S. L. 2004. "The Spatial Dispersion of Native Americans in Urban Areas: Why Native Americans Diverge from Traditional Ethnic Patterns of Clustering and Segregation". MA thesis, Graduate School of Architecture, Planning, and Preservation, Columbia University, New York.

Robertson, D., and D. Judd. 1989. *The Development of American Public Policy: The Structure of Policy Restraint.* Glenview, IL: Scott, Foresman.

Robertson, I. 1987. *Sociology*, 3rd ed. New York: Worth.

Rondinelli, D. 1988. "Giant and Secondary City Growth in Africa." Pp.291–321 in M. Dogan and J. Kasarda, eds., *The Metropolis Era*, Vol. 1. Newbury Park, CA: Sage.

Rubin, J. 1970. "Canals, Railroads, and Urban Rivalries." Pp.127–139 in Mohl and Betten, eds., *Urban America in Historical Perspective.* New York: W. and T. Publishers.

Safa, H. 1987. "Urbanization, the Informal Economy and State Policy in Latin America." Pp.252–274 in M. Smith and J. Feagin, eds., *The Capitalist City.* Oxford: Blackwell.

Sale, K. 1975. *Power Shift: The Rise of the Southern Rim and Its Challenge to the Eastern Establishment.* New York: Random House.

Sassen, S. 1989. "New Trends in the Socio-Spatial Organization of the New York Economy." In R. Beauregard, ed., *Economic Restructuring and Political Response.* Newbury Park, CA: Sage.

_____. 1991a. *The Global City: New York, London, Tokyo.* Princeton, NJ: Princeton University Press.

_____. 1991b. "The Informal Economy." In J. Mollenkopf and M. Castells, eds., *The Dual City: Restructuring New York.* New York: Russell Sage.

_____. 1994. *Cities in a World Economy.* Thousand Oaks, CA: Pine Forge Press.

_____. 1998. *Globalization and Its Discontents: Essays on the New Mobility of People and Money.* New York: New Press

_____. 2000. *Guests and Aliens.* New York: New Press.

Sassen-Koob, S. 1984. "The New International Division of Labor in Global Cities." In M. Smith, ed., *Cities in Transformation.* Beverly Hills, CA: Sage.

Schlyter, A. 1990. "Housing and Gender: Important Aspects of Urbanization." Pp.235–246 in S. Datta, ed., *Third World Urbanization: Reappraisals and New Perspectives.* Stockholm: HSFR.

Schmidley, D. 2003. "The Foreign-Born Population in the United States: March 2002." *Current Population Reports* P20-539.

Schneier, G. 1990. "Latin America: A Tale of Cities." *International Social Science Journal* 125:337–354.

Schnore, L. 1957. "Metropolitan Growth and Decentralization." *American Journal of Sociology* 63:171–180.

_____. 1963. "The Socio-Economic Status of Cities and Suburbs." *American Sociological Review* 28:76–85.

_____. 1965. *The Urban Scene.* New York: Free Press.

Schteingart, M. 1990. "Production and Reproduction Practices in the Informal Sector: The Case of Mexico." Pp.105–117 in S. Datta, ed., *Third World Urbanization: Reappraisals and New Perspective.* Stockholm: HSFR.

Schwartz, D., P. Ferlauto, and D. Hoffman. 1988. *A New Housing Policy for America: Recapturing the American Dream.* Philadelphia: Temple University Press.

Schwirian, K. (ed.). 1974. *Comparative Urban Structure: Studies in the Ecology of Cities.* Lexington, MA: D. C. Heath and Company.

Scott, A. 1980. *The Urban Land Nexus and the State.* London: Pion.

_____. 1988. *Metropolis: From the Division of Labor to Urban Form.* Berkeley and Los Angeles: University of California Press.

Scott, J. 1972. *Comparative Political Corruption.* Englewood Cliffs, NJ: Prentice-Hall.

Scott, M. 2005. *Lords of Lawndale: My Life in a Chicago White Street Gang.* Bloomington, IN: Authorhouse.

Sennett, R. 1994. *Flesh and Stone: The Body and the City in Western Civilization.* New York: W. W. Norton.

Serrin, W. 1992. *Homestead: The Glory and Tragedy of an American Steel Town.* New York: Times Books.

Shannon, T., N. Kleiniewski, and W. Cross. 1991. *Urban Problems in Sociological Perspective*, 2nd ed. Prospect Heights, IL: Waveland Press.

Shaw, C.S. 1930. *The Jackroller: A Delinquent Boy's Own Story*. Chicago: University of Chicago Press.

Shevky, E., and W.E. Bell. 1955. *Social Area Analysis: Theory, Illustrative Application, and Computational Procedures*. Westport, CT: Greenwood.

Shevky, E., and M. Williams. 1949. *The Social Area of Los Angeles: Analysis and Typology*. Berkeley: University of California Press.

Short, J. R. 2004. *Global Metropolitan: Globalizing Cities in a Capitalist World*. London: Routledge.

Shover, J. 1976. *First Majority-Last Minority: The Transformation of Rural Life in America*. DeKalb: Northern Illinois University Press.

Simmel, G. 1950. "The Metropolis and Mental Life." Pp.409–424 in K. Wolff, ed., *The Sociology of Georg Simmel*. Glencoe, IL: Free Press.

Simon, D. 1989. "Postcolonial Africa and the World Economy." *International Journal of Urban and Regional Research* 13:68–92.

Singer, A. 2004. *The Rise of New Immigrant Gateways*. Washington, D.C.: Brookings Institution, Center on Urban and Metropolitan Policy. http://www.brook.edu/metro/publications/20040301–gateways.htm.

Sjoberg. 1960. *The Pre-Industrial City*. New York: Free Press.

Sleeper, J. 1990. *The Closest of Strangers: Liberalism and the Politics of Race in New York*. New York: W. W. Norton.

Smith, C. 1985. "Theories and Methods of Urban Primacy: A Critique." Pp.87–117 in M. Timberlake, ed., *Urbanization in the World Economy*. Orlando, FL: Academic Press.

Smith, D. 1992, October 15. "Valley of Gloom." *Press Enterprise*, pp. A1, A7.

Smith, D., and M. Timberlake. 1993. "World Cities: A Political Economy/Global Network Approach." In R. Hutchison, ed., *Urban Theory in Transition*. Greenwich, CT: JAI.

Smith, M., and J. Feagin. 1987. *The Capitalist City: Global Restructuring and Global Politics*. Oxford: Blackwell.

South, S., and D. Poston. 1982. "The United States Metropolitan System." *Urban Affairs Quarterly* 18:187–206.

Sowell, T. 1981. *Ethnic America*. New York: Basic Books.

Spain, D. 1992. *Gendered Spaces*. Chapel Hill: University of North Carolina Press.

Spear, A. 1967. *Black Chicago: The Making of a Negro Ghetto: 1890–1920*. Chicago: University of Chicago Press.

Squires, G. D. 1989. "Public-Private Partnerships: Who Gets What and Why." Pp.1–11 in G.D. Squires, ed., *Unequal Partnerships: The Political Economy of Urban Redevelopment in Postwar America*. New Brunswick, NJ: Rutgers University Press.

———. 1991. "Partnership and the Pursuit of the Private City." Pp.196–221 in M. Gottdiener and C.G. Pickvance, *Urban Life in Transition*. Newbury Park, CA: Sage.

_____. 1992. "Economic Development Is Killing Education." *In These Times*, December 28, pp.28–29.

Stahura, J., K. Huff, and B. Smith. 1980. "Crime in the Suburbs." *Urban Affairs Quarterly*, March 15, pp.291–316.

Steele, S. 1990. *The Content of Our Character: A New Vision of Race in America.* New York: St. Martin's Press.

Stone, C. 1989. *Regime Politics: Governing Atlanta, 1946–1988.* Lawrence: University of Kansas Press.

Storper, M. 1984. "The Spatial Division of Labor: Labor and the Location of Industries." In L. Sawers and W. Tabb, eds., *Sunbelt/Snowbelt.* New York: Oxford University Press.

Storper, M., and R. Walker. 1983. "The Theory of Labor and the Theory of Location." *International Journal of Urban and Regional Research* 7:1–41.

_____. 1989. *The Capitalist Imperative.* Oxford: Blackwell.

Strauss, A. 1976. *Images of the American City.* Somerset, NJ: Transaction Publishers.

Strong, A. 1971. *Planned Urban Environments.* Baltimore: Johns Hopkins University Press.

Strong, J. 1891. *Our Country.* New York: Baker and Taylor.

Stubbing, R., and R. Mendel. 1986. *The Defense Game.* New York: Harper & Row.

Sullivan, M. 1991. "Crime and the Social Fabric." In J. Mollenkopf and M. Castells, eds., *The Dual City: Restructuring New York.* New York: Russell Sage.

Suro, R., and A. Singer. 2003. "Changing Patterns of Latino Growth in Metropolitan America." Pp. 181–210 in B. Katz and R. E. Long, eds., *Redefining Urban and Suburban America: Evidence from Census 2000.* Washington, DC: Brookings Institution.

Susser, L. 1982. *Norman Street: Poverty and Politics in an Urban Neighborhood.* New York: Oxford University Press.

Suttles, G. 1972. *The Social Construction of Communities.* Chicago: University of Chicago Press.

_____. 1990. *The Man Made City.* Chicago: University of Chicago Press.

Sweetser, F.L. 1965. "Factorial Ecology: Helsinki, 1960." *Demography* 2:372–385.

Taeuber, K., and A. Taeuber. 1965. *Negroes in Cities: Residential Segregation and Neighborhood Change.* Chicago: Aldine.

Taylor, G. 1915. *Satellite Cities: A Study of Industrial Suburbs.* New York: Appleton.

Taylor, R. 1991. "Urban Communities and Crime." Pp.106–134 in M. Gottdiener and C.G. Pickvance, eds., *Urban Life in Transition.* Newbury Park, CA: Sage.

Thorne, B. 1993. "Girls and Boys Together . . . But Mostly Apart: Gender Arrangements in Elementary Schools." Pp.115–126 in C. Richardson and V. Taylor, eds., *Feminist Frontiers III.* New York: McGraw-Hill.

Thrasher, F. 1927. *The Gang: A Study of 1,313 Gangs in Chicago.* Chicago: University of Chicago Press.

Tobio, C. 1989. "Economic and Social Restructuring in the Metropolitan Area of Madrid: 1970–1985." *International Journal of Urban and Regional Research* 13:324–335.

Toennies, F. 1957 [1887]. *Community and Society [Gemeinschaft und Gesellschaft]*. Edited by Charles P. Loomis. East Lansing: Michigan State University.

———. 1971. *Ferdinand Toennies on Sociology: Pure, Applied, and Empirical*. Edited by W.J. Cahnman and R. Heberle. Chicago: University of Chicago Press.

United Nations, Department of International and Social Affairs. 1985. *Estimates and Projections of Urban, Rural, and City Populations, 1950–2025: The 1982 Assessment*. (ST/ESA/SER.R./58). New York.

United Nations. 2002. *World Urbanization Prospects: The 2001 Revision*. New York: United Nations, Department of Economic and Social Affairs, Population Division.

United Nations. 2003. *World Urbanization Prospects: The 2003 Revision*. New York: United Nations, Department of Economic and Social Affairs, Population Division.

UNFPA. 1996. *Changing Places: Population, Development and the Urban Future*. New York: United Nations, United Nations Population Fund (The State of the World's Population 1996).

U.S. Bureau of the Census. 1970. *Census of Populuation*. United States Department of the Commerce, Bureau of the Census. Washington, DC: Government Printing Office.

U.S. Bureau of the Census. 1980. *Census of Population*. United States Department of the Commerce, Bureau of the Census. Washington, DC: U.S. Government Printing Office.

U.S. Bureau of the Census. 1990. *Census of Population*. United States Department of the Commerce, Bureau of the Census. Washington, DC: U.S. Government Printing Office.

U.S. Bureau of the Census. 2000. *Census of Population*. United States Department of the Commerce, Bureau of the Census. Washington, DC: U.S. Government Printing Office.

U.S. Immigration and Naturalization Service. 1985. *Statistical Yearbook*. Washington, DC: U.S. Government Printing Office.

———. 1988. *Statistical Yearbook*. Washington, DC: U.S. Government Printing Office.

———. 1993. *Statistical Yearbook*. Washington, DC: U.S. Government Printing Office.

———. 1998. *Statistical Yearbook*. Washington, DC: U.S. Government Printing Office.

———. 2003. Yearbook of Immigration Statistics. Washington, DC: U.S. Government Printing Office.

USA Today. 1991. "Segregation: Walls between Us," November 11, pp.A1–3.

Vance, J. 1977. *This Scene of Man: The Role and Structure of the City in the Geography of Western Civilization*. New York: Harpers College Press.

———. 1990. *The Continuing City: Urban Morphology in Western Civilization*. Baltimore: Johns Hopkins University Press.

Veblen, T. 1899. *The Theory of the Leisure Class*. New York: Viking Press.

Vidich, A.J., and J. Bensman. 1968 [1958]. *Small Town in Mass Society: Class, Power, and Religion in a Rural Community*. Princeton, N.J.: Princeton University Press.

Vigil, J. 1988. *Barrio Gangs: Street Life and Identity in Southern California*. Austin: University of Texas Press.

Wade, R. 1959. The *Urban Frontier: The Rise of Western Cities, 1790-1830*. Chicago: University of Illinois Press.

Wallerstein, I. 1976. *The Modern World System*. New York: Academic Press.

Walton, J. 1982. "The International Economy and Peripheral Urbanization." Pp.119–135 in N. and S. Fainstein, eds., *Urban Policy Under Capitalism*. Beverly Hills, CA: Sage.

_____. 1987. "Urban Protest and the Global Political Economy: The IMF Riots." Pp.364–386 in M. Smith and J. Feagin, *The Capitalist City*. Oxford: Blackwell.

Warner Jr., S.B. 1962. *Streetcar Suburbs: The Process of Growth in Boston*. Cambridge, MA: Harvard University Press.

_____. 1968. *The Private City: Philadelphia in Three Periods of Its Growth*. Philadelphia: University of Pennsylvania Press.

Weber, A.F. 1899. *The Growth of Cities in the Nineteenth Century*. New York: Macmillan.

Weber, M. 1958. *The Protestant Ethic and the Spirit of Capitalism*. New York: Scribner's.

_____. 1966. *The City*. New York: Free Press.

_____. 1968. *Economy and Society*. New York: Bedminster Press.

Weiss, M. 1987. *The Rise of Community Builders: The American Real Estate Industry and Urban Land Planning*. New York: Columbia University Press.

_____. 1988. *The Clustering of America*. New York: Harper & Row.

Wellman, B. 1979. "The Community Question." *American Journal of Sociology* 84:1201–1231.

_____. 1988. "The Community Question Re-evaluated." Pp.81–107 in M. Smith, ed., *Power, Community, and the City*. New Brunswick, NJ: Transaction.

Wellman, B., and B. Leighton. 1979. "Networks, Neighborhoods, and Communities." *Urban Affairs Quarterly* 14:363–390.

Whitt, J.A. 1982. *Urban Elites and Mass Transportation: The Dialectics of Power*. Princeton, NJ: Princeton University Press.

Whyte, M., and W. Parish. 1984. *Urban Life in Contemporary China*. Chicago: University of Chicago Press.

Whyte, W.F. 1955. *Street Corner Society: The Social Structure of an Italian Slum*. Chicago: University of Chicago Press.

Whyte, W.H. 1956. *The Organization Man*. Garden City, NY: Simon & Schuster.

_____. 1988. *City: Rediscovering the Center*. New York: Doubleday.

Williams, T., and W. Kornblum. 1985. *Growing Up Poor*. Lexington, MA: D.C. Heath.

Wilson, J. 1992. "Anarchy Spreads on Day 2." *Press Enterprise*, May 1, p.A1.

Wilson, W.J. 1987. *The Truly Disadvantaged: The Inner City, the Underclass, and Public Policy*. Chicago: University of Chicago Press.

_____. 1996. *When Work Disappears: The World of the New Urban Poor*. New York: Random House.

Wirth, L. 1928. *The Ghetto*. Chicago: University of Chicago Press.

_____. 1938. "Urbanism as a Way of Life." *American Journal of Sociology* 44:3–24.

Wohl, R., and A. Strauss. 1958. "Symbolic Representation and the Urban Milieu." *American Journal of Sociology* 63:523–532.

World Bank. 2002. *World Development Indicators, 2002.* New York: World Bank.

Wright, T. 1998. *Out of Place: Homeless Mobilizations, Subcities, and Contested Landscapes.* Albany: State University of New York Press.

Yago, G. 1984. *The Decline of Transit: Urban Transportation in German and United States Cities: 1900–1970.* New York: Cambridge University Press.

Yeh, Anthony Gar-on, and Xu Xueqiang. 1984. "Provincial Variation of Urbanization and Urban Primacy in China." *Annals of Regional Science* 23(3):1–20.

Yeung, Y. 1988. "Great Cities of Eastern Asia." Pp.155–186 in M. Dogan and J. Kasarda, eds., *The Metropolis Era.* Newbury Park, CA: Sage.

Zhou, M. 1992. *Chinatown: The Socioeconomic Potential of an Urban Enclave.* Philadelphia: Temple University Press.

Zhou, Yixing. 1991. "The Metropolitan Interlocking Region in China: A Preliminary Hypothesis." Pp.89–111 in Norton Ginsburg, Bruce Koppel, and T. G. McGee, eds., *The Extended Metropolis: Settlement Transitions in Asia.* Honolulu: University of Hawaii Press.

Zorbaugh, H. 1929. *The Gold Coast and the Slum: A Sociological Study of Chicago's Near North Side.* Chicago: University of Chicago Press.

Zukin, S. 1990. *Loft Living: Culture and Capital in Urban Change.* Baltimore: John Hopkins University Press.

INDEX

ABOUT THE AUTHORS

Mark Gottdiener is professor of sociology at the State University of New York–Buffalo. He received his Ph.D. from the State University of New York–Stonybrook and taught at the University of California–Riverside before moving to Buffalo. Mark is the author of more than fifteen books and edited volumes in urban sociology, urban semiotics, and urban theory, including *Life in the Air*; *Key Concepts in Urban Studies*; *Las Vegas: An All American City*; *The Social Production of Urban Space*; *The Theming of America*; and *Postmodern Semiotics*. He teaches courses in urban sociology, contemporary theory, and cultural studies. Mark is married and has two children.

Ray Hutchison is professor and chair of urban and regional studies at the University of Wisconsin–Green Bay. He received his Ph.D. in sociology from the University of Chicago and taught at DePaul University and the University of California–San Diego before moving to Green Bay. Ray is series editor of *Research in Urban Sociology* (now in the ninth volume) and senior editor of the three-volume *The Encyclopedia of Urban Studies* (at press). He is the author of more than twenty-five articles and book chapters on urban sociology, immigration and refugee populations, and street gangs. He teaches courses in urban sociology, the city through time and space, and ethnic and racial identities. Ray is married and has three children.